Rountree

INTERMEDIATE ECONOMIC ANALYSIS

Intermediate

Economic Analysis

Resource Allocation, Factor Pricing, and Welfare

by
JOHN F. DUE
Professor of Economics
University of Illinois

and

ROBERT W. CLOWER
Professor of Economics
Northwestern University

FIFTH EDITION—1966

RICHARD D. IRWIN, INC.

HOMEWOOD, ILLINOIS

FIFTH EDITION

First Printing, March, 1966

PRINTED IN THE UNITED STATES OF AMERICA
Library of Congress Catalog Card No. 66–14543

PREFACE

The primary purpose of this book is to provide a summary exposition of contemporary economic theory at a level intermediate between the beginning principles courses and graduate courses in economic theory. It is intended for use in undergraduate courses designed to provide a more intensive training in economic analysis than is possible in the elementary course. The emphasis, as in the previous editions, is upon value and distribution theory. The level of analysis is based upon the assumption that the students have had an elementary course in economics, but basic concepts are reviewed in order to provide a common background of terminology. The treatment is largely nonmathematical, beyond simple geometrical tools and equations. In order that the book may be kept within manageable length, no attempt is made to develop the historical antecedents of contemporary theory, nor to analyze in detail the current controversies in the field, although the more important of these are pointed out.

The present edition is comparable in coverage to the previous edition. The introductory chapters have been condensed, and considerable material which duplicated that in elementary texts has been removed. The discussion of the demand schedule for the product of the individual firm has been integrated with the material on pricing in various types of markets. The theory of consumer demand has been broadened and expanded. The chapters on price and output determination have been substantially rewritten to improve presentation, tighten the reasoning, and introduce new material in the field. The chapter on factor pricing has been completely revised and rewritten in light of recent approaches to the question. The two chapters on wage theory have been condensed into one chapter, and those on investment and interest theory significantly revised. Chapters 18, 19, and 20, largely new in the previous edition, have been left almost unchanged. Chapter 21, on welfare theory, has been completely rewritten in light of contemporary welfare theory.

As in previous editions, the lists of references at the ends of chapters are not intended to be exhaustive, but are designed to suggest additional reading for students. Instructors will find useful illustrative material in the *Wall Street Journal, Fortune,* and *Business Week,* and in case books for courses in managerial economics, such as W. W. Haynes, *Managerial Economics* (Homewood, Ill.: The Dorsey Press, 1963).

The authors would like to express appreciation to the numerous readers of the previous edition who took the trouble to call our attention to errors or unclear statements; to Professors Edward Budd of Pennsylvania State University and Mary Crawford of Indiana University who supplied detailed comments on the previous edition; to Professor M. M. Davisson of the University of California for his encouragement of the earlier editions; to the art and editorial staffs of Richard D. Irwin, Inc.; and to Joanne Jones for her excellent work in typing the manuscript.

Urbana and Evanston
March, 1966

TABLE OF CONTENTS

PART I. INTRODUCTION

CHAPTER
PAGE

1. NATURE AND FUNCTIONS OF THE ECONOMIC SYSTEM 3

Economic Institutions. The Problem of Choice. Human Wants. The Means to Satisfy Human Wants. The Functions of the Economic System. The Nature of the Market Economy. The Economic System of Socialism.

2. NATURE AND SCOPE OF ECONOMIC THEORY 12

The Nature of Economic Theory. Analytical Principles. The Relationship between Empirical Studies and Economic Analysis. The Usefulness of Economic Analysis. The Terminology of Economic Analysis: Definitions and Classifications. Positive and Welfare Economics. The Major Segments of Positive Theory. Dynamic versus Static Analysis.

3. GOALS OF ECONOMIC UNITS AND MARKET STRUCTURE 25

The Basic Units. The Functions of Business Firms. The Performance of Functions within the Firm. GOALS OF ECONOMIC UNITS: Maximization of Consumer Satisfaction. Maximization of Factor Income. Maximization of Business Profits. RELATIONSHIPS AMONG UNITS—MARKET STRUCTURE: The Concept of a Market. Bases of Market Classification. Major Classes of Markets. PERFECTION IN MARKET CONDITIONS: Imperfect Knowledge. Mobility of Factor Units. The Approach to Price Theory.

PART II. COMMODITY PRICE AND OUTPUT DETERMINATION

4. DEMAND CONCEPTS 45

The Concept of Demand. The Demand Function. Changes in Demand. ELASTICITY OF DEMAND: Price Elasticity. Classification of Segments of Demand Schedules on the Basis of Elasticity. Income Elasticity.

5. THE THEORY OF CONSUMER BEHAVIOR AND THE DETERMINANTS OF DEMAND 56

The Law of Demand. THE LAW OF DIMINISHING MARGINAL UTILITY: The Allocation of Consumer Income. The Relationship between Price and Quantity Demanded. THE INDIFFERENCE CURVE TECHNIQUE: The Indifference Schedule. The Convexity of Indifference Curves and the Principle of Diminishing Marginal Rate of Substitution. Indifference Curves with More than Two Commodities. The Pattern of Indifference Curves. The Budget Restraint or Consumption Possibilities Line. The Quantities Purchased. Indifference Curves and the Demand Schedule. The Income Effect and the Substitution Effect. DETERMINANTS OF ELASTICITY OF DEMAND—SUBSTITUTABILITY: Other Influences on Elasticity. THE LEVEL OF THE DEMAND SCHEDULE: CHANGES IN THE PARAMETERS: Consumer Preferences. Income. Income Elasticity of Total Consumption. Prices of Other Commodities. Expectations about Future Prices. Number of Potential Consumers. The Collection of Demand Schedule Data. APPENDIX: HOUSEHOLD SAVINGS BEHAVIOR.

6. THE THEORY OF PRODUCTION 89

THE PRODUCTION FUNCTION: Typical Output Behavior. The Explanation of the Behavior of Output with Varying Proportions: The Law of Diminishing Returns. The Stage of Increasing Returns. The Stage of Diminishing Returns.

ix

CHAPTER   PAGE

The Stage of Negative Returns. OPTIMUM FACTOR COMBINATIONS: The
Marginal Rate of Factor Substitution. The Principle of Diminishing Marginal
Rate of Factor Substitution. The Isoquant Graph. The Isoquant Graph: In-
creasing and Diminishing Returns. The Optimum Factor Combination.
Tangency of the Isoquant with an Isocost Line. Factor Price Changes and Factor
Substitution. The Scope of Applicability of the Law of Diminishing Returns.
ADJUSTMENTS IN ALL FACTORS: THE PRINCIPLE OF RETURN TO SCALE: The
Isoquant Presentation and the Expansion Path. Increasing Returns to Scale.
Constant Returns to Scale. Decreasing Returns to Scale. The Validity of the
Principle of Returns to Scale.

7. NATURE AND BEHAVIOR OF COST   115

THE NATURE OF COST. EXPENDITURE AND NONEXPENDITURE COSTS: Ex-
penditure Costs. Nonexpenditure Costs. THE ADJUSTABILITY OF COSTS IN
RESPONSE TO CHANGES IN OUTPUT: Fixed Costs. Variable Costs. COST
SCHEDULES: The Parameters of Cost Schedules. SHORT-RUN COST SCHED-
ULES: Average Fixed Cost. Average Variable Cost. The Behavior of Average
Cost. The Behavior of Marginal Cost. The Applicability of the Assumptions.
Empirical Studies of Short-Run Cost Behavior. COST SCHEDULES WITH LONG-
RUN ADJUSTMENTS COMPLETED: The Nature of the Long-Run Cost
Schedule. The Behavior of Long-Run Average Cost. The Significance of the
Assumptions. Empirical Studies of Long-Run Cost Schedules. COST CONDI-
TIONS OF THE INDUSTRY: Increasing Cost Industries. Decreasing Cost In-
dustries. Constant Cost Industries. FURTHER COMPLEXITIES OF COST.

8. PRICE AND OUTPUT DETERMINATION UNDER CONDITIONS OF PURE

COMPETITION   149

Competitive Price Determination: General Considerations. MARKET PRICE
DETERMINATION: The Average Revenue Curve of an Individual Seller. The
Concept of Supply. Supply Schedules in the Market Period. Market Price
Determination. OUTPUT AND PRICE IN A SHORT-RUN PERIOD: Short-Run
Supply. The Short-Run Supply Schedule. The Short-Run Equilibrium. The
Relations between Price and Cost in the Short-Run Period. OUTPUT AND
PRICE IN THE LONG-RUN PERIOD: Supply Schedules in the Long-Run Period.
Identity of Lowest Average Cost for All Firms in the Industry. Nature of the
Supply Schedules. The Long-Run Equilibrium Price. THE ADJUSTMENT OF
MARKET PRICE TO THE LONG-RUN EQUILIBRIUM LEVEL: Readjustment to
a Change in Demand. Adjustments to Cost Changes. IMPERFECTIONS IN AD-
JUSTMENTS IN PURELY COMPETITIVE INDUSTRIES: Knowledge of Future
Prices and Time Lags in Supply Adjustments. The Cobweb Theorem. Other
Imperfections.

9. NONPURELY COMPETITIVE MARKETS: MONOPOLY   181

NONPURELY COMPETITIVE MODELS: GENERAL CONSIDERATIONS: Average
Revenue and Marginal Revenue. PRICE AND OUTPUT DETERMINATION:
UNREGULATED MONOPOLY: Monopoly Price Determination in the Market
Period. Short-Run Pricing—the Average Revenue Function of a Monopolist.
Long-Run Adjustments. PRICE DISCRIMINATION: The Conditions Necessary
for Discrimination. The Profitability of Discrimination. First-Degree Discrim-
ination. Third-Degree Discrimination. ADJUSTMENT OF PRODUCT AND
SELLING ACTIVITIES: Adjustment of the Physical Product. Selling Activities.
RESTRAINTS UPON MONOPOLY PRICE. REGULATED MONOPOLIES.

10. NONPURELY COMPETITIVE MARKETS: MONOPOLISTIC COMPETITION   205

General Characteristics of Monopolistic Competition. MARKET PERIOD PRICE
DETERMINATION. OUTPUT AND PRICE DETERMINATION IN THE SHORT RUN:
Industry Adjustments. LONG-RUN PRICE AND OUTPUT ADJUSTMENTS: The
Tangency Case. Excessive Entry of New Firms. Restrictions to Completely Free
Entry. Industry Cost Conditions. SELLING ACTIVITIES AND MONOPOLISTIC
COMPETITION. THE SIGNIFICANCE OF MONOPOLISTIC COMPETITION.

CHAPTER   PAGE

11. NONPURELY COMPETITIVE MARKETS: OLIGOPOLY 220

Classification of Oligopoly Markets. COMPLETE OLIGOPOLY: Obstacles to the Attainment of Maximum Joint Profits. PARTIAL OLIGOPOLY: The Case of the Kinked Demand Curve. Approaches to Pricing: Price Leadership. Price Following or Imitative Pricing. The Cost-Plus, Average Cost, or Markup Approach. The Advantages of the Average Cost Approach. Average Cost Pricing and Profit Maximization. The Significance of Average Cost Pricing. Introductory Pricing. Adjustment of Product to Price. Strategical Moves in Oligopoly. Other Objectives of Oligopolists. PRODUCT VARIATION AND SELLING ACTIVITIES: Mutual Interdependence in Selling Activities. The Significance of Selling Activities. PRICE DISCRIMINATION. LONG-RUN ADJUSTMENTS: Long-Run Cost Adjustments. Tendencies toward the Elimination of Excess Profits. Entry Restriction. Common Costs and the Level of Average Cost. Elimination of Losses. Nonuniformity of Price. PURE OLIGOPOLY. MONOPSONY AND OLIGOPSONY: Monopsony and Large Numbers of Sellers. Oligopsony with Large Numbers of Sellers. Bilateral Monopoly and Bilateral Oligopoly.

PART III. FACTOR PRICE DETERMINATION

12. INTRODUCTION TO THE THEORY OF FACTOR PRICES AND INCOME DISTRIBUTION 261

Factor Prices and the Distribution of Income. FACTOR DEMAND: The Basic Rule of Optimum Factor Use by the Firm. Average and Marginal Outlay. Average and Marginal Revenue Product. Cost Minimization and the Demand for Factor Inputs. The Behavior of Marginal Revenue Product in the Short Run. Behavior of Marginal Revenue Product over a Longer Period. The Demand Schedule for a Factor by an Individual Firm. Changes in Factor Demand. Total Demand for a Factor. The Marginal Revenue Product Principle and Business Policy. FACTOR SUPPLY. FACTOR PRICE DETERMINATION: Deviations from Pure Competition. TWO OVERALL QUESTIONS OF FACTOR PRICING: The Adding-Up Problem: Euler's Theorem. Long-Run Trends in Labor's Share of Output and the Cobb-Douglas Production Function.

13. THEORY OF WAGES 284

WAGE DETERMINATION UNDER PURELY COMPETITIVE CONDITIONS: The Determinants of the Aggregate Supply of Labor. Supply of Labor of Particular Types. Demand Considerations. Purely Competitive Wage Levels. Occupational Wage Differentials. Geographical Wage Differences. Long Period Aggregate Supply of Labor. NONPURELY COMPETITIVE INFLUENCES IN THE LABOR MARKETS: Employer Domination. The Determinants of the Extent of Employer Dominance. Labor Immobility and Monopsonistic Competition. Oligopsony. LABOR UNIONS AND WAGE DETERMINATION: Employer Policies. Union Wage Policies. The Actual Money Wage Level. The Effects of Unions upon Money Wage Levels. Labor Unions and Wage Differentials. Unions and Economic Stability. THE REAL INCOME OF LABOR.

14. CAPITAL INVESTMENT AND CAPITAL BUDGETING 314

Sources of Productivity of Capital Goods. Determinants of Investment. Risk Considerations. The Cost and Availability of Money Capital. The Functional Relationship between the Amount of Money Capital Used and the Cost. Total Investment. The Prices of Capital Goods. Changes in the Demand for Capital Goods. The Payments for Capital Goods and Factor Incomes.

15. THE THEORY OF INTEREST 329

The Nature of Interest. DECISIONS AFFECTING THE INTEREST RATE: Allocation of Income between Consumption and Saving. Liquidity Decisions. The Significance of the Interest Rate for Liquidity Decisions. Money Creation. DETERMINATION OF THE INTEREST RATE: The Supply of Money Capital. The Demand for Money Capital. The Equilibrium Interest Rate Level. Ad-

CHAPTER   PAGE

ditional Requirements for Interest Rate Stability. Equilibrium Relationships
of the Interest Rate. The Structure of Interest Rates. Interrelationships among
Interest Rates in Various Segments of the Money Capital Market. Changes in
the General Level of Interest Rates. Functions of the Interest Rate.

16. RENTS AND QUASI RENTS 354

Marginal Productivity Analysis Applied to Land. The Selling Price of Land.
The Differential Theory of Land Rent. Differences in Fertility and Location.
Nonagricultural Production. The Merits of the Two Approaches to Rent Determination. Land Rent as a Distinct Functional Return. Quasi Rent. The Concept of Rent as a Generalized Surplus Return. Summary.

17. THE THEORY OF PROFITS 370

BUSINESS PROFITS AND IMPLICIT COSTS: Interest Return on the Money
Capital of the Owners. Implicit Wages. Implicit Rents. THE PORTION OF
BUSINESS PROFITS IN EXCESS OF IMPLICIT COSTS: Monopsony Profits.
Monopoly Profits. Innovations as a Source of Pure Profits. Uncertainty as the
Source of Pure Profits. The Absence of Pure Profits and Monopoly Profits in
Perfect Competition. PROFITS AS A FUNCTIONAL RETURN: The Role of Profits
in the Economy. NEGATIVE PROFITS OR LOSSES: The Various Situations of
Losses. Causes of Losses.

PART IV. CONCLUDING PERSPECTIVES

18. GENERAL EQUILIBRIUM 389

Consumer Price Interdependencies. The Relationship of the Prices of Con-
sumption Goods and Factors. THE FRAMEWORK OF GENERAL EQUILIBRIUM
THEORY: The Demand Equations. The Supply Equations. Solution of the
Demand and Supply Equations. Further Extensions. The Usefulness of General
Equilibrium Theory. Limitations of General Equilibrium Theory. CHANGES
IN THE DETERMINANTS: Changes in Consumer Preferences. Techniques of
Production. Changes in Factor Supplies. Changes in Competitive Relation-
ships. Theories of Change in the Determinants of General Equilibrium.

19. LINEAR PROGRAMMING 404

LINEAR PROGRAMMING AND ECONOMIC ANALYSIS: Establishment of Linear
Relations. Scope of Linear Programming. LINEAR PROGRAMMING: SOME EX-
AMPLES: The Selection of an Optimal Diet. Choosing an Efficient Production
Process. Selection of an Efficient Shipping Schedule. THE TECHNIQUE OF
LINEAR PROGRAMMING: More Complex Problems. INPUT-OUTPUT ANALYSIS
AND OTHER APPLICATIONS: The Theoretical Structure of Input-Output Anal-
ysis. Empirical Content. Limitations to the Analysis. Interindustry Economics.

20. ECONOMETRICS 427

THE PURPOSE AND SCOPE OF ECONOMETRICS: The Nature and Purpose of
Econometrics. The Scope of Econometrics. CONCEPTS AND GENERAL AP-
PROACH OF ECONOMETRICS: Preliminary Research and Data Collection.
Theoretical Considerations. Necessary Modifications in the Theoretical Analysis.
THE FORMULATION OF ECONOMETRIC MODELS: A Typical Model. Models
and Structures. Shock Models. The Complexity of the Models. PROBLEMS OF
ESTIMATION: The Identification Problem. The Problem of "Goodness of Fit."
Choice of Estimation Techniques. CONCLUSION.

21. WELFARE ECONOMICS 447

SOCIAL GOALS AND THE ECONOMIC SYSTEM. FREEDOM OF CHOICE. MAX-
IMUM SATISFACTION OF WANTS: Optimum Efficiency in the Use of Resources.
Optimum Adjustment of Production in Terms of Consumer Preferences.
Optimum Degree of Factor Utilization. Attainment of an Optimum Rate of
Economic Growth. INTERPERSONAL COMPARISONS AND WELFARE CRITERIA.

CHAPTER   PAGE

THE OPTIMUM PATTERN OF INCOME DISTRIBUTION: The Lerner Argument.
The Attitudes of Society—the Social Welfare Function. Concluding Observations.

INDEX   471

PART 1

Introduction

Chapter 1

NATURE AND FUNCTIONS OF THE ECONOMIC SYSTEM

Social institutions, like air, food, and other commonplace phenomena, are taken for granted by most of us—except when they fail to work properly, or when they seem to impose needlessly harsh restrictions on our freedom to behave as we please. Among social scientists, however, social institutions are regarded as anything but commonplace, and are never taken for granted. For the ultimate presupposition of all social science is that individual conduct is capable of rational explanation and prediction on the basis of logic and past experience; and social institutions are thought to be among the more important "molds within which individual conduct is shaped."[1] By the same token, description of relevant social institutions serves as a natural point of departure for expositions of specific social science disciplines, such as the account of economic analysis presented in this book. For it is only in terms of particular social institutions that the scope and content of specific disciplines can be demarcated.

Economic Institutions

It is convenient for purposes of discussion to classify social institutions into separate categories suggested by everyday experience: religious, political, legal, family, economic, and so forth. A certain amount of overlapping is inevitable because all aspects of human behavior are interdependent. But each type of institution has its own peculiar features, so the classification is meaningful even though it does some violence to reality.

In this book we shall be concerned primarily with _economic institutions;_ that is to say, _institutions through the operation of which various resources—scarce, relative to the demand for them—are utilized to satisfy the wants of men._ Like all social arrangements, economic institutions not only condition and control but also coordinate individ-

[1] H. R. Bowen, _Toward Social Economy_ (New York: Rinehart, 1948), p. 16.

3

ual behavior. To emphasize the last of these functions, we refer to the set of economic institutions, considered as a unit, as the economic system.

The Problem of Choice

Were all *goods*—physical objects and services capable of satisfying human wants—present in quantities in excess of the amounts which persons desire, as is air, for example, economic institutions would be nonexistent; all wants would be satisfied without effort and without interference with other persons. Increased use of a good by one person would not reduce the amounts which other persons could obtain to satisfy their wants. No organization would be necessary to regulate the use of the resources, and no control would be required over this phase of human behavior. But the world is not of this character. So long as most goods are scarce relative to the demand for them, conflicts of interest over their possession will occur, and institutions for controlling individual action will be necessary. If each person could satisfy his wants by his own activities, obtaining directly from nature by his individual efforts the goods which he required, economic institutions would play a minor role in human life. But modern economic society is characterized by a very high degree of interdependence. Each person performs a highly specialized task in the production system and, by the use of the income received for the performance of this task, purchases goods which he desires. For such a system to function, an elaborate mechanism of economic institutions is necessary to coordinate the choices of individuals. It is the study of this system which constitutes economics.

Human Wants

Persons are born with certain basic desires, such as: for food, for warmth, for security. The choices which a person makes of particular goods to satisfy these wants, however, are determined to a great extent by the customs of the society in which the person lives. Some ways of satisfying wants are socially (and legally) acceptable; others are not. A person has a basic desire to avoid the discomfort of extreme cold; but the type of clothing which he wears is likely to be dictated very largely by the customs of the community in which he is living. Similarly, a person has a basic desire to obtain recognition from his fellowmen; but depending on the society in which he lives, recognition may be determined by the number of wives he acquires, the size of the house he builds, or the extent of the business empire he controls.

Individual choices are subject not only to general cultural influences, but also to pressures exercised by the producers of goods, in the form of advertising and other sales effort. Some of this activity is designed to encourage persons to satisfy one desire instead of another, or to utilize one particular method to satisfy a desire in preference to alternatives. Much advertising, however, attempts primarily to induce the buyer to use the brand of one producer in the field instead of that of another.

The Means to Satisfy Human Wants

Material objects and services which are capable of satisfying human wants are called *goods;* the property or capacity of goods which enables them to satisfy wants is known as *utility*. A few commodities, for example, air, exist in nature in quantities that exceed a person's desire, even when they can be obtained free of charge, in the form, place, and time desired for consumption. Such commodities are called *free goods*. But most commodities are scarce relative to the demand for them; i.e., most commodities are *economic goods*. Few *consumption goods*—commodities which directly satisfy personal wants—are available at all in nature in the form, place, and time desired.[2] Instead, there are available *factors of production*—commodities that can be used to produce goods which will directly satisfy wants.

The factors of production provided by nature can be classified into two general groups: (1) the capacity of human beings to perform various activities and (2) natural resources—material objects which can be utilized directly or indirectly in want satisfaction.

In early societies, persons satisfied many of their wants by utilizing directly their own activities in obtaining goods from natural resources. But with the passage of time, man developed two additional aids to production: greater *skills* in carrying on productive activity, and *capital goods*—material objects produced by human effort to facilitate further production. Man discovered that he could obtain more goods to satisfy his wants if he devoted a portion of his activity to making capital goods to assist him in producing consumption goods rather than devoting all his working time to direct want-satisfying activities.

In the present-day economy, the factors of production—the means used to produce goods to satisfy wants—can be classed into three general groups:

[2] There are exceptions: the land upon which homes in a city are built may exist in the form, place, and time desired but in limited quantities relative to demand.

1. <u>Natural resources</u>:[3] all economic goods used in production which are found directly in nature, as, for example, land used in wheat production, coal in the veins of a mine, or a waterfall which can be harnessed to generate electric power, such as Niagara Falls.

2. <u>Labor</u>: all human activity utilized in production. The nature of the labor service being rendered is controlled not only by the native capacity of human beings to work, but also by the skill which they have acquired. It is neither possible nor necessary to separate labor services into the parts for which each of these two elements is responsible. It is useful, however, to distinguish *entrepreneurial* activity, the undertaking of *business* organization and management, from labor activity of a more routine kind.

3. <u>Capital goods</u>: all material goods produced by man to be used in production, such as factory buildings, machinery, and trucks.

Money capital is regarded not as a distinct factor of production or as a consumption good, but rather as an instrument of exchange—a means by which other commodities are acquired. Money is essential for efficient exchange of goods among households, business firms, and other economic decision units, but it does not itself enter into any technical processes of production or consumption.

The Functions of the Economic System

Every economic system performs certain basic functions:

1. *Resource Allocation.* Most factors can be used to produce a wide variety of goods. From iron ore, for example, can be made automobiles or washing machines, railroad cars or paper clips. The services of a carpenter can be used on house construction, the building of new service stations, or government public works. There must be some method in the economy for determining the uses to which resources will be put or, in other words, for selecting the goods to be produced and determining the output of each.

2. *Production Methods.* Since at any time there are available a number of possible methods for producing particular goods, there must be some system for selecting actual methods to be used. Is coal to be mined by hand labor or by machinery? Is a factory to use oil or coal for fuel? Selection must be made not only among particular techniques but also among various possible methods of organizing the conduct of production. Shall production of a commodity be centered in one locality or scattered throughout the country? Shall production be concentrated

---

[3] The term *land* is often used in economic analysis to refer to the entire group of natural resources, as defined.

in the hands of a few large producers or distributed among many small firms?

3. *Distribution of Output.*   There would be no problem of sharing the outputs of the economy among the various members of society if production were sufficiently great for each person to obtain as much of every product as he desired. Since products are in fact scarce relative to the demand for them, however, some method of allocating them must be devised.

These three functions are performed by every economic system. But the exact manner in which they are performed varies from one economic system to another. The type of system with which we are primarily concerned is that of the market economy, or capitalism.

The Nature of the Market Economy

The market economy is characterized by private ownership of the factors of production, by private initiative, guided by the profit motive, in the conduct of production, and by freedom of choice among households as regards spending and saving decisions. More specifically, this type of economy has the following characteristics:

1. The legal institution of private property: in consumption goods, such as houses; in factors of production, such as labor, capital equipment and land; and in money capital, the means by which producing units obtain physical goods and human services needed to carry on production. Individuals are protected by law in the enjoyment of rights to own, use, and employ both their wealth and talent to gain an income.

2. Private enterprise in the organization and conduct of production: except for a limited number of governmentally rendered services, goods are produced by businesses that are owned directly or, in the case of the corporation, indirectly, by individuals. Firms are free to acquire necessary means of production by purchase or hire and to dispose of products as they see fit. Incentive to carry on production arises from the desire of the owners of businesses to gain income in the form of profits.

Because of private ownership of the factors of production and private initiative in production, a market economy is characterized by a very large number of independently reached individual decisions and an equally large number of exchange transactions. Decisions are made by individual factor owners about hiring or selling units of the factors of production to business firms; decisions are made by individual business firms about products and volumes of output, selection of methods of production, acquisition of factor units, and, in many cases, price.

Decisions are made by individual consumers about what goods to buy, how much to save, etc. Market transactions must thus be carried on more or less continuously between factor owners and business firms, among business firms themselves, and between business firms and consumers.

3. Control of the functioning of the economy by the price system: the control functions which an economy must perform, as described above, are carried out primarily by the operation of the price system. Price relationships provide signals that guide the direction of production into various channels, and thus determine resource allocation; the selection among alternative production techniques; and the distribution of total output among various persons in society. This feature will be discussed in detail in subsequent sections.

4. Market competition: the force which prevents exploitation of some groups in the economy by others is market competition—the struggling of various individuals against one another to increase their own economic well-being. Thus, if firms seek to raise prices in order to gain profits higher than the average, new firms will enter the industry and reduce prices and profits. In practice, market competition does not work with complete effectiveness, but it serves as a force of great importance. Interferences with competition will be discussed in later chapters.

5. Limited role of government: the market economy is characterized by a relative absence of government control over economic activity, particularly over prices and production. In the laissez-faire capitalism of the last century, governmental interference was extremely limited. Little control was exercised over private production, and governmental production was restricted mainly to such areas as national defense and police protection. In the economic system of today, the extent of government control is greater, yet relatively slight compared to the sphere of private initiative. Some government controls regulate the conduct of private economic activity, presumably in the interests of society as a whole. For example, the government seeks to prevent monopoly, and thus to insure more fully the protection of particular groups from exploitation by others. Some governmental measures are designed to improve relationships between business firms and persons supplying labor services to them. Others are intended to prevent the sale of goods regarded as detrimental to the welfare of the community.

In addition to regulatory actions, governments in all countries undertake some direct production of goods and services. This is confined primarily to the provision of *social goods*—commodities which benefit the community as a whole, but which do not provide direct separable benefits to individuals, and thus cannot be produced on a profit-making basis. National defense is the traditional example. In other cases, governments have taken over certain activities because the cost involved in selling the services to users is prohibitive (as is true of highways), or because production would tend otherwise to pass into monopoly control. But despite these actions, the government sector in the United States is relatively insignificant compared to that of private enterprise. A person is legally free to start any business he desires, provided the product is not considered harmful and the business is not in one of the few industries, such as the public utilities field, in which the number of firms is restricted. He can use any method of production he desires and, with certain exceptions, set prices as he sees fit. He can obtain units of the factors of production from any supplier and pay the amount that he and the supplier agree upon, subject to certain restrictions on wages. He can produce any quantity of goods, and choose the quality, if the product is not considered harmful and is not misrepresented. He can cease production whenever he pleases, unless he operates in the public utilities field.

The exact nature of the market economy varies considerably with time and place. The American economy has undergone marked changes in the last century in the extent and nature of competition, the degree of governmental interference with prices, the conduct of production, and the amount of direct governmental production. Nevertheless, the basic nature of the economy remains unchanged. In the western world, wide variations are to be found in the nature of competition, the functioning of the price system, and the role of government in the economy; these variations inevitably affect the manner in which the system operates.

The Economic System of Socialism

Although this study is primarily concerned with the functioning of a market economy, it is desirable to note briefly the characteristic features of the socialist form of economic society.[4] As distinguished from a market economy, the basic feature of socialism is the conduct of all or most production activity directly by the government rather than by private business. In addition, under the usual concept of socialism, private ownership of the factors of production (other than human

---

[4] There are, of course, many possible forms of socialism. The characteristics indicated in this section are those generally regarded as fundamental features of any socialist system. In Africa, particularly, the term has taken on a somewhat different meaning, stressing the role of government in economic development, but with less emphasis on government ownership of economic activity.

services) is replaced by government ownership, and thus property ceases to be a source of individual income.

When ownership and control of production rest in the hands of government and individual freedom in the conduct of production is eliminated, the price system ceases to provide an automatic control mechanism over the operation of the economy. The government—or more specifically, those in control of the government—can determine the commodities to be produced and the techniques of production on any desired basis, and can allocate the output of production by arbitrary standards. Actually, however, if reasonable efficiency in production is to be obtained and production is to be directed toward those goods for which there is greatest desire, the price system must be retained in the sale of commodities to consumers, and elsewhere allowed to perform functions almost as important as those which it performs in a market economy.

Under the usual concept of a socialist society, persons would be paid money wages for their services. Since other factor units would be owned by the government, money wages would be the sole source of individual income. The persons receiving wages would use them for the purchase of government-produced goods, which would be sold for money prices, as is the output of business firms in a capitalist economy. Prices would be set by the government at levels which would insure that total demand would equal the total supply being produced, and production would be adjusted to such figures that the costs of production would equal the selling prices. Only by this means could the government insure that production was being directed to those goods most desired by consumers. For the selection of the most efficient methods of production and types of organizational structure, the costs of the various methods would be determined. Thus the government would utilize the price system to control production and as a device for distributing income. But the importance of the price system in socialism would not be an inevitable consequence of the form of the economy, as it is in capitalism, but rather the result of deliberate choice on the part of the government.

SELECTED REFERENCES

BOWEN, H. R. *Toward Social Economy,* chap. i. New York: Rinehart, 1948.
KNIGHT, F. H. *The Economic Organization,* pp. 3–30. New York: Kelley and Millman, 1951.
STIGLER, G. J. *The Theory of Price,* chap. i. 3d ed. New York: Macmillan, 1965.

QUESTIONS

1. How do economic institutions differ from other institutions in society?
2. What is the economic system?
3. In what sense is scarcity the basis of economic activity?
4. Distinguish between the terms *utility* and *good*.
5. What is the distinguishing characteristic of economic goods?
6. Distinguish between consumption goods and factors of production.
7. What are the three major groups into which factors of production are typically classified?
8. What is entrepreneurial activity?
9. Explain the major functions which the economic system performs.
10. What are the principal characteristics of a market economy?
11. What are social goods? Why have governments undertaken their production?
12. How does the capitalism of the present-day United States differ from that of one hundred years ago? From the present-day economic system of Great Britain?
13. What is the basic regulating mechanism of a market economy? How does it function?
14. Contrast the role of the price system in socialism and the market economy.

Chapter

2

NATURE AND SCOPE
OF ECONOMIC THEORY

Every empirical science rests on an organized body of theoretical knowledge that serves as an instrument for the arrangement of ideas about those aspects of experience that fall within the purview of the science. Such is the relation, for example, between theoretical mechanics and physics or between probability theory and statistics. Economic theory is much less abstract and far more informal than theoretical mechanics or probability theory, but it bears precisely the same relation to the remainder of economics as these disciplines bear to physics and statistics. The object of this chapter is to examine the nature, scope, and methods of economic theory.

The Nature of Economic Theory

It is the purpose of economic theory to provide tools for analyzing and explaining observed economic behavior. Economic theory thus seeks to isolate relationships among observable data which will provide an explanation of various events and facilitate prediction of the reactions which are likely to occur in response to changes in particular data. For example, suppose that coffee prices rise sharply. The theory of price determination does not in itself explain why the rise occurs. But by indicating the various forces which influence the prices of commodities, it provides a guide to the selection of data (such as changes in supply) which might provide an explanation, and facilitates the formulation of an explanation by demonstrating how changes in the various determinants of price will affect the price level.

Relationships which result from economic analysis are called *economic principles*. More specifically, economic principles are generalizations which express relationships among various elements of an economic system. Thus, for example, the principle that over a long-run period in pure competition, price tends to equal average cost, expresses a

12

relationship between price, on the one hand, and cost, on the other, under the assumed conditions.

There are two types of such generalizations. The first type is analytical or demonstrative, and expresses conclusions which follow logically from certain assumptions. In the example given in the previous paragraph, with various assumptions about technology and human motivation, the principle that price will equal average cost follows as a matter of logical necessity. The set of assumptions and the conclusions which are derived from it is called a *model.* The second type of generalization is empirical or inductive—a statement of relationships observed to hold between actual data. Thus, if a large number of observations show that price reductions lead to increases in consumption, the empirical generalization may be advanced that price reductions increase consumption. But unlike the analytical generalization, in which the conclusion follows as a matter of necessity from the assumptions, the empirical proposition is merely a statement of a tendency which, although valid in particular instances, may not be true in general.

Generalizations of the empirical type, which are direct products of inductive study of actual data, are often reformulated into analytical principles by selecting appropriate assumptions and determining the logical conclusions which follow. Thus the price-consumption relationship expressed above as an empirical generalization would not necessarily apply in all cases. But if it were reformulated as an analytical principle, built on certain assumptions about consumer motivation and behavior, the principle would be necessarily valid (provided that the logic by which it was obtained was correct) in all cases to which the assumed conditions were applicable.

Analytical Principles

Formulation. The first step in the formulation of an analytical principle is the determination of the problem, that is, the selection of the question with which the principle is to deal. If economic analysis is to be anything more than an exercise in logic, the problems selected must be of significance for the actual world. For example, there would be little gained from developing a theory of possible causes of unemployment if no one had ever been unemployed.

The next step is to select the assumptions from which the conclusions will be derived. If the principles are to be helpful in guiding empirical research, in explaining actual behavior in the economy, and in providing a basis for economic policy, the assumptions must bear an adequately close relationship to actual conditions. For example, if the relationship of price and cost in certain industries is to be explained, the assumptions made about the nature of competition in the industries must reflect actual conditions in the industries.

This rule must often, as a matter of necessity, be tempered by the need for simplification. The economic system is a very complicated mechanism. If economic analysis is to be manageable and is to provide generalizations which are significant in any substantial number of cases, rather broad assumptions must be made, assumptions which recognize the major features of a number of situations rather than exact characteristics of individual circumstances. Accordingly, the principles cannot offer very detailed conclusions. The alternative—the selection of very detailed assumptions—would allow more detailed conclusions but would require an extremely large number of principles, no one of which would be significant in a substantial number of cases. In Boulding's terminology, economic analysis presents a "map" of reality rather than a perfect picture of it: "Just as we do not expect a map to show every tree, every house, and every blade of grass in a landscape, so we should not expect economic analysis to take into account every detail and quirk of real economic behavior."[1] Thus, in developing analytical principles, we must compromise between the use of assumptions which resemble actual conditions as closely as possible, on the one hand, and the need for simplification and the development of generalizations of reasonably broad scope, on the other.

Once the assumptions have been selected, the final step is to develop by a process of logical reasoning the implications of the assumptions, that is, to determine logical relationships among the elements in the problem and to express them in the form of economic principles. Thus, given the assumptions of pure competition and of the action of businessmen on the basis of profit maximization, the generalization can be developed by a process of logical reasoning that price will equal average cost, once long-run equilibrium has been attained.

Validity. As implied in the definition of an analytical principle given above, the sole test of the *correctness* of such a principle is that of logical consistency: Does the conclusion follow logically from the assumptions? But the *applicability*—that is, the validity of the use of the principle in a particular situation—depends upon agreement between the assumptions of the principle and the conditions of the actual situation. Regardless of its logical consistency, a principle is not useful

---

[1] K. E. Boulding, *Economic Analysis* (3d ed.; New York: Harper, 1955), p. 13.

in a particular case if its assumptions are not in adequate agreement with the conditions present, and an attempt to apply it may lead to erroneous results. For example, the theory of price-cost relationships in pure competition is based upon certain assumptions (to be discussed in later chapters) about the nature of pure competition. If, in a particular industry, conditions are such that one or more of these assumptions are not realized in practice, the principle—that price will equal average cost in the long run—will not necessarily be valid. The general usefulness of a principle will normally depend upon the number of situations in which the actual conditions are in adequate agreement with the assumptions of the principle.

The most frequent source of error in the use of economic analysis, as well as in policy based upon it, is the failure to consider carefully whether or not the principles are applicable to the particular situation. In some cases the exact nature of the assumptions has not been realized, while in others, too little attention has been paid to their relation to actual conditions. The subsequent misapplication of the principles has served to discredit economic analysis, since conclusions developed from misapplied theories are so obviously contrary to actual occurrences. Such procedure promotes the popular statement that economic principles are "fine in theory, but don't work in practice." A principle is not "fine" for a particular purpose unless its assumptions agree to an adequate extent with actual conditions. If they do, the conclusions advanced by the principle will be realized (granted its logical correctness). Apparent discrepancies between theory and practice arise from misapplications of theory, of using it in situations for which it is not relevant.

As indicated above, if economic principles are to be of significance for any substantial number of situations, the assumptions must involve some simplification of reality. As a result, when the attempt is made to use a principle to analyze a particular situation, usually no precise answer can be given by use of the principle because of the generalized nature of the assumptions. Thus the principles relating to the incidence of taxation cannot provide directly the answer to such questions as the actual incidence of the federal excise tax on cigarettes. For such problems the general principles indicate which facts must be collected and studied (for example, those relating to the exact nature of competition in the industry) before any specific answer to the question is possible. Then, by applying that portion of the general analysis whose assumptions are as nearly as possible in agreement with the situation, it may be feasible to reach a provisional conclusion. But in all likelihood the assumptions will still be too generalized to allow precision in the conclusion. The varieties of competition, for example, are too numerous to make it possible for a general theory of tax incidence to cover all of them. As a result, to obtain greater precision, it is necessary to refine the general principles in terms of the particular situation, to consider the significance of the various features in the situation, and to refine the general conclusions of the theory by reference to particular characteristics of the situation under study.

The Relationship between Empirical Studies and Economic Analysis

Earlier in this chapter, a distinction was made between empirical generalizations and analytical principles. There has been controversy for many years over the relative desirability of the two general approaches to the furtherance of economic knowledge. The institutionalist school of thought emphasized the importance of the development of empirical studies and empirical generalizations, while the classical tradition stressed the importance of analytical tools. However, it is now recognized that the progress of economic knowledge requires use of both empirical and analytical studies, each being necessary if successful use is to be made of the other. Today the disagreement is mainly over the relative importance of the two, rather than over the desirability of the exclusive use of one approach or the other. Empirical studies undertaken without an analytical framework to guide the selection of relevant data are completely futile; analytical studies made without reference to empirical data are mere exercises in logic, without possible significance or usefulness.

The Functions of Empirical Studies for Analytical Work. More specifically, empirical studies serve several important functions for the development of analytical principles. First, they indicate the problems which require solution. For example, if studies show that a significant portion of the labor force is unemployed, or that farmers' incomes have been dropping steadily, development of tools to analyze the reasons for these changes is clearly warranted.

Second, studies of the economy suggest assumptions upon which the analysis must be based if it is to be useful. As noted, the more closely these assumptions agree with actual conditions, the more useful the analysis is likely to be for interpreting particular concrete situations and explaining the behavior involved.

Finally, empirical studies provide a check upon the validity and applicability of the principles. If studies of reactions to a particular change show responses which differ from those anticipated on the basis of the theoretical analysis, a review of the analysis is necessary. For example, suppose that a certain principle of price determination leads to the conclusion that an increase in demand will raise prices. However, empirical studies of the response of price to demand changes show that prices do not increase when demand increases. Reexamination of the principle and its applicability to the particular case is obviously necessary. If the principle is found to be logically correct, the difficulty lies in the relation between assumptions and actual conditions. Careful reexamination of the assumptions of the theory may show that the assumptions were not clearly understood. Or it may show that the principle was not applicable because there was not a sufficiently close similarity between the assumptions and the conditions, perhaps because of the great degree of simplification in the assumptions.

While disparity between expected and actual results indicates that the principle is not valid for the particular case, similarity between the two does not "prove" that the principle is logically correct and applicable to the situation. In the first place, there may be accidental mutual offsets; for example, an error in the logic may be offset by a difference between the conditions and the assumptions of the principle. In the second place, there is always the possibility that there may be a better principle, in the sense of more universal validity, or the provision of more precise statement of relationships. For example, suppose that there is developed a principle that a flow of gold into a country will cause a rise in the general price level by increasing the total money supply. A flow of gold into the country occurs, and the general price level rises. But a far more satisfactory explanation of the rise might be one which attributes it to increased demand for goods coming from foreign buyers, the gold flow being regarded merely as an indicator of the excess of exports of goods over imports. Furthermore, the correlation may be purely accidental; the rise in price and the gold flow may occur in the same period due to completely unrelated causes.

The Contributions of Analytical Studies to Empirical Work. As far as empirical research itself is concerned, analytical studies are of major importance. A theoretical framework is needed as a guide to the selection of facts; without it the investigators would be lost in a sea of completely unmanageable individual occurrences. Just as all analytical work is based upon certain assumptions about actual behavior, likewise all empirical work is guided by an analytical framework. Moreover, the development of empirical generalizations itself requires some analytical work. No matter how carefully data are collected, generalizations do not "leap out" of them; the generalizations can be derived only by a careful study of the relationships.

Further advancement in knowledge of the functioning of the economy requires extensive use of both empirical and analytical studies, in close cooperation with one another. Empirical work will suggest further problems for analysis and will test present hypotheses, many of which are built upon rather flimsy assumptions and have not been carefully tested empirically. On the other hand, additional analytical work is required to guide the collection of significant facts and to develop generalizations on the basis of the facts uncovered by the empirical work. The development of all knowledge of social institutions is hampered by our inability to conduct experiments, because of the impossibility of holding constant variables other than those which are under study. But careful collection of data, the study of them by advanced statistical techniques, and further development of analysis on the basis of more realistic assumptions can allow substantial progress.

Chapter 20 reviews the recently developed field of *econometrics,* in which theoretical analysis and empirical research are combined in a unified approach to the study of the economy.

The Usefulness of Economic Analysis

Apart from providing increased knowledge of the world in which we live, economic analysis is of primary significance in indicating the consequences of alternative actions and thus providing an intelligent basis for choice among them. To the businessman, the consumer, the worker, the union official, and those responsible for governmental policy, economic analysis provides a guide to rational planning. Given the desired goals of the individuals concerned, the utilization of economic principles allows an evaluation of various policies for efficient attainment of the goals.

Closely related to the function of guiding choice is that of providing a basis for predicting future events. Application of economic principles to existing circumstances should facilitate improved estimates of future conditions. A business firm is interested in future trends in costs of goods which it purchases and in future prices of its products. A study of price-determining forces in the type of industry in which the firm operates, and the utilization of economic principles to analyze the facts of the particular situation provide the best available basis for prediction. Almost all persons in the economy are interested in the trend of the general price level. If, on the basis of economic analysis, we know that a general increase in demand for goods not accompanied by a comparable increase in supply will lead to price increases, we can expect the general price level to rise during a war period, in which this type of imbalance of supply and demand forces develops.

Knowledge of principles is particularly important as a basis for governmental action affecting economic activity. If the economy is in some manner failing to produce results desired on the basis of accepted goals, the initiation of governmental control measures to produce more satisfactory operation requires knowledge of the operation of the economic system. Thus, to continue the example of the preceding paragraph, if during a period of high defense spending the general price level is rising rapidly and such a rise is considered to be undesirable, some knowledge of the causes of the increase is essential if effective control measures are to be introduced. Only by the use of economic analysis is it possible to predict the consequences of alternative policies and thus to select those policies that are most likely to yield desired results. Policies that superficially appear to offer satisfactory remedies may in practice produce highly objectionable consequences that can be foreseen only by the use of economic analysis.

Finally, economic analysis provides a basis for judging the performance of various segments of the economy and of the economic system as a whole. For example, if the maximization of real income is accepted as a goal of the economic system, it is necessary that all persons seeking employment be able to find jobs. If, at any time, many persons are found to be unemployed, a knowledge of the principles which control the determination of the level of employment is necessary in order to decide whether the unemployment is due to an inherent weakness in the economy or to some minor maladjustment in its operations, such as unwise union or government policy.

But care must be taken not to expect too much of economic analysis. The economic system is too complex to allow explanation of its operation by a few simple laws. The principles are primarily tools of analysis, to be applied in particular cases as an aid in selecting the data which require study, and in developing a solution to the problem. As J. M. Keynes once said:

The object of our analysis is, not to provide a machine, or method of blind manipulation, which will furnish an infallible answer, but to provide ourselves with an organised and orderly method of thinking out particular problems; and, after we have reached a provisional conclusion by isolating the complicating factors one by one, we then have to go back on ourselves and allow, as well as we can, for the probable interactions of the factors amongst themselves. This is the nature of economic thinking.[2]

The Terminology of Economic Analysis: Definitions and Classifications

The criterion of *correctness* cannot be applied to definitions, which are merely short descriptions of particular concepts. One definition may be more convenient, comprehensive, or unambiguous than another, but it cannot be "right" or "wrong" in any absolute sense. From this, it follows that a person is entitled to define a term as he wishes, provided that the definition is clear. The only criterion of a "good" definition is that of usefulness for purposes of analysis, and thus the most satisfactory definition of a term is the one which facilitates clarity of exposition to the greatest extent. There is, of course, obvious merit in using definitions which are consistent with general usage in the field (if there is any), provided that this procedure does not interfere with exposition. This spares the reader the inconvenience of reorienting himself to new meanings of old terms, and so lessens the chances of confusion and misunderstanding.

Just as definitions are neither "right" nor "wrong," so there is no "right" or "wrong" classification of data. In order to facilitate analysis, it is often desirable to classify material into certain groups. There may be a large number of ways in which a classification can be made, no one of which is the sole "correct" classification. The criterion of a classification is the same as that of a definition: Does the classification best facilitate the analysis for which it is developed? For some purposes, one classification of certain data may be better; for other purposes, another.

Positive and Welfare Economics

The body of contemporary economic analysis may be classified into two general types, according to the purpose involved. The first type, *positive* theory, consists of the analysis of the operation of the economy, without regard to the desirability or undesirability of the results in terms of goals. It deals with *what is* rather than *what ought to be*. The second type, *welfare* theory, is concerned with the evaluation of the economy in terms of assumed standards. Thus the positive theory of monopoly seeks to explain price and output determination under conditions of monopoly, whereas welfare theory as applied to monopoly evaluates the monopoly price-output levels in terms of desirability from the standpoint of assumed goals of society.

[2] *General Theory of Employment, Interest and Money* (New York: Harcourt, Brace, 1936), p. 297.

Social goals are not themselves derived from economic analysis; their selection is an aspect of ethics, not of economics. There are certain goals, outlined in Chapter 21, which have come to be generally accepted or, in other words, to represent the consensus of opinion in present-day society. *But these are assumptions of an ethical character, not products of scientific analysis.* Any evaluation of various phenomena in the economy is valid only in terms of the particular goals which are assumed.

Reference to welfare economics suggests the long-debated question: should economists make policy recommendations? On the one hand, it is argued that such recommendations are beyond the scope of economics as a scientific study, since they can be made only in terms of goals which must be assumed, rather than determined by scientific analysis. On the other hand, it may be argued that persons who are trained in economic analysis are in a particularly advantageous position to make policy suggestions. As a practical matter, few economists have ever refrained from dealing with policy questions. But it must be recognized that the making of policy recommendations is not a part of scientific economic analysis as such, since such recommendations involve ethical judgments. Fortunately, in some instances the ethical content of welfare judgments is so slight relative to the scientific content as to make the entire issue of "science versus ethics" of minor concern.

The Major Segments of Positive Theory

Contemporary positive economic theory may be divided into two major segments, *macro-* and *micro*economic theory, respectively. The former is concerned with the behavior of individual households and firms, and with the working of the price system in the determination of prices and quantities of factor inputs and commodity outputs.

Macroeconomics (also called *national income theory, employment theory,* or *aggregative economics*) seeks to explain the level of national income in both real and monetary terms, and thus the level of employment. It is also concerned with changes in the level of aggregate real output and with changes in the general price level. The two segments of economic theory overlap in analyzing the role of money in the economy, the determination of interest rates, and the establishment of the general price level; this sphere of the overall body of theory is commonly referred to as *monetary theory.* Of growing importance in the last decade is the portion of aggregative economics which is known as *growth theory* or the *theory of economic development,* which deals with changes in economic activity and national income over time. A substantial portion of growth theory has concentrated on the developing economies.

There are two general approaches to the explanation of price and output determination. The first, *partial analysis* (also called *partial equilibrium* analysis), deals with separate markets and stresses the determination of the prices and outputs of particular commodities on the assumption that the prices and outputs of other goods are given. In contrast, the second approach, known as *general analysis* (or *general equilibrium* analysis), is concerned with the price and output structure of the economy as a whole. It deals with systems of interconnected markets and emphasizes mutual interrelationships among the prices and outputs of various goods and factors. The two approaches—partial and general—are not mutually exclusive and can be integrated together; the difference between them is primarily one of emphasis.

Dynamic versus Static Analysis

Economic analysis, particularly in the field of price theory, has been traditionally *static* in nature rather than dynamic; in recent years, particularly in the analysis of national income behavior, increasing emphasis has been placed upon dynamic considerations. The static approach seeks to define *equilibrium* positions, that is, the set of relationships among the various elements which, once attained, will continue so long as the determinants remain unchanged. Static analysis typically refers, at least implicitly, to the process by which equilibrium is reached, and also describes differences between one equilibrium and another reached subsequent to a shift in the determinants. The latter aspect of static analysis is often designated as comparative statics. For the most part, however, static theory deals with the definition of equilibrium positions and the requirements for equilibrium, and abstracts from time, in the sense that equilibrium values are not dependent upon the passage of time or upon previously attained values. For many purposes, particularly in the field of price analysis, the static approach is fairly adequate.

By contrast, dynamic analysis introduces the element of time in an essential way; that is, values of the variables other than their equilibrium values are considered to be actually attainable, and the values of the variables at any particular moment are assumed to be dependent in part upon their values at past moments of time. Thus, time becomes an element in the system, and emphasis is placed on processes of adjustment rather than upon the determinants of equilibrium. For some portions of economic analysis, particularly problems of national income and economic growth, the dynamic approach is essential.

The present book is devoted largely to static price theory, with major stress on partial analysis. However, a survey of general equilibrium analysis is presented in Chapter 18. The book as a whole is concerned mainly with positive as contrasted with welfare economics, but a broad survey of contemporary welfare theory is given in the final chapter.

SELECTED REFERENCES

COHEN, K. J., AND CYERT, R. M. *Theory of the Firm,* chap. ii. Englewood Cliffs, N.J.: Prentice-Hall, 1965.

FELLNER, W. *An Introduction to Probability Theory and Its Application,* pp. 1–6. 2d ed. New York: Wiley, 1957.

KEYNES, J. N. *The Scope and Method of Political Economy.* 4th ed. London: Macmillan, 1930.

LANGE, O. "The Scope and Method of Economics," *Review of Economic Studies,* Vol. 13 (1945–46), pp. 19–32.

MACHLUP, FRITZ. "Equilibrium and Disequilibrium: Misplaced Concreteness and Disguised Politics," *Economic Journal,* Vol. 48 (March, 1958), pp. 1–24.

RUGGLES, R. "Methodological Developments," *A Survey of Contemporary Economics* (ed. B. F. HALEY), Vol. II. Homewood, Ill.: Irwin, 1952.

QUESTIONS

1. What is the purpose of economic theory?
2. What are economic principles? An economic model?
3. Distinguish between analytical and empirical principles.
4. What considerations influence the selection of the assumptions upon which an analytical principle is based?
5. What compromise must be made in the selection of the assumptions?
6. Distinguish between the test of *correctness* of a principle and the test of *applicability* of a principle.
7. If the results anticipated from the use of an economic principle in a particular case do not occur, what is likely to be the source of the difficulty?
8. Explain the statement: "Economic theory does not provide the answers to a particular question, but rather serves as a guide to the facts necessary to obtain an answer."
9. In what respects do empirical and analytical studies complement each other?
10. In what sense can empirical studies show that a principle is not applicable in a particular case, yet never prove that a principle is applicable?
11. Why is empirical work completely futile without some analytical framework?

12. Economists debated for years the question of whether there are two, three, four, or some other number of factors of production. Is there one correct number which careful analysis can discover? If not, what is the correct criterion of evaluation of a particular classification?

13. Can a definition be "right" or "wrong"? Explain.

14. Distinguish between positive theory and welfare theory.

15. Can economic analysis alone be used as the sole basis for policy recommendations? Explain.

16. Distinguish between partial and general equilibrium theory.

17. What aspects of the behavior of the pendulum of a "grandfather" clock would you mention if you were analyzing its static properties (i.e., how would you describe the equilibrium position of the pendulum)? Would a dynamic analysis of the behavior of the pendulum involve anything more in the way of general principles? Discuss.

Chapter 3

GOALS OF ECONOMIC UNITS AND MARKET STRUCTURE

Before undertaking the task of explaining the price system and the allocation of resources we must devote some attention to the basic decision-making units of the economic system, the goals which they are presumed to follow, and the nature of their market relationships with each other.

The Basic Units

There are three primary types of decision-making units or transactors. First, those which carry on consumption activities are known as *households* or *consumers*—persons, or, more commonly, families, which utilize funds obtained from current or past income to acquire consumption goods for the satisfaction of personal wants. The expenditures made by consumers are known as *consumption expenditures.*

A second group consists of factor owners, persons possessing factor units (or money capital) which can be made available for use in production. Each household ordinarily contains at least one factor owner, whose provision of factor units to business firms yields income for purchasing consumption goods. The factor owner may supply labor services, services of land or capital goods, or money capital.

The third group consists of business firms, enterprises which undertake and carry on production activities. A firm may be a single person, e.g., a dentist, or an extensive organization with the legal status of a corporation. The expenditures by firms to obtain factor units constitute costs. In contrast to consumption expenditures made by consumer units, cost payments by firms constitute incomes for the ultimate recipients. The concept of the firm must be distinguished from that of entrepreneurial activity. The former is the enterprise—as a unit —which carries on production; entrepreneurial activity is the work involved in controlling the operations of an enterprise.

For purposes of analysis, it is desirable to group firms into

25

industries—groups of firms producing commodities which are technically similar or close substitutes for one another. Thus the retail grocery industry consists of firms operating retail grocery stores; the steel industry consists of the steel-manufacturing enterprises. Some difficulty is encountered in defining the boundaries of an industry when the products of firms are not identical. The products of one industry may shade off gradually into those of another, and the brands at opposite ends of the quality scale may be poorer substitutes for one another than each is for some other commodity. Sellers of low-priced cars may compete more directly with bus companies, for example, than with the sellers of the most expensive cars. As a rule, however, the coverage of an industry is relatively clear-cut. For example, various brands of washing machines are substituted for one another much more readily than they are substituted for stoves.

For some purposes it is also convenient to distinguish certain kinds of transactors other than households, firms, and factor owners: cooperatives, labor unions, charitable institutions, governments, and the like. These other transactors play an important role in economic activity but do not fit precisely into any of the three categories mentioned above. The behavior of such units has been studied a great deal in recent years, but with little success in the development of useful rules of behavior to characterize probable responses to changing economic circumstances.

The Functions of Business Firms

The business firm, considered for the moment as an entity distinct from the individuals who own and manage it, performs several functions. First, it acquires ownership of the various factor units, or their services, and retains title to the products until they are disposed of in the market. In order to acquire factor services prior to the sale of products, the firm must have money capital, which may be obtained from the owners of the firm, from profits earned, or by borrowing.

Second, the business firm coordinates production activities. In a market economy decisions must be made by firms about type and qualities of products, methods of production (and thus the types of factors to be used, relative proportions of factors, and levels of investment), volumes of output, and frequently prices. The enterprise initiates production and suspends it if adequate profits are not earned. The decisions of the enterprise are conditioned by price relationships or, more specifically, by relationships between costs and revenues.

Third, the business firm must appraise future conditions and make present decisions despite uncertain expectations about the future.

In a static society the management functions of the firm would involve only routine decisions, once a satisfactory program of products, factor combinations, outputs, and prices had been attained. But in a dynamic economy, the firm must constantly make estimates of future conditions and adjust its policies in the light of uncertainties. These decisions may be made on the basis of informed judgments about the future, but the firm can never be certain about the correctness of its estimates of future circumstances.

As a consequence of the role which the firm plays in undertaking production and making decisions in a dynamic economy, it bears a major share of any danger of financial loss. Because the firm contracts to pay for factor services, and makes most of its payments prior to the sale of goods produced, it runs the greatest chance of loss if operations are not successful. Even the lenders of money capital have prior claim to earnings before they are available to the firm. Of course, other factor owners run some chance of loss; workers may not get their full pay, and bondholders may not receive their interest payments if a business is unsuccessful. But the greatest chance of loss is incurred by the firm itself —the coordinating unit in the conduct of production.

The Performance of Functions within the Firm

Decisions obviously must be made by human beings. Which person or groups of persons within the firm actually perform the management and entrepreneurial functions noted above? To answer this question we must classify business firms into two groups: those in which the owners and the managers of the firm are the same persons, and those in which the two groups are largely separate.

In the first group, regardless of the legal form of organization, the persons who own the enterprise constitute the entrepreneurial group making the policy decisions, and thus perform the functions of management and estimation of future conditions. Since, as owners, the entrepreneurial group directly controls the disposition of earnings, it obtains the profits in the event of success and bears the greatest loss in the event of failure. Under proprietorship and partnership forms of business organization, even the personal property of the owners may be taken to satisfy the debts of the enterprise.

The second group is characterized by a separation between ownership and management. The typical large corporation is owned by large numbers of small stockholders who are not in a position to influence the management of the enterprise, and are not, as a rule, interested in doing so. Even the holders of relatively large amounts of stock are often not interested in management policies, but only in dividend payments and increases in the market price of their stock. The typical part-owner of a large corporation performs no entrepreneurial functions beyond the purely technical one of ownership, plus the provision of money capital. His position, in fact, differs very little from that of a bondholder, except that he runs a somewhat greater risk of loss. The stockholder does, of course, receive a share of the earnings, provided the persons controlling the enterprise decide to make dividend payments; however, profits earned by the enterprise do not necessarily accrue directly to the stockholders. Most large corporations are avid savers, on their own account.

The primary functions in the large corporation are performed by the executive group—top management officials, or business leaders of the enterprise. These persons often are not major owners, although they usually own some stock in the corporation. Accordingly, while they may receive relatively small amounts from the profits of the enterprise, most of their income is derived from salaries and bonuses. Technically these executives are responsible to the stockholders, but as a matter of practice the influence exercised by the latter, even as a group, is often very limited.

GOALS OF ECONOMIC UNITS

The development of a coherent system of economic analysis requires assumptions about the economic goals pursued. It must be recognized initially that no assumption of a single goal pursued by each type of economic unit can be entirely satisfactory as an explanation of motivation. But some assumption is necessary, and the most satisfactory procedure is to focus attention on a goal which appears to be common if not universal. When there are obvious deviations from this goal, the analysis can be modified to take them into account.

Economic analysis traditionally assumes that each unit of the economic system seeks to maximize its own economic well-being. The application of this assumption to consumers and factor owners encounters relatively few difficulties. Its application to business firms is somewhat complicated, however, especially with separation of ownership and management.

Maximization of Consumer Satisfaction

As applied to households, the maximization assumption is taken to imply the pursuit by each consuming unit of maximum satisfaction from the use of funds available. In a given period of time, each household has available, from income received and past accumulations, a certain sum of money. It is assumed that the household seeks to allocate this money between savings and consumption and among purchases of various consumption goods in such a manner as to maximize satisfaction. Among other things, this requires that households purchase units of any given commodity from the cheapest available source of supply, due allowance being made for differences in the quality of goods provided by different sellers, extra services rendered, etc. It is not assumed that satisfaction from the use of the income is actually maximized, but merely that households attempt to do so.

Maximization of Factor Income

Factor owners and holders of money capital are assumed to make factor units available in such quantities and in such a manner as to maximize the net gain received.

If workers are to maximize satisfaction from the provision of labor services, they must provide such a number of labor hours that the satisfaction associated with a marginal gain in income from the provision of additional hours just offsets the dissatisfaction of the additional labor. Since the provision of labor hours (at least beyond a certain point) involves increasing disutility of work, eventually a point will be reached (short of the maximum number of hours the persons could possibly work) at which the additional utility from income just balances the additional disutility from work, and the person will supply no additional labor. Thus, it cannot be assumed that workers seek to maximize income, but rather that they seek to maximize overall gain from work and leisure. Attainment of this adjustment is restricted by the fact that many workers have little discretion about the number of hours worked. Since standard work periods are set for groups of workers, it is not always possible for each person individually to strike an optimum balance between work and leisure. However, families may make some adjustment in this regard (e.g., by "moonlighting," sending wives or children out to work, etc.). The maximization assumption also requires that each worker supply his services to the business firm which offers the highest reward, taking into consideration not only wages, but other conditions of work such as prestige, job security, and working conditions.

The maximization assumption requires that holders of money capital allocate it between liquid (monetary) holdings and various forms of loans and other uses in such a manner as to maximize net income, subject to various qualifications. Since the holding of wealth in liquid form in itself offers certain advantages (discussed in Chapter 14), the quantity made available will not necessarily be the amount which will maximize dollar income, but rather the amount which balances income gains from making funds available to business firms against liquidity advantages of keeping funds in monetary form. It is also assumed that money will be made available to those users who offer the maximum return, with due allowance for different degrees of risk. For owners of land and capital goods, maximization relates simply to money income received, net of any costs associated with maintaining assets intact.

Maximization of Business Profits

As applied to business firms, the maximization assumption requires that firms seek to maximize the net income—the total profits—of the enterprise. In a sense, this rule is merely an extension of the maximization-of-factor-income rule. However, examination of its application suggests that certain modifications are necessary.

Disutility Incurred in Gaining Additional Profits. In small businesses, the gaining of additional profits may require greater personal effort on the part of the owner-manager. If, in order to gain additional dollar profit, the owner must devote more time to the business and less to leisure, he will seek a balance between additional money income on the one hand and gains from additional leisure on the other.

Uncertainty and Profit Maximization. Under conditions of uncertainty about the future, the concept of maximization of profit is by no means precise. It is obvious that the enterprise is not concerned merely with the maximization of current profits, since pursuit of this objective might result in failure to maximize gains over a longer period of time. Rather, we assume that the firm attempts to maximize the sum of profits over a period of time, the various segments being discounted to the present. However, the firm cannot be certain of the gains from various policies. Not only will expected profit from alternative policies differ, but also expectations about the likelihood of actually earning the profit. One policy, for example, may offer the possibility of high gains but little certainty that they will be made. Another policy may promise much lower profits with a high degree of certainty. In choosing among alternative policies, the firm must not only consider gain expectations and the likelihood of their receipt, but also the possible consequences for the firm if the policy it selects turns out to be wrong.[1]

Separation of Ownership and Management in Large Enterprises. Much more important than the two modifications just noted is the effect of the separation of ownership and management in large corporations. The typical owner—the stockholder—has little voice in the making of decisions, and the typical executive owns little or no stock in the enterprise and so receives relatively little of any profits earned. Salaries and bonuses comprise the primary income of the executives, while the profits accrue initially to the corporation, and may ultimately be paid out as dividends to the stockholders. The extent to which this separation of ownership and management affects the applicability of the profit-maximization assumption must be considered.

Continued Importance of the Profit-Maximization Goal. The profit-maximization assumption appears still to be applicable in large measure to the corporation, despite the fact that the persons who make the decisions may not receive the profits. First, there is a tendency on the part of corporation officials to regard the corporation as a separate entity, distinct from the stockholders who own it, and to identify their own welfare with that of the corporation, even though they do not receive the profits. It is almost universal in the business world for management officials to regard the profits made by their firm as the best measure of their own professional success. Second, the attainment of a high rate of profit may directly affect the economic position of the executives. Continued failure to earn as good a rate of return as informed stockholders believe to be possible may lead stockholders to revolt and seek to replace top management personnel. Failure to earn profit may endanger the continued existence of the firm, or at least lead to bankruptcy and reorganization. Finally, a satisfactory rate of profit is essential for continued expansion of the firm. Profits directly provide funds for expansion and facilitate the acquisition of additional capital. Growth of the enterprise not only increases the income of the executives but also raises their prestige and power, as discussed below.

Management may strive harder to obtain profits if the actual rate earned is below a figure regarded as "satisfactory" than if the current rate earned exceeds this figure. In the latter case, the position of management is secure, and expansion will be possible if the firm wishes to undertake it. Attempts to push profits up may be regarded as more

[1] See K. J. Cohen and R. M. Cyert, *Theory of the Firm* (Englewood Cliffs, N.J.: Prentice-Hall, 1965), chap. xv, for an analysis of this question.

trouble than they are worth. If profits are less than the figure regarded as satisfactory, a strong effort will almost certainly be made to restore them to this level, particularly because failure to do so may weaken the position of the management and possibly endanger the continuation of the firm.

Conflicts between Maximization of Profits and the Interests of Executives. The goal of profit maximization is likely to be pursued with vigor only so long as it is consistent with the interests of the management group. When divergencies arise, executives are likely to follow policies that promise maximum gains to themselves rather than maximum gains to the enterprise.[2] A projected expansion—though obviously profitable over a period of time—may imperil the solvency of the firm by imposing heavier fixed charges, or may bring in new dominant stockholders who may gain control and eliminate the present management. In other instances, current assets may be disposed of at a heavy loss in order to obtain funds to meet pressing obligations. Finally, complete liquidation of a business may be delayed by management long beyond the point at which it should be undertaken in the interest of stockholders. The managers not only dislike seeing the firm to which they have long been attached disappear, but also seek to avoid the loss of their positions. Through undermaintenance of plant and equipment, depletion of inventories, failure to cover depreciation charges, and sale of assets, the firm may continue to operate until the equity of the owners is completely dissipated, whereas earlier liquidation might preserve a substantial portion of the stockholders' money capital.

Vigor in the Pursuit of Goals. In the large-scale business organization the vigor with which the goal of profit maximization is pursued may be less than in the small owner-managed enterprise. Management of a large-scale business can easily become overcautious; the desire to maintain the *status quo*—to protect the positions of the executives—may encourage managers to avoid changes which appear profitable for fear that the expected gains will not be realized. Since profits do not accrue to the executives to any extent, the dynamic qualities of management characteristic of smaller enterprises may be overwhelmed by the desire to avoid disturbance of conditions that are "satisfactory." As a consequence, desirable readjustments in the conduct of the business may be avoided. The very complexity of the structure of

[2] This point of view is stressed in the article by R. J. Monsen and A. Downs, "A Theory of Large Managerial Firms," *Journal of Political Economy,* Vol. 73 (June, 1965), pp. 221–31.

the large corporation may itself slow down readjustments. The goals of top, middle, and lower management may diverge, and it is difficult for top management to gain adequate information from lower echelons, and to ensure that their policies are carried out with vigor.

Other Goals. If profit maximization is not accepted as the primary goal, what alternatives warrant consideration? Several have been proposed.

1. *The Goal of "Satisfactory" Profits.* Business firms may aim primarily for a "satisfactory" rate of profit rather than for the maximum figure. Not only do they strive more diligently for profits when earnings are less than satisfactory, but in some instances the "satisfactory" goal comes to be regarded as the dominant one. Top management may be more concerned with a steady growth in earnings than higher but fluctuating earnings.

Short-run acceptance of a goal of "satisfactory" profits does not necessarily involve failure to seek maximum returns over a long-run period. The importance of this goal may result from the belief that, over a long-run period, profits are likely to be greater if the firm avoids full exploitation of all temporary situations (which might allow high profits for a time, but would encourage the development of new firms). However, emphasis upon "satisfactory" profits does affect the reactions of firms in the short-run period. An increase in demand will almost of necessity lead to a price increase if firms are attempting to maximize profits. But if they are temporarily seeking only "satisfactory" profits, prices may be left unchanged.

2. *Sales Maximization.* Several students of the question, particularly W. J. Baumol,[3] have argued in recent years that maximization of sales, rather than profits, is the primary goal of the management of larger businesses, subject to the constraint of earning a satisfactory rate of profit, one sufficient to keep the stockholders satisfied. Sales represent a measure of success of management, particularly in light of acceptance of the doctrine that the share of the market obtained by a company is of primary importance for its long-term success. Baumol also suggests that there is a much closer correlation between the salaries of the executives and the gross sales of their businesses than between their salaries and the net profits; thus executives are more concerned about the former

---

[3] See W. J. Baumol, "On the Theory of Oligopoly," *Economica,* Vol. 25 (August, 1958), pp. 187–98. This argument is disputed by W. C. Pardridge, whose study of profit/sales ratios in management-controlled and closely held companies showed no difference in the ratios between the two groups. See "Sales or Profit Maximization in Management Capitalism," *Western Economic Journal,* Vol. 2 (Spring, 1964), pp. 134–41.

than the latter. Some empirical evidence favoring this position was found by McGuire, Chiu, and Elbing.[4]

3. *Nonpecuniary Goals.* In both small owner-managed enterprises and large corporations, the persons making decisions are without doubt in some cases influenced by nonpecuniary motives, which may take precedence over profit maximization. For example, prestige may be very important to the executives; they may thus undertake policies which will enhance their standing in the community or in the industry even though the policies do not contribute to profit maximization. Closely related is the desire of business leaders for power over as large a "business empire" as possible. While in many cases profit maximization is the best path to expansion, in other cases it may not be. History offers many examples of business firms which undertook unprofitable expansions merely because the executives wished to exercise authority over more extensive empires. Such policies are more likely to be followed in large corporations, in which executives do not directly benefit from the profits, than in small enterprises; but they are not absent even in the latter.

Large firms sometimes follow policies which they regard as best serving the interests of the community or nation as a whole, even though not directly advantageous for profit maximization. Thus, firms may be reluctant to cut wages or lay off men in a depression, in the belief that such action may aggravate the decline in economic activity. Or, for purely humanitarian reasons, they may not fire aged employees.

Businessmen operate within a complicated and restrictive framework of legal and social institutions. Except in rare instances, they will not seek to maximize profits by taking illegal action, although the latter is not unknown. Furthermore, they are likely to avoid certain practices which, although legal, are contrary to accepted standards of business practice. Thus, they may avoid price cutting if such practices are generally frowned upon by other firms.

4. *Preference Maximization.* These various qualifications suggest that for a more satisfactory analysis, the profit-maximization assumption should be replaced by a more general assumption of preference maximization, in which various goals, including profit maximization, could be integrated. Such an assumption would be particularly desirable when uncertainty prevails, and the profit-maximization rule is inadequate because executives are confronted by a group of possible outcomes, with different degrees of uncertainty, rather than a single profit-

[4] See J. W. McGuire, J. Y. S. Chiu, and A. O. Elbing, "Executive Incomes, Sales and Profits," *American Economic Review,* Vol. 52 (September, 1962), pp. 753–61.

maximization potentiality. Further progress in economic analysis may require such an assumption. But the complexity of the overall analysis would be tremendously increased by replacement of the profit-maximization goal by a broader one.[5] For purposes of the present analysis the assumption of profit maximization will be retained in the interests of simplicity, but recognition will be given to the effects of major deviations from the assumption.

RELATIONSHIPS AMONG UNITS—MARKET STRUCTURE

The determination of prices and outputs of various commodities and prices of factors is affected by the structure of the markets, that is, relationships prevailing among transactors in various markets. The price and the output of a commodity will obviously be different if the entire supply is controlled by one firm than if it is provided by a large number of small sellers, all acting independently of one another. The number of buyers and the relationships prevailing among them will likewise affect price and output. The nature of markets for factor units will affect the prices paid for them, and thus the costs of producing the products made with them and the distribution of income among factor owners. Market behavior will depend upon the extent to which information about market conditions, past and present, is available to buyers and sellers and upon the mobility of factor units from one employment to another.

The Concept of a Market

A market consists of a group of buyers and sellers in sufficiently close contact with one another for exchange to take place among them. For some commodities, as for example, gravel, there are numerous more or less isolated markets. Buyers are in contact only with local producers, since transportation costs are so high relative to selling prices that the commodity cannot be shipped any substantial distance. Thus, price and output are determined in a number of small markets, and total production of gravel is the sum of the amounts of output determined separately in each of the markets. In other industries, markets are nationwide; automobile manufacturers, for example, sell to dealers throughout the country and determine price and output on the basis of considerations relating to the entire economy.

---

[5] See J. De V. Graaff, "Income Effects and the Theory of the Firm," *Review of Economic Studies,* Vol. 18 (2), No. 46 (1950–51), pp. 79–86; also R. W. Clower, "Mr. Graaff's Producer-Consumer Theory . . . ," *Review of Economic Studies,* Vol. 20 (1), No. 51 (1952–53), pp. 84–85.

+ Bases of Market Classification

Market situations differ from one another primarily on the basis of the extent to which individual buyers and sellers can by independent action influence price. The extent of such influence, in turn, depends primarily upon four considerations: the homogeneity of the product, the number of sellers, the number of buyers, and the extent of coöperative action or interdependence among the various buyers and sellers.

Homogeneity—the extent to which buyers regard the products of all sellers as being identical, and the extent to which sellers have no preferences as to the buyers to whom they sell—is of primary importance in controlling the degree of freedom which firms have to act independently of their competitors. The development of differentiation —that is, of preferences on the part of buyers and sellers for particular varieties of product and for dealing with particular firms—increases the freedom of firms to act independently and thus increases the control which they have over their own prices. The greater the differentiation, the less easily will customers shift from one firm to another in response to price changes.

The numbers of buyers and sellers determine the extent to which each is aware of the effects of his own policies on those of his competitors and thus the extent to which each expects his action to affect the prices and outputs of his competitors. If sellers are numerous, for example, they will not expect their own policies to have sufficient effect upon their competitors to affect their policies. If the number is small, each firm will expect competitors to react to its policies. The number of buyers and sellers also affects the extent to which certain standard practices (cost accounting methods, for example) will be adopted by firms, as well as the likelihood of outright agreements on price and output. When collusive policies are followed, their exact nature is of primary importance for the character of market relationships and thus of price and output determination. Collusive policies depend not only upon the number of competitors but also upon the nature of the product, the attitudes of officials of competing firms toward coöperative action, the relationships of the firms in past years, and government antitrust policy.

Major Classes of Markets

The number of possible types of market situations is very great, because of the large number of possible degrees of differentiation of

product and of variations in numbers of buyers, sellers, and relationships among them. For purposes of analysis, however, the various
possible situations may be grouped into two classes, *purely competitive*
and *nonpurely competitive* markets. In the first, neither individual
buyers nor sellers have any direct control over market prices. In the
second, individual buyers, or sellers, or both, do exercise such control.

The purely competitive model is useful for purposes of analysis,
although actual conditions approximate it in only a small segment of
the economy. It is a simple, clear-cut case, the analysis of which will
serve to clarify basic theoretical relationships more easily than would
analysis of more complex structures.

Nonpurely competitive markets consist of a heterogeneous collection of situations, which may be grouped into four categories:

1. *Monopolistic competition,* characterized by differentiation of
product, and a sufficiently large number of sellers that each determines
his policies independently of any effects which they may have upon
the policies of competitors.

2. *Oligopoly,* a situation in which the number of firms is
sufficiently small that there is mutual interdependence among them;
that is, each firm, in determining its own policies, takes into consideration the possible effects which these policies may have upon the actions
of competitors. The products of the various firms may be either
homogeneous or differentiated.

3. Complete *monopoly,* a situation in which there is a single
seller.

4. *Monopsonistic* markets, characterized by the exercise of influence upon price by individual buyers. This influence may arise
because of smallness in the number of buyers, or because of preferences
on the part of sellers for dealing with particular buyers. Markets which
contain monopsonistic elements may be purely competitive on the side
of the sellers, or contain any of the forms of nonpure competition noted
above.

Since deviations from purely competitive conditions appear to be
more common on the sellers' side than on the buyers' side, primary
attention will be given to analytical models relevant for cases 1 to 3,
above, with the assumption that individual buyers are unable to
influence price, except where otherwise noted.

It must be emphasized that we are concerned with analytical
models, based upon simplified assumptions. Hence the analysis of price
and output determination in the various models must not be regarded as
an exact description of actual conditions. The analysis of price and

output to be manageable must be developed in terms of a relatively small number of simple models, the assumptions upon which each is based being derived from studies of market structures.

PERFECTION IN MARKET CONDITIONS

Price and output determination are affected not only by market relationships prevailing among buyers and sellers, but also by the absence or presence of other institutional factors that affect the behavior of transactors. There are two major considerations of this type: the extent of knowledge about market conditions, and the mobility of various factor units. Deviations from perfect knowledge or perfect mobility of factors are known as *imperfections*.

A market characterized by complete absence of imperfections, as well as by purely competitive market conditions, is described as *perfectly competitive*. All sellers and buyers have perfect knowledge of market conditions, and frictions checking immediate adjustment of price and output are completely absent. Producing units have complete knowledge of costs and market conditions, and so are able to maximize profits at all times. Factor units are freely mobile, and so will always move to the most attractive employments.

The concept of perfection in markets may be applied to nonpurely competitive markets as well. In monopolistic competition, for example, perfection requires perfect factor mobility and complete knowledge on the part of sellers about cost and demand conditions. In oligopoly, perfection requires that firms know the reactions of their competitors to their own policies, as well as other data pertinent to profit maximization.

The assumption of perfection is frequently useful as a first approximation in the development of an analysis, in order to make it manageable. Actually, all markets are characterized by substantial imperfections which interfere with the attainment of the goals of business firms, households, and factor owners. There are two major types: imperfect knowledge and imperfect mobility.

Imperfect Knowledge

Factor owners and business firms rarely, if ever, possess all information necessary to attain maximization goals. Workers may be unaware of employment alternatives. Persons about to establish new business enterprises have only limited knowledge of profit possibilities. Despite improved techniques, sellers have inadequate knowledge of potential sales at various price levels and imprecise knowledge of cost behavior. Information about income possibilities, sales, and costs depends upon the institutions of the period—the state of education, the state of market research and cost analysis techniques, the activity of government agencies in preparing and distributing information about job and profit possibilities, trends in national income, etc. As a consequence of imperfect knowledge, outputs of various goods are different from what they would otherwise be, and both resource allocation and income distribution are affected. Too many producers enter some lines of production, for example, and others make unwarranted plant expansions or fail to make other changes which would be profitable. Prices may be set at levels which do not maximize profits, and production may exceed the quantities which can be sold at profitable prices.

Mobility of Factor Units

There are numerous restrictions, in practice, on the movement of factors of production from one use to another. Many specialized factors of production are not easily adaptable to changing conditions. Machinery constructed for one purpose is frequently completely unsuited for any other use. A railroad grade, including expensive bridges and tunnels, is ordinarily useless for any purpose except railroad operation. Apple trees cannot produce anything but apples. In some instances the transfer of resources, although possible, is not feasible because of costs of transference; streetcar rails on abandoned lines are often left in the pavement because costs of removal are prohibitive. As a result of nonadaptability, resources will be continued in a particular use long after they have ceased to yield the return which was necessary to bring them into the field.

Labor likewise is not entirely adaptable. Persons trained in certain lines of work cannot easily shift to employment requiring different skills. Geographical mobility of labor is seriously restricted by costs of moving, by family ties, and by preferences for living in certain areas. Workers are typically reluctant to shift away from present occupations and employers to move to other areas.

The significance of these various imperfections will be indicated in succeeding chapters.

The Approach to Price Theory

Our analysis of price and output determination will be divided into two general segments. The first portion deals with the prices and outputs of consumption goods produced by business firms. The second portion deals with the prices and quantities utilized of various types of factor services. The first segment is known as price theory; the second, as the theory of factor pricing, or distribution theory. The interrelationships of output and factor prices, and the nature of the price system as a whole, will be summarized in Chapter 18.

The prices of produced commodities depend in general upon two sets of forces, those relating to the demand for commodities and those relating to cost of production and supply. Each of these two forces is best analyzed separately before consideration is given to the manner in which their interaction determines equilibrium price and output.

SELECTED REFERENCES

A very extensive literature has appeared in the last decade on the question of the goals of business firms:

BAUMOL, W. J. *Business Behavior, Value and Growth.* New York: Macmillan, 1959.

———. *Economic Theory and Operations Analysis,* chap. xiii. 2d ed. Englewood Cliffs, N.J.: Prentice-Hall, 1965.
   A good brief summary.

COHEN, K. J., AND CYERT, R. M. *Theory of the Firm,* chaps. xv–xvii. Englewood Cliffs, N.J.: Prentice-Hall, 1965.
   A detailed summary of the recent work.

CYERT, R. M., AND MARCH, J. G. *A Behavioral Theory of the Firm.* Englewood Cliffs, N.J.: Prentice-Hall, 1963.
   An advanced analysis.

GORDON, R. A. *Business Leadership in the Large Corporation.* Washington, D.C.: Brookings, 1945.
   An earlier study of policy determination and goals in the large corporation.

MARCH, J. G., AND SIMON, H. A. *Organizations.* New York: Wiley, 1958.
   An excellent general treatment of the theory of formal organizations.

SIMON, H. A. "New Developments in the Theory of the Firm," *Proceedings of the American Economic Association for 1961,* pp. 1–15.

———. "Theories of Decision-Making in Economics and Behavioral Science," *American Economic Review,* Vol. 49 (June, 1959), pp. 253–81.

WILLIAMSON, O. E. *The Economics of Discretionary Behavior.* Englewood Cliffs, N.J.: Prentice-Hall, 1964.

QUESTIONS

1. Distinguish between *firm* and *industry.*
2. As the term *industry* is employed in the analysis, does potato farming constitute an industry? Do law firms?
3. Would you regard the firms producing toasters, refrigerators, and air condi-

tioners as constituting separate industries, or all constituting elements in the electrical appliance industry? Discuss.

4. Give some examples of firms operating in more than one industry.

5. Indicate the major functions of business firms.

6. Indicate the principal characteristics of the two major types of business firms.

7. What is meant by the maximizing assumption? Apply the assumption to consumers and to factor owners.

8. Why is it incorrect to state that we assume that workers seek to maximize their money incomes?

9. Suppose that you operate a small restaurant. What may serve as a constraint on the goal of profit maximization?

10. What is the significance of uncertainty for the goal of profit maximization?

11. In a large-scale firm, is it more realistic to assume that top management is seeking to maximize profits of the firm, or personal income of the management personnel? Why may the two goals in large measure not be conflicting? In what types of situations may they conflict?

12. What is the sales-maximization goal? Does this statement refer to physical units or dollar volume? Does acceptance of this goal suggest that the firm will disregard the profits goal? Explain.

13. Are large firms or small firms more likely to be influenced by nonpecuniary goals? Explain.

14. Explain the concept of preference maximization. In view of its theoretical superiority over profit maximization, why has it not been employed more extensively in economic analysis?

15. Explain the concept of a market.

16. Indicate the likely geographical scope of the markets for the following: (*a*) typewriters, (*b*) used cars, (*c*) sugar beets, (*d*) haircuts, (*e*) university education, (*f*) movie theater services, and (*g*) books.

17. Indicate the primary determinants of the nature of market structures.

18. Define and indicate the characteristics of a purely competitive market.

19. Distinguish between oligopoly and monopolistic competition. Give examples of each.

20. Distinguish between pure and perfect competition.

21. Indicate major market imperfections.

22. Would you classify the following market structures as ones of pure competition, oligopoly, monopolistic competition, monopsony, or monopoly?
    a) Wholesale markets for wheat.
    b) Automobiles (manufacturing level).
    c) Sugar beets.
    d) Women's dresses.
    e) Men's shirts.
    f) Bakery products.
    g) Restaurants in large cities.
    h) Electric power, in a particular area.
    i) Glass containers (manufacturing level).
    j) Medical service.

Part II

Commodity Price and Output Determination

Chapter 4 — DEMAND CONCEPTS

In a market economy, characterized by freedom of choice, consumer demand plays a major role in determining product prices and the allocation of resources. Firms will produce only those goods for which demand is adequate to support prices at levels that will cover production costs, and the quantities produced will in turn influence the employment and earnings of factor units. To help clarify the concepts and relationships we begin our discussion of consumer demand with an account of the nature and determinants of demand and related concepts of demand elasticity. A more formal analysis of consumer behavior underlying demand is presented in the next chapter.

The Concept of Demand

The demand of an individual buyer for a product, known as *individual demand*, is a schedule of the amounts of the product which the person would buy at various possible alternative prices in a particular interval of time.[1] A shopper enters a store to buy oranges for use during the coming week; she finds the price to be 30 cents a dozen, and she buys four dozen. Had the price been 40 cents for oranges of the same grade, she would have bought a certain quantity—perhaps three dozen. Had it been 50 cents, she might have bought none at all; at 20 cents, she might have bought five dozen. Her demand for oranges at the particular time is the schedule of the various amounts that she would purchase at the various possible prices. Such a schedule is illustrated in Table 4–1. The fact that the shopper is not aware of the amounts that she would purchase at prices other than the prevailing one does not alter the fact that she has a schedule, in the sense that she would have bought various other amounts had other prices prevailed. It must be

---

[1] Demand schedules may be considered in terms of a particular moment of time or, more realistically, in terms of a short period.

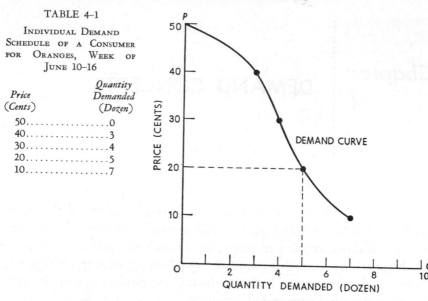

TABLE 4–1

INDIVIDUAL DEMAND
SCHEDULE OF A CONSUMER
FOR ORANGES, WEEK OF
JUNE 10–16

Price (Cents)	Quantity Demanded (Dozen)
50................	.0
40................	.3
30................	.4
20................	.5
10................	.7

FIGURE 4–1
INDIVIDUAL DEMAND SCHEDULE OF A
CUSTOMER FOR ORANGES OF A CERTAIN
GRADE, WEEK OF JUNE 10–16

emphasized that the schedule is a list of alternative possibilities; at any one time, only one of the prices will prevail, and thus a certain determinate quantity will be purchased.

The data in Table 4–1 can be plotted graphically, as shown in Figure 4–1. The data as given provide a series of points, which, when connected by a continuous curve, constitute the demand curve. This procedure provides by interpolation estimates of quantities demanded at prices between those for which information is given. In the graphs employed for price and output analysis, price is always plotted on the vertical axis, and quantity on the horizontal axis.

In the typical market, there are numerous buyers, each with his own individual demand schedule. The sum of these schedules, known as *market demand,* or more commonly, *demand,* is thus a schedule of total amounts that would be purchased by all buyers in a particular market at various possible prices in a given time interval. The market demand for oranges in a particular market for a certain week might appear as shown in Table 4–2 and illustrated graphically in Figure 4–2. Although the actual quantities which would be purchased at prices other than the prevailing one may not be known, the schedule is nevertheless determinate in the sense that total purchases would shift to various other definite amounts if the price were to change.

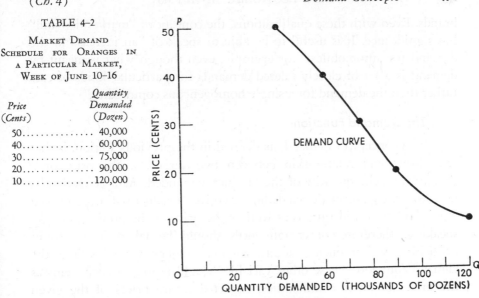

Price (Cents)	Quantity Demanded (Dozen)
50	40,000
40	60,000
30	75,000
20	90,000
10	120,000

TABLE 4-2

MARKET DEMAND SCHEDULE FOR ORANGES IN A PARTICULAR MARKET, WEEK OF JUNE 10–16

FIGURE 4–2

MARKET DEMAND SCHEDULE FOR ORANGES OF A CERTAIN GRADE IN A PARTICULAR MARKET, WEEK OF JUNE 10–16

When a commodity is homogeneous, in the sense that buyers have no preferences for particular brands of the commodity and thus no preference for the product of any particular seller, the concept of market demand is precise; the various individual demand schedules can be added without conceptual difficulty. But when the product is differentiated, the concept of market demand, although still useful, becomes less precise. With differentiation, individual buyers have preferences for brands of particular producers; a buyer's schedule is not, for example, for "cigarettes," but for a particular brand of cigarettes. The amount that he is willing to buy depends upon the brands available, and he may use less of the commodity if his favorite variety cannot be obtained. Likewise, with differentiation, the selling prices of firms may not be identical; in one situation some brands may sell for 25 cents, some for 30 cents, and others for 20 cents; in another situation they may sell for 18, 23, and 13 cents, respectively, etc. Thus there is no clear-cut market demand schedule of certain amounts being purchased at particular prices. Instead, the schedule must be regarded as showing the total amounts of particular brands that would be purchased at various possible levels of a pattern of prices, with the fact recognized that the amounts which individuals will buy are different for the various brands. Even with these qualifications, the concept of "market demand" has significance. It is useful to be able to speak of "an increase in the demand for automobiles," for example, even though what is meant by demand is a set of closely related demands for particular kinds of cars rather than the demand for a single homogeneous commodity.

The Demand Function

The concept of demand, as defined in the previous section, is that of a functional relationship between two variables: the price of a product, and the quantity of the product demanded. As a general rule, however, the quantity demanded of any given product will depend on a host of other considerations as well as the price of the product. Strictly speaking, therefore, other influences should be taken into account explicitly by introducing additional independent variables into the demand function. These other variables would represent such items as the prices of other commodities, expected future prices of the given commodity, expected future prices of other commodities, the level and distribution of income and wealth, the age and family characteristics of households, etc. Depending on the problem we wished to consider, we might then treat demand not only as a function of price alone (all other variables fixed in value), but alternatively as a function of income alone (prices, etc., constant) or as a function of other prices alone, and so forth. When we speak of demand (or the demand function) without further qualification, however, we mean by this the special and simple form of the demand function in which price is the only explicit independent variable and all other influences are implicit "shift" parameters (i.e., variables which, if their values are altered, produce a shift on the graph of the demand function relating quantity to price).

Changes in Demand

Since *demand* is defined as a schedule of amounts which would be purchased at various alternative prices, a change in demand occurs only if persons will buy larger or smaller quantities at particular prices as a result of a change in one or more of the "shift" parameters noted in the preceding section. A change in demand may affect the entire schedule or only portions of it. An increase in demand is shown in Table 4–3, and is illustrated graphically in Figure 4–3. The change in demand is reflected in an entirely new demand curve ($D'D'$ in Figure 4–3).

A change in demand must be distinguished clearly from a change in *quantity demanded* resulting from a price change. The latter is illustrated by a movement along an existing curve from one point to another. A change in the price of a good cannot cause a change in the

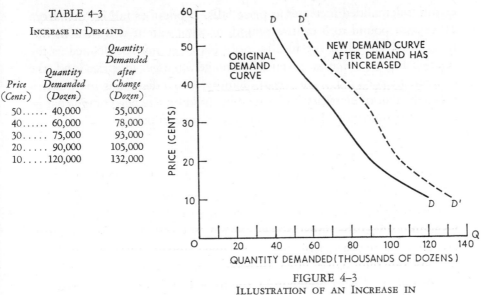

TABLE 4–3

INCREASE IN DEMAND

Price (Cents)	Quantity Demanded (Dozen)	Quantity Demanded after Change (Dozen)
50	40,000	55,000
40	60,000	78,000
30	75,000	93,000
20	90,000	105,000
10	120,000	132,000

FIGURE 4–3
ILLUSTRATION OF AN INCREASE IN
DEMAND

demand for the good, since demand is defined as the entire schedule of the quantities which would be purchased *at various possible prices.*

ELASTICITY OF DEMAND

The concept of elasticity relates to the responsiveness of a given variable (e.g., quantity demanded, quantity supplied) to changes in the value of another variable to which it is functionally related. With the basic demand function relating quantity demanded to price, for example, elasticity refers to the relative response of quantity demanded to a change in price. With a demand function relating quantity demanded to income, price being treated as a given parameter, elasticity refers to the relative response of quantity demanded to a change in income. With a demand function relating the quantity demanded of one commodity to the price of another commodity, elasticity refers to the relative effect of a change in the price of one commodity on the quantity demanded of the other. The terms *price elasticity* (or, more commonly, *elasticity*), *income elasticity,* and *cross-elasticity* are given to these three concepts. Each will be considered in turn.

Price Elasticity

For reasons explained in the next chapter, a reduction in price typically results in an increase in the quantity demanded. The question of price elasticity, therefore, is the question of the extent to which quantity demanded increases as price falls. If potatoes fall in price from 10 cents a pound to 5 cents a pound, to what extent will persons buy more potatoes? More specifically, price elasticity may be defined as the relationship between a given percentage change in price and the consequent percentage change in quantity demanded; thus the numerical coefficient of elasticity is obtained by dividing the percentage change in quantity demanded by the percentage change in price:

$$e_p = \frac{Q - Q'}{Q} \div \frac{P - P'}{P},$$

where Q and P represent the initial quantity and price, and Q' and P' represent values of the same variables after the change. The negative sign, indicating the inverse relationship between price and quantity demanded, is in practice often omitted.

When the changes in price and quantity are of any significant magnitude, the exact meaning of the term *percentage change* requires interpretation, and the terms *price* and *quantity* in the formula above must be defined more precisely. The question is: Should the percentage change be figured on the basis of price and quantity before or after the change has occurred? For example, a price rise from $1.00 to $1.50 constitutes a 50 percent change if the original price ($1.00) is used in figuring the percentage, or a $33\frac{1}{3}$ percent change if the price after the change ($1.50) is used. The most common approach is the use of the midpoints between the old and the new figures for both price and quantity demanded. In the formula the sums of the prices ($1.00 plus $1.50 in the example) and of the quantities before and after the change, respectively, may be used instead of the averages of these, since the result will be exactly the same. A fraction is not altered by dividing both the numerator and the denominator by 2. The formula thus becomes:

$$\text{Elasticity} = \frac{\dfrac{\text{Change in quantity demanded}}{\text{Original quantity plus quantity after change}}}{\dfrac{\text{Change in price}}{\text{Original price plus price after change}}},$$

or

$$e_p = \frac{Q - Q'}{Q + Q'} \div \frac{P - P'}{P + P'}.$$

Behavior of Total Outlay. The elasticity of demand for a commodity is reflected in behavior of the total outlay or expenditure on the commodity (price times quantity purchased) as the price changes. When the elasticity exceeds one (numerically), total outlay will rise as the price declines, since the quantity demanded increases at a relatively greater rate than that at which the price falls. If a price is cut in half and the quantity demanded more than doubles, obviously more money is being spent on the commodity than before. If elasticity is less than one, the total outlay will be less at low prices than at high, since a given price reduction will be accompanied by a proportionately smaller increase in quantity demanded. If the elasticity is one, the relative changes in price and quantity are the same, and total outlay will be the same regardless of the price.

Classification of Segments of Demand Schedules on the Basis of Elasticity

On the basis of elasticity, particular segments of demand sched-ules[2] can be grouped into three major classes:

1. *Elastic* demand segments—those with elasticity numerically greater than one. Thus the price change is accompanied by a more than proportionate change in quantity demanded, and total outlay is greater at lower prices than at higher ones. In the limiting case of *perfect elasticity*, an increase in price causes the quantity demanded to fall to zero; at a certain price and at any lower figure the quantity demanded is infinite.[3] In Table 4–4 a typical elastic demand is illustrated, as well as a perfectly elastic schedule.

TABLE 4–4

Price (Cents)	Typical Elastic Demand		Perfectly Elastic Demand	
	Quantity Demanded	Total Outlay	Quantity Demanded	Total Outlay
50	8	$4.00	0	0
40	12	4.80	0	0
30	20	6.00	0	0
20	35	7.00	Infinite	Infinite
10	80	8.00	Infinite	Infinite

2. *Inelastic* demand segments—those with elasticity less than one. Thus the price change is accompanied by a less than proportionate

---

[2] An entire demand schedule would rarely have the same elasticity throughout.

[3] Strictly speaking, the quantity demanded is not defined, but is said to be infinite. Individual and total demand schedules cannot be perfectly elastic; the fact that incomes are limited prevents persons from buying infinite amounts of any good. The demand schedules confronting individual sellers may appear to be perfectly elastic, from the standpoint of the sellers themselves.

change in quantity demanded, and total outlay is greater at higher prices. The limiting case is a *perfectly inelastic* demand; the quantity demanded is the same, regardless of the price. Individual demand schedules are often perfectly inelastic within certain price ranges. An increase in the price of gasoline, for example, from 29 to 30 cents will not affect the volume of purchases of many buyers. A typical inelastic schedule and one of perfect inelasticity are illustrated in Table 4–5.

TABLE 4-5

Price (Cents)	Typical Inelastic Demand		Perfectly Inelastic Demand	
	Quantity Demanded	Total Outlay	Quantity Demanded	Total Outlay
50	8	$4.00	8	$4.00
40	9	3.60	8	3.20
30	11	3.30	8	2.40
20	14	2.80	8	1.60
10	19	1.90	8	0.80

3. *Demand segments of unitary elasticity*—those with a numerical expression of elasticity of one. The percentage change in quantity demanded is the same as the percentage change in price. For example, if price is cut in half, the quantity demanded doubles, and total outlay is the same regardless of the price. It is unlikely that a demand schedule would possess exactly unitary elasticity over a substantial range, the case merely constituting the dividing line between elastic and inelastic segments. Table 4–6 shows a demand of unitary elasticity.

TABLE 4-6

DEMAND OF UNITARY ELASTICITY

Price (Cents)	Quantity Demanded	Total Outlay
50	8	$4.00
40	10	4.00
30	$13\frac{1}{3}$	4.00
20	20	4.00
10	40	4.00

In any given range of a graph, an inelastic demand will appear as a steeper curve than an elastic demand. A perfectly inelastic demand will appear as a vertical line, and a perfectly elastic demand as a horizontal line. A demand of unitary elasticity appears as a rectangular hyperbola. These are illustrated in Figure 4–4. Great care, however, must be taken in estimating elasticity from the slope of the curve,

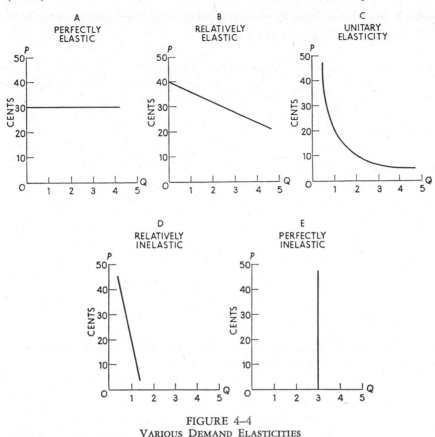

FIGURE 4–4
VARIOUS DEMAND ELASTICITIES

beyond the extreme limiting cases; when segments of curves appear on different portions of the graph, the relative slope tells nothing about elasticity. A straight-line demand curve which is sloping will change elasticity continuously along its course, since the denominators of the fractions in the formula are continuously changing while the numerators remain unchanged. The determinants of elasticity will be analyzed in the next chapter.

Income Elasticity

While the most widely employed demand function is that relating price and quantity demanded, use is also made of the function which relates quantity demanded to income. The concept of income elasticity relates to the nature of the functional relationship involved; more specifically, it is a measure of the relationship between a relative change in income and the consequent relative change in quantity demanded, price being a parameter. Expressed symbolically, the income elasticity of demand is given by the formula

$$e_y = \frac{\dfrac{q - q'}{q + q'}}{\dfrac{y - y'}{y + y'}}$$

i.e., the percentage change in purchases (quantity demanded) divided by the percentage change in income. The response may be positive or negative. Presumably for most commodities, an increase in income will result in an increase in purchases, but the degree of elasticity may vary substantially, for reasons explained in the next chapter. As distinguished from "normal" goods, the relationship for "inferior" goods is inverse; as incomes rise, persons will buy fewer units of the goods. These are "cheap" goods which persons buy only when they cannot afford anything better—poor cuts of meat, poor quality clothing, etc. As their incomes rise they will shift to preferred substitutes.

Cross-Elasticity of Demand

Another useful demand function relates the price of one commodity to the quantity demanded of another; the concept of cross-elasticity is that of the behavior of this functional relationship. As apple prices fall, to what extent does the demand for oranges increase?

More specifically, cross-elasticity of demand may be defined as the relationship between a certain percentage change in the price of one commodity and the consequent percentage change in the quantity demanded of another good:

$$e_{p(x,y)} = \frac{Q_x - Q_x'}{Q_x + Q_x'} \div \frac{P_y - P_y'}{P_y + P_y'}.$$

The determinants of cross-elasticity will be discussed in the next chapter.

SELECTED REFERENCES

See Chapter 5.

QUESTIONS

1. Distinguish carefully between the terms *demand* and *quantity demanded.*
2. The usual demand function expresses the relationship between price and quantity demanded. What are the principal parameters of this functional relationship?

3. Distinguish between an increase in demand and an increase in quantity demanded. Show each graphically.

4. Indicate several possible causes of a decrease in demand.

5. Why, on the basis of the terminology employed, can an increase in price not cause a decrease in demand?

6. Indicate the general meaning of the concept of elasticity as relating to demand and supply schedules.

7. Distinguish price elasticity, income elasticity, and cross-elasticity of demand.

8. Indicate the formula used to obtain a numerical coefficient of price elasticity of demand.

9. Suppose that when a firm reduces price, its total revenue from the sale of the product increases. Will the coefficient of demand elasticity be positive or negative? Will it exceed or be less than one? Why?

10. A store finds that if it raises the price of bread from the present price of 24 cents a loaf to 25 cents, it sells none at all. What is the nature of the elasticity of demand for bread from this firm?

11. With an elastic demand, will total revenue (price times quantity) be greater at low prices or at high prices? Why?

12. With a demand of unitary elasticity, what happens to total revenue as price changes? Why?

13. Indicate the formula for income elasticity of demand. Is the relationship negative or positive? Explain.

14. Indicate the formula for cross-elasticity of demand.

Chapter 5

THE THEORY OF CONSUMER BEHAVIOR AND THE DETERMINANTS OF DEMAND

The previous chapter reviewed the major concepts relating to demand schedules. The important task remains of explaining the underlying determinants of demand and demand elasticity. To do so requires an analysis of consumer behavior, that is, decision making by the household. The analysis is built upon the assumption that consumers act rationally, seeking to maximize satisfaction gained from given incomes.

The Law of Demand

As noted in the previous chapter, quantity demanded typically increases as the price declines; that is to say, demand curves ordinarily slope downward from left to right. This relationship is supported by extensive empirical evidence; it can also be inferred by deductive reasoning from the assumptions that (1) consumers seek to maximize satisfaction; (2) incomes are limited; and (3) the marginal utility— the addition to satisfaction from acquiring an additional unit of a commodity—falls as additional units of a commodity are acquired. The Law of Demand can be explained in rather simple terms on the basis of the Law of Diminishing Marginal Utility, or in more sophisticated terms by the use of indifference curves and the Law of Diminishing Marginal Rate of Substitution.

THE LAW OF DIMINISHING MARGINAL UTILITY

Marginal utility is defined as the addition to total utility or satisfaction which results from the acquisition of an additional unit of a good in a given period of time. While marginal utility is not directly measurable in any usual sense, the concept has meaning in the sense that marginal utilities of various goods can be compared and ranked. In other words, it is an *ordinal* rather than a *cardinal* measure. Thus a person can compare the satisfaction gained from another car with that obtained from the first car purchased, and the gain from the car with the satisfaction from a trip to Europe or new furniture.

The Law of Diminishing Marginal Utility describes the behavior of marginal utility as the quantity of a good possessed by an individual varies. According to the law, as a person obtains additional units of any good, the marginal utility declines; that is, each successive unit adds less to the person's satisfaction than did the previous unit. The law is relevant for a particular period of time. The first automobile that a consumer acquires may yield him a great deal of satisfaction by providing a form of transportation more suitable for many purposes than alternative forms. If the person acquires a second car (in the same period of time), it will increase his satisfaction to a certain extent, because, for example, two members of the family can now use cars at the same time. But the marginal utility—the increase in satisfaction resulting from the acquisition of the second car—is likely to be far less than that resulting from the purchase of the first car.

The Law of Diminishing Marginal Utility may be explained in terms of the mutual interaction of two factors: individual wants are satiable, and different goods are not perfect substitutes for one another in the satisfaction of particular wants. As a person uses more and more units of a good to satisfy a given kind of want, the intensity of the want diminishes. But units of the good cannot be transferred to the satisfaction of other wants and produce as much satisfaction as they yielded initially in the satisfaction of the first want, because the good is not a perfect substitute (and possibly not one at all) for goods best designed to satisfy the second want.[1] For example, as a person consumes more and more salt, his desire for it in his food is eventually satisfied. Additional amounts can be used for other purposes, such as removing ice from sidewalks, but will yield less satisfaction than the initial units used for food.

The Allocation of Consumer Income

Because marginal utility diminishes as additional units of a good are acquired, a person, if he is to maximize satisfaction from his income, must avoid extending purchases of any one good beyond the point at which other goods will yield greater satisfaction, and thus exercise care in the allocation of income among various commodities. More precisely, for maximization of satisfaction, income must be allocated in such a

---

[1] This could occur if two goods were perfect substitutes for one another and thus, in an economic sense, essentially the same good.

way that the marginal utility of a unit-of-money's worth (for example, 10 cents' worth) is the same for every commodity. When this situation is realized, 10 cents' worth of gasoline will yield the same satisfaction— the same marginal utility—as 10 cents' worth of bread or apples or theater tickets or soap or any other commodity that is purchased. If this situation is not attained, the person can increase total satisfaction by buying more of some goods and less of others. If, for example, the marginal utility of 10 cents' worth of apples is less than that of 10 cents' worth of bread, total satisfaction can be increased by buying more bread (and thus lowering the marginal utility of bread) and fewer apples (and thus raising the marginal utility of apples).

This principle may also be stated in terms of the relationship between the marginal utilities and the prices of the various goods. Maximum satisfaction requires allocation of income in such a way that the marginal utilities of units of the various goods purchased are proportional to the prices of the goods. That is, if potatoes cost twice as much per pound as spinach, the consumer must adjust his purchases of the two commodities until the marginal utility of a pound of potatoes is twice as great as the marginal utility of a pound of spinach. It must be recognized that many goods, such as pianos and automobiles, are not available in small, inexpensive units and thus perfect adjustment of marginal utilities is not possible. The equilibrium can be shown by an equation:

$$\frac{MU_1}{P_1} = \frac{MU_2}{P_2} = \frac{MU_3}{P_3} \cdots \frac{MU_n}{P_n}.$$

The Relationship between Price and Quantity Demanded

It follows as a matter of logic from the Law of Diminishing Marginal Utility and the principle of income allocation outlined above that a price reduction will lead to an increase in the quantity of the good demanded. The price reduction necessitates a reallocation in the use of income, since the old equilibrium has been disturbed.

If the price of coffee declines from 80 cents to 40 cents a pound, 10 cents' worth of coffee is now one quarter of a pound instead of one eighth of a pound, and thus may exceed the marginal utilities of 10 cents' worth of substitute commodities whose prices remain unchanged. Accordingly, a readjustment in the relative purchases of coffee and other goods is necessary to restore the equality of the marginal utilities of 10 cents' worth of all goods purchased. In addition, since coffee is cheaper than before, the buyer can buy more of various commodities with a given income and some of the income freed may be spent on coffee.

THE INDIFFERENCE CURVE TECHNIQUE

A more sophisticated approach to the explanation of the allocation of consumer income and the nature of the demand schedule utilizes indifference schedules and curves to illustrate consumer behavior.[2] The use of indifference curves facilitates explanation of various demand and consumer behavior relationships, avoids the implication of the marginal utility approach that utility can be measured cardinally, and stresses the interrelationships among the demands for various articles.

The Indifference Schedule

An indifference schedule indicates various combinations of two goods which will yield a consumer the same total satisfaction. For example, a household may obtain the same satisfaction from the use of three loaves of bread plus four pounds of steak a week as from the use of one loaf of bread and five pounds of steak, or ten loaves of bread and two pounds of steak, etc. The person's indifference schedule for these two commodities, shown in Table 5–1, contains various possible combinations of the two commodities which will yield the same satisfaction. For another level of satisfaction, there is another pattern of combinations.

This schedule can be plotted on a graph, one commodity being plotted on the vertical axis, the other on the horizontal. The curve connecting the various points is known as an *indifference curve.* The curve in Figure 5–1 includes points representing the various combinations contained in Table 5–1. *The curve shows nothing about the absolute amounts of satisfaction obtained but merely indicates the various combinations which will yield equal satisfaction.*

Indifference curves slope downward from left to right, under the assumption that, in order to maintain the same satisfaction, as more units of one good are added, less units of the other will be required. The actual slope measures the *marginal rate of substitution* between the two

[2] This approach was first outlined in the writings of V. Pareto, *Manuel d'economie politique* (1909) and later developed in detail by the Russian economist Slutzky (1915). It was restated and popularized by J. R. Hicks and R. G. D. Allen, "A Reconsideration of the Theory of Value," *Economica,* Vol. 1 (February and May, 1934), pp. 52–76, 196–219; see also J. R. Hicks, *Value and Capital* (2d ed.; Oxford: Oxford University Press, 1946), chaps. i, ii.

TABLE 5-1

Various Combinations of Bread and Steak
Yielding a Given Level of Satisfaction
to a Consumer

Steak (Pounds)		Bread (Loaves)
6	plus	0
5	plus	1
4	plus	3
3	plus	6
2	plus	10
1	plus	15
0	plus	25

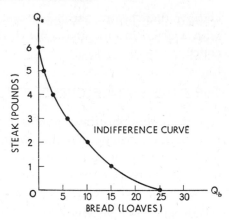

FIGURE 5-1
An Indifference Curve of a Consumer for Bread and Steak

TABLE 5-2

The Marginal Rate of Substitution between Bread and Steak for a Particular Consumer

Steak	Bread	Marginal Rate of Substitution of Steak for Bread*
0	25	
		10
1	15	
		5
2	10	
		4
3	6	
		3
4	3	
		2
5	1	
		1
6	0	

* The number of units of bread necessary to replace a unit of steak and maintain a given level of satisfaction.

commodities—the number of units of one of the commodities necessary to replace one unit of the other commodity in order to maintain the same total satisfaction. For example, the marginal rate of substitution of steak for bread is the number of units of bread which must be added to replace a unit of steak and maintain the same level of satisfaction. Thus, in Table 5–2, with four pounds of steak, three loaves of bread must be added when one pound of steak is eliminated if the same amount of satisfaction is to be obtained. With one pound of steak, ten loaves of bread must be added, if the one pound of steak is eliminated, to maintain satisfaction. When a large number of units of bread are necessary to replace a unit of steak, the indifference curve is nearly horizontal; if the number of units of bread required to replace a unit of steak is relatively small, the curve will be nearly vertical.

The Convexity of Indifference Curves and the Principle of Diminishing Marginal Rate of Substitution

A second characteristic of indifference curves is their convexity to the point of origin, that is, the left-hand portion is relatively steep while the right-hand portion is relatively horizontal. In other words, the greater the number of units of bread acquired, the smaller the number of units of steak necessary to replace a unit of bread in order to maintain the same total satisfaction. Likewise, the greater the number of units of steak, the smaller the number of units of bread necessary to replace a unit of steak. This rule, known as the *Principle of Diminishing Marginal Rate of Substitution,* may also be stated in terms of the behavior of the marginal rate of substitution; as additional units of one commodity are added, the marginal rate of substitution of this commodity for the other falls; that is, progressively less of the other commodity will be necessary to replace units of the first in order to maintain the same satisfaction.

The principle follows as a matter of logical necessity from the assumptions that particular wants are satiable, that various goods are not perfect substitutes for one another, and that increased quantities of one good do not increase the want-satisfying power of the other. As more units of one good are added, the ability of additional units of this good to satisfy wants falls because the want for which the good is best suited becomes more completely satisfied. Thus a relatively small quantity of the other good (the desire for which is relatively intense, per unit, with few units being acquired) is necessary to replace a unit of this good and maintain satisfaction. If the consumer has relatively little of the first good and large quantities of the second, a large additional amount of the second must be added if another unit of the first is eliminated, in order to maintain the same level of satisfaction.

However, the assumption that the ability of one good to satisfy a want is not dependent upon the quantity of the other good possessed is clearly not universally valid. Many goods are *complementary* to each other; that is, the desires for the two goods are interrelated, in the sense that the use of more units of one encourages the acquisition of additional units of the other. Under such circumstances, units of one good cannot be acquired without affecting the want-satisfying power of

TABLE 5-3

INDIFFERENCE SCHEDULE OF TWO COMMODITIES WHICH
ARE PERFECT SUBSTITUTES FOR EACH OTHER

X	Y	MRS
1......................6		
	1	
2......................5		
	1	
3......................4		
	1	
4......................3		
	1	
5......................2		
	1	
6......................1		

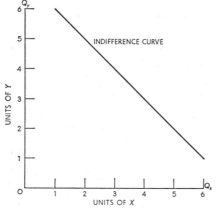

FIGURE 5-2
AN INDIFFERENCE CURVE OF PERFECT
SUBSTITUTES

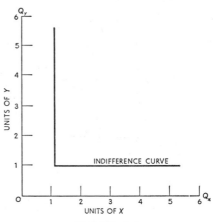

FIGURE 5-3
AN INDIFFERENCE CURVE OF COMMOD-
ITIES WHICH ARE NOT SUBSTITUTABLE

other goods. Gasoline and oil in a car, bread and butter are examples of complementary goods.

The degree of convexity of an indifference curve, that is, the extent to which the curve deviates from a straight line, depends upon the ease of substitution of the two goods for each other. If two commodities are perfect substitutes, the indifference curve is a straight line, as shown in Figure 5-2 based upon the data in Table 5-3, since the marginal rate of substitution is the same, regardless of the extent to which one good is replaced by the other.

At the other extreme are two commodities which are not substitutes at all or, in other words, are perfect complements, as, for example, to many persons, coffee and cream. Since it is impossible to replace units of one by units of the other and maintain satisfaction, the marginal rate of substitution is indefinitely large, and the indifference curve contains a right-angle turn convex to the point of origin, as shown in Figure 5–3. The left portion is vertical, in the sense that an infinite amount of Y is necessary to replace one unit of $X;$ the right portion is horizontal, since an infinite amount of X is necessary to replace a unit of Y. In more typical cases, in which the two commodities can be substituted for each other but are not perfect substitutes, the indifference curve will be bent. The more easily the two commodities can be substituted for each other, the nearer the curve will approach a straight line; in other words, it will maintain more closely the same slope throughout.[3]

Indifference Curves with More than Two Commodities

The usual indifference curve shows the relationship between two commodities only, because of the limitations of a two-dimensional surface. But the relationships portrayed for two commodities are valid for relationships among all of the various commodities which a person is interested in acquiring. This rule can be illustrated by following the procedure of showing one commodity on the horizontal axis and all other commodities, represented by dollars of expenditure on all other commodities, on the vertical axis.[4] Given prices of other commodities are assumed. The indifference curve then shows various combinations of purchases of this commodity and total expenditures on all other commodities which will yield the same satisfaction; and the slope of the curve shows the person's marginal rate of substitution between this good and expenditure on all other goods or, in other words, the person's marginal valuation of the good, relative to the total amount he has available for spending and saving.[5]

The Pattern of Indifference Curves

The discussion up to this point has been in terms of a single indifference curve, representing a particular level of satisfaction. But actually, there is, for each consumer and for each pair of goods, a whole

[3] Although there is some sense in the view that *perfect* substitutes and *perfect* complements stand at opposite ends of the substitution scale, there is no simple way of contrasting substitute with complementary goods in the intermediate cases. The matter is explained in detail by Hicks, *Value and Capital, op. cit.*, pp. 42–43 and 46–48.

[4] For purposes of explaining the allocation of income, saving may be regarded as a type of expenditure.

[5] Another way to look at the matter is to regard "all other goods" as, say S & H Green Stamps. The consumer may then be considered to buy either "good A" (say), or "green stamps," the latter "good" then being redeemable for a wide variety of ordinary goods at a redemption center.

TABLE 5–4

A PATTERN OF INDIFFERENCE CURVES OF A CONSUMER FOR STEAK AND BREAD
(Pounds and Loaves, Respectively)

Schedule A		Schedule B		Schedule C		Schedule D	
Steak	Bread	Steak	Bread	Steak	Bread	Steak	Bread
6	0	6	3	6	6	6	10
5	1	5	4.5	5	8.5	5	12
4	3	4	7	4	11.5	4	15.5
3	6	3	10.5	3	16	3	20.5
2	10	2	15.5	2	22	2	28
1	15	1	23	1	31	1	42.5

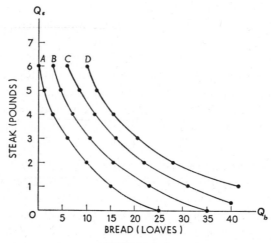

FIGURE 5–4
A PATTERN OF INDIFFERENCE CURVES OF A CONSUMER FOR
STEAK AND BREAD

pattern or family of indifference curves, each indicating <u>different levels of satisfaction</u>. Four schedules are presented in Table 5–4, including the one given in Table 5–3 above, and illustrated graphically in Figure 5–4. The successive indifference curves *A, B, C,* and *D* never intersect, since each portrays various combinations which yield a particular degree of satisfaction. <u>*Transitivity* of indifference curves is also assumed</u>, that is, <u>consistency of the consume</u>r. If the consumer is indifferent between one apple and two oranges and between two oranges and one grapefruit, he must also be indifferent between one apple and one grapefruit. There is no way of knowing—and no need to know—the quantitative differences in satisfaction yielded by combinations that lie on separate indifference curves. The schedules merely show that combinations on one curve yield *more* or *less* satisfaction than combinations on another.

If a given combination on one curve contains more of both commodities than any combination on another curve, the curve containing the first combination is said to be *higher than* the second. Moreover, since more goods will always be preferred to less, *all* combinations on the higher indifference curve will be preferred to *any* combination on lower curves. Geometrically, this means that any combination that lies to the "northeast" (or "north" or "east") of another combination will lie on a higher indifference curve and will therefore represent a greater quantity of satisfaction.

The Budget Restraint or Consumption Possibilities Line

A person's schedule of preferences, or pattern of indifference curves for various goods, is assumed to be independent of his income and of prices. But his actual purchases depend upon the level of his income and the manner in which he allocates the income among different commodities. Possible patterns of expenditures of a given sum of money on two commodities may be illustrated on the indifference graph by the use of a *budget restraint* or *consumption possibilities line,* a line which shows the various combinations of quantities of the two commodities which can be purchased with a certain expenditure, given the prices of the two goods. For example, if $5.00 is to be spent on bread and steak, and bread costs 20 cents a loaf and steak $1.00 a pound, 25 loaves of bread can be purchased if no steak is bought, five pounds of steak if no bread is bought; or various combinations of the two, such as three pounds of steak and ten loaves of bread; one pound of steak and twenty loaves of bread, etc. The various combinations are shown in Table 5–5 and illustrated in Figure 5–5. Under the assumption that the prices of the commodities are independent of the quantities purchased, the budget restraint will necessarily be a straight line.[6] The slope of the curve is dependent upon the ratios of the prices of the two commodities. The same principle applies to the expenditure of a person's entire income on a wide range of commodities; for example, if a person has an annual income of $8,000, there are a large number of different combinations of goods which could be purchased with this amount, given the prices of the goods.

The Quantities Purchased

Given the pattern of indifference curves of the consumer for two commodities, together with the budget restraint showing the various

[6] If they are not, because of quantity discounts, or because additional purchases drive up prices, the budget restraint will be a curved line.

TABLE 5–5

EXPENDITURE SCHEDULE ON
BREAD AND STEAK, TOTAL
EXPENDITURE OF $5.00

Bread (Price 20 Cents) Loaves	Steak (Price $1.00) Pounds
0	5
2.5	4.5
5	4
7.5	3.5
10	3
12.5	2.5
15	2
17.5	1.5
20	1
22.5	0.5
25	0

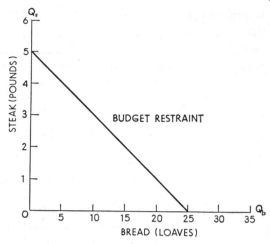

FIGURE 5–5

BUDGET RESTRAINT, SHOWING VARIOUS COMBINATIONS OF BREAD AND STEAK WHICH CAN BE PURCHASED WITH A TOTAL EXPENDITURE OF $5.00.
BREAD: 20 CENTS PER LOAF.
STEAK: $1.00 PER POUND

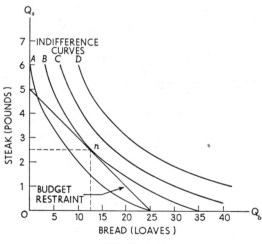

FIGURE 5–6

THE OPTIMUM COMBINATION OF PURCHASES
OF TWO COMMODITIES

quantities of the two which can be purchased out of the expenditure allocated by the person to the two commodities, the equilibrium quantities of each which will be purchased can be determined. By the same principle, given the indifference relationships among all commodities purchased and the person's income (and the prices of all goods), the equilibrium quantities of all goods purchased are determinate. The point of tangency between the budget restraint and an indifference curve indicates the quantities of each good which will be purchased, if total satisfaction is to be maximized. In Figure 5–6 the budget restraint is tangent to indifference curve *B* at point *n;* the person will acquire $2\frac{1}{2}$ pounds of steak and $12\frac{1}{2}$ loaves of bread. In order to maximize satisfaction, the consumer must reach the highest indifference curve attainable with a given expenditure of money. The highest curve which can be reached is that curve to which the budget restraint is tangent. Any other possible combination of the two goods either would be on a lower indifference curve and thus yield less satisfaction, or would be unobtainable with the given expenditure. The same principle applies to all goods, provided that the Principle of Diminishing Marginal Rate of Substitution is valid.[7]

At the optimum combination, defined by a point of tangency between the budget restraint and an indifference curve, the marginal rate of substitution between the two commodities is equal to the ratios of their prices. As shown in Figure 5–6, at point *n*, the marginal rate of substitution between bread and steak is 5 to 1, that is, five loaves of bread must be added if one pound of steak is eliminated; this is equal to

[7] To the extent that the principle is not valid, and thus indifference curves are not convex to the point of origin, there may be no single equilibrium combination of commodities corresponding to a particular set of prices and level of expenditures.

For example, suppose that an indifference curve is of the character of *A* in Figure 5–7A below, being convex in part, concave in part. With budget restraint line *L*, there are three distinct points of tangency and thus three equilibrium points, all yielding the same level of satisfaction, but the analysis does not indicate which of these will be selected by the consumer. Or suppose that the indifference curve and budget restraint appear as in Figure 5–7B. There is one equilibrium point, *s*, but this is not a point of tangency.

Under such circumstances as these, the equilibrium of the consumer cannot be described in terms of the preceding analysis, additional assumptions being required to handle the peculiar types of cases.

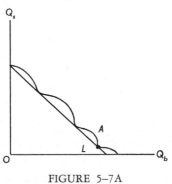

FIGURE 5–7A   FIGURE 5–7B

the price ratio (100/20, or 5/1). This relationship follows from the fact that since the curves are tangent at this point, they have the same slope. If this relationship did not obtain, the consumer could gain satisfaction by purchasing more of one of the commodities and less of the other. If, for example, the consumer were buying such quantities of steak and bread that the marginal rate of substitution was 12 to 1, while the price ratio was 5 to 1, the addition of one pound of steak would necessitate the loss of only five loaves of bread, whereas the person would be willing to sacrifice twelve loaves in order to gain the pound of steak. Thus, substitution is obviously desirable, and will continue until equality of the two ratios is obtained. The rule of equality between marginal rates of substitution and price ratios applies to each pair of commodities purchased, and thus to all commodities.

Indifference Curves and the Demand Schedule

The relationship between the budget restraint and the pattern of indifference curves indicates the equilibrium amounts of each of the two commodities which will be purchased, given the prices of the two commodities and the consumer's total expenditures. For different possible prices for one of the commodities, given the price of the other and given total expenditures, various quantities of the two will be purchased. A change in the price of one of the commodities will alter the slope of the budget restraint, since a different amount of the commodity can be purchased with a given level of expenditures. If, for example, the price of X falls, the budget restraint will become more nearly horizontal, since more units of X can be purchased than previously with a given expenditure. Likewise, at all points except that at which no units of X are purchased, the line will be to the right of the old one. Thus the new point of tangency with an indifference curve will be on a higher indifference curve. In Figure 5–8 the point of tangency moves from *n* to *n'* as a result of the decline in price of X from 20 cents to 10 cents; the equilibrium quantity of X purchased increases from two to five units.

Figure 5–9 shows a series of points of tangency of the budget restraint with indifference curves, under the assumption of various possible prices for X (50 cents, 20 cents, 13.3 cents, and 10 cents), the price of Y remaining unchanged (at 10 cents). A relation, known as the *price-consumption* curve (*CC*), may be drawn through these points of tangency, indicating the equilibrium quantities of X (and Y) at various possible prices of X (given the price of Y). From this price-consumption curve can be derived the usual demand curve for the

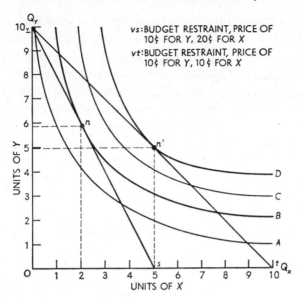

FIGURE 5–8

THE EFFECT OF A DECLINE IN THE PRICE OF *X* UPON THE QUANTITIES OF
X AND *Y* PURCHASED

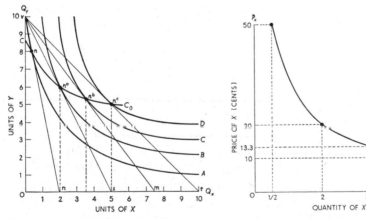

FIGURE 5–9	FIGURE 5–10
THE VARIOUS COMBINATIONS OF COM-MODITIES *X* AND *Y* WHICH WILL BE PURCHASED AT VARIOUS PRICES OF *X*	THE DEMAND SCHEDULE FOR COMMOD-ITY *X* DERIVED FROM THE PRICE-CON-SUMPTION CURVE IN FIGURE 5–9

commodity. Thus, from Figure 5–9, it can be ascertained that if the price of *X* is 10 cents, five units of *X* will be purchased; if the price is 13.3 cents, $3\frac{1}{2}$ units will be purchased; if the price is 20 cents, two units will be purchased; if the price is 50 cents, one-half unit will be purchased. These data may be plotted, as in Figure 5–10, as a demand curve of the usual form. It should be noted that in Figure 5–10 the price of X is measured on the vertical axis, and quantity purchased on the horizontal axis, whereas the axes of Figure 5–9 refer to quantities of the two commodities. It should also be emphasized that the quantities demanded, as shown in Figure 5–10, are those with the consumer expenditures in equilibrium at the various prices. Essentially, the demand curve is made up of various price and quantity equilibrium points, in the sense that it indicates the quantities which the consumer will buy at various prices when he has attained equilibrium adjustment of expenditures among the various commodities.[8]

The demand curve in Figure 5–10 is of limited significance, since it is based upon an analysis of the adjustments between the commodity in question and one other, in terms of expenditures of a certain sum of money on the two, rather than on all commodities purchased. However, if the Y axis in Figure 5–9 is interpreted to represent expenditures on all other commodities, rather than on one, and the budget restraint is assumed to represent total expenditures, rather than those on two commodities only, the demand curve which is derived from the price-consumption curve reflects the reactions of the quantities of the commodity purchased in response to changes in the price of the commodity, with adjustments made between purchases of this commodity and all others, as of a given level of total expenditures.

The Income Effect and the Substitution Effect

With indifference curves, the two distinct types of effects through which a price reduction influences the quantity demanded can be distinguished clearly. When the price of a commodity declines, the *income* effect enables the person to buy more of this (or other) commodities with a given income; the price reduction has the same effect as an increase in money income. This is reflected by the movement onto a higher indifference curve. For example, in Figure 5–9, if price falls from 20 cents to 13.3 cents, the consumer is enabled to move from indifference curve B to curve C, and thus to a higher level of satisfaction. It is possible, of course, that the entire amount of purchasing power freed may be used to purchase other goods. This will occur if the marginal rate of substitution drops very sharply for additional units of the good whose price has changed. In some cases the purchasing power freed might be used to buy better quality substitutes for the

---

[8] A major difficulty in constructing demand curves by observing actual consumer behavior is that observation alone will not indicate whether or not the consumer is in equilibrium, and thus whether the observed price-quantity point lies on or off the demand curve.

commodity whose price changes, and thus the quantity of the commodity purchased would fall. This case of negative influence will be discussed in more detail in the section dealing with the effects of income changes upon demand.

The second influence of the price decline upon the quantity demanded is the *substitution* effect. The lower price encourages the consumer to buy larger quantities of this commodity to replace units of other commodities. To the extent that this reaction is significant in a particular case, the point of tangency of the budget restraint with the indifference curve is moved farther to the right. Thus, in Figure 5–9 the budget restraint that is parallel to line *vt* would be tangent to indifference curve *C* farther to the right than the point at which *vm* was tangent. Thus the decline in the price of *X* would lead to an increase in quantity purchased even if none of the income freed by the lower price were spent on the commodity. The greater the substitutability of other goods with *X,* the less will be the curvature in the indifference curve, and thus the greater the extent to which the point of tangency will shift to the right (that is, in the direction of a greater quantity of *X* purchased) as the price of *X* falls.

The substitution effect is completely distinct from the income effect, and always acts to increase the quantity of *X* purchased as its price falls. When the income effect is positive, the two effects reinforce each other in leading to a greater quantity being demanded at low prices than at high. When the income effect is negative, as noted above, the substitution effect may more than offset it, if substitution is sufficiently great. It may not, however, and in this event the demand schedule will be the reverse of the typical pattern; the quantity demanded will *fall* as the price falls. One other situation will also lead to this result: when the assumption that preference schedules are independent of price is not valid. This will occur when persons judge quality by price and thus assume that the quality is inferior if the price is lower, or when preference is largely a prestige matter so that the more expensive an item is the greater the prestige of having it.

DETERMINANTS OF ELASTICITY OF DEMAND— SUBSTITUTABILITY

The elasticity of demand for a commodity depends primarily upon the ease of substitution of this commodity for other goods in the satisfaction of wants. When several commodities are regarded by consumers as more or less equally desirable for the satisfaction of particular wants, the demand schedules for each of the goods will tend to be elastic, since changes in their relative prices cause substantial shifting of relative purchases. Thus, an increase in the price of oranges will cause many consumers to purchase apples or bananas instead of oranges, and the sale of oranges will drop substantially. When no satisfactory substitutes are available, price changes will have less effect upon the quantity demanded.

The effects of substitutability upon the elasticity of demand may be illustrated by the indifference curve technique. The greater the ease with which the commodity in question can be substituted for others (and other goods may be substituted for it), the less will be the curvature of the indifference curve; that is, the curve will more closely approach a straight line. The smaller the curvature, the greater the extent to which the point of tangency of the budget restraint with an indifference curve will shift to the right when the price of the good falls; and thus the greater the extent to which the purchases of the commodity will increase in response to the price reduction.

The significance of curvature is illustrated in Figure 5–11, A and B. In order to show the significance of substitutability, it is necessary to eliminate the income effect by drawing a budget restraint (p') parallel to the new budget restraint (p) after the price change, at a location such that the former is tangent to the old indifference curve (A). In Figure 5–11, where the curvature of the indifference curve is slight, the tangency of p' with A (at b) is much farther to the right of the

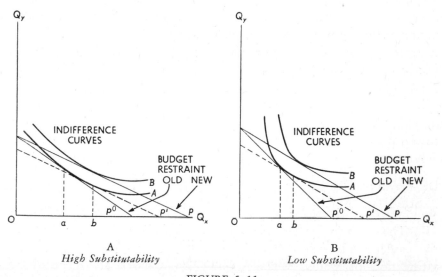

A	B
High Substitutability	*Low Substitutability*

FIGURE 5–11
THE SIGNIFICANCE OF SUBSTITUTABILITY FOR THE RESPONSE OF THE QUANTITY
OF COMMODITY X PURCHASED TO CHANGES IN THE PRICE OF X

original tangency of p^0 with A (at a) than it is in Figure 5–11B, on which the curvature is great because the commodities are poor substitutes.

The same relationships may be expressed in terms of marginal rates of substitution. If the rate falls rapidly, as it will if the commodities are poor substitutes, a decline in the price of one commodity will result in only a relatively slight readjustment in quantities of the two goods purchased to restore equality of the price ratios and the marginal rate of substitution. If the marginal rate of substitution falls slowly, a much greater readjustment in relative purchases will be necessary.

Other Influences on Elasticity

Elasticity is likewise affected by the satiability of the want for which the good is being acquired or, in terms of utility, the rate of decline in marginal utility as additional units of the good are acquired. The more quickly the want is satiated and thus the more rapidly the marginal utility and the marginal rate of substitution fall, the less elastic will be the demand. The marginal utility of bread, for example, appears to fall more quickly, for most persons, than the marginal utilities of various forms of recreation. The possibility of alternate uses —that is, the ability to use the good to satisfy other wants as well as the original one—lessens the rate of decline in marginal utility.

Elasticity is affected by the closely related considerations of durability of the product and the time interval for which the schedule is relevant. When goods can be used for a number of years, individual consumers are not in the market for additional units for a considerable period of time after they have made a purchase. But if the goods are not durable, consumers can adjust their rates of purchase at any time and thus are more sensitive to price changes. As a consequence, demand schedules for durable goods are more elastic over a longer period of time. The demand for nondurable goods used in conjunction with durable equipment is affected in a similar manner. If a person has installed an oil-burning furnace, he cannot shift from oil to gas without substantial additional expense. Thus, changes in relative prices of oil and gas will not cause immediate replacement of one fuel by the other. But once the furnace requires replacement, substitution of the cheaper fuel for the more expensive one, and of one type of furnace for the other, may occur.

Apart from considerations of durability, the importance of habit in consumer purchasing causes the demands for many goods, durable or not, to become more elastic over a period of time than they are in a shorter period. Persons become accustomed to buying certain articles, and do not reconsider at frequent intervals the desirability of continuing or adjusting certain purchases. Thus, price changes may bring little immediate response. But over a longer period, there is greater chance of reconsideration of the desirability of purchases and of seeking substitutes, and the effects of changes in relative prices will be greater. Thus, if cheese falls greatly in price, most consumers at first will not consider replacing butter or oleomargarine by cheese. But if the price remains at a low level over a period of time, more and more persons may revise their purchase patterns to take advantage of the low price of cheese. Furthermore, over a longer period, persons are more likely to become better informed about the existence of lower prices.

The elasticity of the total demand schedule for a commodity is determined by the elasticities of the individual schedules which underlie it. As the price of a good falls, much of the increase in quantity demanded may come from new purchasers—persons not buying the good at all at higher prices. These may be persons with relatively low incomes or ones whose desires for the good are relatively weak. For some commodities the demand schedules of individual buyers are extremely inelastic, yet the total demand is elastic, since many additional buyers will enter the market at lower prices. Thus the demand for electric refrigerators is relatively elastic, even though few individuals buy more than one regardless of the price. At lower prices, many persons acquire the product who would not do so at all at higher price levels.

THE LEVEL OF THE DEMAND SCHEDULE: CHANGES IN THE PARAMETERS

As noted in the previous chapter, a given demand schedule relating price and quantity demanded is valid only for given values of the prices of other goods and a host of other "shift" parameters. It is useful to consider the relationships between changes in these "givens" and consequent changes in the position and form of the demand schedule. The problem may be approached by considering the functional relationship between each of these parameters and quantity demanded, price being regarded as a parameter instead of a variable.

Consumer Preferences

The quantities of various commodities purchased are dependent upon the intensity of the preference of consumers for the commodities, which will depend upon a wide variety of social, climatic, demographic, and economic factors about which we have little knowledge. In the actual process of decision making, moreover, habit plays an extremely important role, in part because habit buying saves time for the customer. Various studies have shown a wide variation in the extent to which decisions, particularly on consumer durables, are based upon careful consideration of alternatives; in many instances, of course, they are not.[9] Decisions are also subject to outside deliberate influence, in the form of advertising.

Changes in preferences, of course, result in shifts in demand schedules. A person may grow tired of one type of recreation and try another type. Or he may become dissatisfied with the type of fuel that he is using to heat his home and shift to another variety. Changes in occupation, number of dependents, state of health, and age will alter preferences. The birth of a baby may cause a family to spend less on recreation and more on food. Illness will lessen the purchases of some commodities and increase the demand for medicine. A cold winter will increase the demand for fuel. Changes in customs and traditions will affect preferences; changing styles in clothing, for example, produce significant modifications in the demand for various types. Successful advertising campaigns will divert purchases from some products to others. Development of new products draws consumer preference away from other goods; the automobile very quickly eliminated consumers' preferences—and demand—for buggies.

Income

A second major determinant of consumption demands is household income. The functional relationship between quantity demanded and income (all other influences being regarded as given), and thus the income elasticity of demand, varies greatly among different commodities in terms of the nature of consumer preferences and the behavior of marginal utility as additional units are acquired. The more rapid the rate of decline in marginal utility and thus of the marginal rate of substitution, the lower will be the income elasticity. High positive income elasticity is characteristic of many so-called luxuries: items not imperative for a minimum living standard but highly desired once incomes reach a certain level. Low income elasticity is characteristic of goods the desire for which is quickly satisfied.

The response of demand to income changes is illustrated with the use of indifference curves by showing progressively higher budget

---

[9] See R. Ferber, "Research in Household Behavior," *American Economic Review,* Vol. 52 (March, 1962), pp. 49–51.

restraint lines, indicating larger amounts available for spending, with a given pattern of indifference curves, and drawing an income-consumption curve connecting the various points of tangency. Figures 5–12 and 5–13 show, respectively, commodities of high and low positive income elasticity.

As noted in the previous chapter, for commodities known as inferior goods, the income elasticity is negative; the quantities purchased will fall as income rises. These are goods which persons will buy only because they cannot afford more expensive substitutes. Cheap cuts of meat, inexpensive clothing and shoes are examples; as incomes rise, persons will shift to more expensive, preferred substitutes, and the demand for the inferior goods will fall. Such a case is shown in Figure 5–14.

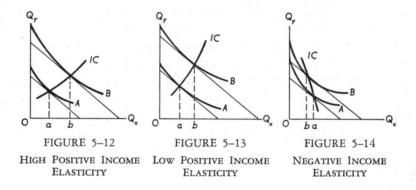

FIGURE 5–12   FIGURE 5–13   FIGURE 5–14

HIGH POSITIVE INCOME   LOW POSITIVE INCOME   NEGATIVE INCOME
ELASTICITY   ELASTICITY   ELASTICITY

Studies of income elasticity of demand for various commodities were among the oldest empirical studies in economics. The pioneer work was that of Engel; the relationships which he discovered have since been referred to as Engel's laws, or, graphically, as Engel curves. Greater availability of data has allowed much more exhaustive research on the question in recent years. One of Engel's laws, that food consumption rises less rapidly than income, has been confirmed many times. The same rule for housing has also been confirmed by various studies, but the most recent one, by Margaret Reid, questions the conclusion, and suggests that housing constitutes a major avenue of "luxury" spending as income rises.[10] Most studies have found elasticities approaching unity for clothing and education, and high elasticities for recreation, personal care, home operation, and other services. There are,

[10] See M. Reid, *Housing and Income* (Chicago: University of Chicago Press, 1962).

of course, significant variations among families, in terms of family characteristics and preferences.

Income Elasticity of Total Consumption

The concept of income elasticity can also be applied to the behavior of total consumption expenditures as incomes rise. Conclusions on this subject that were once generally accepted have been the object of widespread criticism in recent years. We may summarize briefly three points of view that presently play an important role in empirical research.

1. The traditional view—usually called the *absolute income hypothesis*—holds that as a person's absolute income increases he will increase his consumption, but by a lesser amount than the increase in income.[11] This hypothesis is supported by casual inspection of time-series data on aggregate income and consumption expenditure, and also by cross-section data on income and consumption expenditure by families with different incomes. Unfortunately, the cross-section data indicate that the *proportion* of income spent on consumption tends to decline as income increases (i.e., that the income elasticity of consumption is less than unity), whereas the time-series data suggest that the proportion of income spent on consumption is relatively constant (the value of the consumption-income ratio in the United States, for example, has tended to remain at about .90 since at least 1900). This apparent contradiction between one set of empirical results and another has led to the formulation of new and more general theoretical hypotheses.

2. One way out of this dilemma is to argue that the consumption expenditures of a household depend on its *relative* position in the income scale. This view,[12] usually referred to as the *relative income hypothesis*, is supported by commonsense observation (i.e., what one spends on consumption is obviously influenced by what one's neighbors

[11] The historical origins of this view are uncertain, but it owes its modern popularity to J. M. Keynes and his *General Theory of Employment, Interest, and Money* (New York: Harcourt, Brace, 1936).

[12] Suggested first by Dorothy Brady and Rose Friedman in 1947, but proposed independently in different guises at about the same time by Franco Modigliani and James S. Duesenberry. See D. S. Brady and Rose Friedman, "Savings and the Income Distribution," Nat. Bur. Econ. Res. *Stud. in Income and Wealth,* 1947, pp. 247–65; F. Modigliani, "Fluctuations in the Savings-Income Ratio," Nat. Bur. Econ. Res. *Stud. in Income and Wealth,* 1949, pp. 371–443; J. Duesenberry, *Income, Saving, and the Theory of Consumer Behavior* (Cambridge: Harvard University Press, 1949).

spend, by one's impressions about how other people live, etc.), and it provides a suitable explanation of the findings of the cross-section studies mentioned above (households with below-average incomes have more unsatisfied desires than households with above-average incomes, for minimal standards are set by average-income households.) Moreover, the hypothesis also accounts for the relative constancy of the consumption-income ratio as indicated by time-series studies; for on this hypothesis, changes in absolute income would be expected to lead to changes in the consumption-income ratio only if accompanied by significant changes in the distribution of income—and changes in income distribution have not in fact been significant in the United States during the past few decades. Changes in income distribution have occurred in Great Britain, where there has been a noticeable increase in the ratio of personal consumption to personal income since 1946. Unfortunately, there have been many other changes in British society, including numerous welfare schemes that could hardly help but alter household attitudes towards the relative desirability of consumption and saving. Thus the relative income hypothesis, although consistent with a wide range of empirical findings, has by no means become established doctrine as of the present time.

3. Another way out of the dilemma posed by empirical studies is to argue that current consumption expenditures are influenced not only by current income but also by previously accumulated wealth (see below, pp. 81–86); or, what is essentially the same, that consumption is a function not of current income but of "expected" or "permanent" income—i.e., actual earnings over fairly long periods of time. This view,[13] variously referred to as the *permanent income hypothesis* or the *wealth-income hypothesis,* explains *short-run* variations in the income-consumption ratio (and also the findings of the cross-section studies) by reference to variations in income. If consumption depends on permanent income (or wealth) rather than current income, the current consumption-income ratio will vary when current income varies because permanent income and wealth do not themselves change significantly except over fairly long periods of time. The long-run constancy of the consumption-income ratio is then explained by assuming that consumption is directly proportional to permanent income. It is the latter aspect of the permanent income hypothesis that has come in for most criticism,

[13] Developed and argued most effectively by Milton Friedman, *The Theory of the Consumption Function* (Princeton: National Bureau of Economic Research, 1959), but independently presented in other forms by Franco Modigliani, James Tobin, and a host of other writers.

for to assume that consumption is a constant fraction of long-run income or wealth looks suspiciously like assuming one's conclusions. Furthermore, the concepts of "permanent income" and "wealth" are much too ambiguous to suit many students of household behavior.

Prices of Other Commodities

The third major determinant of the height of a particular demand schedule is the level of prices of other commodities. The influence of the prices of other goods is in part dependent upon the extent to which the latter can be substituted for the particular commodity. Price levels of close substitutes are far more significant than those of goods not directly substitutable. The demand for oranges is affected much more by prevailing prices for apples than by those for theater tickets.

The nature of the cross-elasticity of demand between two goods depends upon the relative influences of the income and substitution effects. When the price of one good falls, the income effect, representing the freeing of purchasing power by the price reduction, encourages the purchase of more units of both commodities. But the fact that the price of the first commodity has fallen relative to the price of the second encourages persons to substitute the first for the second, and thus to buy less of the second. If the substitution effect outweighs the income effect, the cross-elasticity is positive, and the two commodities are regarded as substitutes for each other. This situation is illustrated in Figure 5–15. The higher the cross-elasticity, the greater is the ease of substitution. If the articles are perfect substitutes (and thus essentially the same commodity, from the standpoint of the users), the cross-elasticity is infinite.

There are two types of situations in which cross-elasticity will be negative, in the sense that a decline in the price of one good will lead to an increase in the quantity of the other good purchased. First, the income effect of the price change may outweigh the substitution effect: as the price of X falls, if little substitution occurs and the demand for X is inelastic, less total purchasing power will be spent on X than before, and the amount of Y purchased may increase. This case is shown in Figure 5–16.

The other case of negative cross-elasticity is that of *complementary* goods—those of such nature that increased use of one gives rise to the use of additional units of the other, as, for example, greater use of bread encourages the purchase of additional butter. When two goods are complementary, a decline in the price of the one, by stimulating increased use of the good, will raise the marginal utility of the other

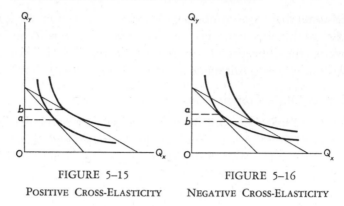

FIGURE 5–15
POSITIVE CROSS-ELASTICITY

FIGURE 5–16
NEGATIVE CROSS-ELASTICITY

good and increase the quantity of the latter purchased. The purchases of other commodities must, of course, decline to free the necessary purchasing power, if total expenditure on the two items rises.

Expectations about Future Prices

The height of a demand schedule is also affected by expectations about future prices. This influence is, in a sense, transitory, since consumers will not continue indefinitely to buy in anticipation of future wants, nor will they continue to postpone purchases of desired goods if expected price decreases fail to materialize. But at any given time expectations may be of substantial importance, and changes in them may produce major shifts in demand schedules. If consumers expect price increases, they may buy large quantities in anticipation of the increases and thus cause substantial increases in demand. If decreases come to be expected, buyers may reduce current purchases drastically.

Number of Potential Consumers

A final consideration affecting total demand schedules is the number of consumers in the market. The number depends in part upon population and in part upon the accessibility of various persons to the market. Thus, population growth will increase total demand, as will reductions in import controls or similar barriers to trade, which allow more persons to enter a particular market.

The Collection of Demand Schedule Data

At any time a certain demand schedule exists for each commodity, in the sense that if definite prices prevail, consumers will wish to purchase certain definite quantities. It is impossible, however, to determine with any degree of accuracy what the schedule actually is. With most goods, the total sales in particular markets with existing prices can be ascertained; many data of this type are collected by various private and government agencies at the present time. But the figures may not represent equilibrium quantities, in the sense that consumers may not have completed adjustments to the governing circumstances. Moreover, quantities that would be demanded at other prices can only be estimated with the aid of statistics of sales at various prices in the past. The greatest care must be used in interpreting these statistics, since the changes in sales from one period to another are due not only to price changes but also to shifts in the various determinants of demand. Incomes, preferences, prices of other goods, and expectations are constantly changing. In part, it is possible to isolate the effects of these other changes by various statistical techniques. But such techniques are by no means entirely accurate or reliable. Particularly, there is no possible way of determining satisfactorily the effects on sales of changes in preferences which occur during a period for which data are available. Thus, statistical estimates of demand schedules, of necessity, involve a substantial margin of error. But such work is of great value in providing additional information about demand behavior.

APPENDIX: HOUSEHOLD SAVINGS BEHAVIOR[14]

Up to this stage in the discussion, we have treated saving—the use of income to acquire assets—as a kind of consumption expenditure. This is questionable in principle and can lead to misunderstanding and confusion in practice. Additions to current wealth in the form either of money or securities, unlike current spending on food, entertainment, etc., increase a household's potential future purchasing power. In theory, therefore, current saving and asset accumulation should have an effect on future consumption much like that of a future increase in income. In order to clarify this issue, and also to provide an example of the flexibility of the indifference curve approach to consumer behavior theory, we shall present a simplified model of household saving.

Let us assume initially that money balances (M) are the only asset in which households can invest current savings, and that the only alternative to holding money is to spend it on current consumption (C). The preferences of the household may then be represented by an indifference map such as that shown in Figure 5–17, where quantities of

[14] This section may be omitted without affecting the continuity of the analysis.

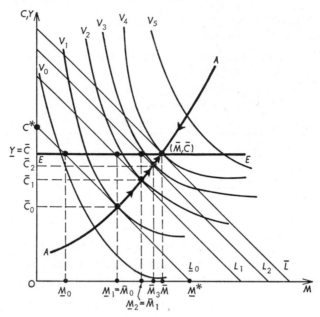

FIGURE 5–17
HOUSEHOLD PREFERENCES FOR CON-
SUMPTION AND MONEY BALANCES, AND
THE PROCESS OF CONVERGENCE TO A
POSITION OF STATIONARY EQUILIBRIUM

money are measured horizontally and quantities of current consumption (expressed in money units) are measured vertically. The budget restraint corresponding to a given money income, $\underline{Y}$ (assumed to be paid at the beginning of each of a series of market periods), and a given initial quantity of money balances, $\underline{M}_0$, are represented in the same diagram by the line $\underline{L}_0$.

If the household spent nothing on consumption in the initial market period, its money balances at the beginning of the next period would be $\underline{M}^*$; if it spent its entire income plus its initial money balances on current consumption, its consumption would be $\underline{C}^*$ and its money balances at the beginning of the next period would be nil, etc. If the preferences of the household between consumption and end-of-period money balances are as shown by the indifference curves V_0, V_1, V_2, . . . , in Figure 5–17, in order to maximize current satisfaction the household will choose to spend only a portion of its current income on consumption in period 0, namely $\overline{C}_0$, and it will save the remainder $(\underline{Y} - \overline{C}_0)$ in the form of increased money balances. At the beginning of the next period, therefore, the household will have money balances of $\underline{M}_1 = \overline{M}_0$, and its budget restraint will shift accordingly from L_0 to L_1 (income in this period being the same as in the previous period, namely, $\underline{Y}$). If the preferences of the household remain unchanged, consumption will be larger in period 1 than in period 0 ($\overline{C}_1$ instead of $\overline{C}_0$). As before, however, a portion of income, namely $\underline{Y} - \overline{C}_1$, will be saved and added to previously accumulated money balances; hence, money balances at the outset of period 2 will be $\underline{M}_2 = \overline{M}_1$, the budget line will shift from L_1 to L_2 (income being fixed still at $\underline{Y}$), consumption will again increase (from $\overline{C}_1$ to $\overline{C}_2$), and so on.

Provided that money balances and consumption are both "superior" goods, this process of adjustment over time will converge along the *decision locus AA* (i.e., the locus of points of tangency of the various budget lines with various indifference curves). Thus the household will gradually approach a point of stationary equilibrium ($\overline{M}, \overline{C}$) in Figure 5–17 where consumption equals income and desired holdings of money equal actual money balances. This type of behavior—saving out of a given level of income gradually tending towards zero—may be regarded as the "normal" case in an economy in which the only form in which assets may be accumulated is money balances. However, if the household is "miserly"—i.e., if consumption is a superior good only up to a certain point, and then assets become objectives in themselves, the process of asset accumulation may never end. For example, if the decision locus takes a form such as that shown by the curve *BB* or *CC* in Figure 5–18, money will be accumulated indefinitely, starting from any given level of initial money balances (e.g., $\underline{M}_0$), and consumption will either level off at a value slightly less than income (as indicated by the decision locus *BB*), or decline steadily over time (decision locus *CC*). Which of these cases occurs (i.e., whether the decision locus looks like *AA, BB,* or *CC* in Figure 5–18) will depend partly on the preferences of the household, partly on the level of income.

Perhaps the most interesting conclusion to be drawn from this analysis is that consumption is not a function simply of the level of current income. More generally, we may say that in the "normal" case (i.e., consumption and money balances both superior goods), saving is a *transitory* phenomenon, for in the long run, for any one person consumption tends to equal income, and savings tend to disappear entirely.[14a]

A similar line of argument may be used to analyze household

[14a] Another way to state the same conclusion is to say that the long-run average propensity to consume is unity.

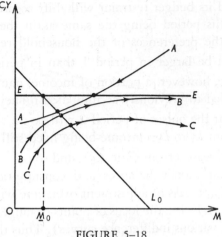

FIGURE 5–18
CONVERGENT AND DIVERGENT
SAVING PROCESSES

saving behavior in an economy where savings are invested in income-earning assets rather than in money balances. The only difference between this situation and that analyzed above is that current saving will not only lead to increased holdings of assets, but also to increased money income in every subsequent period. Funds that are deposited in a savings account, for example, will earn interest income, as long as the money is left on deposit. In such circumstances, the locus of possible asset-income combinations—represented by the horizontal lines EE in Figures 5–17 and 5–18—becomes an upward sloping curve (or line). The slope of this *endowment locus* at any point will measure the increment in asset income resulting from a unit increase in asset balances. If all funds are invested in an asset that yields 10 percent per period, for example, the slope of the EE curve will be .10; at the other extreme, if all funds are invested in money (i.e., an asset that has a zero rate of return), the slope of the curve will be zero, etc.

If the endowment locus is upward sloping, the saving process may fail to converge to a point of stationary equilibrium even though consumption and assets are both superior goods. Whether it does so or not will depend as before on household preferences and the level of nonasset income. If the decision locus is relatively flat as shown by AA in Figure 5–19 (more precisely, if the increase in consumption associated with an increase in asset balances is less than the rate of return on assets), with the EE curve as shown the process of saving and asset accumulation will be a permanent phenomenon. We might

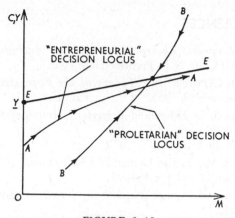

FIGURE 5–19
"Entrepreneurial" and "Proletarian"
Savings Processes

describe this kind of behavior as "entrepreneurial"; for one of the essential characteristics of entrepreneurship is willingness to acquire and hold quantities of disposable resources vastly greater in dollar value than the annual income yield of the resources. The more usual case, at least among households with moderate incomes, is probably that shown by the "proletarian" decision locus *BB* in Figure 5–19, which implies a kind of behavior qualitatively the same as that described by Figure 5–17; i.e., saving tends gradually towards zero if income from sources other than assets remains constant from one period to another. Households having preferences of this kind will tend to save and accumulate assets during those years when wage and salary incomes are substantial and rising, and will then decumulate assets (dissave) following the retirement of the head of the household. This is the kind of behavior that characterizes most households in the United States and Great Britain; i.e., virtually all households save at some stage during the life of the household, but only a small proportion of households (less than 5 percent in the United States) continue to save and accumulate assets during their later years.

The preceding analysis might be made far more elaborate and extended in a variety of directions to deal with various issues in monetary theory and policy, with policies to promote saving in underdeveloped countries, with dynamic aspects of the demand for durable goods, etc.; but these matters lie outside the scope of the present book.[15]

[15] For further discussion of some of these questions, see R. W. Clower, "Permanent Income and Transitory Balances," *Oxford Economic Papers,* Vol. 15 (May, 1963), pp. 177–90.

SELECTED REFERENCES

BAUMOL, W. J. *Economic Theory and Operations Analysis,* chaps. xix, xxii. 2d ed. Englewood Cliffs, N.J.: Prentice-Hall, 1965.

COHEN, K. J., AND CYERT, R. M. *Theory of the Firm,* chap. v. Englewood Cliffs, N.J.: Prentice-Hall, 1965.

FERBER, R. "Research in Household Behavior," *American Economic Review,* Vol. 52 (March, 1962), pp. 19–63.
    A review of the literature.

FRIEDMAN, M. "The Marshallian Demand Curve," *Journal of Political Economy,* Vol. 57 (December, 1949), pp. 463–95.

HICKS, J. R. *Value and Capital,* chaps. i, ii. 2d ed. Oxford: Oxford University Press, 1946.
    A detailed presentation of the indifference curve approach.

HENDERSON, J. M., AND QUANDT, R. E. *Microeconomic Theory,* chap. ii. New York: McGraw-Hill, 1958.
    A mathematical presentation of the theory of consumer behavior.

MARSHALL, A. *Principles of Economics,* Book III. 8th ed. London: Macmillan, 1936.
    The classic presentation of the marginal utility approach.

SIMON, H. "Theories of Decision-Making in Economics," *American Economic Review,* Vol. 49 (June, 1959), pp. 257–58.

QUESTIONS

1. What is the "law of demand"? What are the assumptions from which it is derived?
2. Explain the concept of marginal utility. What is meant by the statement that it is an ordinal rather than a cardinal measure?
3. What is the Law of Diminishing Marginal Utility? Explain the underlying rationale.
4. Explain, in terms of the marginal utility approach, the pattern of allocation of consumer income that is necessary to allow maximization of satisfaction.
5. Why does optimum allocation require that the marginal utilities of the various goods purchased be proportional to their prices?
6. Explain the law of demand in terms of the marginal utility approach.
7. What is meant by an indifference schedule?
8. Why do indifference curves slope downward from left to right? Why do they not intersect?
9. What is meant by the term "marginal rate of substitution"? What is its relation to the slope of an indifference curve?
10. Why are indifference curves convex to the point of origin? What principle is involved in the explanation?
11. What determines the degree of convexity of an indifference curve?

12. What would be the nature of an indifference curve of two commodities which are perfect substitutes?
13. What is meant by transitivity of difference curves?
14. Explain the "budget restraint" line. Upon what assumption is it typically drawn as a straight line?
15. Why is the point of tangency of the budget restraint line and an indifference curve the point of optimum satisfaction? Explain.
16. What is the relationship between the ratio of the prices of two articles and the marginal rate of substitution between them at the point of optimum satisfaction? Explain.
17. Distinguish between the price-consumption curve and the demand curve.
18. Explain how the demand schedule can be derived from schedules of indifference curves and budget restraint lines.
19. Distinguish carefully between the income and substitution effects of price changes, and distinguish between the two effects by the use of an indifference curve diagram.
20. What is meant by a "negative" income effect of a price change?
21. Illustrate the significance of substitutability for demand elasticity by means of the indifference curve technique.
22. On the basis of commonsense observations, would you expect the overall elasticity of demand for the following to be high or low? Why?
    a) Cigarettes
    b) Fur coats
    c) Tonsillectomies
    d) Movie theater admissions
    e) Insulin
    f) Frozen orange juice
23. Again, on the basis of commonsense observations, would you expect the income elasticity of demand for the following to be positive and relatively high, positive but relatively low, or negative? Why?
    a) Intercity bus travel
    b) Potatoes
    c) Expensive cuts of meat
    d) Cigarettes
    e) Inexpensive domestic wine
    f) Imported liqueurs
    g) Used clothing
    h) Outboard motors and boats
    i) Laundry service
24. What is the absolute income hypothesis? What led to doubts about its validity?
25. How does the relative income hypothesis differ from the absolute income hypothesis?
26. Explain the permanent income hypothesis.
27. Under what circumstances is cross-elasticity of demand between two goods positive? Under what circumstances is it negative? Explain.

28. Indicate some of the difficulties encountered in making empirical studies of the elasticity of demand for commodities.

29. Under the assumption that savings are held in the form of money, why will a typical family cease to save after a certain level of accumulated savings has been attained? What determines this point? Under what circumstances would the household continue to make net savings?

30. Distinguish between "entrepreneurial" and "proletarian" household savings behavior.

Chapter 6

THE THEORY OF PRODUCTION

Having completed our discussion of consumer demand, we turn now to the output and supply side of final product markets— the theory of production and cost. Our point of departure is the principle of profit maximization: the assumption that the object of the business firm in purchasing factor inputs with which to carry on production is to maximize the difference between total revenue and total cost. This requires, among other conditions, that the firm combine inputs in such a way that the total cost of producing any particular level of output is the lowest possible figure, given existing technological and institutional conditions. This chapter is concerned with the reactions of output to changes in inputs of various factors. The behavior of cost in response to changes in output will be discussed in Chapter 7. The determination of market prices through the mutual interplay of demand and output-supply considerations will be examined in Chapters 8–11.

THE PRODUCTION FUNCTION

We begin by supposing that the maximum amount of any product that a firm can produce with any given collection of factor inputs is determined by prevailing institutional circumstances and by the existing state of technical knowledge. The relationship between the inputs and outputs is expressed symbolically by a *production function* of the general form

$$x = f(v_1, v_2, \cdots, v_n),$$

where the variables $v_1, v_2, \ldots, v_n$ represent quantities of various factor inputs, and the variable x represents the maximum output that the firm can produce with a given set of the input variables. We may assume that the effect of an increase in any of the input variables is, at least up to some limit, to increase output. We may also assume that the proportions

89

in which various factor inputs can be combined to produce a given quantity of output are normally variable. Cases of fixed proportions are found in certain chemical processes; but apart from this (and perhaps a few other exceptions), experience indicates that input proportions can be varied significantly with output at a constant level. Thus one type of material can be substituted for another in the production of cigarette lighters; capital equipment may be substituted for labor in the production of long-distance phone calls, etc.

In order to facilitate further analysis of the properties of the production function (i.e., to describe the relationship between changes in inputs and consequent changes in output), it is useful to introduce two new concepts at this point: *average physical product* and *marginal physical product*. By *average physical product*, or *average product*, is meant the *total product per unit of a variable factor* (or factors). With ten men employed, and total output of 300 units per day, *the average product per man* is 30 units. By *marginal physical product*, more commonly known as *marginal product*, is meant the *addition to total product* which results from the utilization of one additional unit of a factor, given the quantities of the other factors. Thus, if output is 70 units a day with nine men employed, and rises to 73 units if a tenth man is added, the marginal product of the tenth man is three units. More precisely, the marginal product of three units is a result of the *change* in manpower from nine to ten; but customarily, we speak of it in relation to the additional factor unit added—the tenth man in the example.

Typical Output Behavior

What is the typical behavior of total output as inputs of some factors are increased, while inputs of other factors remain unchanged? Both economic analysis and empirical studies suggest the following pattern, as shown in Table 6–1 and Figure 6–1 :

a) Initially output rises at an increasing rate, and at a rate in excess of the rate of increase in inputs.

b) Ultimately the rate of increase in output commences to decline, and beyond a certain point falls below the rate of increase in inputs.

This pattern of behavior of total output results in the following pattern of behavior of marginal product and average product per unit of the variable factor:

a) Marginal product, which is the measure of the rate of change in total product, rises so long as total product is increasing at an increasing rate, commences to fall when the rate of increase in total product falls, and becomes negative at the level of output at which *total product* commences to fall.

b) Average product rises so long as output rises more rapidly than inputs, and thus over a greater range of output than that in which marginal product rises, and then falls as the rate of increase in inputs falls below the rate of increase in output.

c) Marginal product is above average product so long as the latter is rising, is equal to marginal product at the output level at which average product commences to fall, and is below it beyond this level of output.

↳ AVE PROD. 7

TABLE 6–1

TYPICAL OUTPUT BEHAVIOR WITH ONE VARIABLE FACTOR

Units of Variable Factor	Total Output	Average Physical Product	Marginal Physical Product
1.	12	12	12
2.	28	14	16
3.	52	17.33	24
4.	74	18.50	22
5.	91	18.20	17
6.	104	17.33	13
7.	114	16.29	10
8.	120	15	6
9.	121	13.44	1
10.	115	11.50	− 6

The behavior of output as a variable factor is increased can be separated into three stages, delimited by the broken lines in Figure 6–1.

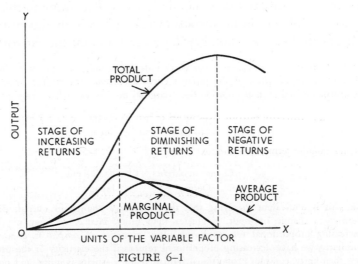

FIGURE 6–1

PRODUCT BEHAVIOR AS VARIABLE FACTOR UNITS ARE INCREASED

In the first stage, that of *increasing returns,* average product and marginal product increase. In the second stage, that of *diminishing returns,* marginal product declines continuously, eventually reaching zero, while average product increases to its maximum and then declines. Total product reaches its maximum at the point at which marginal product becomes zero. The third, or *negative returns,* stage is that in which total product is diminishing, and thus marginal product is negative.

The first and second stages may also be defined in terms of average rather than marginal product. By this approach, the stage of increasing returns extends to the output level at which average product commences to decline. The delineation between diminishing and negative returns remains the same as with the marginal definition.[1]

The Explanation of the Behavior of Output with Varying Proportions: The Law of Diminishing Returns

What forces are responsible for this behavior of output as proportions of the factors are varied? There are two primary considerations:

1. Certain factor units cannot be utilized effectively without a certain minimum number of units of other factors.
2. The operation of the Law of Diminishing Returns.

The first consideration is obvious; the second requires examination.

The law of Diminishing Returns is one of the oldest and most widely accepted laws in economic analysis. According to this law, if the quantities of certain factors are increased, while the quantities of other factors are held constant, beyond a certain point the rate of increase in

---

[1] An alternative classification of various stages may be established in terms of the concept of the *elasticity* of the product curve at various points. The stage of increasing returns is defined by the condition that marginal product exceeds average product; i.e.,

$$\frac{\text{Change in output}}{\text{Change in input}} > \frac{\text{Output}}{\text{Input}}$$

or, rearranging terms, the condition that

$$\frac{\text{Change in output}}{\text{Output}} > \frac{\text{Change in input}}{\text{Input}}$$

But this is equivalent to saying that the *percentage* change in output, divided by the *percentage* change in input, is greater than unity. Hence, we may say that we have increasing proportional returns if the *input elasticity of output* is greater than unity. Similarly, we have decreasing proportional returns if the elasticity of the product curve is less than unity, constant proportional returns if the elasticity is unity, and negative returns if the sign of the elasticity is negative rather than positive.

output, and thus the marginal product of the variable factors, will decline. Since the decline in the rate of increase in output will continue once it commences, eventually the rate of increase in output will drop below the rate of increase in the inputs of the variable factors, and average physical product will also fall.

The law is strictly relevant only to those situations in which factor proportions are varied, that is, where some factors are increased in quantity relative to the quantities of others, and is not applicable if all factors are varied in the same proportion—for example, if the quantities of all factors employed are doubled.

The Law of Diminishing Returns is based upon two premises. First, given technology is assumed; the law is relevant to the behavior of output when factor inputs are varied in the framework of available methods and techniques. For clarity of analysis, it is necessary to distinguish clearly between the effects of changes in factor proportions, as such, and those of the introduction of improved technological methods. Although, in any given period of time, both types of changes may occur, the effects of the one are distinct from those of the other. Second, it is assumed that units of the various factors employed are homogeneous, any unit being of equal efficiency and thus interchangeable with any other unit. The effects of using factor units of varying efficiency are distinct from those of varying factor combinations.

What is responsible for the operation of the Law of Diminishing Returns? Essentially, marginal physical product decreases because each successive unit of the variable factor has a smaller quantity of fixed factor units with which to work. Once the point is reached at which the number of variable units is adequate to utilize the available fixed factor units efficiently, further increases in the variable factor will add progressively less to total product.

With this preliminary survey of the Law of Diminishing Returns completed, it is now possible to analyze the behavior of average and marginal product in the successive stages of increasing, diminishing, and negative returns.

The Stage of Increasing Returns

The initial rise in marginal and average product is due in part to the operation of the Law of Diminishing Returns working negatively relative to the variable factor, and in part to the more effective use of fixed (and possibly variable) factor units as the number of variable units is increased.

When the number of variable factors is extremely small, the Law of Diminishing Returns operates negatively relative to the variable factors or, in other words, in a positive way relative to the fixed factor. That is, the quantity of the fixed factor is so great that efficiency of operation is interfered with, and production would actually be greater if some of the fixed factor units were disposed of. There are so many units of fixed factors that in effect they get in the way of other factors. If one man tried to operate a large department store alone—doing work of all types necessary in the store—his energies would be spread so thinly in so many directions that total output (sales) might be less than if he were operating a smaller store (i.e., working with less capital). As successive men were added, up to a certain number, each man would add more to total product than the previous one.

More significantly, the stage of increasing returns can be attributed to the greater efficiency in the use of certain fixed and variable factor units as they are combined with large quantities of other factors. For example, certain types of capital equipment may require a minimum number of men for efficient operation, or perhaps any operation at all. With a small number of variable factors, machines cannot operate at all, or only at a low level of efficiency. As additional variable factor units are added, machines are brought into efficient operation, and thus marginal product of the variable factors rises sharply.

Similarly, additional units of the variable factors may permit more effective utilization of their services.[2] Some tasks are inherently difficult for one person alone to perform, and the adding of a second person may far more than double output. This is true, for example, of bricklaying on the wall of a house. Without a helper, the bricklayer will waste a great deal of time and energy climbing up and down with bricks. Similarly, two persons can get the hay crop into a barn in much less than half the time required for one person, with given equipment and techniques.

In some lines of production the stage of increasing returns may never manifest itself at all. If the variable factor units cannot be obtained in small units (for example, if men cannot be hired for periods shorter than a day or a week), the first unit of the variable factor may carry production out of the increasing returns stage, and thus the firm is never aware that such a stage exists. Only if the variable factor could be

---

[2] In a sense, this is an aspect of specialization, discussed below. But since the primary advantages of specialization are obtained only when all factors can be adjusted, the principal discussion of this question is postponed until later in the chapter.

added in much smaller units would the stage be noticeable. Thus, in a small store the adding of one clerk may carry operations into the decreasing returns stage, and the marginal product of a second clerk will be less than that of the first. Likewise, if the fixed factor units are divisible into very small units, increasing returns may never be encountered, since it may be possible to set aside a portion of them, and concentrate the work of variable units on only a small portion of fixed factors.

The Stage of Diminishing Returns

The second stage, that of diminishing returns, results from the operation of the Law of Diminishing Returns, once the point is reached at which the number of variable factor units is sufficient to allow efficient utilization of the fixed factors. Further increase in the number of variable factor units beyond this point results in a decline in marginal product, because the number of fixed factor units is inadequate for the number of variable units.

The exact behavior of total product, and thus marginal and average product, and the actual output figures at which marginal and average product commence to diminish, depend upon the nature of the production process and the character of the fixed and variable factor units involved. If the fixed factor consists of a large number of machines of a type which can be operated with small amounts of variable factors (materials and labor primarily), marginal product is likely to be more or less constant over a substantial range as variable factors are increased, since additional units will be used to operate previously idle machines. Similarly, in a department store (with given physical plant), portions of the store might simply be closed off if the number of clerks is small; as more clerks are hired, additional portions of the store would be utilized. Thus, for a substantial range, each successive clerk might make possible the same increase in sales volume.

On the other hand, if the fixed factors consist of a large, indivisible, and unadaptable[3] unit—that is, if the group of fixed factors requires certain amounts of variable factors if it is to be used at all— marginal product, after initially rising rapidly, will fall very sharply, once the necessary number of variable units has been obtained. For example, if a bus company is to operate one bus run a day between two

---

[3] A good example of this practice is found in restaurants. When the volume of business is light and only a few waitresses are needed, portions of the dining rooms will be closed off, so that the waitresses will not have to cover unnecessarily large areas.

points, one driver and a certain amount of gasoline are necessary, but the marginal productivity of a second employee on the bus or of additional gasoline is virtually zero.

The Stage of Negative Returns

The third stage, one which a firm will never knowingly allow itself to reach, is that in which the use of additional factor units actually reduces total output, and marginal product is therefore negative. In such a situation, there are so many units of the variable factor that efficient use of the fixed factor units is impaired. Too many clerks in a store will make it difficult for customers to get in; too many workers in a factory will get in one another's way. In such a situation a reduction in the number of variable units will increase total output, just as in the stage of increasing returns a reduction in the number of units of the fixed factor will increase output if the condition of increasing returns is due solely to an excessive number of fixed factor units.

OPTIMUM FACTOR COMBINATIONS

Since marginal product and average product change as factor proportions are varied, certain factor combinations are more economical than others for the production of a *given* level of output. A major task of the business firm is the selection of the factor combination which is the optimum, in the sense of allowing lowest cost of producing a given output. The optimum factor combination cannot be determined solely on the basis of the production function—that is, on the basis of technological conditions and the behavior of physical output—since the relative efficiency of different combinations is also dependent upon the prices which must be paid for various factor units.

The Marginal Rate of Factor Substitution

Explanation of the optimum factor combination can be facilitated by the use of the concept of the marginal rate of substitution as applied to factors: the number of units of one factor necessary to replace a unit of another factor and maintain the same level of output.

Let us suppose that steel and aluminum are substitutes in the manufacture of automatic washers. For the production of a given number of washers, various possible combinations of the two metals (together with given quantities of other factors) may be used, as illustrated in Table 6–2. At one extreme, if only steel were used, ten tons would be required. At the other extreme, if only aluminum were used, five tons

TABLE 6–2

VARIOUS COMBINATIONS OF ALUMINUM AND STEEL WHICH WILL PERMIT
AN OUTPUT OF 200 AUTOMATIC WASHERS PER DAY

Aluminum Tons	Steel Tons	Marginal Rate of Substitution of Aluminum for Steel
0	10	
		4
1	6	
		3
2	3	
		2
3	1	
		$\frac{3}{4}$
4	$\frac{1}{4}$	
		$\frac{1}{4}$
5	0	

would be required. There are various intermediate combinations; for example if two tons of aluminum are used, three tons of steel will be needed. It must be emphasized that the various combinations are alternative possibilities for the production of a given quantity of the product, 200 washers in the example.

For each quantity of aluminum used, there is a marginal rate of substitution of aluminum for steel, that is, the quantity of steel which must be added to allow replacement of a ton of aluminum and yet produce the same amount of output. The third column in Table 6–2 presents the marginal rates of substitution of aluminum for steel. For example, if five units of aluminum are now being used (and no steel), only one quarter of a ton of steel must be added to allow the elimination of one ton of aluminum. On the other hand, if two tons of aluminum (and three tons of steel) are now being used, three additional tons of steel must be added to allow reduction of aluminum input to one ton.

The Principle of Diminishing Marginal Rate of Factor Substitution

As illustrated by the data in Table 6–2, the greater the quantity of aluminum used, the smaller the quantity of steel which must be added to allow the elimination of one ton of aluminum. In other words, the greater the extent to which steel is replaced by aluminum, the lower will be the marginal rate of substitution—the quantity of steel necessary to replace a unit of aluminum and maintain output. This relationship is known as the *Law of Diminishing Marginal Rate of Factor Substitution*. It is essentially an extension of the Law of Diminishing

Returns to the relationship between two factors. The law may be stated more precisely in this manner: As the quantity of any one factor is increased relative to the quantity of the other, output being constant, the number of units of the second which can be replaced by one unit of the first falls, because the marginal product of the first factor falls relative to that of the second.

For purposes of simplicity, Table 6–2 is set up with a diminishing marginal rate of substitution of aluminum for steel over the entire range of the table. Actually, if in a particular case there is a stage of increasing marginal returns for the variable factor, the marginal rate of substitution will rise initially, since the replacement of aluminum (of which there is too much) by steel (of which there is too little) will facilitate efficiency in production. As soon as the stage of diminishing returns for the factor which is being increased is encountered, however, the marginal rate of substitution will fall.

The rate at which the marginal rate of substitution falls is a measure of the extent to which the two factors are substitutes for each other. If they are perfect substitutes, that is, if either factor can be used equally well to produce the product, the marginal rate of substitution will not fall. If steel and aluminum can be used equally well to produce all of the metal parts of a washer, the marginal rate of substitution will remain unchanged—regardless of the extent to which substitution is carried in either direction.

At the other extreme, two factors may not be substitutes at all for a particular purpose; the marginal rate of substitution is undefinable, since output cannot be maintained if one factor is replaced by the other. If this relationship exists among all factors used by the firm, the factor combination employed is dictated entirely by technological conditions, and no substitution is possible.

If two factors are partial substitutes for one another, the marginal rate of substitution will vary as factor proportions are altered, ranging from infinity to values near or equal to zero. Suppose, for example, that in the production of washers, either steel or aluminum can be used for most purposes, but steel is essential for some purposes because aluminum lacks sufficient strength for performing the task. In this case, once the quantity of steel has been reduced to the minimum amount required, the marginal rate of substitution will become infinite, since output cannot be maintained if substitution is carried further.

For purposes of simplification, the explanation of the marginal rate of substitution and its behavior has been set up in terms of two factors. When a firm is using a large number of factors, there are

separate marginal rates of substitution between each two factors
employed, and the principles outlined above apply to any two factors,
and thus to all of them.

The Isoquant Graph

The various combinations of two factors which will allow the
production of a given quantity of output can be illustrated graphically,
measuring the quantity of one factor on the vertical axis, the quantity of
the other on the horizontal axis. The curve showing the various factor
combinations which will produce the given output is known as an
isoquant. In Figure 6–2, tons of aluminum are measured on the vertical

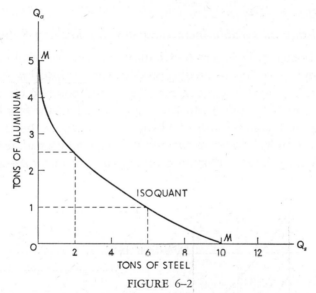

FIGURE 6–2

ISOQUANT SHOWING VARIOUS COMBINATIONS OF ALUMINUM
AND STEEL WHICH CAN BE USED TO PRODUCE 200
AUTOMATIC WASHERS

axis, and tons of steel on the horizontal axis; isoquant *MM* shows the
various combinations of the two factors which will allow the production
of 200 washers per day (with given quantities of other factors), based
upon the data in Table 6–2.

The slope of the isoquant at any particular point shows the
marginal rate of substitution between the two factors at this point.
Under ordinary circumstances, the isoquant will be convex to the point
of origin, because of the Law of Diminishing Marginal Rate of Factor
Substitution. The greater the quantity of one factor used, the smaller is
the quantity of the other factor which is needed to replace a unit of the

first factor and maintain output. Thus the right-hand portion of the isoquant is almost parallel to the horizontal axis, while the left-hand portion is almost parallel to the vertical axis. However, if the two factors are perfect substitutes, the isoquant will be a straight line, since the marginal rate of substitution will not vary. At the other extreme, if the two factors cannot be substituted the isoquant will contain a right-angle bend, showing that a given minimum quantity of each factor is required to produce a given output. The more easily the two factors may be substituted for one another, the less will be the curvature of the isoquant. The isoquants are drawn in terms of two factors, but the relationships they indicate apply to each pair of factors used, and so to all factors.

The Isoquant Graph: Increasing and Diminishing Returns

The isoquants in Figure 6–3 indicate alternative combinations of factors b and a that can be used to produce various *integral* amounts 1, 2, 3, 4, . . . , of an output x. Starting at the point R on the input expansion path RS (along which the quantity of factor b is held constant at two units), one unit of factor a is needed to increase output from 2 to 3 units. To *increase* output by an additional unit (from 3 to 4) then requires *less* than an additional unit of factor a—indicating

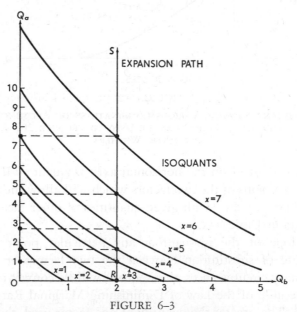

FIGURE 6–3

INCREASING AND DIMINISHING RETURNS
AS SHOWN BY THE ISOQUANT
TECHNIQUE

increasing returns. To increase output by yet another unit (from 4 to 5), however, requires *more* than unit increase in factor *a*, and similarly thereafter—indicating that diminishing returns set in after output exceeds 4 units. These relationships are indicated in Figure 6–3 by that fact that the *distance* between successive isoquants first decreases and then increases as we move along the expansion path *RS*.

The Optimum Factor Combination

Knowledge of the marginal rates of substitution between two commodities does not, in itself, indicate the optimum quantities of each to use, in the sense of that combination which will allow the firm to produce a given level of output at lowest cost. This combination can be defined only if the costs of the various factors are known as well as the

TABLE 6–3

RELATIVE COSTS OF PRODUCING 200 AUTOMATIC WASHERS WITH
VARIOUS COMBINATIONS OF STEEL AND ALUMINUM

Aluminum (Tons)	Steel (Tons)	Cost of Aluminum* (Dollars)	Cost of Steel† (Dollars)	Other Costs (Dollars)	Total Cost (Dollars)
0	10	0	300	9,000	9,300
1	6	60	180	9,000	9,240
2	3	120	90	9,000	9,210
3	1	180	30	9,000	9,210
4	$\frac{1}{4}$	240	$7\frac{1}{2}$	9,000	$9,247\frac{1}{2}$
5	0	300	0	9,000	9,300

* Assuming a price of $60 a ton.
† Assuming a price of $30 a ton.

marginal rates of substitution among them. In the automatic washer example presented in Table 6–2, let us assume that aluminum costs $60 a ton, and steel costs $30 a ton. In Table 6–3 the total costs of producing the given number of washers are shown with various combinations of steel and aluminum, the assumption being made that other costs are the same regardless of the combination of metals employed.

With these data, the least-cost point, and thus the optimum factor combination, is attained when two tons of aluminum and three tons of steel, or, alternatively, three tons of aluminum and one ton of steel, are used. If the data were broken down in this bracket to fractions of a ton, a single combination could be discovered which would allow absolute minimum cost.

Examination of the data in Tables 6–2 and 6–3 will show that the range of combinations allowing lowest cost is that in which the marginal rate of substitution is 2 to 1, and is thus equal to the ratio of the prices of the two factors (60 to 30). This relationship between the factor-price ratio and the marginal rate of substitution is essential for attainment of the least cost combination. Any deviation from this point will result in an increase in the cost of the added factor of greater magnitude than the reduction in the cost of the replaced factor, and thus in an increase in total cost. For example, on the basis of the data in Table 6–3, if the quantity of aluminum were cut back from two tons to one, the saving in aluminum costs would be $60, whereas the cost of additional steel required to allow production of the same output would be $90 (three tons at $30 per ton). An increase in the quantity of aluminum from three tons to four would add $60 to the cost of the aluminum but would reduce steel costs by only $22.50.

Tangency of the Isoquant with an Isocost Line

The optimum factor combination can be shown graphically by adding to the isoquant graph *isocost* (equal cost) lines to show the various possible quantities of the two factors which can be purchased with a given outlay of money. The isoquant shown in Figure 6–2 is reproduced in Figure 6–4 and isocost lines are added, showing the various quantities of steel and aluminum which can be purchased with a given outlay of money on the assumption that the prices of aluminum

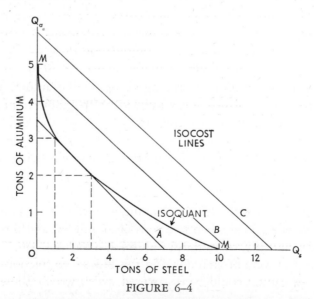

FIGURE 6–4

THE OPTIMUM COMBINATION OF ALUMINUM AND
STEEL TO PRODUCE 200 WASHERS PER DAY

and steel per ton are \$60 and \$30, respectively. If the given outlay is \$210, for example, the isocost line is represented by the line *A* in Figure 6–4, which indicates that 3½ tons of aluminum can be purchased if only aluminum is purchased, 7 tons of steel if only steel is purchased, 2 tons of aluminum if 3 tons of steel are used, etc. The isocost relation is a straight line as a matter of mathematical necessity so long as prices paid for factor units are the same regardless of the quantities purchased. There are various possible isocost lines, one for each potential level of outlay on factors, the successive lines being parallel to each other, as indicated by the lines *A, B,* and *C* in Figure 6–4. The farther to the right a line is located, the higher is the level of outlay which it represents.

Minimum cost is achieved for a given level of output by choosing that combination of factor inputs which is cheaper than any alternative combination which could be used to produce the given output. This combination is represented graphically by the lowest isocost line (the one farthest to the left) which touches the isoquant representing the quantity to be produced. Thus the optimum factor combination will be represented by a point of tangency between the given isoquant and the lowest possible isocost line (provided that the isoquant is a smooth curve; if not, there may be more than one point of tangency and thus more than one "optimum" combination of factors). In Figure 6–4 the tangency condition does not define a single point, but rather a range of points between three tons of steel and two of aluminum, and one ton of steel and three of aluminum. As shown above in Table 6–3, it is within this range that the optimum factor combination must lie. With figures for intervals within this range available, tangency would appear at a single point, as illustrated in Figure 6–5.

The isocost line which is just tangent to the isoquant is that which allows the acquisition of the necessary factor units with the lowest possible outlay. Any lower line would not allow the purchase of sufficient factors to produce the desired output, while any higher isocost line would entail unnecessarily high factor costs. At any point on the isoquant other than the point of tangency, the outlay on the factors to produce the given output would be higher than that at the tangency point. At tangency, the slope of the isoquant (which represents the marginal rate of substitution between the two factors) is equal to the slope of the isocost line (which represents the ratio of the prices of the two factors), and thus the marginal rate of substitution is equal to the ratio of the factor prices. It must be emphasized that the isoquant shows the various quantities of the two factors necessary to produce a given

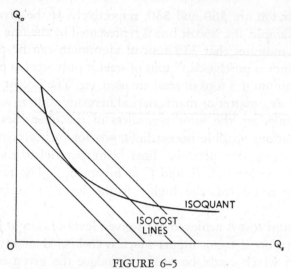

FIGURE 6–5

THE OPTIMUM FACTOR COMBINATION, WITH SINGLE-
POINT TANGENCY

output, while each isocost line shows the various quantities of two factors which can be acquired with the expenditure of a given sum of money.

Factor Price Changes and Factor Substitution

The explanation of the optimum factor combination in the preceding section has, of necessity, been based upon the assumption of given factor prices. It is possible, however, to extend the analysis to consider changes in the relative prices of the two factors and consequent changes in quantities of the two factors acquired.

A change in the price of any factor, total output and the prices of the other factors remaining unchanged, will necessitate a readjustment in factor proportions, since the price change will destroy the equality of the price ratio and the marginal rate of substitution. The readjustment will continue until this equality is restored. The slower the rate of decline in the marginal rate of substitution between two factors, the relatively greater will be the extent of substitution of one factor for another as their relative prices change.

In graphical terms, the change in the price of one factor changes the point of tangency between the isoquant and the isocost line, as shown in Figure 6–6, and thus results in a new optimum combination. If the factors are good substitutes, and thus the isoquant has little curvature, the shift of the point of tangency will be substantial (from *Oa* to *Ob* in Figure 6–6), and the increase in the quantity utilized of the factor which has become cheaper will be relatively great. If the two factors are poor substitutes, the curvature will be sharp and the shift in the quantity of the factor acquired will be relatively slight (from Oa to Ob in Figure 6–7).

The Scope of Applicability of the Law of Diminishing Returns

The Law of Diminishing Returns is relevant to the behavior of output only when factor proportions are varied; that is, when one factor or several factors are increased (or reduced) in quantity while the inputs of the others remain the same. The law is therefore significant

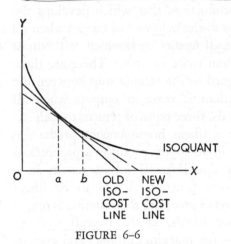

FIGURE 6–6

READJUSTMENT OF THE OPTIMUM FACTOR COMBINATION IN RESPONSE TO A CHANGE IN THE PRICE OF ONE FACTOR. HIGH SUBSTITUTABILITY

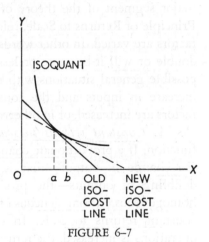

FIGURE 6–7

READJUSTMENT OF THE OPTIMUM FACTOR COMBINATION IN RESPONSE TO A CHANGE IN THE PRICE OF ONE FACTOR. POOR SUBSTITUTABILITY

under all circumstances (except those of fixed coefficients of production) for relative adjustments of inputs of various factors needed to obtain the optimum factor combination, since adjustments to attain this combination necessarily involve changes in the relative quantities of the various factors used.

The law is also relevant, however, for the behavior of total output in any situation in which it is not possible for a firm to increase all factors of production in the same proportion. As explained more carefully in the next chapter, in a relatively short period of time, some factors of production, particularly capital equipment, cannot be adjusted. Accordingly, as a firm increases output by adding additional inputs of those factors which can be adjusted, the Law of Diminishing Returns is encountered in the behavior of product outputs relative to inputs of the variable factors. Accordingly, the operation of the law is significant for the behavior of cost per unit of output as a firm increases output under circumstances in which the inputs of some factors are fixed (as explained in the next chapter).

ADJUSTMENTS IN ALL FACTORS: THE PRINCIPLE OF RETURN TO SCALE

The discussion of the previous sections of this chapter has related to situations in which factor proportions have been varied. The other major segment of the theory of production, that which develops the Principle of Returns to Scale, relates to the behavior of output when all factors are varied. In other words, if all factors are doubled, will output double or will it be more or less than twice as great? There are three possible general situations with regard to the relationship between the increase in inputs and the consequent increase in outputs when all factors are increased, or in other words, three types of returns to scale.

1. *Constant returns to scale:* a linear homogeneous production function. If a proportionate change in all inputs produces a proportionate change in output—that is, if doubling all inputs results in a doubling of outputs—the production function is said to be linear homogeneous or homogeneous of first degree, and the situation is one of constant returns to scale. In other words, as the overall scale of operations is increased, the returns—the marginal product and average product of each factor—are constant.

2. *Increasing returns to scale:* an increase in inputs of all factors results in a more than proportionate increase in output.

3. *Decreasing returns to scale:* an increase in inputs of all factors results in a less than proportionate increase in output.

It is widely believed that in a typical production activity, when scale of operations is first increased, increasing returns to scale are encountered; ultimately, with the exhaustion of all economies, returns to scale are constant; if expansion is carried far enough, returns to scale decrease.

The Isoquant Presentation and the Expansion Path

With constant returns to scale, the isoquants representing successive unit increases in output (with adjustments of all factors) will be equidistant on any line extended from the point of origin. Thus in Figure 6–8 segments Op, pr, rs, etc., are of equal length; doubling the inputs results in a doubling of outputs. As shown in Figure 6–9, with

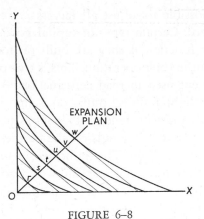

FIGURE 6–8

EXPANSION PATH. CONSTANT RE-
TURNS TO SCALE

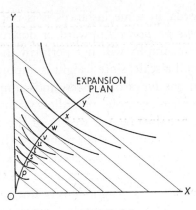

FIGURE 6–9

EXPANSION PATH. "NORMAL"
PATTERN

increasing returns to scale the segments between isoquants (each successive isoquant representing the same increase in output) decrease in length. With decreasing returns the segments increase in length.

Figure 6–8 shows the expansion path of a firm as it increases output with increases in all inputs, assuming constant returns to scale. The expansion path is a straight line under these assumptions and the ratios of the factors remain the same. Doubling the expenditure on inputs will double the output in all ranges of the graph and the factor combination will remain unaltered. This figure is, of course, based upon the assumption that increases in the use of factors do not lead to changes in the prices paid for the factors.

When returns to scale are not constant, the expansion path is not a straight line; in the "typical" case, with successively increasing, constant, and decreasing returns to scale, the expansion path is concave to the horizontal axis, as illustrated in Figure 6–9. Initially, doubling the expenditure on inputs will more than double output; ultimately, doubling expenditure results in less than a doubling of output.

Increasing Returns to Scale

A situation of increasing returns to scale can be attributed to two considerations: indivisibilities of some factors and advantages of specialization.

1. *Indivisibilities.* The inability to divide certain factor units into smaller units without either complete loss of usefulness in production or partial loss in efficiency results in a relatively low output per unit of input when operations are conducted on a very small scale. In other

words, in some instances it is not possible to adjust all factors *in the same proportion* upward or downward. Certain types of capital goods, for example, will not perform their function if they are built on too small a scale, since weight is important in their operation. This is true of various types of presses, and equipment used in road construction. As another example, regardless of how light railroad traffic on a line is expected to be, the weight of the rails must be at least 45 pounds per yard if standard equipment is to be operated. Yet rails on the heaviest traffic lines may not exceed 135 pounds in weight. The traffic density on a heavily used line may be 2,000,000 ton-miles per mile of track annually; on a light-density line the traffic may not exceed 20,000 ton-miles. The latter is only 1 percent of the former; yet the rail required is 33 percent as large. A rail only 1 percent of the weight of the 135-pound rail would not stand the weight of a handcar.

With other capital equipment, small units can be made, but the output per unit of factors used to make and operate them is low. A 5-H.P. diesel engine cannot be built for 1 percent of the cost of a 500-H.P. diesel. For physical reasons, larger machines require less material per unit of output for their construction than smaller machines; and they likewise require less labor for their construction per unit of product, since it takes little or no additional time to assemble the parts of a machine designed to produce 100 units a day than to assemble the parts of a similar machine designed to produce 50 units. If the size of the machine is very small, more time may actually be required because of the difficulty of working with small parts. When machinery is small in size, necessary precision in measurements is difficult to obtain. Strength-weight relationships produce the same effects. To continue the railway rail example introduced in the previous paragraph: For rails above the minimum size necessary, strength and wearability increase much more rapidly than weight. A study made by the Canadian National Railways showed that rail weighing 132 pounds per yard would, on the average, carry a total traffic of 400,000,000 gross ton-miles before replacement was necessary, whereas rail of 100 pounds weight would carry only 150,000,000 gross ton-miles.[4] Similar patterns are found in warehouse construction; doubling the building material will more than double the amount of usable space. With a rectangular building, costs of walls will need to increase only 50 percent for the capacity of the area to double.

Indivisibilities are not confined to capital goods. Labor units are not completely divisible. One operator may be required for each machine,

[4] *Canadian National Railways Magazine,* October, 1955, p. 4.

regardless of its size. A freight train requires one engineer, regardless of the tonnage of the train; there is no way of using a fraction of an engineer on a train of light tonnage. Within limits, in small enterprises, employees may be used to perform several different tasks. But as a practical matter, there are severe limitations to such possibilities. A switchboard operator may serve as receptionist and do some stenographic work, but she can scarcely be used at the same time as an elevator operator and window cleaner. A clerk in a store may be busy only one third of the time, yet he must be paid for the entire day. In any type of business, it is difficult to utilize each worker to the maximum of his productivity at all times. As an establishment grows, the percentage of labor time not utilized should fall, if management policies are effective.[5]

Indivisibilities are also encountered in advertising, research work, and financing. Advertising on a small scale is relatively less effective than on a large scale, as explained in Chapter 9. Research activities cannot be carried on effectively on a small scale. Indivisibilities are likewise encountered in the financing of a business. The cost of floating a bond issue, for example, is to a large extent independent of the size of the issue. Thus, this method of financing—the cheapest method when large amounts of capital are to be obtained—is expensive to a firm until it has expanded beyond a certain size. The refusal of many investors to consider the bonds of any except well-known companies increases the difficulty of bond financing by small businesses.

2. *Specialization.* The other and closely related cause of increasing returns to scale is the advantage offered by specialization. In a very small business, employees must perform a wide variety of tasks. As the size of the enterprise increases, each employee can be used in a relatively specialized job, with a consequent increase in output per worker. The advantages of specialization of labor have been recognized since the days of Adam Smith.[6] The primary advantages include the greater skill acquired with specialization, the avoidance of wasted time in shifting from one task to another, and the employment of persons best suited to particular types of work. In managerial activity as well as in other phases of work, advantages of specialization are encountered. As a firm grows in size, personnel relations will be conducted by a specialist;

[5] Union rules sometimes increase indivisibilities of labor and lessen effective utilization of labor time. Thus a freight train must have a crew of a stated size, though less men may be needed in certain operations.

[6] His classic example deals with the advantages of specialization in the manufacture of pins (see his *Wealth of Nations* [Modern Library ed.; New York: Random House], pp. 7–8).

traffic management will be in the hands of a full-time traffic expert instead of being performed by a person who also has a half dozen other tasks. The owner of a small retail store selects the location for the store primarily upon a guesswork basis, placing it where he thinks his sales volume should be high or where he happens to find an empty low-rent building. In contrast, larger chains have store sites selected by experts who have experience in analyzing the factors which affect the relative desirability of different sites. Specialization is also possible with capital equipment. As a firm increases its scale of operations, it becomes possible to replace nonspecialized equipment which is capable of performing a number of tasks by specialized equipment designed for various specific operations, with a consequent increase in output per unit of input.

The importance of the phase of increasing returns depends in large measure upon the type of production process involved. In almost any type, increasing returns are likely to be encountered to some extent when a business expands from a very small initial size because of indivisibilities of labor. If, however, a business utilizes relatively little capital equipment, and if few advantages of specialization of labor are obtainable, increasing returns may very quickly come to an end. On the other hand, if a firm uses extensive amounts of capital goods of types which cannot be used efficiently on a small scale, very substantial increasing returns extending over a great range of output may be encountered. Thus, increasing returns are very important in steel, cement, and automobile production, while they are of less importance in agriculture and retailing.

Constant Returns to Scale

As a business continues to expand its scale of operations, it gradually exhausts the economies responsible for increasing returns. A firm will eventually grow to the point at which it is using the best type of capital equipment available and is gaining full advantages of specialization of labor. Beyond this point, further increases in the scale of operations are likely to produce more or less constant returns for a substantial range of output, the production function being linearly homogeneous. If the entire scale of operations is doubled, output will approximately double also.[7] It must be emphasized that constant

---

[7] Even in the phase of constant returns, small increases in scale may produce decreasing returns or increasing returns because of indivisibilities—the inability to add small quantities of certain factors. A railroad cannot build half of a new track between two points; if two tracks are inadequate, it may build a third track, which initially will not be used to capacity.

returns to scale are relevant only for time periods in which adjustment of all factors is possible. If a firm doubles output in a short period with a fixed physical plant which was previously utilized to normal optimum capacity, returns per unit of the variable factors will decline because of the operation of the Law of Diminishing Returns. But if all factors are varied, as may be possible over a long-run period, the Law of Diminishing Returns is not relevant.

Decreasing Returns to Scale

As a firm continues to expand its scale of operations, beyond a certain point there is apparently a tendency for returns to scale to decrease, and thus a given percentage increase in the quantities of all factors will bring about a less than proportional increase in output. In some types of production, decreasing returns may follow directly after the increasing returns phase, with no significant intervening period of constant returns. It is believed, however, on the basis of limited evidence, that a long phase of constant returns is typical.

Decreasing returns to scale for a particular plant must be distinguished from such returns for the firm as a whole. The former are attributable almost entirely to physical relationships. The greater area over which production operations must be coordinated and the greater territory from which labor supplies must be drawn will ultimately result in lower product per unit of input in a given plant. A classic historical example of failure to consider decreasing returns to scale of plant was provided by the Portuguese vessels in the East Indian trade in the sixteenth and seventeenth centuries. The Portuguese continued to increase the size of their ships in order to provide greater cargo space. But strength and maneuverability could not be maintained as the vessels became larger, and the ships became increasingly vulnerable to storms and attractive to pirates. As a consequence, losses of vessels increased disastrously; and the Dutch, with smaller, faster ships, proceeded to capture the trade.[8]

Decreasing returns to scale for the firm itself are usually attributed to increased problems and complexities of large-scale management. Continued increases in entrepreneurial labor activity beyond a certain point encounter more and more serious problems and difficulties. An increasing percentage of the total labor force will be required in administrative work, in order to provide coordination of the activities of the enterprise and necessary control over the large numbers of em-

[8] See James Duffy, *Shipwreck and Empire* (Cambridge: Harvard University Press, 1955).

ployees. A growing concern, once it reaches substantial size, encounters a fundamental problem of management; final authority for basic policy must remain in the hands of a group of men who control the operation of the business, yet these men are far removed from the actual level of operations. They are forced to make decisions on the basis of second-hand information, on subjects with which they have no direct contact. Furthermore, substantial delay can occur in the making of decisions, since the request for a decision, plus necessary information, must pass up through the chain of command to the entrepreneurial group, and the decision must then pass down to the operating unit.

In order to reduce to a minimum the amount of red tape and delay in making decisions by those out of contact with the situation, it becomes necessary to delegate responsibility for many decisions to subordinate officials. But to the extent that such a policy is followed, the decisions are made by persons who lack both the knowledge of general business policy and the experience which the men at the top level of management possess. As a result, there arises a lack of coordination and unity of policy among various parts of the enterprise. Modern business management attempts to carry delegation to limits which are consistent with reasonable unity of policy, but the problem can never be eliminated. Scientific management principles merely lessen its seriousness.

The growth of a business likewise increases the amount of division of responsibility and serves to lessen initiative, especially on the part of persons in lower-level jobs who are in a position to note desirable changes. With increased size comes loss of personal contact between management and workers, with consequent loss of morale and increase in labor strife.

The Validity of the Principle of Returns to Scale

The Principle of Returns to Scale has not enjoyed the general acceptance afforded the Law of Diminishing Returns. The initial increase in output per unit of factor which occurs as a firm first increases its scale of operations appears to be confirmed both by commonsense observation and by empirical studies. The ultimate exhaustion of economies of scale likewise seems inevitable. But whether or not an ultimate decline in output per unit of input is inevitable, or is confined to those fields (such as certain types of agriculture) in which management problems are particularly serious because of space considerations is still an open question.

SELECTED REFERENCES

BAUMOL, W. J. *Economic Theory and Operations Analysis,* chap. xi. 2d ed. Englewood Cliffs, N.J.: Prentice-Hall, 1965.

CASSELS, J. M. "On the Law of Variable Proportions," *Readings in the Theory of Income Distribution* (eds. W. FELLNER AND B. F. HALEY), pp. 103–18. Philadelphia: Blakiston, 1946.

COHEN, J. J., AND CYERT, R. M. *Theory of the Firm,* chap. vii. Englewood Cliffs, N.J.: Prentice-Hall, 1965.

RYAN, W. J. L. *Price Theory,* chap. ii. London: Macmillan, 1964.

QUESTIONS

1. What is the subject matter of the theory of production?
2. What is a production function?
3. Distinguish between production functions with fixed coefficients of production and those with variable coefficients. Give an example of the former.
4. Distinguish between average physical product and marginal physical product.
5. Explain and illustrate with a graph the typical behavior of total product as the input of one factor is increased, with given quantities of the other factors.
6. Why is marginal product equal to average product at the highest level of average product?
7. Why does marginal product fall if the rate of increase in total product falls?
8. Can average product be rising while marginal product is falling? Explain.
9. Explain the Law of Diminishing Returns, indicating the premises upon which it is based.
10. Distinguish between the stages of *increasing returns* and *increasing returns to scale,* and indicate the causes of each.
11. *a)* Contrast the causes of the stage of diminishing returns and those of decreasing returns to scale.
    b) Distinguish between decreasing returns to scale for the plant and for the firm. Why is the latter the more significant of the two?
12. What is meant by the stage of "negative returns"? What can be responsible for negative returns if a firm expands far enough?
13. What is meant by the term *optimum factor combination?*
14. Explain carefully the meaning of the term *marginal rate of substitution* with respect to factors.
15. Why may the marginal rate of substitution of y for x fall as the quantity of y is increased? Why may it rise initially?
16. What is the relationship between the rate of decline in the marginal rate of substitution and the degree of substitutability of the two factors for each other?

17. What is the marginal rate of substitution among the various factors in a situation of fixed coefficients of production?
18. What is an isoquant? Distinguish between an isoquant and an indifference curve.
19. What does an isocost line show?
20. Why is an isoquant convex to the point of origin?
21. How is the optimum factor combination defined, in terms of the marginal rate of substitution? In terms of the isoquant graph?
22. For what circumstances is the Law of Diminishing Returns applicable?
23. In what circumstances is the Principle of Returns to Scale applicable?
24. What are "indivisibilities"? How do they cause increasing returns to scale?
25. When is a firm likely to encounter constant returns to scale?
26. What is responsible for decreasing returns to scale?
27. What is a linear homogeneous production function?
28. What is the "expansion path"?
29. Indicate the difference between the expansion path with constant returns to scale and that with decreasing returns to scale.

Chapter 7

NATURE AND BEHAVIOR OF COST

To obtain factor inputs for use in production, a firm must compensate factor owners. The compensations constitute *incomes* to the factor owners and *costs* to the firm. The quantity of output which a firm decides to produce and offer for sale depends upon the relationship between prices and costs. Costs, in turn, depend on the quantities of various factors necessary to produce the given output and on the prices paid for factor units. The behavior of cost per unit of output as the firm varies output is determined by the extent of changes in inputs as output changes. The relationship between price and cost not only governs the output of the firm, but also influences decisions for the undertaking of new business enterprises and the liquidation of old ones. In order to provide a foundation for discussion of the determinants of output and supply, therefore, we must introduce relevant concepts of cost and describe how various types of costs vary with changes in output.

THE NATURE OF COST

The term *cost* has a wide variety of meanings. To a businessman, items included in cost for the purpose of some decisions are very different from those included for other purposes.[1] For the determination of profit, "cost" includes only the usual business expenses (including depreciation, interest, rent, and taxes).[2] However, when a firm is figuring the profitability of undertaking a particular expansion or buying new equipment, there is included in addition to other cost elements an item of return on the money capital used for the

[1] See National Bureau of Economic Research, *Cost Behavior and Price Policy* (New York, 1943), pp. 20–27.

[2] In determining net income in the calculation of income tax liability, the amount of the income tax itself, of course, cannot be treated as a cost.

investment, even though the money is supplied by the owners of the business. The same procedure is followed in pricing various products.[3] On the other hand, for some purposes cost includes far less than it does for profit calculations. If a firm with an idle plant considers whether or not to accept additional orders which can be obtained only at a very low price, it may take into consideration, so far as cost is concerned, only the direct out-of-pocket costs associated with the additional output. When a railroad decides whether to continue operating a particular passenger train, it considers only the cost resulting directly from operation of that train and not the train's "share" of track maintenance, administrative expenses, interest on investment, etc.

For purposes of economic analysis, the most satisfactory definition of cost is broader than the concept used in financial accounting, but is similar to the concept used by business firms for many purposes. Specifically, by the term *cost is meant the compensations which must be received by the owners of money capital and the units of the factors of production used by a firm if these owners are to continue to supply money capital and factor units to the firm.*

Two elements in this definition require emphasis. The phrase "compensations which must be received by the owners" is used rather than "payments which must be made to the factor owners" because in some instances no formal payment occurs. A person operating a business does not "pay" himself interest on funds which he invests in his own business. Yet, if he does not receive a return on such funds equivalent to the amount which he could get by lending them to others, he will eventually liquidate the business. Likewise, the phrase "continue to supply the factor units" is used in the definition rather than "supply the factor units," because factor owners may supply factor inputs for a period of time to a firm even though they are getting little or no compensation. The firm will not be able to obtain factor inputs indefinitely, however, if it cannot offer a return comparable to that available in other industries. The owners of a business not yielding a normal return will often continue to operate it for some time because they cannot quickly withdraw money capital which has been invested in specialized capital goods. Once the capital goods are worn out, however, the money capital will not be reinvested.

From the standpoint of a particular business firm, the amount of compensation which owners of factor services must receive is deter-

---

[3] This is not meant to imply that firms can set their prices on a basis of cost considerations alone. But cost is an element considered; and for this purpose, cost usually includes a "profit" on the firm's own capital.

mined by other opportunities which they have—specifically, by the amounts which they could obtain by supplying factor inputs to other business firms. Thus, if the market price for bar copper is 8 cents a pound, a manufacturer who wishes to use bar copper must pay this price, since sellers of the input will not supply it to him for less when they can get 8 cents from other buyers. If the current wage rate for laying brick is $24 a day, a contractor must pay $24 a day in order to obtain bricklayers. The same principle applies to factor inputs owned by the firm itself or supplied to it by the owners of the firm. A businessman who invests $20,000 in his own business could have bought stock— perhaps in General Motors, for example—for this sum and received $800 a year in dividends. This sum constitutes a cost for which his business is responsible.

EXPENDITURE AND NONEXPENDITURE COSTS

There are two types of elements in total cost: (1) those such as wages which take the form of contractual payments by the business firm to factor owners and are designated *expenditure* or *outlay costs;* and (2) those which, when covered, accrue directly to the firm itself, or its owners, with no contractual obligation for payment. The second type may be called *nonexpenditure* or *implicit costs*.

Expenditure Costs

The first group consists of the items other than depreciation charges that are usually treated as costs in financial accounting: wages and salaries paid; payments for raw materials, fuel, and goods purchased for resale; payments for transportation, utilities, advertising, and similar services; interest on borrowed capital; rent on land and capital equipment leased; taxes. However, not all payments made by business firms are costs. Those made for the purchase of capital equipment involve merely a change in the form of the firm's assets and hence are not costs of producing the output of the particular period in which the assets are purchased. They are charged to capital account, and a depreciation charge—a nonexpenditure cost—is set up to recover the amount paid over the period of years during which the equipment will be used. Payments of dividends to stockholders are not costs,[4] but merely withdrawals of profits from the firm by stockholder-owners.

---

[4] As indicated below, a normal return on the funds invested by the stockholders is a cost of the nonexpenditure type.

Nonexpenditure Costs

Costs take the nonexpenditure form when factor units and money capital are owned by the firm itself or the owners of the firm. Although the firm is not obligated to make a contractual payment for these factor units, the units are responsible for costs, since they could be supplied to other producers if they were not used in the business.

In the typical large-scale enterprise operated under the corporate form of organization, the two major nonexpenditure costs are depreciation and an average return on money capital supplied by the stockholders. Depreciation charges, which will be discussed in greater detail in Chapter 14, are sums which must be recovered over the life of a capital good to maintain intact the capital sum invested in the item. The sums involved, if actually earned, may be used by the firm for any purpose. But the charges constitute costs and must be earned if the firm is to continue to operate indefinitely.

Likewise, the owners of the firm must earn an adequate rate of return on their invested money capital, that is, a rate equal to the figure obtainable from other investments of comparable risk. If the owners of a firm have invested $10,000 in the business they are forgoing a return on this money which they could otherwise have made by lending the money, directly or through the purchase of bonds, by purchasing stock in other corporations, by buying land or buildings, etc.

In smaller businesses, especially those organized as partnerships or individual proprietorships, an additional nonexpenditure cost may be important, namely, the wage which the owner of the firm could make by hiring himself out to another business. A grocer must be able to earn as much from his own store as he could by working for a chain store or, more exactly, the wage he could get less the value which he attaches to the privilege of working for himself. A person is often satisfied with a somewhat smaller return from his own business because he prefers to be his own boss. But this preference has a definite value to the person; if the differential between the earnings of the store and the available wage exceeds a certain figure, the alternative of taking a job will become preferable.

When a firm is earning an amount in excess of all costs, including those of a nonexpenditure nature, the additional amount constitutes "excess profit" or "economic profit" and is not in any sense a cost, since the business will be operated on a permanent basis whether or not any such excess sum is earned.

THE ADJUSTABILITY OF COSTS IN RESPONSE TO CHANGES IN OUTPUT

Of fundamental importance for cost behavior is the extent to which a firm is able to adjust the inputs of various factors, and thus the total magnitudes of the various cost elements, as it varies output. This, in turn, is affected by the length of time involved. Over a period of time long enough to allow adjustment to be made in all factors, called a *long-run period,* all costs are *variable,* that is, they will change as output changes. The time necessary for adjustments to be made in all factors will vary according to the length of life of the capital equipment, the ability to obtain additional skilled workers and managerial personnel, and the extent to which capital goods are specialized, that is, usable only for particular purposes. In general, the type of factor which requires the longest period for adjustment is the specialized and relatively indivisible form of capital equipment—blast furnaces, dies used in the making of automobile parts, railroad tracks, hydroelectric plants, steamships, grain elevators, etc.

In contrast, in the *short-run period,* some factor units are not adjustable in amount. New capital equipment cannot be obtained or built overnight. Often, additional skilled labor and management personnel can be secured only by training new men. Likewise, with a downward adjustment, specialized capital equipment rarely can be sold for the amount of money invested in it; the firm has the alternative of suffering a heavy loss of invested funds or using the equipment over a long period at a low return. The latter alternative is often preferable.

Fixed factors—those not readily adjustable—consist primarily of capital equipment and top management personnel, and are thus often designated by the term *plant.*

Fixed Costs

The costs for which fixed factor units are responsible are known as *fixed costs,* while those arising from the use of the variable factors are known as *variable costs.* More precisely, fixed costs may be defined as those which are the same in total amount regardless of the volume of output, even if nothing is produced. The various cost items which are usually fixed in a short-run period may be classified into two major groups, those of a *recurrent* nature, involving actual outlay of money during the period, and those which are *allocable* to the period, the total outlay having been incurred at one time for the benefit of production during several time periods.

Recurrent fixed costs include interest on money borrowed; taxes which are independent of output, such as capital stock taxes, flat-sum occupation levies, and, to a large extent, the general property tax; the portions of heat, utility, and insurance costs which are independent of output; most rent; and the portions of labor cost that are not affected by output changes. Even if a plant produces nothing at all, some labor will be necessary: watchmen, maintenance employees, clerical and accounting personnel, portions of the administrative staff. These recurrent fixed costs give rise to cash outlays; the firm must obtain the funds from some source—current revenue, accumulated cash surplus, disposition of noncash assets, or borrowing—if it is to continue to operate.

In contrast, allocable fixed costs do not usually necessitate cash outlays during the period, and the firm can continue to operate for a time even if they are not covered. Nevertheless, these items constitute costs in the sense that they must be covered ultimately if the firm is to continue operations. One major example is the portion of depreciation which is a function of the passage of time rather than of usage. The economic life of capital equipment is in part independent of usage, being controlled by the rate of development of new techniques, which render old equipment obsolete. The portion of depreciation which is dependent upon usage is a variable cost, but many firms make no effort to separate the time and usage elements in total depreciation, and assign the entire amount on the basis of time alone, thus in effect treating depreciation entirely as a fixed cost.

The other major allocable fixed cost element is the necessary return on capital supplied by owners. This sum does not have to be earned or paid out in any particular period, but it must be earned over a period of time if the firm is to continue operation. Given the average rate of return and the quantity of money capital invested by the owners, the necessary profit is the same for each year, regardless of the volume of output. The actual profit earned may fluctuate widely, but the necessary return is essentially a fixed cost.

Variable Costs

Variable costs, those for which the variable factors are responsible, are dependent upon the volume of output, and are eliminated if production is not carried on. The major short-run variable costs are those for materials, fuel, electric power, and transportation; most wages, especially for work in direct physical production; and taxes which vary with output, such as those levied upon sales and gross receipts. In addition, other cost items which are primarily fixed costs may be partly variable. Depreciation, for example, is a short-run variable cost to the extent that the actual rate of depreciation is affected by usage.

A distinction is sometimes made between *fully variable costs*—those, such as raw material costs, which vary more or less in proportion to output—and *semivariable* costs, those which change relatively little as output changes. The latter resemble fixed costs but are distinguished by the fact that if production is temporarily suspended, they can be eliminated, whereas fixed costs continue unchanged even if nothing is produced.[5] Semivariable costs reflect indivisibilities of variable factor units; once an indivisible variable factor unit is acquired, it is not fully utilized until output reaches a certain level, and thus the variable cost item for which it is responsible does not vary with small changes in output. For example, if a railroad is to operate freight service at all on a line, a certain train crew—perhaps four men—will be required. As volume of traffic on the line increases over a very substantial range, the same crew will be required, and wages will remain approximately the same. With a small volume of traffic the potential services of the crew are not utilized fully; hence, as output increases, the costs for which the crew is responsible do not increase significantly. The wages of the crew are variable costs, however, rather than fixed costs, since they are not paid if the train does not operate.

As indicated earlier, the distinction between fixed and variable costs is significant only in a short-run period, since over a longer period all factors, and all costs, are variable.

COST SCHEDULES

A cost schedule indicates the total cost of producing various volumes of output and thus shows the response of cost to changes in output. A short-run schedule is relevant to a situation with a given plant, while a long-run schedule shows the costs of producing various amounts of output in a time interval sufficiently long to allow adjustments in all factors necessary to obtain the optimum factor combination for each output level.

The Parameters of Cost Schedules

The actual data in a cost schedule—the costs of producing various amounts of output—depend primarily upon three considerations: the

---

[5] Under a broader definition of fixed costs, the concept might include some items treated here as semivariable costs.

technique of production, the efficiency of the factor units employed, and the prices paid for factor units, including the necessary compensation for factor units owned by the firm.

Profit maximization requires the use of the particular technique of production which will allow the optimum combination of factors, as explained in the previous chapter. In a short-run period the optimum combination for any given level of output is the least-cost combination possible with the fixed factor units which the firm has, but is likely not to be the absolute optimum attainable if all factors could be adjusted. The short-run optimum combination is therefore influenced by the nature of the fixed factor units which the firm has on hand at the particular time. Over a longer period, all factors can be varied, and the firm is free to select the combination which is the absolute optimum, in terms of existing technological conditions and factor prices.

Cost levels are affected not only by available methods of production but also by the efficiency of factor units—the quality of natural resources employed, the types of capital goods available, and the skill of all types of labor, including managerial personnel. The better the quality of the resources, for example, the greater will be the output obtained from a given quantity of resources at the optimum factor combination, and the lower will be the cost of production.

Finally, the prices paid for factor units will influence cost in monetary terms. The cost of factor units to any one producer is the price which the owner of the unit could obtain from making it available in the next-best use.

Any particular cost schedule is based upon the assumption that factor prices and other underlying determinants of costs are given. When a change in these underlying determinants occurs, the cost schedule of the firm will be shifted. An increase in factor prices, for example, will raise cost schedules; the development of new methods of production, the discovery of better quality resources, or increased training of workers will lower cost schedules. It is essential to distinguish clearly between a shift in a cost schedule caused by a change in factor prices or technology and a change in costs resulting from a change in output by the firm. The former is represented graphically by a shifting of a cost curve, the latter merely by movement along a given cost curve.

SHORT-RUN COST SCHEDULES

A short-run cost schedule for an individual firm shows the behavior of cost when output is varied with a given plant, as illustrated

TABLE 7–1

DAILY COST SCHEDULE OF A PRODUCER

Units of Output	Total Fixed Cost	Total Variable Cost	Total Cost	Average Fixed Cost	Average Variable Cost	Average Cost	Marginal Cost
0*	$20	$ 0	$ 20	....	....	....	....
1	20	30	50	$20.00	$ 30	$ 50.00	$ 30
2	20	56	76	10.00	28	38.00	26
3	20	75	95	6.67	25	31.67	19
4	20	80	100	5.00	20	25.00	5
5	20	105	125	4.00	21	25.00	25
6	20	132	152	3.33	22	25.33	27
7	20	182	202	2.86	26	28.86	50
8	20	320	340	2.50	40	42.50	138
9	20	720	740	2.22	80	82.22	400
10	20	3,000	3,020	2.00	300	302.00	2,280

* If no units are produced, total fixed cost is the same as it would be if production were carried on. No variable costs are incurred. The unit cost columns are blank for zero units because the concept of cost per unit has no meaning if no units are produced.

in Table 7–1. For most purposes, unit cost data are more convenient to use than total cost data. *Average cost*[6] is equal to total cost divided by the number of units of output; it consists of two elements, *average fixed cost* (total fixed cost divided by the number of units of output) and *average variable cost* (total variable cost divided by the number of units of output).

The last column in Table 7–1 shows data on *marginal cost*—the increase in total cost which results from the production of an additional unit of output. For example, with five units of output, total cost is $125; with six units, it is $152. Thus the marginal cost of the sixth unit—the amount which the production of the sixth unit adds to total cost—is $27 ($152 − $125). Marginal cost depends solely on changes in total variable cost, since total fixed cost is, by definition, the same for every level of output. A typical pattern of cost curves for a firm is shown in Figure 7–1.

The analysis of short-run cost behavior is based upon the following assumptions:

1. The firm has only a fixed quantity of certain factors, and therefore certain cost items are fixed in total.
2. The fixed factor units require a certain minimum quantity of variable factor units for efficient operation, but have at least some degree of adaptability for utilization with varying quantities of other factors.
3. Some types of variable factors cannot be acquired in infinitesimally small units. For example, workers often cannot be hired for periods of less than one day.

[6] For simplicity, the term *average cost* is used rather than *average total cost*.

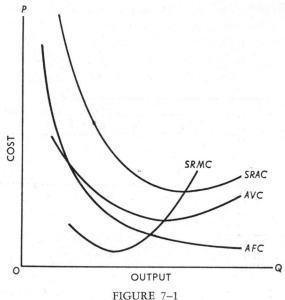

FIGURE 7–1

SHORT-RUN COST CURVES OF A FIRM

Major parameters of a given cost schedule include:

a) Technological conditions.
b) Factor prices.
c) Efficiency of factor units.

Under these assumptions, as output is increased, average cost will decline initially, and ultimately increase, the overall curve being **U**-shaped. The reasons for this behavior can best be explained in terms of the reactions to changes in output of the component parts of average cost—average fixed cost (AFC), and average variable cost (AVC).

Average Fixed Cost

As output increases, AFC declines continuously, since a given sum of total fixed cost is being spread over successively larger volumes of output. The curve is a rectangular hyperbola.

Average Variable Cost

Under the assumptions made, AVC will decline initially but ultimately increase. Its precise behavior is dependent upon the behavior of average physical product (APP) per unit of the variable factors, under the assumption of given prices for the factor units. If APP increases as more units of the variable factors are added, AVC will fall, since, as each additional unit of output is produced, the quantity of variable factors required per unit of output falls. On the other hand, if APP falls, AVC must rise. If APP is constant, AVC will be unaffected by output changes. These relationships are illustrated in Table 7–2. Each unit of the variable factors (consisting, perhaps, of one worker plus a certain quantity of materials and electric power) is assumed to cost $20. Since APP of the variable factor rises when the number of factor units is increased from 1 to 3, total variable cost rises at a slower rate than output, and thus AVC falls. In the range from 3 to 5 units of the variable factor, APP remains constant; total variable cost and total product rise at the same rate, and thus AVC remains constant. With 6

TABLE 7–2

RELATIONSHIP OF THE BEHAVIOR OF AVERAGE PRODUCT OF THE
VARIABLE FACTORS AND AVERAGE VARIABLE COST

Productivity Schedule			*Schedule of Variable Cost*		
Units of Variable Factor	Output	Average Product per Unit of Variable Factor	Output	Total Variable Cost	Average Variable Cost
1	5	5	5	$ 20	$4
2	15	7½	15	40	2.67
3	30	10	30	60	2
4	40	10	40	80	2
5	50	10	50	100	2
6	54	9	54	120	2.22
7	56	8	56	140	2.50
8	57	7⅛	57	160	2.81

or more units of the variable factor, diminishing average returns are encountered, APP falls, and AVC rises.

Under the assumptions made, AVC will pass through three successive phases as output is increased:

1. *The Phase of Declining Average Variable Cost.* Under the assumption that the fixed factor units cannot be used effectively without a certain minimum quantity of variable factor units, APP will rise as additional variable units are added, since more effective use is made of fixed factor units. Thus, AVC will fall, since the rate of increase in output exceeds the rate of increase in variable factor units. For example, a plant may have a certain set of machines which require five men for efficient operation. With only two or three men hired, the machines can be used only very ineffectively, and the output per man will be relatively small. But as the fourth and fifth men are hired, operation of

the machinery reaches a high level of efficiency, so that output per man is higher and variable cost per unit of product is lower.

The tendency for AVC to fall will be strengthened if the variable factors must be acquired in relatively large indivisible units. It is difficult, for example, to hire workers for only a few hours, or to use particular men on a large number of different tasks. Accordingly, when output is low, a portion of the manpower will not be utilized fully, and a particular percentage increase in output will not require an equivalent percentage increase in labor employed. Thus, output per worker will rise, and AVC will fall. Extreme examples are found in certain service industries. One bus driver is required whether one passenger or fifty are carried in a bus; and as the load increases, the manpower cost per passenger falls. A theater must have at least one cashier on duty while the theater is open, regardless of the number of customers.

2. *The Phase of Constant Average Variable Cost.* When the inputs of variable factors have reached such levels that the fixed factors can be employed effectively, and when each variable factor unit is likewise fully utilized, further increases in output, over a considerable range, may be associated with a more or less constant level of AVC. Through this range of output, a doubling of the variable factors will more or less double the output, and thus the APP and AVC will be constant. This stage will be encountered at relatively low levels of output if fixed factor units are divided into small units, so that only a small number of variable units are required to operate each fixed unit. If a plant consists of a large number of small identical machines (such as those used in some lines of textile production), efficient operation with a small volume of output can be obtained with only a small labor force. As output is increased, more men are added and more machines brought into use, and variable cost will be more or less constant per unit of output.

If the nature of a production process is such that operations can be carried on in three shifts of eight hours each in length, output can be tripled, more or less, from the quantity at which the plant was fully utilized on an eight-hour basis, without any significant change in AVC. The ability to vary the speed at which production is carried on likewise increases the range of constant AVC.

Empirical studies of cost functions in recent years have confirmed the importance of the phase of constant AVC. The phase is not always encountered, however. If the fixed capital is of such nature that a certain number of variable units is required for efficient operation, yet further increases in the number of variable factor units will increase output very little, the initial phase of decreasing AVC will be followed directly by the phase of increasing AVC.

If we abandon the assumptions that fixed factors require a certain minimum quantity of variable factors for efficient operation and that variable factors cannot be obtained in very small units, the phase of constant AVC could be encountered initially. It is widely believed, however, that these assumptions are realistic ones, although their significance undoubtedly varies widely in different lines of production. The more divisible the units of both fixed and variable factors; the less significant will be the stage of declining AVC.

3. *The Phase of Increasing Average Variable Cost.* Eventually, in any type of business, as output is increased with a fixed plant, AVC will commence to rise because of the decline in APP of the variable factors which results from the Law of Diminishing Returns. The plant is designed for a certain volume of production; when output is carried beyond this level, the increase in the variable factors necessary to produce the additional output will be relatively greater than the output increase, and AVC will rise. In some production processes the increase will be gradual, as equipment will be used longer hours than intended and machinery will be operated at a faster rate. Obsolete reserve equipment will be placed in use. These adjustments will involve some increase in AVC, since maintenance costs are certain to rise more than proportionately when machinery is run at a higher than optimum rate, and the use of older equipment will necessitate higher variable costs. But such adjustments make possible further increases in output without large changes in cost. In other lines of production, however, it will be almost impossible to produce more than the quantity for which the plant was designed; AVC will rise rapidly because substantial increases in the quantities of the variable factors will be required to produce a few more units of output. Once absolute capacity[7] is reached, there are no meaningful AVC figures for larger volumes of output, since such quantities of output cannot be produced. Or, in alternative terms, AVC is said to be infinite.

The Behavior of Average Cost

Since average cost (AC) is the sum of AVC and AFC, its behavior reflects the combined influence of changes in the two constituent elements. As a firm first increases output, AFC must necessarily fall;

---

[7] The term *capacity* is sometimes used in reference to the "optimum" or "low-cost" level of operation, in other cases to the absolute maximum output level possible with the plant.

and under the assumptions indicated above, AVC will also fall. As a consequence, AC must fall as well, as illustrated in Table 7–1 and Figure 7–1. The rate of decline will depend upon the relative importance of fixed and variable cost elements, the extent to which fixed factor units consist of large unadaptable units which require several units of variable factors for efficient operation, and the extent to which the variable factors can be obtained in small units. The rate of decline in AC will be particularly great in large manufacturing establishments with heavy fixed costs and equipment of such nature that effective operation requires a relatively large labor force.

If AVC does not decline initially, or becomes relatively constant

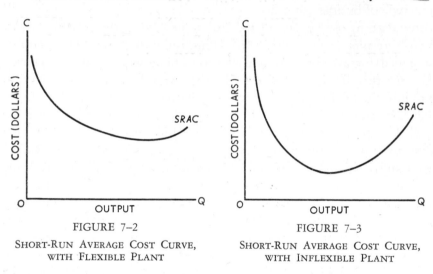

FIGURE 7–2	FIGURE 7–3
SHORT-RUN AVERAGE COST CURVE, WITH FLEXIBLE PLANT	SHORT-RUN AVERAGE COST CURVE, WITH INFLEXIBLE PLANT

once output has reached a certain level, AC will still decline because of the fall in AFC, but the rate of decline will be very low once output has expanded to the point at which fixed costs are a minor element in total costs.

If production is carried far enough, AC must eventually rise. AVC will commence to increase once the optimum plant capacity output is reached, and eventually offset the continuing decline in AFC. The speed at which AVC and AC rise will depend primarily upon the nature of the production process, and particularly upon the flexibility of the fixed plant—the ability to expand production beyond the optimum capacity level without a substantial increase in variable factors.

In summary, the short-run average cost (SRAC) curve is U-shaped; or ᴗ-shaped when AVC is more or less constant over a substantial range of output. Figure 7–2 illustrates the second case. Figure 7–3 illustrates the first case, in which AC falls and rises sharply, because the capital equipment is of such a nature that a substantial number of men are required for efficient operation; yet, once the equipment is brought into effective operation, additional output cannot be obtained except by using substantially greater quantities of the variable factor.

The Behavior of Marginal Cost

Since the behavior of marginal cost (MC) depends upon that of total cost, its determinants are the same as those of AC. Certain relationships between MC and AC should be noted, however. When AVC is falling, MC must be less than AVC (but not necessarily falling); likewise, when AC is falling, MC must be less than AC. On the other hand, when AVC is rising, MC will be greater than AVC (but not necessarily rising), and when AC is rising, MC must of course exceed AC. Marginal cost is equal to AVC at the lowest point of AVC and is equal to AC at the point of lowest AC. Thus the MC curve intersects both the AVC curve and the AC curve at their respective low points. This relationship is simply a matter of arithmetic; when a number (the marginal cost) being added into a series is smaller than the previous average of the series, the new average will be lower than the previous one; when the number added is larger than the average, the average will rise.

If AVC is constant, MC and AVC will be identical, since the production of an additional unit will add to total cost the same amount as the previous average of the variable cost.

On the assumption of constant factor prices, the behavior of MC bears a definite relationship to the behavior of the marginal physical product of the variable factors (MPP). When MPP is rising, MC is falling, because each successive unit of the variable factors adds more to total product than did the previous unit, and thus the increase in total cost due to the production of another unit of output will be less than the increase resulting from the production of the previous unit. If the addition of a sixth man raises output by 45 units a day and the addition of a seventh man raises output by 65 units, the marginal cost of each of the 65 units is less than that of each of the 45. When MPP is constant, MC will be constant; when MPP is declining, MC will be rising because successive factor units will add progessively less to total output.

The Applicability of the Assumptions

The usefulness of short-run cost analysis depends upon the applicability of the assumptions to actual situations. The first assumption—that certain factor units are fixed in quantity—follows from the definition of a short-run period, and describes the situation which confronts a going concern in relatively short time intervals.

The second and third assumptions (page 123) relate to the nature of fixed and variable factor units. It was assumed that a certain minimum quantity of variable units is required to utilize the fixed factor units effectively, and that at least some of the variable factor units, especially manpower, cannot be obtained in very small units. The assumption about fixed factors is relevant to many types of capital equipment in manufacturing; an automobile assembly line, for example, cannot be utilized at all without a certain minimum amount of manpower. In other lines of production, however, this consideration is of much less importance. In retailing, for example, there is typically no equipment that requires a substantial number of workers to operate. In this type of industry, therefore, there is less likelihood of an increase in APP, and thus an initial decline in AVC from this cause. AFC will, of course, fall as output increases.

The assumption that variable factor units cannot always be obtained in very small units is more likely to be realized. It is not possible, for example, to hire half a man or, in many cases, to hire a man for less than a day. Accordingly, the time of the first units of manpower added will not be fully utilized initially; and as output is increased, proportionate increases in inputs of variable factors will not be required, and AVC will fall.

The treatment of technological conditions, factor unit efficiency, and factor prices as given data or parameters is necessary to distinguish the functional relationship of output and unit cost from cost changes due to variations in technology, factor prices, and efficiency. However, in some instances the prices paid for various factor units will change *as a result* of changes in output by the firm; hence the changes are relevant for the nature of a particular cost schedule. When materials are purchased in larger quantities, lower prices are often obtainable. Rate schedules for electric power provide lower rates per unit for larger quantities than for smaller amounts. The ability to ship in carload and truckload quantities reduces freight costs per unit. When quantity discounts are available, the net cost per unit of the variable factors falls as more units are acquired, and the decline in AVC due to the initial rise in APP per unit of the variable factors is reinforced. In retailing and some other lines of business, the quantity discount feature is of particular importance and is likely to be of greater significance in bringing about an initial decline in AVC than the behavior of APP, because of the relative unimportance of capital equipment in these lines of business.

As a firm continues to expand, however, eventually all available quantity discounts will be obtained, and a point may ultimately be reached at which further increases in factor purchases may drive factor prices upward. For example, if a large firm is the principal employer of skilled labor in a certain area, it may eventually exhaust the local supply of this type of labor, and further increases in output will necessitate the payment of higher wages to draw workers from other plants or from more distant areas. To the extent that factor prices are increased as output increases, AVC will tend to rise. This effect will reinforce the increase produced by the decline in APP.

Not only may factor prices rise as a firm increases output, but the additional factor units also may be less efficient. The assumption of homogeneous factor units is by no means necessarily realized in practice. Presumably a firm will hire the most efficient workers first. As additional men are hired, successive workers are likely to be less skilled and less capable. Thus the decline in APP and the rise in AVC will be greater than would result from the Law of Diminishing Returns alone, unless the prices paid for less efficient factor units are proportionately lower than those paid for better units. But often they are not.

Empirical Studies of Short-Run Cost Behavior

The determination of the data in an actual cost schedule of a particular firm is a difficult task, far more so than might appear at first glance. A firm usually has a reasonably accurate knowledge of average cost at existing output levels, but nothing more than a rough estimate of costs at other output levels. Frequently, no serious attempt is made to ascertain these data; and even if an effort is made, the difficulties involved in doing so prevent the results from being entirely accurate. The firm must, however, base its policy upon some estimate of cost behavior. Various studies of business policy suggest that firms frequently do not attempt to ascertain marginal cost as such, but seek to determine optimum price and output levels with the use of total and average cost and revenue data. On the whole, however, it is likely that firms have a much better knowledge of their cost schedules than of their demand schedules, since the latter are dependent upon often unpredictable reactions of customers and competitors.

A number of studies have been made of cost schedules in

particular industries, primarily to determine whether the pattern of cost behavior developed by economic analysis accords with actual behavior. The problems which such studies have encountered are, however, very serious. A major one arises out of changes in the underlying determinants of cost schedules—factor prices, techniques of production, etc.—during the period for which the study is made. Statistical techniques to isolate changes in cost due to output changes from changes due to shifts in the parameters are not entirely satisfactory. Also, in any particular period, costs may be affected by the *rate* at which output changes; a sudden increase may cause temporary additions to cost which can be avoided once production is adjusted to the higher volume. Changes in the size of orders may affect costs materially in some lines of manufacturing. The problem of the time periods in which costs are recorded gave rise to difficulties. Raw materials may be purchased in large quantities and charged as expenses in a period in which output is low (but an increase is expected), while in the later period, when output actually does rise, few materials purchases may be made. The measurement of units of output likewise is a source of difficulty. Most firms produce more than one type of product, and the relative importance of various types produced is likely to change during the period. Finally, the range of output may be relatively narrow, and only a small segment of the schedule can be computed; the data obtained cannot safely be projected into ranges of output for which no data are available.

The most important discovery which has been made is the importance of the phase of constant AVC. Within the ranges of output for which data were available, AVC and thus MC were found to be relatively constant. Therefore, the typical AVC curve would appear to contain an extensive horizontal section rather than being U- or V-shaped. But the difficulties encountered in the studies were so great that too much significance cannot as yet be attached to the conclusions. It is maintained by some writers that the statistical techniques employed created a bias in favor of constant AVC.[8]

---

[8] See J. Johnston, *Statistical Cost Analysis* (New York: McGraw-Hill, 1960).

A study by W. J. Eiteman and G. E. Guthrie, "The Shape of the Average Cost Curve," *American Economic Review,* Vol. 42 (December, 1952), pp. 832–38, sought to discover, by questionnaire, the businessman's typical belief about the nature of his short-run average cost curve. The largest number reported AC curves of the types illustrated in Figures 7–4 and 7–5, below. In Figure 7–5 the curve would, of course, rise if carried beyond the "capacity" line. Unfortunately, the authors of this article drew unwarranted conclusions from these findings, as noted in a series of comments in the September, 1953, issue of the *American Economic Review.* It is by no means clear whether the respondents

COST SCHEDULES WITH LONG-RUN ADJUSTMENTS COMPLETED

As indicated above, the long-run period is defined as a period sufficiently long that the business firm can make desired adjustments in all factors of production employed. The actual time interval depends upon the nature of the productive processes and particularly upon the extent to which specialized types of capital equipment requiring a substantial period to construct and having a life of a number of years are utilized. The time necessary to allow adjustment of all factors is much greater for a steel mill, a railroad, or an ocean shipping company, than for a service station or a grocery store. Over a long-run period, since all factors are adjustable, all costs are variable.

The Nature of the Long-Run Cost Schedule

The long-run cost schedule shows, for each level of output, the *lowest possible cost* of producing the particular amount of output, given a sufficient time interval that all factors can be adjusted and the absolute optimum factor combination for the particular output level attained. In Table 7–1 the total cost of producing ten units is $3,020, with the particular plant. But this plant was designed for a much smaller volume of output (four units per day). With the plant best suited for ten units, one considerably larger, the total cost of producing ten units per day might be $190. This figure, since it is the lowest possible cost of producing ten units, is the appropriate cost figure for this level of output in the long-run cost schedule. Similarly, for other levels of output, there are certain figures of lowest possible total cost, with the plant size—the

---

to the questionnaires interpreted the term *capacity* to mean "optimum operating capacity" or "absolute capacity."

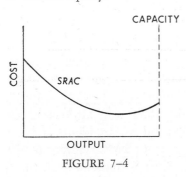

FIGURE 7–4

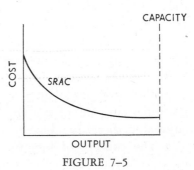

FIGURE 7–5

combination of all factors—best suited to the particular output levels. A typical long-run cost schedule for a firm is illustrated in Table 7–3. The data are obtained from a number of short-run cost schedules, one for each possible size of plant. The data taken for the long-run schedule from each of the short-run schedules are the cost figures for those levels of output for which the particular plant allows the most satisfactory factor combination and lowest cost. From the short-run schedule shown in Table 7–1 the cost data for four, five, and six units of output might go into the long-run schedule, since the plant is designed for this output range and allows a lower cost for this output range than any other. But for a daily output of seven or eight units, a somewhat larger plant

TABLE 7–3

TYPICAL LONG-RUN AVERAGE COST SCHEDULE OF A FIRM

Units of Output	Total Cost	Average Cost	Marginal Cost
5	$125	$25.00	...
10	190	19.00	$13.00*
15	263	17.35	14.60
20	340	17.00	15.40
25	418	16.72	15.60
30	498	16.60	16.00
35	579	16.54	16.20
40	664	16.60	17.00
45	751	16.69	17.40
50	845	16.90	18.80

* The increase in total cost of $65 resulting when five additional units are produced, divided by five.

would be more suitable; and the long-run cost figures, taken from the short-run cost data for the larger plant, would be lower than the figures for producing these amounts of output with the smaller plant. For output of three units or less a day, a plant smaller than that for which the data are given in Table 7–1 would allow lower cost.

Long-run average cost (LRAC) for any output level is determined by dividing the figure of long-run *total cost* for this output by the number of units of output. Long-run average cost may be defined as the lowest possible average cost of producing a particular amount of output, with the optimum plant size, and thus factor combination, for that particular amount of output. Since, in the long run, all factors are adjustable, there are no fixed costs, and AVC and AC are identical.

The concept of long-run marginal cost (LRMC) refers to the increase in total cost which occurs when a shift is made to a one-unit-higher scale of production, with optimum factor combinations both before and after the change. Since changes in scale ordinarily cannot be made economically in small increments, LRMC may be regarded more realistically as the increase in total cost which occurs when a transition is made from one scale of output to the next highest scale, divided by the number of units of increase in output which results. That is, if with a scale of plant designed for 20 units per day, total cost is $340, and with the next largest feasible scale, one designed for 25 units, total cost is $418, LRMC is $15.60 a unit ($78 increase in total cost divided by five units increase in output).

Long-run marginal cost bears the same relation to LRAC as does short-run marginal cost (SRMC) to short-run average cost (SRAC). Generalization about the relationship of LRMC to SRMC schedules for the various possible plants is more difficult. For any given plant, SRMC will be lower than LRMC for ranges of output up to a certain level, since SRMC is affected only by cost elements which are variable in the short run, whereas all cost elements enter into LRMC. Beyond a certain point, however, LRMC will be less than SRMC, since the latter is affected by the effort to get more and more output from a given plant capacity, and thus is subject to the Law of Diminishing Returns.

The graphical presentation of the LRAC schedule should facilitate an understanding of the concept. A firm has a large number of alternative possible scales of operation, or plant sizes, which it may build and operate. For each scale or plant size, there is an appropriate SRAC schedule and curve. The pattern of these curves, for various scales of operation, may be drawn on a single graph, as illustrated in Figure 7–6. For simplification, cost curves for only seven possible scales are shown, under the assumption (not unrealistic for many industries) that indivisibilities of some factor units prevent the use of scales of operation intermediate to those for which curves are plotted. Certain relationships among the successive curves should be noted. For output of ten units or less, average cost is lowest with plant size A. Costs with plant size B (and larger) are relatively high for these levels of output because the plants are far too large for the particular level of output, and machinery, buildings, etc., would be poorly utilized. But beyond ten units of output, costs with plant size B are lower than those with A. If 18 units were produced with plant A, the plant would be operated beyond designed capacity, and AVC would be high. In contrast, plant B, designed for a larger volume of output, would be operating close to optimum capacity. Beyond 19 units of output, cost is lower with plant C, since production of this volume would carry B beyond designed capacity, whereas C is suitable for a larger volume.

For each level of output, LRAC is represented by the appropriate point on that SRAC curve which reaches the lowest level for the particular output. If a perpendicular line is extended upward from the output axis on a graph containing the various SRAC curves for different-sized plants, the point at which it first strikes an SRAC curve indicates the relevant value of LRAC for that output level. Thus in Figure 7–6, for five units of output the lowest average cost point is on curve *SRAC–A;* for 22 units, it is on *SRAC–C,* etc. Thus the *LRAC* curve is identical with *SRAC–A* up to ten units of output (the intersection of *SRAC–A* and *SRAC–B*); it is identical with *SRAC–B*

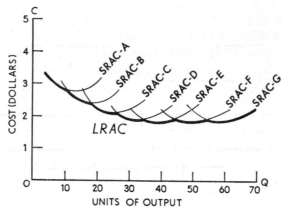

FIGURE 7–6
THE SHORT-RUN AND LONG-RUN AVERAGE
COST CURVES

up to the point at which the latter intersects *SRAC–C,* etc. The entire long-run average cost curve *LRAC* (for the output range covered) is indicated in Figure 7–6 by the heavily shaded line. If the LRAC curve is plotted directly from an LRAC schedule, such as that presented in Table 7–3, the only portions of the short-run curves which will appear are those which comprise portions of the long-run curve itself. It is important to note that the long-run schedule contains no data which are not to be found in the various short-run schedules of the firm; in mathematical language, the long-run curve is the *envelope* of the short-run curves.

When all factors are divisible into small units, the successive scales of operation will be close to another, as illustrated in Figure 7–7; and the *LRAC* curve will be smooth, as shown in Figure 7–8. When indivisibilities prevent small adjustments in plant scale, the short-run curves will be farther apart; and the long-run curves will be irregular,

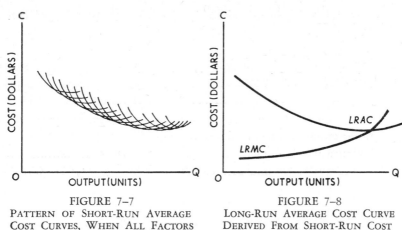

FIGURE 7–7
PATTERN OF SHORT-RUN AVERAGE
COST CURVES, WHEN ALL FACTORS
ARE DIVISIBLE

FIGURE 7–8
LONG-RUN AVERAGE COST CURVE
DERIVED FROM SHORT-RUN COST
CURVES IN FIGURE 7–7

as illustrated in Figure 7–6, above. In Figure 7–8, the *LRMC* curve is included.

The LRAC curve is often called a *planning curve,* since it represents the cost data which are relevant to the firm when it is planning policy relating to scale of operations, output, and price over a substantial period of time. At any particular time a firm already in operation has a certain plant and must base its current price and output decisions upon the cost schedule with the existing plant. But when the firm considers the possibility of adjustment in scale of operations, long-run cost estimates are necessary.

It is important to recognize that the LRAC schedule does not consist of historical data showing what cost has been in the past with various-sized plants; it shows alternative possibilities at the present time—what cost would be for various levels of output if various-sized plants were built.

The Behavior of Long-Run Average Cost

The behavior of LRAC in response to changes in output is controlled by considerations substantially different from those which affect cost behavior with a particular plant. Short-run cost behavior is conditioned very largely by the presence of constant quantities of some factors, which are responsible not only for certain costs being fixed in amount but also for the nature of the reactions of variable costs to output changes. In a period of time sufficiently long for the scale of operations to be adjusted, all factors are adjustable, and the consideration of fixed factors is no longer relevant for cost behavior.

The analysis of long-run cost behavior is based upon the following assumptions:

1. All factors are variable in quantity.
2. Certain factors are indivisible, in the sense that they cannot be obtained in infinitesimally small units, or are relatively inefficient if reduced in size below a certain figure.
3. An increase in the quantities of all factors allows greater specialization in the utilization of particular factor units.
4. The managerial factor cannot be multiplied in the same manner as other factors because of the need for maintaining unified control over the entire enterprise.

The major parameters are the same as those of the short-run schedules: factor prices, technological conditions, and equal efficiency of successive factor units.

Given these assumptions, the primary determinant of the behavior of LRAC is the manner in which the Principle of Returns to Scale operates in the particular production activity, and thus the behavior of changes in output as the inputs of all factor units are changed. As indicated in the previous chapter, a firm typically experiences increasing returns to scale as it expands its operations initially, in part because of indivisibilities of some factors, especially capital equipment, which make operation on a small-scale basis inefficient and costly, and in part because of advantages of specialization of labor. As a consequence, since output rises at a faster rate than the rate of increase in factor units, total cost rises at a slower rate than output, and average cost falls. Typically, as a firm expands, short-run cost curves for successively larger plants will be lower in the range of output for which the plant is designed than cost curves with smaller plants in the output ranges for which these were designed. In other words, the low-cost points for the cost curves for successively larger plants will be progressively lower. This is illustrated in Figure 7–6; the low segment of *SRAC–B*—the segment which constitutes a portion of the *LRAC* curve—is lower than the low segment of *SRAC–A;* and that of *SRAC–C* is lower than that of *SRAC–B.* Hence the *LRAC* curve slopes downward from left to right in the initial stage.

Eventually, however, the economies of large-scale production will be exhausted. The best available types of capital equipment will be employed and utilized to capacity, and full advantage will be gained from specialization. Once a point is reached at which all workers are performing tasks sufficiently limited in scope, further increases in output merely require additional men doing the same tasks. When output reaches the level at which the stage of increasing returns to scale is succeeded by that of constant returns, total cost and output will increase at the same rate, and average cost will be constant. Especially in industries in which little capital equipment is used, and thus few economies of large-scale production are available, the stage of constant average cost may be encountered at relatively low levels of output and will extend over a very substantial range. In instances in which there are important indivisibilities and gains from labor specialization, constant average cost will be encountered only after a long phase of decreasing cost.

Eventually, if expansion is carried far enough, decreasing returns to scale, caused, as explained in Chapter 6, by the complexities of large-scale management, will cause LRAC to become progressively greater for successively larger output levels. This rise is likely to be very gradual, however, and is not at all comparable with the rapid rise in average cost in the short run, when expansion of output beyond the designed capacity causes a sharp increase in variable cost and therefore in average cost.

The necessity of selling in a progressively wider market, covering a greater geographical area, may also tend to raise average cost as output expands. As a firm increases its output, additional sales must frequently be made to buyers at greater distances from the plant. As a consequence, transportation costs increase and raise average cost of production. The firm may seek to avoid this by building additional plants in other areas; but if the original location was the one most suited to the particular type of production, costs will be higher in the new plants.

Under these assumptions, the LRAC curve is ‿-shaped, the rate of decrease on the left-hand portion being much greater in some industries than in others, the rate of increase in the right-hand portion being very gradual. The exact shape of the curve in any particular case depends upon the manner in which the Principle of Returns to Scale operates—that is, the extent to which economies of large-scale production are available, the level to which output must be expanded before economies are completely exhausted, and the extent to which complexities of large-scale management are encountered. Thus, in some industries the lowest possible cost can be obtained with a small volume of output, and the industry will be characterized by the presence of a large number of small firms. In other cases, low cost is obtained only when output reaches a substantial figure; and as a consequence, firms tend to grow large in size, with small firms having difficulty remaining in the industry.

The Significance of the Assumptions

The significance of this analysis depends upon the applicability in particular situations of the assumptions upon which it is based. Each of the assumptions will be examined briefly.

1. *Variability of Factors.* The assumption that all factors can be varied in the long-run period is valid except in rare cases of unique, specialized resources.

2. *Factor Indivisibility.* The assumption that small units of certain factors cannot be obtained, or are relatively inefficient, appears to be applicable in many lines of production. It is not possible, for example, to build all types of capital equipment on a small-scale basis; and some, while they can be built this way, provide relatively low output per unit of input. Manpower often cannot be obtained in very small units, such as man-minutes. While these considerations are more important in some lines of production than in others, both casual observation and careful empirical studies suggest that some indivisibilities are encountered in virtually all lines of production.

3. *Gains from Specialization of Factor Units.* Economies appear typically to be obtainable by utilization of labor and other factor units in specialized fashion.

Despite the obviously extensive validity of assumptions 2 and 3, it must be recognized that if, in a particular instance, neither assumption is valid, LRAC cannot be expected to decline.

4. *Adjustment of the Managerial Factor.* The assumption that the managerial factor cannot be adjusted in the same manner as other factors, with consequent increasing complexities and cost of management as an enterprise grows, is subject to greater question. The problems of large-scale management are, of course, very real. But as business firms grow in size, attention is given to the development and application of the principles of management in an effort to overcome these problems. By this means, firms may succeed in preventing an increase in average cost for a very substantial range of output. Whether this increase can be prevented indefinitely as output is extended farther and farther is doubtful. But there is by no means conclusive evidence that an eventual rise in average cost is inevitable.

Empirical Studies of Long-Run Cost Schedules

Few producers have precise data about long-run cost behavior. But only a small segment of the cost schedule is of direct concern to a producer at any time. He knows that costs with a very small plant would be prohibitively high, but he does not care exactly how high they are. A seller in nonpurely competitive markets knows that there is no need to consider the costs with a plant ten times the present size, as he is aware that he could not possibly sell the increased output at a profitable price. Attention centers on a much narrower range of plant sizes. If a producer suspects that a change might be desirable, he will attempt to figure the cost with various scales of operation, aided by engineering estimates and by data on costs of other firms with larger or smaller scales of operation than his own. Once a plant adjustment is made, the decision is irrevocable for a period of time, even if the cost estimate upon which it is based proves to be erroneous, since additional time is required for further changes.

Empirical studies have been made of long-run cost behavior, but the results have not been at all conclusive. The problems encountered are even more serious than those which arise with short-run cost studies. Any attempt to determine the actual long-run cost function of a single firm from observations of cost with different scales of operation over a period of time is almost entirely futile. Because of the length of the time period necessary to get any substantial number of observations, other determinants of cost—particularly methods of production—change so much that statistical adjustment for them is impossible. As a consequence, actual studies, for the most part, have taken cost data for several firms of different sizes at a particular time, in an effort to build up a cost schedule typical of firms in the industry. This approach also encounters serious problems. Some firms will be operating closer to capacity than others, and thus the cost differences will reflect variations in the degree of utilization of plant, as well as variations due to differences in plant size. Differences in age of equipment, quality of product, management efficiency, cost accounting methods, and prices paid for factors, will prevent exact attainment of the desired results, since the effects of these differences cannot be adequately eliminated.

Two surveys of empirical studies in the field conclude that while there is clear evidence that LRAC declines as the scale of operations is increased from a very small size, there is little evidence to prove (or disprove) the thesis that average cost must eventually rise as the scale of operations is expanded because of increased complexities of management and consequent decreasing returns to scale.[9] There is some evidence that LRAC does eventually rise as operations are expanded,

[9] See C. A. Smith, "Survey of the Empirical Evidence on Economies of Scale," *Business Concentration and Public Policy* (Princeton: Princeton University Press, 1955), pp. 213–39; and Johnston, *op. cit.*

but primarily as a result of the tendency of prices paid for factors and of distribution costs to rise.

COST CONDITIONS OF THE INDUSTRY

The preceding sections have considered the behavior of cost of the individual firm as it varies output, on the assumptions that prices paid for factor units are given, except insofar as they may be influenced by changes in the output of the firm itself, and that the efficiency of factor units is given. There is much greater likelihood of changes occurring in factor prices and in factor efficiency when the output of an entire industry changes. The term *cost conditions of the industry* is given to the relationship between changes in output of an industry and consequent changes in the height of the cost schedules of the individual firms.

There are three possible industry cost conditions—increasing, decreasing, and constant.

Increasing Cost Industries

In an increasing cost industry, the cost schedules of the individual firms rise as the total output of the industry increases.

Increasing cost conditions result from *external diseconomies* of large-scale production, primarily increases in factor prices which occur as larger quantities of factors are employed in the industry. When an industry utilizes a large portion of a factor whose total supply is not perfectly elastic, factor prices will increase when the industry uses more of the factor. Increasing cost conditions are typical of the "extractive" industries, such as agriculture, fishing, mining, and lumbering, in which large portions of the total supply of specialized natural resources are utilized in the industry. As the output of such an industry expands, the increased demand for the resources, such as land or mineral deposits, raises the prices that must be paid for their use. Since additional resources cannot be produced, greater supplies can be obtained (if at all) only by taking them away from other industries, or by using lower-quality (and thus higher cost) resources. Wheat production is a typical example of an increasing cost industry. As the output of wheat increases, the demand for land suitable for the production of wheat rises, and thus the price paid for the use of land and the sale value of the land increase. Farmers owning their own land prior to the output increase do not experience an increase in their expenditure costs, but their total costs increase just as do those of tenant farmers; the opportunity cost of using the land in their own production instead of renting it to others is now greater than before.

In some instances, increasing cost conditions arise from a reduction in efficiency of production as total output of the industry increases. In an agricultural area irrigated from wells, for example, increased production—and pumping of water—will lower the water table and increase pumping costs for all farmers in the area. Similar problems arise in oil production; an increase in the number of wells in a field will lessen the pressure and increase the difficulty and cost of getting the oil to the surface.[10] As more and more planes use the New York area airports, the greater is the delay in landing, with higher costs and accident hazards.

Decreasing Cost Industries

In a decreasing cost industry, the cost schedules of the firms fall as total output of the industry increases, because of *external economics* of large-scale production, economies, in the sense of cost reductions, which no one firm can gain by its own expansion, but which occur as the total output of the industry increases. Consider a new mining region, developed in an area remote from railroad facilities in the days before the motor vehicle. So long as the total output of the mines was small, the ore was hauled by wagon, an extremely expensive form of transport. But when the number of mines increased, and the total output of the region rose substantially, it became feasible to construct a railroad into the area. The railroad lowered transportation costs and reduced the cost schedules of all the firms. No one mine could possibly have increased its output sufficiently to warrant the building of a railroad; but when the total output of the industry increased sufficiently, construction of the road became profitable.

As a practical matter, however, external economies are rarely encountered, from all indications. Some industries may operate under decreasing cost conditions in short intervals of output expansion, when continued growth makes possible the supplying of materials or services at reduced cost. But it is impossible to find examples in which decreasing cost conditions prevail over a wide range of outputs.[11]

[10] Data compiled by the petroleum industry show that, in 1960, the average cost to drill wells under 1,250 feet in depth was $7.57 per foot; for wells between 3,750 and 5,000 feet, $9.19 per foot; for those over 15,000 feet, $38.75 per foot. See Committee on Public Affairs, API Institute, *The Role of Profits in the Petroleum Industry.*

[11] When one firm produces the entire output of a product in a particular market and possesses a completely monopolistic position, the firm may find it profitable to operate at a volume of output less than that of lowest average cost. As a consequence, if the firm

Constant Cost Industries

Constant cost conditions, in which the cost schedules of the firms are not affected by changes in the output of the entire industry, will occur when the industry does not use factors in sufficient quantities for their prices or efficiency to be affected by changes in the output of the industry.

Diagrammatic presentation of the various cost conditions is feasible only for purely competitive industries, and will be deferred to Chapter 8.

FURTHER COMPLEXITIES OF COST

The cost analysis of this chapter has been based upon two simplifying assumptions; effects of changes in certain cost elements upon demand schedules for the product have been ignored, as well as the fact that firms frequently produce more than one product. The cost elements for activities which affect sales are known as *selling* costs, in contrast to *production* costs, those arising from the actual production of the goods. Selling costs are incurred for the purpose of influencing the choice of the buyer for the product which he buys or the firm from which he makes the purchase. Their existence creates an interrelationship between cost schedules and demand schedules, which will be considered in Chapter 11.

The production of more than one product by a firm—a practice which is almost universal—gives rise to *common* costs, those which are incurred for the production of two or more products, no one of the latter being responsible for any particular part of the cost. Thus the cost of maintenance of a railroad line is a common cost for freight and

increases its sales, its average cost falls. The term *decreasing cost industry* is commonly defined to include this case, as well as that described in the previous paragraphs. Thus the electric power industry is frequently called a decreasing cost industry. It should be recognized, however, that in this case the decline in average cost which occurs as output increases involves a movement within a particular cost schedule of an individual firm (and thus along a particular cost curve), whereas the case of decreasing cost due to external economies involves a shifting of the entire cost schedule—in graphical terms, a downward movement of the cost curves of the firm.

The concept of a decreasing cost industry cannot usefully be applied to situations in which individual firms in nonmonopoly situations are operating on the decreasing cost portions of their LRAC curves, as may be typical in many nonpurely competitive fields. Likewise, the concept of a decreasing cost industry is not used in reference to a situation in which average cost declines over a period of time because of the development of new methods of production. This is merely an historical cost change resulting from a shift in one of the determinants of cost.

passenger traffic. The cost of clerk hire in a grocery store is a common cost for the various goods handled. The concept of average cost for each product is no longer precise when common costs exist; average cost is affected by the way in which common costs are allocated among the various products produced. The significance of common costs for price determination will be considered in Chapter 12.

SELECTED REFERENCES

CLARK, J. M. *Studies in the Economics of Overhead Costs.* Chicago: University of Chicago Press, 1923.
    One of the most significant and complete pioneer analyses of cost.

COLBERG, M. R.; FORBUSH, D. R.; AND WHITAKER, G. R. *Business Economics,* chap. iv. 3d ed. Homewood, Ill.: Irwin, 1964.

ELLIS, H. S., AND FELLNER, W. "External Economies and Diseconomies," *American Economic Review,* Vol. 33 (September, 1943), pp. 493–511.
    The most complete discussion of a neglected problem.

HAYNES, W. W. *Managerial Economics,* chap. vii. Homewood, Ill.: Dorsey Press, 1963.

JOHNSTON, J. *Statistical Cost Analysis.* New York: McGraw-Hill, 1960.
    An analysis of cost behavior, with emphasis on statistical studies of actual cost functions.

NATIONAL BUREAU OF ECONOMIC RESEARCH. *Cost Behavior and Price Policy.* New York, 1943.
    A discussion of the problems and conclusions of empirical cost studies.

VINER, J. "Cost Curves and Supply Curves," *Readings in Price Theory* (eds. G. J. STIGLER AND K. E. BOULDING). Homewood, Ill.: Irwin, 1952.
    The pioneer work in clarifying the relation of short-run and long-run cost schedules.

QUESTIONS

1. Explain the meaning of the concept of cost, as used in economic analysis.
2. Distinguish between expenditure and nonexpenditure costs, and give examples of each.
3. What payments made by business firms are not regarded as costs, at least during the period in which they are made?
4. Which implicit cost is treated as a business expense under usual accounting principles?
5. Distinguish between the concepts of short-run and long-run periods.
6. Distinguish between fixed costs and variable costs. The latter are variable with respect to what?
7. List the major fixed and variable cost items.
8. Why are all costs variable in a long-run period?

9. Distinguish between fully variable and semivariable costs; between semi-variable costs and fixed costs.
10. Is depreciation a cost? Explain.
11. What is the opportunity cost to you of attending college? Of taking a vacation this summer instead of working?
12. Would you expect each of the following to be, in typical cases in the short-run, fixed, or variable costs?
    a) Sales taxes.
    b) Property taxes.
    c) Rent on a factory building.
    d) Interest on money borrowed to buy additional materials.
    e) Fire insurance.
    f) Cost of goods sold.
    g) The salary of the president of the company.
13. List the major assumptions in short-run cost analysis. Does the use of these assumptions make the analysis less realistic? Compare these with the assumptions used in the analysis of long-run cost behavior.
14. A firm, with a particular plant, has daily fixed costs of $400. Total variable costs for successive quantities of output, per day, are as follows:

Output	Total Variable Cost	Output	Total Variable Cost
1.................	$200	6................	$ 400
2.................	250	7................	450
3.................	275	8................	550
4.................	300	9................	750
5.................	350	10................	1,500

Determine average fixed cost, average variable cost, average cost, and marginal cost.
15. Why does marginal cost reflect solely on variable cost?
16. Why does the MC curve intersect the AC curve at the lowest point of the latter?
17. If AVC is falling, must MC be falling? Must MC be less than AVC under these conditions? Explain.
18. Why does AFC decline continuously as a firm increases output?
19. Under what circumstances will AVC decline initially as a firm increases output?
20. Why will AVC eventually rise as a firm continues to increase output?
21. Why is the SRAC curve generally believed to be U-shaped?
22. What significance does the Law of Diminishing Returns have for the behavior of SRAC?
23. Why does AVC fall if APP of the variable factor is rising?
24. As a firm adds successive units of variable factors, costing $50 per unit, output increases as follows:

Units of Factor	Total Output
1	8
2	20
3	45
4	54
5	60
6	63
7	64

Determine AVC for the range of output for which information is available.

25. Under what circumstances is a firm likely to experience a long range of constant AVC?

26. Why may AVC fall even though APP of the variable factors is constant?

27. In what respect does the ability to operate an enterprise in more than one shift affect the behavior of SRAC?

28. What difficulties are encountered in making empirical studies of short-run cost behavior?

29. Define carefully the term *long-run average cost.*

30. How is the long-run cost schedule built up from the short-run cost schedules?

31. Why may the LRAC curve be irregularly shaped?

32. Under what conditions will LRAC decline as a firm first expands its scale of operations? Compare the causes of this decline with the causes of decline in SRAC as a firm expands output with a given plant.

33. Under what circumstances would LRAC not fall as a firm first increases its scale of operations?

34. What may cause an eventual increase in LRAC if a firm continues to expand?

35. Why has there been relatively little empirical work on the nature of LRAC curves?

36. Explain the concept of cost conditions of the industry.

37. Under what circumstances will an industry be one of increasing cost conditions? Of decreasing cost conditions?

38. Distinguish between external economies and internal economies.

39. What are common costs?

40. Under what cost conditions is it likely that the following industries operate?
    a) Lumber production
    b) Silver mining
    c) Rubber-band production
    d) Fishing
    e) Parsnip
    f) Corn

41. Does the fact that automobile prices declined greatly from 1910 to 1930 show that during those years automobile production was a decreasing cost industry? Explain.

42. Distinguish between "selling costs" and "production costs."

43. Assume that you have a weekly transit system pass entitling you to an unlimited number of rides, at a cost of $2.25. If you take 23 rides, what is the average cost per ride? What is the marginal cost of the twenty-third ride?

Chapter 8

PRICE AND OUTPUT DETERMINATION UNDER CONDITIONS OF PURE COMPETITION

Having completed our analysis of demand and cost, we proceed to describe price and output determination in various market situations: pure competition, monopoly, monopolistic competition, and oligopoly. This chapter deals with pure competition—a situation in which market prices are regarded as given parameters by all buyers and sellers.

Pure competition is likely to be approximated most nearly in actual practice in markets for standardized commodities that are traded by large numbers of buyers and sellers. The essential condition of pure competition is that buyers and sellers regard the market prices as parameters over which they have no control; that is, their decisions are made on the basis of the assumption that they cannot influence the price by their own actions. They are of course most likely to believe that they cannot influence market price if in fact they cannot do so; however, they may act upon the assumption that they cannot influence prices when in fact they might be able to do so. The assumptions of the purely competitive model are most closely approximated in markets for standardized agricultural products with large numbers of buyers and sellers.

Competitive Price Determination: General Considerations

Actual selling prices—market prices—under pure competition are determined by the interaction of market demand and supply. No individual buyer has any control over price; each bases his behavior upon the assumption that the price is "given" in the market and is beyond his control. The combined but independent actions of buyers and sellers—by determining the relationship between the total quantities that buyers seek to purchase at any price and the total amounts that sellers offer at the same price—govern the behavior of actual market price. Most of the commodities to which the purely competitive analysis is clearly applicable are traded in central wholesale markets, such as the Chicago Board of Trade, where large numbers of buyers and sellers are in continuous contact with one another. The prices determined in these central markets serve as the basic prices for a wide area, in some instances the entire country. Wheat prices, for example, are not determined separately in each locality by local supply and demand conditions. Local prices are simply Chicago prices plus or minus transport costs to or from the Chicago market.

Current prices, determined by prevailing demand and supply conditions, tend over time toward certain equilibrium levels. In a time interval sufficiently long for firms to adjust output but not plant capacity, market price tends toward the *short-run equilibrium* level. In a time interval long enough for firms to adjust output but not plant capacity, market price tends toward the *long-run equilibrium* level. Actual equality of market price with short-run or long-run equilibrium levels may never be attained, and even if it were the adjustment could be maintained only temporarily, because equilibrium levels are themselves subject to change over time. But at any point in time, forces are at work to move actual price in the direction of equilibrium.

MARKET PRICE DETERMINATION

We will consider first the determination of the market price—the actual price prevailing at any particular moment of time.

The Average Revenue Curve of an Individual Seller

In a purely competitive market, the average revenue function of the individual seller, i.e., the relation which indicates for each possible level of output the maximum price per unit for which the seller believes his entire output can be sold, is such that changes in output do not alter the expected price. The seller believes he can sell as much as he wishes to place on the market at the prevailing market price. Or, in other words, the demand as seen by the seller is perfectly elastic. A wheat farmer, for example, will act on the assumption that he can dispose of his entire crop at the current market price, for he knows that any change he makes in the quantity that he offers for sale will have no appreciable effect upon market price. Likewise, he knows that he cannot dispose of his wheat at any figure higher than the current market price—for if he attempted to charge a higher price, prospective buyers would simply purchase their supplies from other sources. Thus, if the prevailing market price of the product were, say, $1.50, the

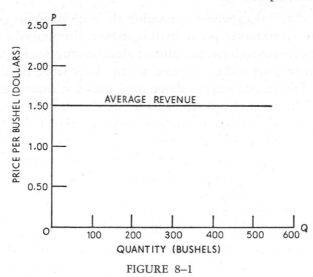

FIGURE 8–1

AVERAGE REVENUE CURVE OF A SELLER OF WHEAT

farmer's average revenue function would be represented geometrically by a horizontal line, as shown in Figure 8–1.

How is it possible for the average revenue curve of an individual seller to be horizontal, when the market demand curve for the product is not? Why will a wheat farmer act on the basis of a belief that he can sell as much wheat as he pleases without affecting the market price if the total quantity of wheat demanded at each price is a finite amount, and larger quantities can be sold only at lower prices? This is possible because of the very large number of sellers, all selling identical products. Each producer is providing such a small fraction of the total supply that a change in his own offerings does not have any noticeable effect on market price, and hence the producer does not realize that his sales have any effect at all. In other words, the effect is imperceptible to him. Thus, his average revenue function appears to be horizontal over the entire range of output that he could possibly produce.

To say that producers under pure competition regard price as a given parameter is not to say that price is constant. The *position* of the average revenue function (as distinguished from its elasticity)—hence, price as seen by the seller—will of course vary with every change in the current market price. In effect, sellers are provided with current information about market demand and supply conditions through the medium of price changes; and it is an essential aspect of the purely competitive model that sellers respond to the signals provided by such price movements. That is to say, sellers alter their behavior over time in the light of actual experience, revising their decisions in conformity with changes in market price. In this respect, the purely competitive model is curiously realistic, for almost alone among models of market price determination it does not assume any knowledge on the part of individual buyers and sellers about total market demand and supply functions. The force of this remark will become clear when we deal in later chapters with price formation under conditions of monopoly, monopolistic competition, and oligopoly.

The concept of *marginal revenue* must also be introduced; by this term is meant the addition to total revenue resulting from the sale of an additional unit of product. In a purely competitive market, since additional units of product can be sold without reducing the price of the product, marginal revenue is in each instance identical with average revenue, and the AR curve on Figure 8–1 may also be labeled the MR curve. As will be explained in succeeding chapters, in nonpurely competitive markets marginal revenue and average revenue are not identical.

The Concept of Supply

Under the assumption that the average revenue function of a seller is given, being determined by market price and not subject to his control, the seller has only to decide the amount to place on the market. At any one period of time, with a given quantity already purchased or produced and on hand, this decision is based upon relative expected gains from holding or selling various quantities of the product. Over a period of time, the decision involves the determination of the amount to produce, and thus is influenced by the costs of producing at various alternative levels of output. Thus, given the relative expected gains from holding or selling, and the firm's estimates of the costs of producing various amounts of output, the quantity which the firm will offer for sale will depend solely upon the market price. Thus we define supply—*the competitive supply function*—as the relation showing for various possible values of market price the quantity which the seller will offer for sale at that price. The *market* or *total* supply function, in turn, may be defined as the relation showing for various possible values of market price the sum of the quantities which sellers in the aggregate will offer for sale at the respective prices. The market supply function is simply the sum of the individual supply functions of all firms selling in a particular market.

So much for definitions and other generalities affecting supply. To say anything specific about the form of competitive supply functions, we must consider the influences which affect profit calculations in market, short-run, and long-run planning periods.

Supply Schedules in the Market Period

We define a *market period* to be a time interval that is too short to allow production of additional units, so that sales can be made only from a fixed stock. In industries in which production is a continuous process, additional output may be quickly adjusted and the market period will be very short. Market price will therefore adjust rapidly to the short-run equilibrium level, and the dichotomy between market price and the short-run equilibrium price is of little significance. In most agricultural industries, however, including many of those for which the purely competitive analysis has the greatest applicability, crops are harvested during a short period of the year, and no additional output is possible for another year. In such industries the period in which only a fixed stock is available and additional output is impossible is relatively long.

With a given stock of goods on hand, a seller has only two alternatives: he can sell the commodity or hold it for possible future sale. A typical supply schedule of an individual in a time interval

TABLE 8–1

SUPPLY SCHEDULE OF AN
INDIVIDUAL SELLER,
FIXED STOCK OF GOODS ON HAND

Price (Dollars)	Quantity Supplied
0.25	0
0.50	800
0.75	1,200
1.00	1,600
1.25	2,000
1.50	2,200
1.75	2,200

relevant for market price determination is shown in Table 8–1. The schedule is illustrated graphically in Figure 8–2.

Determinants of Supply. The actual quantities which a particular seller will place on the market at various possible prices will depend upon the amount he has on hand (under the assumption of a time interval insufficient to allow the production of more units) and his *reservation prices*—the prices below which he will hold, rather than sell, particular parts of his stock of goods. A seller obviously cannot sell more than he has at a particular time. A wheat farmer, on a day in October, cannot sell more wheat for delivery now than he has on hand

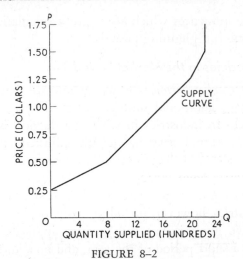

FIGURE 8–2

MARKET PERIOD SUPPLY OF AN INDIVIDUAL SELLER

from this year's harvest. But he will not necessarily sell all that he has available. Whether he does or not depends upon the relationship between the market price and his reservation price, which is controlled primarily by his estimate of future prices. If he believes that prices are going down, his reservation price will be low, since he will wish to dispose of his crop while prices are relatively high, and so avoid a possible price decline, which may be regarded, in a sense, as a subjective cost. On the other hand, if he expects prices to rise, his reservation price will be high, for to sell his stock now would involve sacrificing a prospective gain (another subjective "cost"). Expectations about future prices are affected by many considerations—past experience, current reports on price and business trends, views of other persons, pure guesswork, etc. When sellers become accustomed to receiving prices within a certain range over a period of years, they are likely to regard any price below this figure as unreasonably low and will expect a price rise. Unusually high prices are frequently regarded as being only temporary.

Reservation prices are also influenced by costs of storage, including rental, interest, and depreciation of goods. The higher these costs, the lower will be the reservation price. If a commodity is highly perishable, costs of storage will be prohibitive, and the reservation price will be extremely low. The seller will prefer to realize something from the good rather than have it spoil. Likewise, the seller's need for cash is significant. If he needs money immediately, his reservation price will be relatively low, regardless of other considerations. If he does not need cash quickly, he is much more likely to take a chance that prices will rise.

Thus the determinants of market period supply include:

1. The stock the seller has on hand.
2. Costs of storage.
3. Perishability of the product.
4. Cash requirements of the seller.
5. Expectations of future prices.

Nature of the Supply Schedule of the Individual Seller. As illustrated in Table 8–1, the higher the price, the greater the quantity which will be offered. The higher the price, the greater is the expectation that the price will fall, and the less is the likelihood that it will go still higher. Accordingly, at successively higher prices, sellers will be willing to part with successively larger portions of their stocks, since they are less certain that the price will go still higher and are more afraid that a decline will occur. Furthermore, the higher the price, the greater the likelihood that it will exceed the figure to which the seller is accustomed. Finally, at relatively high prices, sellers can obtain cash to meet expenses through the sale of only a portion of their stock.

Total Supply Schedules. The sum of the individual supply schedules in the market constitutes the total or market supply schedule. The nature of the total schedule is the same as that of the individual schedules. At successively higher prices, additional amounts will be placed on the market by those who would make some sales at lower prices, and additional sellers whose reservation prices are so high that they will sell nothing at lower prices will offer units for sale. There are likely to be substantial differences among the schedules of individual sellers, due to differences in stocks of goods on hand, storage facilities, need for cash, and expectations about future trends in prices. It is impossible to generalize about the elasticity of the typical market supply schedule, beyond noting that perishability is significant. When a good cannot be stored at all, the entire stock will be offered for sale regardless of price, and higher prices will bring forth no larger quantities in the time period under consideration.

Market Price Determination

The market price tends to a level at which the quantity supplied and the quantity demanded are equal. In a perfect market, with complete knowledge by buyers and sellers about market conditions, the market price would adjust almost instantaneously and the actual selling price and the equilibrium market price would be virtually identical at every instant of time. Where imperfections exist, delay is inevitable. Thus the actual selling price may deviate temporarily from the equilibrium market price. However, the principal wholesale markets for goods sold under conditions approximating those of pure competition are relatively well organized, with imperfections at a minimum. Therefore the adjustment usually requires only a very short period; and equilibrium market price and the actual selling price are usually considered to be identical.

Mathematically, the problem that the "market" solves is that of finding a particular value, $\bar{p}$, of the price variable p which satisfies the demand-supply equality

$$D(P) - S(P) = 0.$$

The precise way in which the market solves this problem varies from one market to another, but the general principle is the same regardless of the mechanics of the process. Specifically, if the actual price is for any reason temporarily at a level above the equilibrium value $\bar{p}$, some sellers will discover that they cannot find buyers at the higher price, because total quantity demanded will be less than the total quantity offered for sale. Consequently, some sellers will offer to sell for slightly less in order to avoid storage, interest, and other costs, and the market price will fall until buyers are willing to purchase the same number of units that sellers wish to sell at the new price. If the price were lower than that at which quantity demanded and quantity supplied were equal, buyers would want to buy more units of the good than sellers would be willing to sell. Accordingly some buyers would offer to pay more in order to get the desired number of units, and the market price would rise until equality of quantity supplied and demanded was attained.

The supply schedule in the market period, and to some extent the demand schedule, are greatly influenced by expectations of future prices. Therefore, market price is typically subject to frequent change as expectations shift.

Cost in the usual sense has little direct influence in the market period. Once a good is produced, there is no way of obtaining money from it except by selling it. A seller may not wish to sell below cost, but it is better for him to do so than to allow the product to spoil. The level of price in the market period is likely to be very sensitive, however, to the subjective "cost" of possible decline in price. This is a highly

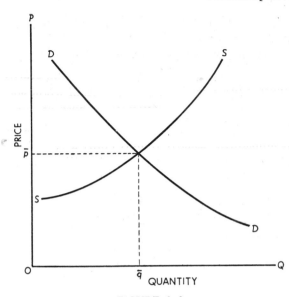

FIGURE 8–3

MARKET PRICE EQUILIBRIUM

significant factor in markets for financial assets as well as certain agricultural commodities.

The determination of the market period equilibrium price is illustrated graphically in Figure 8–3. The curve *DD* represents the demand function $D = D(P)$, and the curve *SS* represents the supply function $S = S(P)$. Price will tend to adjust to $\bar{p}$, the level at which the quantities demanded and supplied are equal, and the quantity exchanged will adjust to the equilibrium level $\bar{q}$.

OUTPUT AND PRICE IN A SHORT-RUN PERIOD

Over a period of time, firms can adjust output; thus the supply function is dependent upon the rate of output, rather than merely upon the willingness of firms to sell from a given stock of goods. In all situations in which output is adjustable—short run or long run—attainment of maximum profit requires the adjustment of output to the point at which any additional increase in output, however small, will increase total revenue less than it increases total cost, and any reduction in output will reduce total revenue more than it reduces total cost. Thus marginal profit—the additional profit resulting from the sales of an additional unit of output—will be zero at the profit maximizing point, and negative for changes in output in either direction from this point.

Thus the supply function is dependent upon the various parameters influencing cost of production at various levels of output.

In a short-run period, which is defined as an interval long enough to allow adjustment in output but not in plant capacity, market price will tend toward the short-run equilibrium price level, the level determined by the relationship between the average revenue function and the short-run supply function. Firms will adjust output in terms of the relationship between price and short-run cost, and changes in market supply resulting from these output adjustments will bring the market price toward the short-run equilibrium figure.

Short-Run Supply

The short period supply function is defined as the relationship between various prices and the quantities which will be offered for sale at these prices, during a time interval long enough to allow the existing firms to adjust output with given plant capacity. As noted above, because the firms can adjust output, a new determinant of supply becomes significant, namely, cost of production.

The firm will not produce at all unless the price obtainable at least covers *average variable cost* (AVC). These costs will cease if production is suspended, and thus operation at a price which does not cover them will worsen the financial position of the firm. If a firm cannot obtain enough revenue from the sale of the product to cover the direct wage, raw material, and power costs necessary to produce it, each additional unit produced will reduce the firm's capital or increase its debt. Even if the owners of a business desire to continue operation under such circumstances, they cannot do so for very long except through use of cash reserve or by incurring debt. Firms will continue to operate when price is below AVC only if the owners believe that prices will rise in the near future, and wish to avoid costs associated with closing and reopening the plant and losing experienced personnel.

At price levels equal to or in excess of AVC, a firm will produce in the short-run period even if total average cost is not completely covered. Since fixed costs continue whether the firm produces or not, it is preferable to earn enough to cover a portion of these costs rather than earn nothing at all. Immediate liquidation of a business is usually not economically feasible. Money capital invested in specialized capital equipment cannot be withdrawn quickly except at great loss because used capital goods, as a rule, have little sale value.

In the range of prices at which production will be carried on—those which are equal to or above AVC at some level of output—the firm

will adjust its output to a level at which *marginal cost* (MC) with the
existing plant is equal to *marginal revenue* (MR), which, in pure
competition, is equal to average revenue (AR), i.e., market price. Until
this volume of output is reached, each additional unit produced results
in a greater *addition* to the total revenue of the firm (marginal
revenue) than to its total cost (marginal cost), and hence is profitable
to produce, provided that price covers AVC. If output is carried beyond
the level at which MR = MC, additional units will add more to total

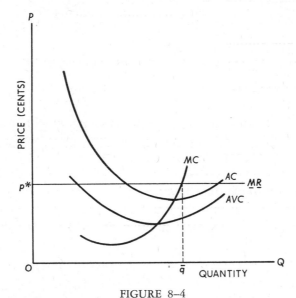

FIGURE 8–4

EQUILIBRIUM OUTPUT OF THE FIRM IN THE SHORT RUN

cost than to total revenue and will thereby either reduce profits or
increase losses.

The level of operation of a firm in pure competition in the short
run is illustrated in Figure 8–4. The short-run cost schedule, comparable
to those discussed in the previous chapter, is plotted on the same chart
with the revenue schedule. The AR curve is a horizontal line at the
level of the current market price p^*. This line also indicates marginal
revenue, which is identical with average revenue in pure competition.
Since, in this illustration, price is in excess of AVC for some levels of
output, the firm will operate; it will produce such a number of units,
namely $\bar{q}$, that $MR = MC = p^*$, as indicated on the graph by the
intersection of the MC and MR curves. Price in this particular instance
is also in excess of AC. Figure 8–5 illustrates a case in which price is

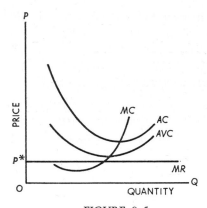

FIGURE 8–5

REVENUE AND COST CURVES OF A
FIRM IN A SHORT-RUN PERIOD, PRICE
LESS THAN LOWEST AVC

FIGURE 8–6

REVENUE AND COST CURVES OF A
FIRM IN A SHORT-RUN PERIOD, WITH
PRICE ABOVE AVC BUT BELOW AC

less than AVC at all ranges of output; hence the firm will not produce
(i.e., $\bar{q} = 0$). Figure 8–6 shows a situation in which price is less than
AC but in excess of AVC ($\bar{q} > 0$).

The Short-Run Supply Schedule

At each possible price above the level of lowest AVC, the firm
will place on the market such a number of units that MC = price. Thus
the firm's supply schedule can be derived directly from its MC schedule,
as illustrated in Table 8–2. The right-hand portion of the table
indicates the supply schedule of the firm, on the basis of the cost data
presented on the left-hand side. At any price below 20 cents, nothing

TABLE 8–2

SHORT-RUN COST SCHEDULE AND SHORT-RUN SUPPLY SCHEDULE OF A FIRM SELLING
IN A PURELY COMPETITIVE MARKET

	DAILY COST SCHEDULE				DAILY SUPPLY SCHEDULE	
Units of Output	Average Variable Cost (Cents)	Average Cost (Cents)	Marginal Cost (Cents)		Price (Cents)	Quantity Supplied
1	30	50	30		12	0
2	24	34	18		20	4
3	20	26.67	12		25	5
4	20	25	20		27	6
5	21	25	25		50	7
6	22	25.33	27		138	8
7	26	28.86	50			
8	40	42.50	138			

would be produced, since AVC would not be covered. A price of 20 cents would cover AVC, and therefore the firm would operate; four units would be produced, since, with a price of 20 cents, MC = MR at an output of four units. At 25 cents, MC = MR with an output of five units. If the price were 27 cents, six units would be supplied; if it were 50 cents, seven units; and so on.

In graphical terms, the short-period supply curve of a competitive seller is identical with that portion of the MC curve which lies on or above and to the right of the point at which the MC curve intersects the AVC curve. As a cost relation, this curve shows the marginal cost of

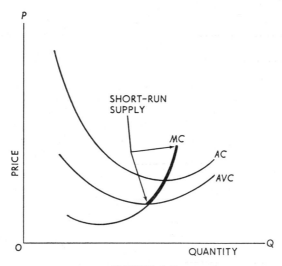

FIGURE 8–7
SHORT-RUN COST CURVE AND SUPPLY CURVE OF A FIRM

producing any *given output;* as a supply curve, it shows the *equilibrium output* that the firm will supply at various prices. Thus, as shown in Figure 8–7, the portion of *MC* above its intersection with *AVC* is the supply curve. The declining portion of the *MC* curve has no significance for supply, because greater profit can be made by extending production to the quantities for the respective prices on the rising portion of the curve. All units of output in the intervening range will add more to total revenue than to total cost.

Since, beyond the point of lowest AVC, the marginal costs of successively larger amounts of output are progressively greater, larger and larger amounts will be supplied only at higher levels of price. The absolute maximum that the firm can supply, regardless of price, is the maximum quantity that can be produced with the existing plant.

The total short-run supply schedule is the sum of the schedules of the individual firms in the industry. By definition, the short run is too brief for new firms to commence production, and hence the total schedule is the summation of the individual schedules of existing firms. One modification to the summation rule arises from the possible effect of higher levels of output of the industry in raising prices which must be paid for factor units used by existing firms. If this occurs, the quantities supplied at higher prices will be somewhat less than they would appear to be on the basis of a summation of existing individual schedules.

In summary, the determinants of short-run supply include:

1. The number of firms.
2. The plant facilities of firms.
3. The cost functions of firms.
4. Factor prices.

The Short-Run Equilibrium

The short-run equilibrium price level is the figure at which the demand for the product and the short-period supply of the product are equal. At this level the total amount which sellers will produce and place on the market in each interval of time with a given plant is equal to the amount buyers will purchase in the same time interval at that price. Once sufficient time has passed for firms to complete output adjustments with given plant capacities, the market price will tend to reach the short-run level (apart from possible effects of market imperfections noted in subsequent sections). If market price is temporarily above this level, output will increase over time, market period supply will shift to the right, and market price will thus tend to fall back toward the short-run equilibrium level. Similarly, if for any reason market price is below the equilibrium level, output will decline to a figure less than the quantity demanded at that price, and market price will tend to rise. Accordingly, only at the short-run equilibrium level will the volume of output coming on the market, with given plant capacities, equal quantity demanded. This equilibrium position, one from which there is no tendency for market price to depart, is illustrated in Figure 8–8 ($\bar{p}_s$). Once short-run adjustments have been completed, the market supply curve will be at the level SS and will intersect the demand curve (DD) at the same point as that at which the latter is intersected by SRS—the short-period supply curve. Figure 8–9 illustrates a case in which market price (p^*) initially exceeds the short-run equilibrium level. Because market supply (SS) is relatively low, the quantity actually

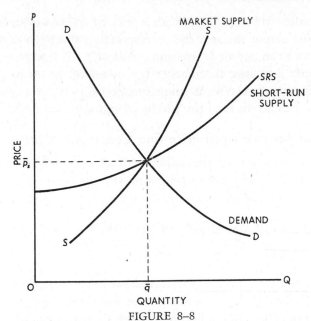

FIGURE 8–8
EQUILIBRIUM MARKET PRICE AND SHORT-RUN EQUILIBRIUM PRICE IN
A PURELY COMPETITIVE INDUSTRY

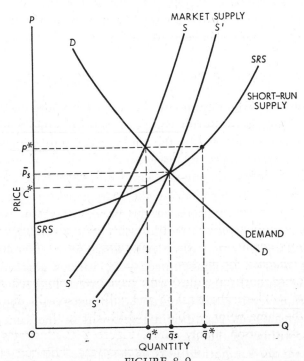

FIGURE 8–9
ADJUSTMENT OF MARKET PRICE TO THE SHORT-RUN EQUILIBRIUM LEVEL

offered for sale will be only q^*. With a price of p^*, however, firms will quickly adjust output towards the corresponding short-run equilibrium level $\overline{q}^*$, since at an output q^* marginal cost (C^*) is less than price. As market supply increases, the market supply curve moves to the right until it reaches the level $S'S'$. With this market supply curve, the market price will be $\overline{p}_s$, and the quantity produced and sold will be $\overline{q}_s$.

The Relations between Price and Cost in the Short-Run Period

As a consequence of the adjustment of output by firms in the short-run period, certain relationships must exist between equilibrium price and costs, once adjustments are complete. Specifically:

(1) $\overline{p} = \overline{MC}$ for each firm, as required for short-run profit maximization;
(2) $\overline{p} \geqq \overline{AVC}$, since firms will not operate unless AVC is covered at the short-run equilibrium output.

At the short-run equilibrium output, market price may be either above or below AC, for there is no necessity that fixed costs be covered except in the long run. The actual relation between short-run equilibrium price and AC in particular cases will depend upon the relationship between demand and short-period supply, as indicated above. If demand is sufficiently great, price will be above AC; if demand is relatively low, price will be in the range between AC and AVC.

OUTPUT AND PRICE IN THE LONG-RUN PERIOD

The long-run equilibrium price level is the figure toward which market price and the short-run equilibrium price tend in a period of time long enough to allow (1) the completion by firms of all desired adjustments in factor units, (2) the entry of new firms, and (3) the departure of old ones. At any one time, adjustments in output with existing plant are tending to bring the market price to the short-run equilibrium figure, as described in the previous section. But over a longer period—one which will allow all firms to make all desired adjustments in plant, and allow new firms to be established and unprofitable ones to be discontinued—the various adjustments will bring market price and the short-run equilibrium figure to the long-run equilibrium level. If all long-run adjustments are completed, the short-run and long-run equilibrium levels will be the same, and the market price will be equal to them.

The long-run equilibrium price is determined by the relationship between demand and long-period supply—the schedule of total amounts that would be forthcoming onto the market at various price levels in each time interval, over a period sufficiently long to allow adjustments in the quantities of all factors used. Demand requires little further consideration. As indicated previously, demand schedules will be more elastic over a longer period than they are at a given time, to the extent that buyers will make greater readjustments to price changes in a longer time interval than they will immediately after the change has occurred. Long-period supply, however, requires more detailed analysis, since its determinants are not identical with those of supply in the short period.

Supply Schedules in the Long-Run Period

In a long-run period, output adjustments of existing firms will differ from those made in the short run, since the ability to adjust the quantities of all factors employed alters the costs which affect output determination. In addition, changes may occur in the number of firms in the industry and alter total quantities supplied at various prices as well as affect the cost schedules and supply schedules of existing firms.

Long-Run Adjustments by Existing Firms. Whereas price in the short-run period need cover only AVC to ensure that firms continue production, over a long-run period price must cover all costs—and thus be at least equal to average cost, or the owners will liquidate the enterprise and reinvest in other fields.

At price levels equal to or in excess of the minimum value of AC, the firm will adjust plant capacity until LRMC and SRMC both equal MR and thus price. The plant will be adjusted to a size which allows equality of LRMC and MR and thus permits the lowest-cost factor combination for any given volume of equilibrium output. The firm will produce at the point at which SRMC with this plant is equal to price. The long-run equilibrium position is illustrated in Figure 8–10. The firm adjusts all factors until the plant with curve *SRAC* is attained and $\overline{q}$ units of output are produced. At this level of output, price $\overline{p}$ (and thus *MR*) is equal to both *SRMC* and *LRMC,* and *AC* is just covered.

Adjustments in the Number of Firms. The rule that the firm will operate after long-run adjustments have been completed at a level at which both LRMC and SRMC are equal to price is a necessary consequence of the assumption that the firm is seeking to maximize profits. Under this assumption the rule is valid whether price equals or exceeds average cost. But adjustments in the number of firms in the industry will force all firms to operate at a point at which price is equal to AC. As long as price is in excess of AC for any firm, excess profits

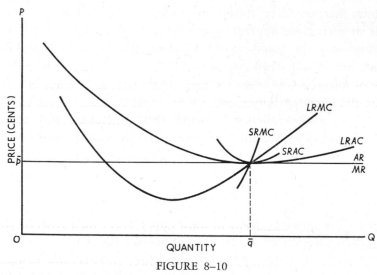

FIGURE 8–10

LONG-RUN ADJUSTMENT OF A FIRM

will be earned and new firms will enter the industry. This process will continue until price falls to the level of AC for every firm.

Not only must price be equal to AC in the long-run period; it must also be equal to the lowest possible AC figure; i.e., firms must be operating at the lowest points on their LRAC curves. The desire for maximum profit causes the firm to operate at a point at which price is equal to LRMC. The flow of firms into the industry gradually forces price to equality with AC. Ultimately, therefore, the firm must operate at a point at which price is equal to both LRMC and LRAC, and these two cost figures are equal to each other only at the lowest point on the LRAC curve.

This relationship is illustrated graphically in Figure 8–10. When long-run equilibrium adjustments have been completed, the AR curve will be tangent to the LRAC curve at its lowest point. At this point of tangency the equilibrium level of output q̄ is such that price is equal to LRAC (at the lowest possible figure), to SRAC with the optimum-sized plant, and to both SRMC and LRMC. Tangency of the AR and AC curves is essential for equilibrium, because if the curves do not touch, AC is not covered, while if they intersect so that the revenue curve cuts through the AC curve, there will be certain output levels at which excess profits can be earned. A horizontal revenue curve can be tangent to a ⌣-shaped LRAC curve only at the lowest point of the latter, and thus tangency is obtained at the point of lowest LRAC.

Identity of Lowest Average Cost for All Firms in the Industry

The reasoning of the preceding paragraphs applies to all firms in the industry. Thus, when equilibrium is attained, price must equal the figure of lowest LRAC for each firm. Therefore, since there is a single market price for the commodity, LRAC must be identical for all firms. The apparent contradiction between this conclusion and common knowledge about differences in the costs of various firms can be explained. In any given period, in which long-run adjustments have not been completed, the statement is not applicable. Many apparent cost differences are short-run phenomena which would disappear over a longer period, since firms having high costs because of obsolete techniques or poor management must either lower their costs or go out of business.

Those firms which appear to have lower costs because of particularly good resources or higher than average management ability do not actually have lower cost schedules if all implicit cost elements are taken into consideration. The owners of superior factor units can command a higher price for them if they are supplied to other firms than is paid for standard-quality units. The price differential will, in general, reflect the difference in efficiency. Hence the implicit costs to the firm using superior factor units are higher than those of firms using standard units, and average cost, including both explicit and implicit elements, is not lower for firms using superior units. A farmer whose land is particularly fertile will have lower labor and capital costs per unit of output than other farmers, but he could rent the land to others at a figure based upon its yield at a price considerably in excess of the rent which could be obtained by the owners of poor land. The rent element in his total cost will be greater by the amount of the reduction in his other costs resulting from the use of the good land, and his average cost will be the same as that of neighbors using poorer land.

Nature of the Supply Schedules

The nature of the long-run industry supply schedule depends on the cost conditions in which the industry operates.

Constant Cost Industries. As explained in the preceding section, once long-run adjustments are complete, each firm will of necessity be operating at the point of lowest LRAC. Therefore, each firm will be supplying to the market the quantity of output which it can produce at the lowest possible LRAC. At a price equal to lowest LRAC, the potential *total* supply—taking into consideration changes in the number of firms in the industry—appears to be infinite, if the industry is one of constant cost. In such conditions, total output will in the long run increase to equal the quantity demanded. Should output be less than this amount temporarily, price will exceed AC, and new firms will enter the industry. As a result, market supply will increase and drive the market price down to the AC level. Hence the long-run supply curve for the entire industry—the curve showing the total potential amounts which will be supplied by all firms at various prices—may be represented by a horizontal line, as shown in Figure 8-11. At lower prices, nothing will

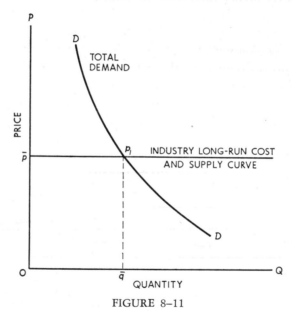

FIGURE 8–11

LONG-RUN EQUILIBRIUM, CONSTANT COST INDUSTRY

be supplied in the long run since the firms cannot cover AC. Higher prices are of no significance, since prices in the long-run period cannot remain above AC. The industry long-run supply curve is identical with the long-run cost curve for the industry—the curve showing the locations of the lowest points of the LRAC curves for the firms in the industry with various amounts of total output of the industry. The actual quantity that will be forthcoming on the market—as distinguished from the potential quantity—in each time interval after long-run adjustments have been completed is indicated by the point of intersection of the demand curve with the industry supply curve ($\bar{q}$ in Figure 8–11).

Increasing Cost Industries. In an industry of increasing cost conditions, the entry of new firms into the industry will raise the cost schedules of all firms by increasing the prices paid for certain factor units or giving rise to certain diseconomies. Accordingly, the height of the lowest cost figure for the firms depends upon the total output of the industry, and will shift as the total output changes.

At price levels lower than LRAC at the minimum output of the industry, nothing at all would be produced, and thus the long-run supply would be zero. At a price level equal to minimum LRAC, and at each price level higher than this, the total quantity supplied would be the amount which would allow AC to equal price. If total output were less, AC would be less than price, so new firms would enter the industry and increase total output. If total output were greater, AC would exceed price, some firms would leave the industry, and the decline in total output would reduce AC.

In Table 8–3 the relationship between the long-run industry cost

TABLE 8-3

LONG-RUN INDUSTRY COST SCHEDULE AND SUPPLY SCHEDULE,
INCREASING COST INDUSTRY

COST SCHEDULE		SUPPLY SCHEDULE	
Total Output for the Industry (Units)	Point of Lowest Long-Run Average Cost for Each Firm (Cents)	Price of the Product (Cents)	Total Quantity Supplied (Units)
1,000,000	25	25	1,000,000
2,000,000	30	30	2,000,000
3,000,000	35	35	3,000,000
4,000,000	40	40	4,000,000

schedule and the long-run industry supply schedule in an increasing cost industry is shown. In Figure 8–12 the industry cost and supply curve is illustrated. With these data, if the total output of the industry were 1,000,000 units, the figure of lowest AC for the firms would be 25 cents. Thus, if the price on the market were 25 cents, over a period of time output would adjust to the 1,000,000 figure, since any larger quantity would result in an excess of cost over price, and any smaller quantity would result in excess profits. If the price were 30 cents, industry output would adjust to 2,000,000 units because with this output, AC would equal price. The same reasoning applies to other price levels.

In this situation the industry supply curve slopes upward from left

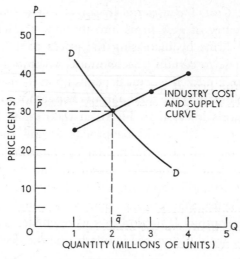

FIGURE 8–12

INDUSTRY COST AND SUPPLY CURVE, INCREASING COST INDUSTRY

to right (Figure 8–12), since the level of AC is higher for successively larger volumes of total output. As in constant cost conditions, the industry cost and supply curves are identical since, at each price level, total industry supply will adjust to the level at which $AC = LRMC = P$.

The third possible case is a decreasing cost industry, one in which the cost schedules of the firms fall as the total output of the industry increases. However, this case is, from all indications, of no practical importance, and it is not worthwhile to develop a detailed analysis.[1]

The Long-Run Equilibrium Price

The long-run equilibrium price is the figure at which the quantity demanded is equal to the long-period supply, the quantity that will be supplied continuously in a given time interval after long-run adjustments are complete. At higher prices, total output would exceed the quantity demanded; at lower prices an insufficient amount would be produced to meet the quantity that persons wished to buy. In Figure 8–12 the long-run equilibrium price level is $\bar{p}$, defined by the intersection of the demand curve with the long-period supply curve, which

[1] The industry cost curve (as shown in Figure 8–13), which slopes downward from left to right, can in this case also be regarded as a supply curve. At each point on the cost curve, the potential supply extends outward to infinity from the point on the cost curve; quantities less than the figure indicated by the point on the cost curve cannot be supplied at the particular price figure, since average cost would be higher than the price. The actual

is, of course, identical with the industry cost curve—the curve which shows the locations of the lowest LRAC figures of the firms with various levels of output for the industry.

In terms of the cost schedules of the individual firms, the long-run equilibrium price level is the figure of lowest possible LRAC, with the cost schedule of the firm at the level appropriate to the figure of total industry output. In a constant cost industry, lowest LRAC and the long-run equilibrium price (which is equal to lowest LRAC) are the same regardless of the demand for the product and the output of the industry. In an increasing cost industry, the greater the demand for the product, and thus the long-run equilibrium output of the industry, the higher will be the cost schedules of the firm, the figure of lowest LRAC, and the long-run equilibrium price. The equilibrium price is, of course, also equal to the LRMC figures of the firms, and to SRMC with the plants of optimum (lowest cost) size.

THE ADJUSTMENT OF MARKET PRICE TO THE LONG-RUN EQUILIBRIUM LEVEL

At any particular time, market price tends toward the short-run equilibrium level as a result of output adjustments with existing plants. But even if price is at the short-run equilibrium level, changes in plant capacities of existing firms and in the number of firms in the industry will lead to more or less continuous price and output adjustments until market price reaches the long-run equilibrium level. The adjustment

---

quantity that would come on the market would be determined by the intersection of the demand curve with the cost curve, and the price indicated by this intersection (point p in Figure 8–13) is the long-run equilibrium price.

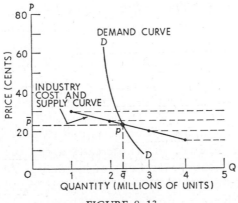

FIGURE 8–13

INDUSTRY COST AND SUPPLY CURVE, DECREASING COST INDUSTRY

toward equilibrium may be illustrated by considering the effects of a change in demand and a change in cost.

Readjustment to a Change in Demand

The explanation of readjustments in response to a change in demand is facilitated if it is assumed that long-run equilibrium has been attained prior to the demand change (as illustrated in Figure 8–14),

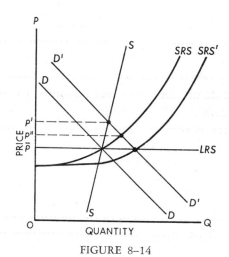

FIGURE 8–14

ADJUSTMENT OF PRICE AND OUTPUT IN RESPONSE TO A DEMAND INCREASE, CONSTANT COST INDUSTRY

price being at the level $\bar{p}$. The adjustment can be broken down into several steps:

1. *Rise in market price.* When the demand for the product increases from DD to $D'D'$, market price rises immediately, since at the old price the quantity demanded exceeds the quantity supplied. Buyers will be unable to obtain as many units as they wish at the old price, and will bid the price up. Equality of market demand and market supply will be attained at a price of p'. At this level, however, the market price exceeds both the short-run and the long-run equilibrium levels.

2. *Increase in output and decline in market price to the short-run equilibrium level.* The rise in price creates a gap between price and marginal cost at the current level of industry output. As a consequence, firms will increase output in order to reestablish equality of price and marginal cost with their existing plants. Therefore the market period supply curve will move to the right, and market price will fall until it

reaches the new short-run equilibrium level, p'', in Figure 8–14. Because of the upward slope of the short-run supply curve, which in turn is due to the higher marginal cost of additional output produced with existing plants, the new short-run equilibrium price will be higher than p. When market price reaches the short-run figure, quantity demanded will equal the current rate of output, with the given number of firms and plant.

3. Increase in the number of firms in the industry, and decline in market price to the long-run equilibrium level.

Even when short-run adjustments are complete, price will exceed average cost; new firms will enter the industry, raise market supply, and bring market price down to the long-run equilibrium figure. The new market supply curves are omitted from Figure 8–14, but the new *SRS* curve is shown as *SRS'*.

If the industry is one of constant cost (as is assumed in Figure 8–14), the new long-run equilibrium price will be at the same level, $\bar{p}$, as prevailed prior to the demand increase. But the output of the industry will be greater, in response to the greater demand.

On the other hand, if the industry is one of increasing cost (see Figure 8–15), an increase in output of the industry as a whole will raise the cost schedules of the firms. Accordingly, the new long-run equilibrium price will be somewhat higher than the old (i.e., $\bar{p}'$ rather than $\bar{p}$ in Figure 8–15).

If the demand for a commodity falls, the adjustment is in the

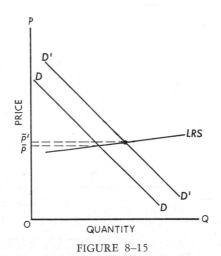

FIGURE 8–15

ADJUSTMENT OF PRICE AND OUTPUT IN RESPONSE TO A DEMAND INCREASE, INCREASING COST INDUSTRY

opposite direction. Market price falls, and firms reduce short-run output. Market supply shifts to the left and the price adjusts upward to the new short-run equilibrium figure, which is less than the original market price. But price is still less than average cost, and some firms leave the industry. Market supply shifts still more, and price is driven down to the long-run equilibrium level. The new long-run equilibrium price is less than the original price if the industry is one of increasing cost, but the same if constant cost conditions prevail.

The adjustments outlined above are, of course, oversimplified. The basic determinants of cost, including factor prices, methods of production, etc., are themselves subject to change, and thus the long-run equilibrium price may change independently of changes in rates of output. As a consequence, market price may rarely reach the level of long-run equilibrium, which itself is constantly changing. The analysis is meaningful, nevertheless, because the direction of movement in market price in any period is controlled by the relationship between the prevailing market price and the short-run and long-run equilibrium price levels.

Adjustments to Cost Changes

When an increase in cost occurs, there is no immediate effect on market price unless the reservation prices of sellers or demand prices of buyers are affected by the expectation that the cost increase will lead eventually to increases in price. However, the cost increase will affect both short-run and long-run equilibrium levels and so will lead ultimately to increases in price, once adjustments have occurred in output and in the number of firms. In the short-run period, firms will contract output, since the cost increase will raise MC above price. Thus the short-run equilibrium price level will be higher, but by an amount less than the cost increase per unit of product, since reductions in output reduce MC. Once short-run adjustments are complete, market price will have risen by a sum less than the amount of the cost increase per unit of product. But AC is not yet covered; so over a period of time the number of firms will decline, and market price will rise until it again equals AC. In a constant cost industry, as illustrated in Figure 8–16, AC will ultimately rise by the amount of the cost increase (per unit of output). In an increasing cost industry (Figure 8–17) the AC schedules of the firms will fall as the output of the industry declines. The ultimate price increase will be somewhat less than the amount of the cost increase. In a decreasing cost industry the rise will be greater than the amount of the cost increase. In all cases, output will be less than it was prior to the cost

LONG-RUN ADJUSTMENT OF PRICE TO COST INCREASE

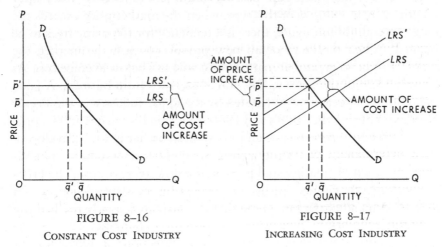

FIGURE 8–16

CONSTANT COST INDUSTRY

FIGURE 8–17

INCREASING COST INDUSTRY

increase. The relative output reduction will be greatest in a decreasing cost industry and least in one of increasing cost conditions.

IMPERFECTIONS IN ADJUSTMENTS IN PURELY COMPETITIVE INDUSTRIES

Our analysis of price and output determination in pure competition has been based on the assumption of an absence of imperfections which interfere with adjustments. Since imperfections are likely to be of considerable significance in some instances, reference to some leading examples is in order here.

Knowledge of Future Prices and Time Lags in Supply Adjustments

In industries with large numbers of small producers, lack of knowledge of market conditions, coupled with the substantial time lag which often occurs between change in inputs and actual change in output reaching the market, may interfere seriously with market adjustments. Farmers, for example, must base output plans on prices prevailing at the time crops are planted. But they are unaware of the actions of other firms relative to output, and thus the total increase or decrease in output made by producers may prove to be too large or too small, relative to demand, when crops actually reach the market.

An extreme example of time lapse in the production process is in the growing of certain types of fruit. Apple and walnut trees, for example, do not reach full bearing until ten to twenty years after planting. In an industry of this type, when the market price exceeds the long-run equilibrium figure, there is a tendency for too many trees to be planted. When the crops of all new producers reach the market, the supply will be so great that market price will fall below average cost. As a result, some of the firms will be forced to retire from business. A good example of this reaction is provided by the apple industry in the Pacific Northwest during the 1920's and 1930's. During the early 1920's, apple prices exceeded average cost, and many new orchards were developed. By the end of the 1920's the increased supply from the new orchards began to reach the market, and prices fell below average cost. The problem was greatly aggravated by the general business depression, which reduced demand at the same time that the increased supply reached the market.

The Cobweb Theorem

A similar reaction, but one of a recurrent nature, occurs frequently with crops that require only one season to reach maturity. If price exceeds average cost at harvest time in any year, the next year's crop may be so large that when it comes to market the price falls below average cost. As a result, in the following year, production may be reduced so much that price will rise above average cost, and so on. This model is known as the cobweb theorem.[2]

For purposes of illustration, suppose that during the current year potato prices exceed average cost. As a result, next year many farmers will shift acreage from other crops to potatoes. When next year's crop is harvested, market supply will be considerably greater than it is this year. The increase may be so great that market price will fall below

[2] The name originates from the appearance of the graphical presentation of price-quantity behavior in a situation of this sort. Figure 8–18A, below, illustrates a case in which the amplitude of the excessive production in alternate years is declining. The RR curve is similar to the usual demand curve; it shows the quantities that will be purchased at various prices in a particular year or, in other words, the prices at which various quantities placed on the market can be sold. Curve TT shows the quantities that will be produced and placed on the market in the second year, on the basis of various prices prevailing during the first year; it is not the same as the usual supply curve. If, in the first year, the actual market price (determined by that year's current supply-demand relationships) is p^1, the quantity that will be supplied the next year is s^1, as indicated by the TT curve. But in the second year, because of the increased supply, the price will fall to p^2. Supply the following year will then be s^2, and price will rise to p^3, only to fall to p^4 the next year, and so on. Eventually, final equilibrium will tend to be reached at price $\bar{p}$ and quantity $\bar{s}$, since each year the amplitude of the fluctuations grows less. Figure 8–18B illustrates a case in which the RR and TT curves have the same shape, so that the fluc-

average cost. As a result, the following year potato acreage will be reduced substantially as farmers shift back to other crops. The reduction may be so great that prices will again rise above average cost and lead to another excessive increase in supply.

Other Imperfections

Knowledge of Cost. Another source of imperfection is lack of knowledge by sellers of their costs. The typical production unit in pure competition is small; the average farmer, for example, has very incomplete records and inadequate knowledge of his costs. As a result, output is frequently not adjusted to the level which will maximize profit, and short-run supply is different from what it would be if farmers calculated marginal cost carefully.

Immobility of Farmers. Another source of imperfection is the unwillingness of small producers, particularly farmers, to abandon farming and turn to other types of activity when they are unable to cover costs. They frequently are not skilled in other lines of work; job opportunities may not be plentiful; personal attachment to farming may prevent them from leaving even though prices are far below average cost. Farmers will typically shift quickly from one crop to another in response to relative price and profit situations, but they are very slow to leave farming entirely. As a consequence, when prices of large numbers of farm products fall below average cost, readjustment to long-run equilibrium is very slow.

Governmental Interference. A new type of imperfection has been introduced in recent years by federal agricultural aid programs. The

tuations continue indefinitely at the same amplitude; Figure 8–18C shows the case in which the fluctuations grow in amplitude, since the slope of the RR curve is greater than that of the TT curve. There is no evidence that this case will be found in practice.

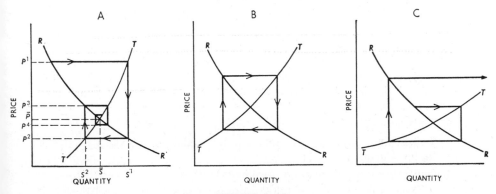

FIGURE 8–18
ILLUSTRATION OF THE COBWEB THEOREM

federal government has sought to prevent prices of various farm products from falling below certain levels by purchasing the commodities. Such programs obviously interfere with supply adjustments and serve to perpetuate maladjustments in allocation of farm land to various crops. When production becomes excessive in certain lines, consequent price declines should bring about a reduction in production. But if the government artificially holds prices up, the supply adjustment fails to occur.

Lack of Complete Control over Output. Finally, the influence of climatic conditions upon crop yield, and the consequent inability of the farmer to control exactly the volume of his output by varying his factor inputs, interferes with the attainment of equilibrium prices and causes substantial price fluctuations unrelated to adjustments toward equilibrium levels.

SELECTED REFERENCES

BRENNAN, M. J. *Theory of Economic Statics,* chaps. xii, xiii, xiv. Englewood Cliffs, N.J.: Prentice-Hall, 1965.

CHAMBERLIN, E. H. *The Theory of Monopolistic Competition,* chaps. i, ii. Cambridge: Harvard University Press, 1933.

COHEN, K. J., AND CYERT, R. M. *Theory of the Firm,* chaps. iv, vi, viii. Englewood Cliffs, N.J.: Prentice-Hall, 1965.

QUESTIONS

1. What is the nature of the AR curve of the individual seller in a purely competitive market? Explain.
2. Explain the concept of a supply function.
3. Does the analysis of pricing in purely competitive markets assume that the sellers have perfect knowledge of total demand and supply functions? Explain.
4. Illustrate graphically the AR curve of an individual seller in pure competition, and the total demand curve for the product of the industry.
5. Explain the concept of market period. For what types of products is the concept of the market period, as distinguished from the short-run period, significant?
6. Explain the determinants of market supply.
7. Explain the effect on the market supply schedule of a sudden flooding of land producing the product.
8. Explain the term "reservation price."
9. Why will sellers tend to hold their crops if the present price is relatively low?
10. Why is the market supply curve perfectly inelastic above a certain point?
11. What is the significance of cost of production for market supply?

12. Draw a supply curve of Christmas trees on the evening before Christmas, assuming a purely competitive market.

13. Suppose that the actual market price is temporarily above the equilibrium market price figure. Explain how it will be brought down to the latter.

14. What is meant by the short-run supply function?

15. *a*) Why must price cover AVC if firms are to continue to operate?
    b) If firms are covering AVC but not all of their fixed costs, will they continue to operate in the short-run period? Why or why not?
    c) Why is it possible for price to remain above average cost in the short-run period?
    d) Why must price equal marginal cost in the short-run period?

16. Explain the relationship between the schedule of marginal cost and the short-period supply function.

17. If market price is above the short-run equilibrium level, by what process will it be brought down to the latter? What determines the length of time which this adjustment will take?

18. Why is the output level at which marginal revenue is equal to marginal cost the level at which profits are maximized?

19. On the basis of the data given below, determine the supply schedule of the firm in the short-run period.

Output	Total Variable Cost	Output	Total Variable Cost
1....................	$22	6.................	$ 85
2....................	32	7.................	115
3....................	40	8.................	155
4....................	50	9.................	205
5....................	65	10................	310

20. Why does the short-run supply curve slope upward from left to right? Why does it start from the vertical axis at a higher point than the market supply curve?

21. Explain the long-run adjustments of an individual firm.

22. Why, if long-run adjustments are complete, will firms in purely competitive markets of necessity operate at the point of lowest average cost?

23. Why, in an increasing cost industry, is the long-run industry supply curve identical to the long-run industry cost curve?

24. Draw the long-run supply curve for the industry on the basis of the cost data given below:

Total Output of Industry	Lowest Average Cost Figure for Each Firm
500,000.........................	$47
1,000,000.........................	52
1,500,000.........................	55
2,000,000.........................	59
2,500,000.........................	63
3,000,000.........................	66

25. What determines the actual long-run output in a constant cost industry, as distinguished from the potential output?

26. Trace carefully, step by step, the effect of a decrease in demand upon (*a*) market price immediately after the change, (*b*) short-run equilibrium price and output, and (*c*) long-run equilibrium price and output, in a constant cost industry.

27. Why, in an increasing cost industry, will price (over a long-run period) rise by an amount less than the amount of a tax levied on the output?

28. Under what circumstances, in pure competition, is price dependent upon demand considerations alone? Upon cost considerations alone? Illustrate graphically.

29. Explain the cobweb theorem. If you were a farmer producing a product whose price is subject to cobweb-theorem fluctuations, what could you do to increase your profits, from a long-run standpoint, provided other farmers do not do the same thing?

30. Why do the present farm programs, designed to hold farm prices up to certain percentages of "parity," interfere with the attainment of long-run equilibrium in the industries? Illustrate graphically.

31. Why does wartime price control give rise to the need for rationing? Illustrate graphically.

32. Why do many farm products fluctuate greatly in price from year to year?

Chapter 9

NONPURELY COMPETITIVE MARKETS: MONOPOLY

Nonpurely competitive models of price and output determination are designed to deal with a broad spectrum of market situations—all situations, indeed, that are considered to lie outside the purview of purely competitive models. Because the empirical significance of purely competitive models is commonly believed to be slight, it would appear that the range of application of nonpurely competitive models is extremely wide. In a potential sense, this is true. But as the situation now stands, the nonpurely competitive models are by no means entirely adequate for analysis of particular industries and for recommendations for public policy. Nevertheless they can make significant contributions to an understanding of the nonpurely competitive industries.

NONPURELY COMPETITIVE MODELS: GENERAL CONSIDERATIONS

As noted in the last chapter, the essential condition for pure competition is that sellers regard price as a parameter, the value of which is determined by forces outside their control. Conversely, the distinctive characteristic of nonpurely competitive markets is that individual sellers consider themselves able by one means or another to exert a perceptible influence on market price—e.g., by varying quantity offered for sale, by engaging in advertising or other sales promotion activities, by lobbying for favorable legislation, by buying out or otherwise eliminating competing sellers, etc. The average revenue functions of purely competitive sellers are defined by a single parameter—market prices; central attention is then focused on the analysis of output decisions of individual sellers. The average revenue functions of nonpurely competitive sellers, however, involve both price and sales as variables, and are influenced by a number of considerations. Accord-

181

ingly, a central problem in the general theory of nonpurely competitive markets is to explain the average revenue functions of individual sellers, that is, the functional relationships, as seen by the sellers, between the amounts placed on the market and the prices at which these amounts can be sold.

The definition of empirically relevant and theoretically consistent average revenue functions is a particularly difficult problem in oligopolistic markets where sellers are so few that the revenue prospects of each seller necessarily depend directly on the actions, anticipated as well as overt, of all other sellers. Such mutual interdependence cannot be entirely ignored even in situations of monopoly and monopolistic competition, but the phenomenon is not of sufficient importance in such situations to require explicit theoretical attention. Sooner or later, of course, we must consider the problem of mutual interdependence of revenue estimates. We begin our discussion of nonpurely competitive markets, however, with the simpler cases of monopoly and monopolistic competition.

Average Revenue and Marginal Revenue

The average revenue function of the firm may be regarded as the demand function for the product of the firm; viewed in the former sense, the function indicates the revenue per unit which can be obtained if various amounts of product are placed on the market; viewed in the latter sense, the function indicates the quantities which the firm can sell at various possible prices. As noted in the previous chapter, the concept of marginal revenue is defined as the additional to total revenue resulting from the sale of additional units of output. Table 9–1 shows a hypothetical demand schedule for the product of the firm and the related revenue schedule, including marginal revenue.

The data in Table 9–1 are illustrated graphically in Figure 9–1. The demand curve for the product of the firm and the AR curve are identical in form, since the two schedules contain the same data, viewed in two different ways.

With the schedule shown in Table 9–1, average revenue declines as additional units are placed on the market; hence marginal revenue is less than average revenue for all units except the first. In the related graph (Figure 9–1), therefore, the MR curve lies below the AR curve and declines at a more rapid rate. Each additional unit sold adds less to total revenue than the price (average revenue) received for it, since the price on all units must be lowered to allow additional units to be sold. In the example, in order to sell eight tires instead of seven, the firm

TABLE 9-1

DEMAND SCHEDULE AND REVENUE SCHEDULE OF A SERVICE STATION FOR
TIRES, STANDARD GRADE, PER DAY

DEMAND SCHEDULE FOR TIRES FROM THE FIRM		REVENUE SCHEDULE			
Price (Dollars)	Number of Tires Purchased by Customers	Number of Tires Sold by Firm	Total Revenue (Dollars)	Average Revenue (Dollars)	Marginal Revenue (Dollars)
17	0	1	16	16	16
16	1	2	30	15	14
15	2	3	42	14	12
14	3	4	52	13	10
13	4	5	60	12	8
12	5	6	66	11	6
11	6	7	70	10	4
10	7	8	72	9	2
9	8	9	72	8	0
8	9	10	70	7	− 2
7	10	11	66	6	− 4
6	11				

must lower the price from $10 to $9; thus, while the eighth tire sells for $9, it adds only $2 (the difference between $70 and $72) to the total revenue of the firm, since seven tires could have been sold for $10 apiece instead of $9.

When the demand schedule for the product of a firm is elastic (elasticity greater than one), marginal revenue will be positive, because

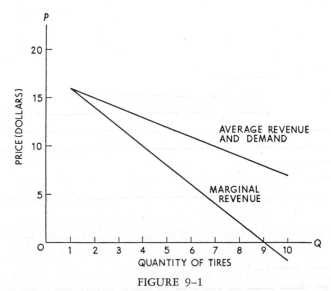

FIGURE 9-1

DEMAND AND REVENUE SCHEDULES FOR A FIRM SELLING TIRES

total revenue is greater at lower prices (and large sales volumes) than at higher prices (and smaller sales volumes). In other words, each additional unit sold will add a positive amount to total revenue. However, when a demand schedule is inelastic, marginal revenue will be negative (at eleven tires in Table 9–1), because the price reduction necessary to sell an additional unit is relatively greater than the quantity increase, and total revenue falls. The total price reduction on units which could have been sold at a higher price exceeds the price received from the sale of an additional unit. If the demand schedule is of unitary elasticity, marginal revenue is zero. The relationship between the elasticity of the demand schedule and marginal revenue is shown in Figure 9–2.

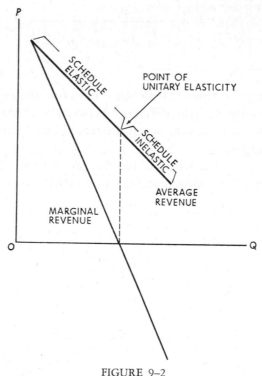

FIGURE 9–2

THE RELATIONSHIP BETWEEN THE ELASTICITY OF AVERAGE
REVENUE AND THE NATURE OF MARGINAL REVENUE

PRICE AND OUTPUT DETERMINATION: UNREGULATED MONOPOLY

Monopoly is defined for purposes of economic analysis as a situation in which a single firm supplies the entire quantity of a good

offered to buyers in a particular market. Monopoly is virtually nonexistent in basic manufacturing industries at this time, but was fairly
common around the turn of the last century—in steel, tobacco,
aluminum, and other areas. It occurs most commonly now in regulated
public utilities and in particular geographical areas where transport
costs or similar factors allow a local seller (e.g., a lumber supply firm or
a lawyer) to act as a monopolist within a certain range of prices.

Since every commodity has a number of more or less close
substitutes, monopoly does not imply complete absence of competition
from other commodities; but it does imply an absence of competing
sellers in the particular market, and a relatively low cross-elasticity of
demand between the product and other products. The lack of seller
competition leads us to emphasize aspects of market behavior different
from those emphasized in our analysis of pure competition, and also to
extend our argument to include certain kinds of activities (e.g.,
advertising and price discrimination) that are entirely absent in purely
competitive markets. Our treatment of monopoly is nevertheless similar
in broad outline to our treatment of pure competition. Analogies
between the two kinds of market situation and major differences will be
emphasized.

Monopoly Price Determination in the Market Period

The concept of a market period is defined for monopoly, just as for
pure competition, as an interval of time so short that adjustments in
output are impractical. We assume a given output rate, not a given
stock of goods on hand, as in the market period purely competitive
model. If, as is usually assumed, the monopolist deals directly with his
customers and so sets his own "asking" price, the price that he sets will
be the market price, and demand conditions will be important only
insofar as they affect the monopolist's view of future revenue prospects.

If quantity demanded at the current price is greater than the firm's
current output, the monopolist may either meet demand by selling from
previously accumulated stock, or choke off excess demand by increasing
his asking (and the market) price. Which alternative is adopted will
depend on the relative advantages of each policy as estimated by the
monopolist. If the monopolist believes that demand is currently
running at an abnormally high level, for example, he may meet it at the
prevailing price in order to maintain the goodwill of his customers and
avoid possible expenditures associated with revisions in price. If the
current level of demand is considered to be permanent, however, the
monopolist will probably raise his asking price, the exact amount

depending on his estimate of demand elasticity, the danger of attracting attention from antitrust authorities, the possibility that high prices may encourage buyers to gravitate towards substitute commodities offered for sale in other markets, etc.

Similar considerations apply in situations in which quantity demanded at the prevailing market price exceeds current output. The monopolist may either hold price at its current level and watch his inventories mount, or cut price in an attempt to reduce storage and other current costs.

Short-Run Pricing—the Average Revenue Function of a Monopolist

The decision problem of the monopolist in a short-run period, i.e., a period sufficiently long to permit output to be adjusted with existing plant, is to choose a profit-maximizing level of output such that MR = MC. Thus the formal decision problem of the monopolist is the same as that of a purely competitive seller. There is a practical difference, however, for whereas a competitive seller, knowing the current market price, can easily estimate his average revenue—and so his marginal revenue—corresponding to any level of sales, a monopoly seller may find accurate estimation difficult if not impossible.

The only objective basis on which a monopolist can arrive at an estimate of his revenue prospects is by referring to past information about actual sales at various prices. If demand conditions are completely stable over time, a little experimentation with different asking prices will provide an accurate impression of the position of the market demand curve and its elasticity in the neighborhood of previously observed price-sales points. If demand conditions fluctuate constantly (because of changes in prices in other markets, changes in aggregate economic activity, changes in preferences, etc.), the monopolist can form only a rough estimate of the probable position and form of the short-period demand function; hence, the average revenue function on which his marginal revenue calculations are based will be largely conjectural.

The Determination of Short-Run Equilibrium Output and Price. With the assumption that the monopolist arrives at an estimate of the relevant short-period average revenue function, we may describe the determination of equilibrium levels of output and price in terms of the relations shown diagramatically in Figure 9–3. The average revenue function of the monopolist is represented by the line *AR;* the marginal revenue function corresponding to the given average revenue function

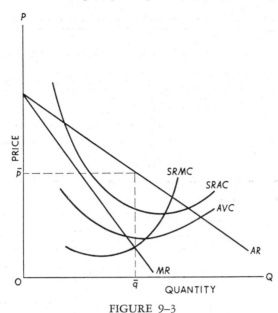

FIGURE 9–3

SHORT-RUN ADJUSTMENT OF PRICE AND OUTPUT BY A MONOPOLIST

is therefore defined by the line *MR*. The factors governing short-period costs of production are assumed to be the same as for an individual seller operating under conditions of pure competition; thus we may regard the short-period variable cost function as given, and assume that it defines the average variable cost curve *AVC* and the corresponding short-run marginal cost curve *SRMC*. Finally, we obtain short-run average cost curve *SRAC* by adding average fixed cost to average variable cost at each possible level of output.

Given the relations shown in Figure 9–3, the short-period equilibrium level of output, $\bar{q}$, is defined by the intersection of the curve *MR* with the curve *MC:* i.e., by the requirement that output be such that *MR = MC,* provided *AVC* is covered. The short-period equilibrium price is then defined by the given *AR* curve as that value of price, $\bar{p}$, at which buyers will be willing to purchase the quantity of output $\bar{q}$ during the short period: i.e., the price at which short-period output will be just equal to short-period quantity demanded.

Differences and similarities with the purely competitive models should be noted. In monopoly as in competition, the equilibrium value of output is defined by the requirement that MR = MC. Since the AR curve of the monopolist is downward sloping rather than horizontal, marginal revenue is less than average revenue at the equilibrium level, whereas marginal revenue is equal to average revenue (and to market price) in pure competition.

An apparent difference between pure competition and monopoly is that the short-period equilibrium output of a monopolist, unlike the short-period equilibrium output of a competitive seller, is a determinant of rather than a function of market price. Thus our theory of monopoly output determination does not lead directly to a definition of the short-period supply function, as does the theory of competitive output determination. On closer inspection, however, it is clear that this supposed difference between pure competition and monopoly is more apparent than real. Under pure competition, there is *just one equilibrium value of output corresponding to any given average revenue function; the same is true in the theory of monopoly*. The supply curve of a competitive seller is generated by *varying* the position of the average revenue function; it indicates for each set of values of the parameters defining the average revenue function of an individual seller the corresponding equilibrium level of output. A similar relation could be established between the equilibrium output of a monopolist and various levels of the parameters that define the monopolist's average revenue function. But such a function is not particularly useful for purposes of analysis and thus is not typically established.

A final point of possible difference between monopoly and pure competition concerns the welfare implications of the fact that price exceeds marginal cost in short-period monopoly equilibrium, whereas price is equal to marginal cost under purely competitive conditions. Provided that the average revenue function of the monopolist accurately reflects actual market demand conditions, the failure to equate marginal cost with price implies a restriction of equilibrium output and an elevation of price as compared with the results that would obtain if the market were purely competitive. The implications of this finding are considered further in Chapter 21.

Long-Run Adjustments

So long as the situation remains one of complete monopoly, long-run price and output adjustments involve nothing more than readjustments by the firm to bring about equality of LRMC and MR, that is, adjustments in plant to a level such that MR = LRMC = SRMC at the long-run equilibrium level of output.

Maximum profits at a given time require operation at the level at which MC with the existing plant is equal to MR. But over a longer period of time, it may be possible to increase profits by adjusting plant size. When this adjustment is complete, MR will be equal both to LRMC and SRMC. Failure to attain equality of MR and LRMC would indicate failure to complete all plant adjustments which are profitable. Failure to attain equality of SRMC and MR would indicate failure to operate at the most profitable output level with the plant constructed. Figure 9–4 indicates the long-run adjustment. Initially, with plant size *D,* the firm produces $\bar{q}_s$ units (for equality of *MR* and *SRMC* with plant *D*) and sets a price of $\bar{p}_s$. But *MR* does not equal *LRMC* at the point of most profitable operation, because the plant is too small relative to the demand for the product. Accordingly, the firm increases its plant to size *H,* with a new

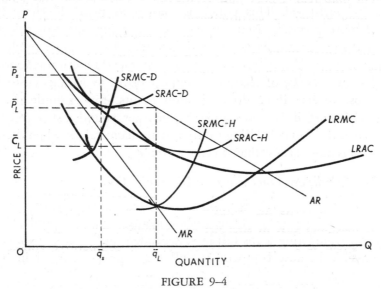

FIGURE 9–4

LONG-RUN ADJUSTMENT OF A MONOPOLIST

SRAC curve *SRAC–H.* With this plant, *MR = SRMC = LRMC* at the point of most profitable operation ($\bar{q}_L$).

Under the assumptions of monopoly, no new firms can enter the industry, and thus no other long-run adjustments will take place. As Figure 9–4 is drawn, the monopolist earns excess profits per unit of output equal to the difference between $\bar{p}_L$ and $\overline{C}_L$. However, a monopolist may or may not have sufficient sales potential to earn more than a normal return on invested capital. Should a monopolist have such a limited sales volume that he cannot earn even a normal return, he will, of course, eventually liquidate the business. Monopoly position in itself is no guarantee of excess profits. If demand is inadequate, lack of competitors is of little benefit to a seller.

PRICE DISCRIMINATION

The preceding discussion is based on the assumption that the firm sells a given product to all buyers at the same price. Under monopoly conditions, however, such a policy is not necessary, and may not be optimal. Some purchasers will be willing to buy at higher prices than others, and most individual purchasers will buy more at lower prices than at higher prices. Thus a monopolist may find it profitable to discriminate among various buyers, charging higher prices to those willing to pay more, and charging individual buyers on a sliding scale for units purchased. This policy is known as price discrimination, defined more precisely as the practice of charging different prices to various customers not in accord with differences in costs of producing and handling goods sold to the various customers. Discrimination thus includes the practice of charging identical prices to various customers when costs differ. Price discrimination occurs, for example, if two buyers are charged 10 cents and 15 cents per pound respectively for sugar when the costs of selling to the two are identical, or when the cost difference is more or less than 5 cents a pound.

The Conditions Necessary for Discrimination

First, discrimination is possible only with monopoly, or if members of a small group of firms follow identical pricing policies. If a number of competing firms follow independent policies, discrimination is impossible because competitors will shade prices charged in high-price markets.

Second, discrimination is possible only if resale from one market to another is impractical; otherwise, goods will flow from the low-price market to the high-price market. Transportation costs may prevent resale. In the diagram below, for example, a monopoly producer located at A may charge a differentially higher price in market B than in market C, up to the amount of the $B-C$ freight rate. Tariff barriers may prevent the return of commodities sold cheaply in a foreign market.

MONOPOLY
PRODUCER
MARKET   MARKET

B————————————A————————————C

The nature of the product may prevent resale; medical service, for example, is not transferable. Finally, resale may be prevented by contractual agreements forced upon the low-price buyer.

The Profitability of Discrimination

As suggested above, discrimination is advantageous because some buyers are willing to pay more for a commodity than others, and because some buyers are willing to pay more for initial units than for subsequent units. One person may be willing to pay $4,000 for an automobile, while another buyer will take the same car only at $3,000; and the first buyer may be induced to acquire a second car only if he can get it for $2,000. If a single, uniform price is charged, some buyers will be pushed out of the market completely, others will buy fewer units than they would at a lower figure, and many of those buying the product at the prevailing price would be willing to pay more for some of the units which they are currently buying. Discrimination is designed to gain additional revenue by varying the price in terms of the demand prices of customers.

Discrimination will be complete, or in the *first degree,* if it yields the maximum sum buyers will pay on each individual unit sold. Or it may be partial, or in the third degree, the buyers being grouped into major classes, and the prices varied according to the class.[1]

First-Degree Discrimination

First-degree discrimination requires that each buyer be induced to pay the maximum possible sum he is willing to pay for any given quantity rather than forgo use of the commodity entirely.

Suppose, for example, that a person will buy each week one gallon of gasoline if the price is $1.00 a gallon, five gallons at a price of 50 cents, and ten gallons if the price is 25 cents. The objective of perfect discrimination is to make him pay $1.00 for one gallon, 50 cents for the next four gallons, and 25 cents for the last five, and thus $4.25 instead of $2.50, which he would pay if he could obtain all ten gallons at a 25-cent figure. In this manner the buyer's individual demand schedule becomes the seller's schedule of marginal revenue from the particular buyer, since it indicates for each quantity the amount the buyer is willing to pay for the additional unit. The optimum amount to be sold to each buyer is that at which marginal cost (assuming it to be constant in the relevant range) is equal to marginal revenue from the sale to the particular buyer, determined as indicated above.

The charge set for the entire group of units sold the customer is

---

[1] The term *second-degree discrimination* is used by some writers for situations in which the seller sets a different price for each customer but does not fully exploit the potential demand prices of the customers.

the sum of the buyer demand prices for each successive unit ($4.25 in the example above), and the buyer is required to pay this sum and take the entire amount, under an all-or-nothing bargain. The buyer has only the choice of paying $4.25 for the ten units, or not buying the commodity at all, since the seller will not sell a smaller number of units to him. Or, in terms of the usual marginal revenue–marginal cost diagram, the monopolist extends production and sales up to the point at which his MC curve intersects the AR (demand) curve, since he can sell additional units at successively lower prices without lowering his price on all units sold. Thus the price charged all buyers except one will be greater than that indicated by the point on the AR curve at which MC = MR.

Market conditions obviously do not permit first-degree discrimination to be carried out to any significant extent. One example on a partial scale is to be found in the practice of doctors who vary charges to their customers according to income status. A breeder of fine horses, dealing individually with relatively uninformed buyers in different parts of the country, may be able to carry on perfect discrimination. But apart from such isolated cases, the analysis of first-degree discrimination is useful merely to illustrate a type of price-setting procedure which would be advantageous to the firm if it could be employed.

Third-Degree Discrimination

While firms can seldom exploit fully their profit possibilities in dealings with each buyer, not infrequently it is possible for a firm to segment its total market into several parts on the basis of demand prices and elasticities and charge different prices to different groups of buyers. Relatively high prices will be charged in segments of the market where demand is inelastic and relatively low prices in segments where demand is elastic. Accordingly, the firm can advantageously sell a larger quantity than under a uniform-price policy. Such a policy is known as *third-degree discrimination;* the optimum price is obtained from groups of buyers, rather than from each individual buyer.

When third-degree discrimination is possible, profits will be maximized by adjusting total output to the level at which the marginal cost of the entire output equals the sum of the marginal revenues in the various markets. Figure 9–5 illustrates the case of two markets. In market *A* the AR curve is *AR–A* and the MR curve, *MR–A;* in market *B* the two curves are *AR–B* and *MR–B,* respectively. Curves *AR–T* and *MR–T* show the sums of the AR and MR schedules, respectively, in the two markets. Total output will be $\bar{q}_T$, if profits are to be maximized, as de-

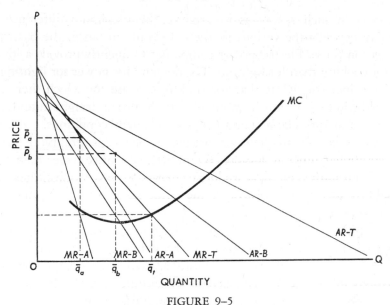

FIGURE 9–5

THIRD-DEGREE PRICE DISCRIMINATION

termined by the intersection of the MC curve (*MC*) and *MR–T*, the curve showing the sum of the marginal revenues in the two markets. The amount sold in each market ($\overline{q}_a$ and $\overline{q}_b$, respectively) is the quantity at which marginal revenue in the market is equal to *MC* at the output level at which *MC* and the sum of the marginal revenues are equal. This figure is indicated by the point of intersection of the MR curve of the market with a line drawn horizontally through the intersection of *MC* and *MR–T*.[2] The price charged in each market ($\overline{p}_a$ in *A*, $\overline{p}_b$ in *B*) is indicated by the point on the AR curve of the market directly above this intersection. It is, of course, the price at which the maximum profit output in the market can be sold. The greater the difference in the elasticities of the demand schedules in the various markets, the greater will be the price differences, and the larger the increase in profit resulting from discrimination. If demand elasticities are the same in all market segments, there can be no gain from discrimination.

The basis upon which markets are segregated depends primarily upon the nature of market conditions and the ability of the seller to prevent resale between market segments. The seller seeks to segregate

[2] The output sold in each market is *not* that at which marginal revenue in that market is equal to the marginal cost of producing the particular amount of output sold in that market; the significant marginal cost figure is that of the entire output sold in the two markets.

customers in such a way as to produce the maximum difference in elasticity between the various markets. In some instances the basis for segregation is use. Electric power companies frequently provide a lower rate for cooking than for lighting. The demand for power for lighting is relatively inelastic, while that for cooking—a use for which there are good substitutes—is much more elastic. Railroad freight rates vary among commodities largely on the basis of demand conditions.

A market is frequently segregated on a geographical basis. Products may be sold in a more distant area at a price lower than that charged near the site of production because more substitutes are available in distant areas or demand is more elastic because of competition.

A third basis is the direct segregation of customers on the basis of buying preferences and incomes by providing several brands of a product (sometimes physically identical), each intended for a certain buying group, with prices adjusted to reflect differences in the elasticity of demand. Price differentials may bear little relationship to cost differences. For example, seats in various portions of a theater are priced in a manner designed to attract different income groups. If a uniform price were charged, lower income groups would not come at all, and those in higher income groups would pay considerably less than they were willing to pay.

A fourth basis is the size of the order. Quantity discounts do not involve discrimination if they merely reflect differences in costs of handling transactions of various sizes; such discounts often exceed cost differences because sellers find it advantageous to make substantial price concessions to large buyers in order to obtain their business—concessions which are not necessary to sell to customers buying smaller amounts.

ADJUSTMENT OF PRODUCT AND SELLING ACTIVITIES

The discussion up to this point has assumed that the product is a standard item, not subject to variation, and that the firm does not engage in activities designed to affect the demand for the product. In other words, the quality and nature of the product and the consumer demand are parameters. Actually, however, both factors are subject to variation by the action of the firm, and the point of absolute maximum profit cannot be attained without optimum adjustment in both product and selling activities.

Adjustment of the Physical Product

Once the firm has selected the product or products it will produce, it must select the exact variety or quality of the product which allows maximum profit. With each potential form of the product, there is a certain cost schedule and a certain demand schedule, and thus a certain possible profit at the level of output for the product at which marginal revenue is equal to marginal cost. In general, the higher the quality of the product, the greater the potential sales at various prices; but the cost per unit for producing various quantities will also be higher. Some one form of the product, with optimum price and output levels for this form, will allow the greatest profit.

Unfortunately, it is very difficult for the firm to estimate sales corresponding to various forms of the product, because of the difficulty of predicting consumer reaction. Since experimentation is seldom feasible, the firm will be forced to select the particular form which, on the basis of rough estimates, appears to yield the greatest net return.

A firm is not, of course, limited to one particular quality; firms often find it advantageous to carry several different brands of the same product, with differences in quality and price. When a firm buys out a previous competitor, it may continue to produce the purchased brands, particularly if they have strongly attached buyers who will be in large measure lost to the firm if the line is abandoned. The provision of several different qualities enables the firm to utilize its plant more effectively, and to gain greater advantages of large-scale production. The importance of having a "full line" so that shoppers can satisfy their wishes for various types of items (colors and varieties of paints, for example) also may encourage the firm to carry a wider variety of qualities.

Selling Activities

Profit maximization also requires optimum adjustment of selling activities, designed to influence the schedule of demand. Costs incurred to carry on these activities are known as *selling costs,* as distinguished from production costs. In practice, a precise line cannot be drawn between the two classes of cost; expenses of packaging, for example, and the salaries of salesmen, fall partly into each category. But the classification is useful for purposes of analysis.

Selling activity, in turn, may be grouped into two major classes, quality-service competition and direct sales promotion. The former involves improving (or giving the impression of improving) the quality of the product, without altering its basic nature, or adding to the service rendered in conjunction with the sale of the product. A major aspect of quality-service competition is the emphasis placed upon style and deliberate changes in styles to make existing models prematurely obsolete. Whenever style can be emphasized, as for example, with women's clothes and automobiles, firms will deliberately change styles from year to year.

No sharp line can be drawn between the process of selection of the optimum physical product, as outlined above, and that of adjustment of quality and service as methods of increasing sales. Both actions affect sales and cost schedules and, if successful, increase the demand for the product. The distinction is essentially one of degree.

Almost universally in monopoly, as in all nonpurely competitive markets, even those with relatively standardized products, firms find it advantageous to increase their sales by advertising, using salesmen and other selling activities. Sales promotion, if successful, can raise the demand schedule for the product of the firm. Consequently, a greater volume can be sold at the existing price and lower production costs per unit obtained, or price can be raised and thus profit per unit increased. If the addition to total cost resulting from selling activities is less than the increase in receipts (net of any change in production cost), the profits of the firm will increase.

Sales promotion is effective primarily because consumers have very limited knowledge of the quality of the goods which they are buying, and their desires are subject to influence. They are not aware of many commodities and frequently have no satisfactory way of judging the relative desirability of products with which they are familiar. Furthermore, consumer wants are themselves subject to modification. Persons have certain basic desires—to eat, to have a place in which to live, etc. But the exact nature of the wants—whether they wish to eat meat or fruit, for example—is subject to change. Many persons have incomes well in excess of the amounts necessary to satisfy the basic needs of life. Great opportunity exists for producers to influence these persons to use a portion of their income to make "luxury" purchases.

The Level of Selling Activities. The adjustment of the level of selling activities is influenced by the manner in which sales react as expenditures on selling activities are increased—the "promotional elasticity" of advertising. Apparently, as a firm first increases sales effort, "returns" typically increase in the sense that additional dollars spent on advertising produce successively greater increases in sales. There are two reasons. In the first place, successful advertising requires repetition, in the sense that repeated suggestions are frequently necessary to influence the actions of the buyers. Thus, if total expenditures on advertising are small, they may have hardly any effect upon sales, but a relatively limited increase may produce a sharp increase in sales because of the repetition effect. Second, as selling expenditures are increased, more effective means can be used. Division of labor produces advantages in selling as well as in other forms of business activity. Advertising experts can be hired, and magazines and radio and television networks with nationwide coverage can be employed.

Eventually, however, it is inevitable that increasing returns must give way to decreasing returns, with additional dollars spent on sales promotion producing progressively smaller increases in sales. The economies will eventually be exhausted, as well as the exploitation of the best portions of the potential market. Additional sales can be made only to persons who are less interested in the product than those who bought it initially, and greater effort will be necessary to induce them to buy. Frequently, the additional customers will be more expensive to contact. The old customers can buy additional units only by sacrificing other purchases which offer greater utility than those forgone in order to buy the initial units of the good. To buy one automobile, a person may need to sacrifice only a portion of the year's savings and a trip to Florida. But to buy a second car, it might be necessary for him to forgo some of the food and clothing to which he has become accustomed.

Attainment of profit maximization requires the selection of the optimum-profit level of selling activities, as well as the most advantageous types. This level, however, cannot be determined independently of decisions on product, output, and price, since the level of selling activities which will maximize profit is not the same at all price levels. Likewise, price cannot be determined independently of the volume of selling activities, since the latter affects both cost and revenue schedules.

At each output level, successively larger selling expenditures will allow higher prices to be obtained but will also increase average cost. For each output level, there will be some level of selling activities at which the relationship between price and average cost will allow maximum profit. If the various possible output levels are considered, there will be one level at which, with optimum selling expenditures for that level, profits are maximized. The price set will be that obtainable with the prevailing level of sales expenditure. At this point, marginal cost, including selling cost, will equal marginal revenue, the demand curve being the one appropriate to that level of selling activities.

In Table 9–2 the profit (or loss) figure is shown for several levels

TABLE 9–2

PROFITS WITH VARIOUS COMBINATIONS OF OUTPUT LEVELS
AND SELLING EXPENDITURES

SELLING EXPENDITURES	UNITS OF OUTPUT					
	1	2	3	4	5	6
	Profit					
$100...............	−$10	−$ 6	−$ 2	−$ 6	−$20	−$60
200...............	− 5	− 1	6	12	8	− 4
300...............	8	18	20	40	20	− 2
400...............	15	17	60	80	60	10
500...............	12	15	50	60	30	− 5

of output, with various levels of selling expenditures. Thus, with one unit of output and selling expenditures of $100, total loss will be $10, etc. Examination of the table will show that profits are maximized with four units of output and selling expense of $400. The price charged (not shown in the table) is that at which the four units can be sold, with $400 of selling expenditures.[3]

The choice of product must also be brought into the picture. For each possible form of product, there will be an optimum price and selling cost combination. For maximum profit, the firm must select that form of product which, with optimum price and selling expenditures, allows the highest profit figure.[4]

Imperfections in the Determination of Selling Activities. Attainment by a firm of the situation in which price, selling activities, and

[3] The tabular presentation is adapted from the method used by G. J. Stigler, *The Theory of Price* (New York: Macmillan, 1946), p. 261.

[4] Diagrammatic presentation of selling cost, price, and output adjustments is difficult with the usual two-variable type of graph. With the use of the indifference curve technique, however, more satisfactory presentation is possible. In the accompanying figure, total selling cost is measured on the horizontal axis, the price of the product on the vertical axis. The SC curves, or sales contours, show the various combinations of total selling cost and price which will allow the sale of particular quantities of output; there is a separate sales contour for each output figure. Thus, SC–80 shows that to sell 80 units a week, $100 of selling cost is necessary if a price of $20 is set, $150 if the price is $25, $200 if the price is $30, etc. The PR lines show various combinations of price and selling costs which will allow particular amounts of production revenue (total revenue minus selling costs). The point n shows the maximum production revenue obtainable. For successively smaller production revenue figures, a given price with either larger or smaller selling costs or a given selling cost with higher or lower prices will be necessary; thus the successive production revenue contours will encircle n. The point of tangency of each sales contour with production revenue contour shows the optimum price and selling cost combination for the

product are all adjusted to levels which allow maximum profits is likely
to be extremely difficult. It is especially hard for a firm to ascertain
optimum selling expenditures. The results of sales effort cannot be
predicted in advance; and even after these expenditures have been
made, the firm cannot be sure of their exact effect upon its demand
schedule. Thus, as a practical matter, the estimate by the firm of the
optimum sales effort is largely guesswork, more so than decisions in
virtually any other phase of business policy. Many firms spend more or
less constant amounts annually for sales promotion; others adjust sales
expenditures to a certain percentage of expected gross sales; and many
firms are influenced by current net profit figures in determining their
sales budgets. In recent years the so-called "objective and task" method
has become widely used; the firm selects certain sales objectives and

---

particular output volume. Line *KK* connects the points showing optimum price and sales
expenditures for each volume of output. The graph does not show the optimum level of
operation. The data shown in the graph, however, indicate the possible production revenues
from each output level, with optimum selling cost and price; from these data a marginal
production revenue curve can be drawn which, in conjunction with the MC curve, determines the optimum output. The latter thus being determined, this graph shows the

FIGURE 9–6

ADJUSTMENT OF SELLING ACTIVITIES

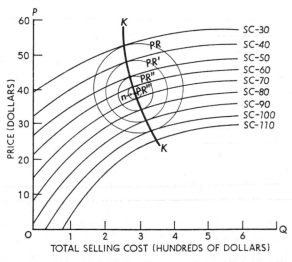

price that will be charged and the volume of selling expenditures. It should be noted that
line *KK* shows the best way to expand from one sales volume to another (whether by
price or selling cost change, or both).

   This presentation of selling costs is based upon the technique utilized by K. E.
Boulding, *Economic Analysis* (3d ed.; New York: Harper, 1955), p. 777. For an al-
ternative approach, see F. H. Hahn, "The Theory of Selling Costs," *Economic Journal*,
Vol. 69 (June, 1959), pp. 293–312.

attempts to estimate the amount of advertising expenditure necessary to obtain them. None of these methods is likely to yield the exact optimum amount, but they are employed because of the lack of more precise techniques for accomplishing the desired goal.

RESTRAINTS UPON MONOPOLY PRICE

Even in fields in which the monopolist is not subject to regulation, there are various considerations which may deter him from seeking maximum profits, and induce him to set a price considerably lower than the one allowing absolute maximum gains. In the first place, barriers against entry are never absolute. If a firm feels there is any chance of new firms developing, it may deliberately hold price below the profit-maximization figure in order to make entry by new firms less attractive and more difficult. Thus the firm is sacrificing temporary gains in the hope of greater long-term gains.

Second, the firm may be deterred by fear of government regulation. Especially in the United States and Canada, in which there are long-standing policies of maintaining competition, and public attitudes to monopoly are basically hostile, a firm may be extremely careful to avoid exploiting a monopoly position to the full in order to ward off the danger of antitrust prosecution.

Third, pressures toward the goal of profit maximization are less severe on a monopolist. With competition, a firm is compelled to undertake measures to maximize profit, since failure to do so is likely to lead to losses and possible bankruptcy. But if a monopolist is earning a good rate of profit, there is much less need to exploit every opportunity to increase profit—especially if the enterprise is a large, widely held corporation. Quite apart from fear of regulation, the monopolist may wish to appear "respectable"—to avoid behavior which seems to the customers to constitute ruthless monopolistic exploitation. A century ago, or even fifty years ago, this attitude was much less prevalent, as indicated by the last-ditch exploitation of shippers by the railroads in the days prior to regulation. But today it would appear that the desire to be regarded as "fair" in exploiting monopoly or semimonopoly positions, like the desire to avoid being regarded as a price chiseler, plays a significant part in molding business behavior and in modifying the profit-maximization goal.

REGULATED MONOPOLIES

In the public utilities field, a single firm is ordinarily allowed a monopoly of its market area, since operation of more than one firm

would prevent the attainment of full economies of large-scale production, and interfere with complete utilization of capacity (which often
must be extended in advance of needs). However, these monopolies are
subject to regulation by governmental agencies, to insure that they
provide adequate service and earn only a "necessary" return on
investment.

In terms of this goal, the aim of the regulatory agencies is to set
the general rate level at the figure at which the rate (the price) is equal
to average cost, including a "fair" or average rate of return on investment. Thus, in Figure 9–7 the rate (assuming no discrimination) would

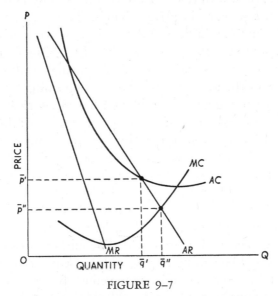

FIGURE 9–7

RATE ADJUSTMENTS OF A REGULATED MONOPOLY

be set at $\bar{p}'$, as indicated by the intersection of the *AR* curve with the *AC*
curve. Because of the difficulty of estimating the elasticity of the demand
schedule and of defining a necessary return, the actual rate level would
only approximate this figure.

It has been argued that the establishment of the rate at the level of
average cost is contrary to the principles of economic welfare, as outlined
in Chapter 21, unless the utility is operating at the point of lowest average cost and marginal cost is equal to average cost. It is argued that optimum utilization of resources requires extension of the output of each
commodity to the point at which MC = P ($\bar{q}''$ in Figure 9–7). If, at
the point at which MC = P, marginal cost is below price, as it would be
if the utility were operating on the downward portion of its AC curve,
additional units of output would add less in cost to the economy (in the

sense of resource utilization) than the price charged for them. Thus, optimum utilization of resources requires production of these additional units.

In practice, however, output is more likely to be set at the point $\overline{q}'$ where AC = P rather than at $\overline{q}''$, with MC = P. For if price is set at the level of marginal cost, the utility may not be able to earn a normal return on its investment, or perhaps even to cover all of its explicit costs. Hence a subsidy would be required to keep the enterprise in operation. The granting of subsidies to private enterprise by governments gives rise to various difficulties, and the taxes necessary to pay the subsidies might themselves interfere with resource allocation. So long as the production of utility service remains in private hands, the use of an average cost basis for price and output determination is almost essential.

Discrimination. The possibility and desirability of rate discrimination greatly complicates the task of controlling utility rates. From the standpoint of the average cost of providing utility services and the optimum use of resources, discrimination has merit, since it allows the utility to gain business which it could not otherwise get, lowers the cost per unit for all of the output (assuming operation under decreasing cost conditions), and may allow operation nearer the point at which marginal cost equals price. In some instances, especially with the railroads, firms would probably be unable to cover costs if discrimination were not practiced. If a single uniform rate were charged on all freight, shipments able to bear only a low rate could not move, and shipments able to bear a high rate would be subject to a lower rate than the shippers would be willing to pay, with consequent overall reduction in volume of business and railway revenue. But rate discrimination raises significant questions of equity and economic effects upon customers, to which answers are not easily supplied by the theory of economic welfare. Especially in the transportation field, some of the most difficult problems of rate regulation center around questions of discrimination among shippers of different commodities, shipments between different points, and shipments of different individuals.

SELECTED REFERENCES

COHEN, K. J., AND CYERT, R. M. *Theory of the Firm.* chap. x. Englewood Cliffs, N.J.: Prentice-Hall, 1965.
    A statement of modern monopoly theory.

COLBERG, M. R.; FORBUSH, D. R.; AND WHITTAKER, G. R. *Business Economics,* chaps. vii, viii. 3d ed. Homewood, Ill.: Irwin, 1964.

HAYNES, W. W. *Managerial Economics,* chap. xi. Homewood, Ill.: Dorsey, 1963.

WESTFIELD, F. M. "Regulation and Conspiracy," *American Economic Review,* Vol. LV (June 1965), pp. 424–43.

QUESTIONS

1. Indicate the difference between the parameters of the average revenue function of a monopolist and of a firm selling in a purely competitive market.

2. Suppose that a firm is the sole supplier of a particular product, but the cross-elasticity of demand between this product and other products is very high. Is the monopoly analysis useful in explaining behavior in this industry? Explain.

3. Suppose that in a market period, a monopolist finds that the demand for his product at the price set exceeds the market-period current output rate. What will he do? Explain.

4. How does a monopolist estimate his average revenue function? Why is his task easier than that of an oligopolist?

5. Explain why the optimum output level is that at which marginal cost equals marginal revenue.

6. In both monopoly and pure competition, the optimum output is at the level at which MR = MC, but only in the latter is the optimum level such that P = MC. Explain.

7. Distinguish between short-run and long-run adjustments of a monopolist.

8. Is it possible to conceive of a monopolist being unable to set a price which will cover average cost? Explain.

9. What is meant by "price discrimination"? Explain.

10. Why can price discrimination not occur in competitive markets?

11. Indicate the conditions necessary for price discrimination to occur.

12. Suppose that all buyers have precisely the same demand schedules for the commodity. Is price discrimination profitable? Explain.

13. Distinguish between first- and third-degree discrimination.

14. Why does first-degree discrimination require an "all or nothing" contract?

15. In third-degree discrimination, why are the optimum output levels in each market NOT the levels at which marginal revenue in that market equals marginal cost of the product sold in that market?

16. Indicate whether or not price discrimination occurs in each of the following situations, and if so, the reasons why discrimination is advantageous, and the basis of segregation of customers:
   a) Family fares on airlines and railroads.
   b) Lower admissions charges for children than adults to movies.
   c) Low per-mile fares for commuters on railroads and bus lines.
   d) Higher prices to American subscribers to foreign periodicals than those charged residents of the countries (the differences exceeding differences in postal charges).

    e) Lower charges for motels in resort areas in off-season periods.

    f) A policy of charging a uniform price throughout the country for a manufactured product.

    g) Lower prices for gasoline in distant market areas than close to the refineries.

17. For some years the major airlines in the United States provided two classes, first class and coach, with a very substantial rate difference. Then United Airlines commenced to eliminate the difference, providing on many routes only one-class service, at rates between coach and first class. Other airlines did not follow. After a few years, United abandoned this policy, and instead moved the other way, following an earlier policy of Continental, in providing three classes. Other airlines have continued their two-class policy, but have greatly reduced the differential between first class and coach.

    Indicate the probable reasoning behind United's one-class policy, and the probable reasons for United's reversal and introduction of a three-class policy. Explain the reduction by all airlines in the first-class coach differential.

18. Explain the reasons for increasing and decreasing returns from selling activities.

19. Explain the problems involved in attaining optimum product, price, and selling activity levels.

20. Why is it particularly difficult for a firm to ascertain the optimum level of selling activities?

21. What may deter a monopolist from seeking maximum profit?

22. Should the aim of utility rate regulation be to obtain equality of the rate level with average cost or marginal cost? Explain.

Chapter 10

NONPURELY COMPETITIVE MARKETS: MONOPOLISTIC COMPETITION

The monopoly and purely competitive models outlined in the two preceding chapters are directly applicable for the analysis of rather limited sectors of the contemporary economy—the former to regulated industries and a few isolated markets, the latter to markets for basic agricultural products and securities. With some modifications the models are applicable over a wider range of markets, in which conditions approach but do not agree entirely with the assumptions upon which the models are built. For the analysis of a major portion of the modern economy, however, models which involve elements of both monopoly and pure competition, in various proportions, are required. Unfortunately, however, these models have not been perfected to the point at which they are as useful as they might appear to be. There are two major types of models which involve both competitive and monopoly elements: monopolistic competition and oligopoly. The former is discussed in this chapter, the latter in Chapter 11.

General Characteristics of Monopolistic Competition[1]

The model of monopolistic competition involves three primary assumptions: (1) products of the various sellers are differentiated, (2) the number of sellers is sufficiently great that each acts independently of the other firms, and (3) entry of new firms is relatively easy. Thus, unlike pure competition, individual sellers do have influence over market price, rather than regarding it as a parameter. The various firms recognize the existence of competitors as a group, which imposes a ceiling on the prices which they can charge and sell a particular level of

---

[1] The theory of monopolistic competition was first elaborated by E. H. Chamberlin; see *The Theory of Monopolistic Competition* (Cambridge: Harvard University Press, 1933). There was some suggestion of the theory in an earlier work by J. M. Clark, *Studies in the Economics of Overhead Costs* (Chicago: University of Chicago Press, 1923), and also in certain journal articles that appeared during the 1920's.

output, yet they do not consider competitors as individuals whose policies will be influenced by their own actions. Because of the relatively free entry of new firms, long-run price and output behavior is somewhat similar to that of pure competition; because of the assumption of a given average revenue function, independent of the policies of the firm, rather than of price as a parameter, the short-run adjustments are more similar to those of a monopolist. In a sense each seller in a market of monopolistic competition may be regarded as a "monopolist" of his own particular brand of the commodity—but unlike the firm of the monopoly model, he is subject to competition by firms producing similar brands, with a high degree of cross-elasticity of demand with his own.

A requisite characteristic of monopolistic competition is differentiation of product—of preferences of buyers for dealing with particular sellers or for purchasing the products of particular sellers. The significant feature of differentiation is the belief on the part of the buyers that the products of the various sellers are not the same, whether the products are actually different physically or not.[2] There are various sources of differentiation. Actual physical differences, of course, constitute one source; brands of ice cream or cigarettes differ significantly in taste to many buyers. There are physical differences among various makes of cars, which lead some buyers to prefer one make, some to prefer another. Prestige considerations are significant; many persons prefer to be seen using the currently popular make, while others prefer the "off brand." Prestige considerations are particularly important with gifts. Location is a major factor in retailing; persons are not willing to travel long distances to shop for items which are minor in the overall expenditure pattern; most people prefer to pay more for a candy bar at a newsstand than to walk two blocks to a supermarket. Service considerations are likewise significant; speedy service is very important to many people. Reliability leads many persons to buy at department stores instead of at discount houses which may be cheaper. Personal attitudes of storekeepers and clerks is an important influence; the attitude or beauty of the waitresses, or the brevity of their dress, may significantly affect choice of restaurants. Since most buyers realize that there is no significant differences among brands of gasoline, their choice of gasoline is often influenced by such considerations as location of service stations and cleanliness of washrooms.

---

[2] A good example of a product of which the various brands are identical but buyers believe them to be different is aspirin.

But despite preferences, relative prices are significant influences on the choice of products, and many buyers will select the sellers who offer the lowest prices. Accordingly, sellers in a market of monopolistic competition may be expected to discover from experience (if not common sense) that relatively small changes in prices produce relatively large changes in sales, if prices of competitors are given. Hence, each seller regards the demand for his product as relatively elastic. By the same token, an individual seller who fails to follow price trends initiated by competitors, or fails to respond to the entry or exit of other sellers into his industry, will experience substantial variations in quantity sold at any given price. The effect will be to encourage individual sellers to revise their estimates of their AR curves in the light of actual sales experience. Thus a seller will act on the assumption that the maximum price he can charge for any given level of output is restricted to a range of values in the neighborhood of the prevailing industry price level, and he will revise his estimate of the position of his AR curve with every significant change in his own sales or in the "industry" price level. Thus in a sense sellers behave as competing monopolists. Each has a less than perfectly elastic demand in his own "market," but his AR curve is nearly horizontal and its position shifts significantly as conditions change in other "markets"—that is, as competing firms change price.

By the nature of monopolistic competition, entry into a given industry is unrestricted in the sense that new firms may easily commence production of close substitutes for existing products, although they cannot produce products which appear identical to existing ones in the eyes of prospective purchasers. Because of relatively free entry excess profits will tend to be eliminated in the long run. As we shall see, however, this tendency will be resisted in a variety of ways; some firms may earn excess profits even in the long run, and those firms that have earned excess profits may lose them not because prices are forced down but because costs are forced up. This theme will be elaborated later.

MARKET PERIOD PRICE DETERMINATION

During an interval of time so short that orders to suppliers or other determinants of output cannot be altered, a seller in monopolistic competition will have a strong incentive to adjust price to ensure that his sales coincide with his current rate of output or purchases, particularly to avoid accumulation of inventory. Because the seller is (by hypothesis) merely one among many, he need not be concerned about possible direct reactions by competitors to a temporary change in his asking price.

If a change in demand causes sales to lag significantly behind current output, the seller may be expected to reduce price sharply in order to bring about a quick adjustment of sales to output. For while demand may be very elastic in the short run, additional customers can hardly be found immediately unless the seller makes important price concessions. Accordingly, special sales of goods at attractive discounts from normal prices, combined with advertising that is designed to attract temporary rather than regular customers, is likely to be a characteristic feature of monopolistic competition.

If a change in demand causes current sales to exceed current output, rather different considerations will apply. The seller will normally distinguish between regular and casual customers, and will be reluctant to run the risk of losing a regular customer for the sake of a temporary and probably minor increase in revenue. Thus upward revisions in price in the market period are unlikely to occur. Instead, the seller will adjust sales to output by simply failing to meet demands by casual customers, available output being rationed to regular customers at the prevailing price.

This asymmetry in price behavior in the market period could not occur in purely competitive markets. Moreover, the phenomenon of frequent temporary reductions in price is unlikely to be found in monopoly or oligopoly. The existence of the kind of behavior described is so familiar in actual retail markets as to demonstrate the usefulness of the monopolistic competition model for market-period price determination in some types of markets. However, in many circumstances, firms will adjust the rate of output or purchases almost simultaneously with changes in sales, and thus the market-period analysis is not significant.

OUTPUT AND PRICE DETERMINATION IN THE SHORT RUN

Since sellers in conditions of monopolistic competition do not regard price as a given parameter, decisions about short-run levels of output must be made in the light of estimates of the probable prices at which various levels of sales can be obtained in conjunction with estimates of cost. This problem is complicated by the fact that the position of the seller's AR curve will depend on the average level of prices in the industry. On what basis do the firms estimate what the "industry" price level will be? There are various approaches. One is recent price experience; if other drive-ins are charging 19 cents for hamburgers and 20 cents for milkshakes and have been doing so in recent months, each drive-in will assume that other firms will typically continue to charge these figures, and will estimate its own potential sales at various price levels on this assumption. Or the firm may reasonably assume that the industry price level will be somewhat above AVC—above by a markup that has become more or less traditional. It may be assumed that with monopolistic competition, since entry of new firms is relatively easy, variable costs (as, for example, cost of goods sold) constitute the major element of total costs. Each seller knows that these costs must be covered if firms are to stay in business; he also knows that certain markups above variable cost are regarded as traditional. Thus, given his estimates of variable costs, he can estimate the typical price level which will prevail, and thus his own average revenue function.

Given the position of an individual's AR curve (conforming with the requirement that the curve must pass through a point that represents expected average sales at the expected industry price level), we may describe the determination of short-run equilibrium output and price in terms similar to those used in the analysis of monopoly output and price determination. Relevant cost and revenue curves of a typical seller may be represented as in Figure 10–1; the intersection of MR and $SRMC$ indicates that the short-run equilibrium output will be q, and the short-run

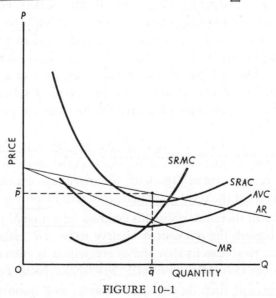

FIGURE 10–1

Initial Short-Run Adjustment of Price and Output

equilibrium price $\bar{p}$. Because the AR curve is relatively horizontal, the excess of equilibrium price over marginal cost will be relatively small as compared with the typical monopoly situation. Since different sellers will form different estimates of the level and position of the AR curve, equilibrium prices will typically differ among firms. The differences are unlikely to be extreme, however, because all firms are likely to have rather similar MC curves under the assumed conditions. As in pure competition, this conclusion is subject to the requirement that price must cover AVC. If, however, failure to cover AVC is regarded as temporary, the firm may continue to operate for a time in order to avoid loss of customers, a consideration not relevant in pure competition.

Industry Adjustments

The equilibrium value of output determined by an individual seller on the basis of his current estimate of average revenue prospects may be expected to vary over time in response to changes in the general level of prices in the industry. The mechanism by which such adjustments occur may be illustrated most conveniently by supposing that the actual sales of a typical individual seller at any given price are indicated not by his average revenue curve, AR, as he anticipates, but rather by an objective sales curve, represented in Figure 10–2 by the relation DD. The definition of the curve DD poses some logical problems, since it cannot be obtained except by making specific assumptions about the prices charged by all other sellers. For the sake of simplicity—and not too unrealistically—we may suppose that the DD curve shown in Figure 10–2 describes for each level of price what the sales of a typical seller would be *if all other firms were charging exactly the same price.* Our analysis of the probable sequence of adjustments in short-run equilibrium output and price by a typical seller (supposing that other sellers always match the given seller's current price) can then proceed as follows.

Starting with an initial expected average revenue curve AR^0, the seller will choose a value of output $\bar{q}^0$, as indicated by the intersection of the marginal revenue curve MR^0 with the marginal cost curve MC. But if price is thus set at the level $\bar{p}^0$, actual sales will be only q^0, or less than $\bar{q}^0$. The seller will therefore revise his estimate of demand. Let us assume that he now regards the relevant AR curve to be AR^1 rather than AR^0, defined by the requirement that the curve which is currently relevant must contain the currently "observed" sales-price point $(q^0, \bar{p}^0)$. Equilibrium output will then be changed from $\bar{q}^0$ to $\bar{q}^1$, and price will be

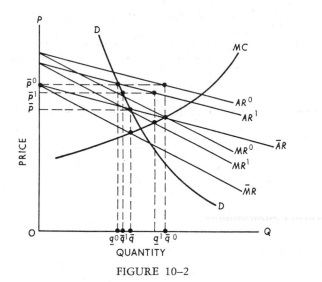

FIGURE 10–2

FINAL SHORT-RUN ADJUSTMENT OF PRICE AND OUTPUT

revised downward from $\bar{p}^0$ to $\bar{p}$. Again, however, sales will be less than output (i.e., $q^1 < \bar{q}^1$); so there will be a further expected AR curve. This process will continue until the seller arrives at an estimate of average revenue prospects represented by the curve $\overline{AR}$ in Figure 10–2; i.e., a curve which produces an equilibrium value of output of $\bar{q}$, and an equilibrium price (for the seller and for the industry) of $\bar{p}$, such that actual sales are just equal to equilibrium output.

    The adjustment process just described is based on very special assumptions. The general character of the process can be shown to be much the same, however, under less restrictive conditions.[3] The precise nature of the process depends on the factors assumed to govern the output and price behavior of every seller. It cannot be doubted, however, that the simplified analysis presented above contains an important element of truth about the way competing sellers may be expected to adapt to sales experience in almost any nonpurely competitive market. Of particular interest in this connection is the conclusion that the AR curve will shift over time as long as equilibrium output at the current price differs from actual sales at the same price. This elementary consistency condition is an essential requirement for any empirically meaningful model of output and price determination. It is not without interest to note, therefore, that the same condition is implicit in the theory of purely competitive markets; it is in fact a direct consequence of the proposition that in pure competition market equilibrium occurs if and only if price is such as to equate quantity demanded with quantity supplied.

LONG-RUN PRICE AND OUTPUT ADJUSTMENTS

In monopolistic competition as in monopoly, adjustments in plant size will be made by existing firms over a long-run period in an attempt to achieve minimal long-run costs for any given level of output. At any given time, maximum profits are sought by establishing output at a level such that $MR = SRMC$ with the existing plant. But this level of output will maximize long-run profit only if the existing plant is that which permits the short-run equilibrium output to be produced at minimum cost. Plant size will be adjusted over time, therefore, so long as SRMC differs from LRMC. Exactly as with monopoly, therefore, attainment of long-run equilibrium requires that $MR = SRMC = LRMC$.

While these conditions for long-run equilibrium are necessary, they are not sufficient. As individual firms are adapting their plant sizes in an attempt to reduce long-run costs, other firms may be considering entry into the industry. Since, as noted earlier, capital requirements are likely to be low and economies of large-scale production rather insignificant in such industries, entry is likely to be fairly free. The main barrier to newcomers is the established reputation of existing firms. The rapid flow of firms into and out of the restaurant field provides a good illustration of this characteristic of monopolistic competition.

To the extent that new firms enter the field, there will be a tendency for any prevailing gap between price and average cost to be closed. Newcomers may find it advantageous to set prices lower than those charged by older firms in order to build up sales volume; and older firms may then find it necessary to reduce prices in order to maintain their sales at a satisfactory level. However, the reductions in price brought about in this fashion will not have a significant effect on total sales of the product unless total demand for the product is sufficiently elastic; the existing sales volume may merely be divided among more firms. Whether or not prices fall, the decline in sales which each firm experiences is likely to force operation at a point farther away from the point of lowest cost, and excess profits will therefore be eliminated in part by a rise in average cost.

The Tangency Case

If entry is sufficiently free to lead to the complete elimination of all excess profits, long-run equilibrium will occur when AR is equal to AC for each firm at a level of output at which each firm's AR curve is just tangent to its AC curve. For if the revenue curve cuts the cost curve at any point, excess profits will be attainable, while if it fails to touch the cost curve, losses cannot be avoided. The adjustment is illustrated in Figures 10–3 and 10–4. In Figure 10–3 the short-run equilibrium output is at $\bar{q}$, and excess profits are being earned. As a consequence, new firms enter, and the *AR* curve of each firm moves to the left, until it is tangent to *LRAC* as indicated in Figure 10–4. The point of tangency is, of necessity, at the same level of output as that at which *MC*—both short

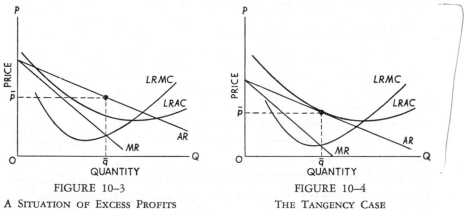

| FIGURE 10–3 | FIGURE 10–4 |
| A SITUATION OF EXCESS PROFITS | THE TANGENCY CASE |

run and long run—is equal to *MR*. The tangency point thus coincides with the point of maximum profit.

Because of the downward slope of the AR curve, the point of tangency will not be at the lowest level of average cost. When long-run adjustments are complete, firms will be operating at levels that do not permit full realization of economies of large-scale production. The existing plant, even though optimal for the particular volume of output, may not be used to capacity. Any attempt to increase output to attain lowest average cost would be unprofitable, since the price reduction necessary to sell the greater output would exceed the cost reduction made possible. Thus, in industries of this type, there is a chronic tendency toward too many firms in the industry, each producing a volume of output less than that which would allow lowest cost. For example, there may be too many grocery stores and too many service stations, in the sense that if the total volume of business were concentrated in a smaller number of sellers, average cost and price would be less.[4]

The significance of the difference between the relationship of LRMC and price in monopolistic competition and in pure competition can easily be exaggerated. So long as preferences for various brands are not extremely strong, the demand schedules for the products of firms will be highly elastic. Accordingly, the points of tangency with the AC curves are not likely to be far above the point of lowest cost, as illustrated in Figure 10–4. Only if differentiation is very strong will the difference between the long-run price level and that which would prevail under purely competitive conditions be relatively great.

It is also possible that excess profits may in part be eliminated by increased expenditures on selling activities, as discussed below.

Excessive Entry of New Firms

In industries in which relatively low capital requirements make entry of new firms comparatively easy, it is possible that so many firms will enter the industry that few if any sellers can earn even normal profits. The extremely high rate of mortality among firms in some lines of retailing, especially in the first two years of operation, suggests a chronic tendency for excessive entry of newcomers.[5] In part, excessive entry may result when excess profits have been earned temporarily. Because of the time required for operation to get under way, too many firms may commence operations, just as farmers may plant too many apple trees when apple prices are high relative to costs. But even when only normal profits are being earned, there may be a tendency for new firms to start, either because newcomers believe they can operate more profitably than existing firms, or because they lack adequate knowledge of profit possibilities and are anxious to develop their own businesses.

[4] This thesis has been attacked by Donald Dewey, "Imperfect Competition No Bar to Efficient Production," *Journal of Political Economy*, Vol. 66 (February, 1958), pp. 24–33. He points out that if firms are operating at less than the output allowing lowest cost, it would be advantageous for them to combine to allow larger-scale operation. But in practice, this may not occur; in fields characterized by large numbers of small firms, the desire for independent operation of one's own business is often paramount.

[5] For example, in California in 1958, 13 percent of all restaurants and taverns in existence at the beginning of the year had been discontinued by the end of the year, and 23 percent changed hands during the year. Twenty-five percent of all service stations changed hands during the year. For retail stores as a whole, 41 percent of those discontinued during the year had been in operation less than a year. See California State Board of Equalization, *Mortality and Business Turnover in California in 1958* (Sacramento, 1960).

Restrictions to Completely Free Entry

Complete adjustment toward equality of price with average cost may be checked by the strength of the reputation built up by established firms. Those firms which are particularly successful in their selling efforts may create such strong consumer preferences that newcomers— even though they are able to enter the industry freely and cover their own costs—will not take away sufficient business from the well-established firms to eliminate their excess profits. Thus, a restaurant which has been particularly successful in promoting customer goodwill may continue to earn excess profits long after the entry of new firms has brought about equality of price and average cost for the others, or even losses. The adjustments toward a final equilibrium situation involving equality of price and average cost do not proceed with the certainty that is characteristic of pure competition.

Industry Cost Conditions

The cost conditions in which an industry operates have the same general significance in monopolistic competition as they have in pure competition. In an increasing or decreasing cost industry, the height of the cost schedule of each firm will be affected by changes in the total output of the entire industry. The actual figure of average cost to which price is equal when long-run adjustments have been completed in a situation of free entry will depend upon the total volume of output for the industry and thus, in part, upon the total demand for the product. Precise industry cost curves which would have any significance cannot be drawn, however, because firms do not operate at the levels of lowest average cost and because costs at the actual points of operation are not uniform among firms. Likewise, the products of various firms are not homogeneous.

SELLING ACTIVITIES AND MONOPOLISTIC COMPETITION

Differentiation is the key characteristic of monopolistic competition, and thus selling activities play a major role. Differentiation is essentially created by adjustment of product, including branding and packaging, and reputation is largely created by selling activity. Increased selling activity not only increases the demand for the product of the firm, but also lessens its elasticity by attaching customers more closely to the particular brand. The formal analysis of sales effort in monopolistic competition is the same as that presented for a monopolist in Chapter 9. But selling activity is likely to be much more significant than it is for a monopolist because of the possibility of taking business away from competing firms.

The effect of the development of selling activities upon prices in monopolistic competition is complex, and generalizations are not so obvious as they might appear to be. Expenditures on selling activities constitute costs, which must be covered by revenues from the sale of the product if an average rate of profit is to be earned. From the standpoint of business firms, selling costs are not significantly different from production costs. However, selling activities will also alter demand schedules. The combined effect of higher cost and higher demand is almost certain to raise prices. But there are possible exceptions. Sales activities may allow firms to operate nearer the point of lowest cost than they would in monopolistic competition without selling activities. It is possible that the decline in production cost will exceed the sales cost, per unit of product. Unless total demand for the product is affected significantly by advertising, other firms will be forced out of business, and sales will be concentrated in the hands of a smaller number of firms. It should be noted, however, that the new price is lower only by comparison with the price existing with monopolistic competition and no sales activity; the price cannot be lower than the figure that would prevail with pure competition, which is the lowest possible average cost figure, with no selling costs.

However, since firms in monopolistic competition are not likely to experience substantial cost reductions as output increases, lower production cost can hardly be expected to offset selling costs if the latter are at all substantial. The chances of a significant reduction in per unit cost are much greater in oligopoly, as discussed in Chapter 11.

While selling activity may increase demand, it is also likely to make demand less elastic by increasing the degree of preference for particular brands. This effect will tend to bring about higher prices.

THE SIGNIFICANCE OF MONOPOLISTIC COMPETITION

The three primary assumptions upon which the analysis of monopolistic competition is based—(1) large numbers of sellers and absence of mutual interdependence, (2) differentiated product, and (3) relatively free entry of firms—are most likely to be approximated in lines of activity in which capital equipment is of relatively minor importance in production. In these fields, comparatively little money capital is required to commence production, and the economies of large-scale production are of limited importance, being fully attained at relatively low levels of output. Thus, various lines of retailing and small handicraft production and repair would appear to be the types of activity most likely to operate under conditions of monopolistic competition.[6]

However, study of these fields raises some doubt about the applicability of the assumptions. Despite the large numbers of retailers, each particular market area rarely has a substantial number, and feelings of mutual interdependence do not appear to be entirely absent, the firms recognizing that their policies will have some effect upon the policies of competing retailers. Interdependence may in some cases be relatively weak, but it is not likely to be completely absent.

The assumption of free entry is regarded by some writers as incompatible with the assumption of product differentiation. It is argued that when consumers have preferences for the products of particular firms, the flow of new firms into the field is inevitably restricted; so the principle that price tends to equal average cost, with the AR curve tangent to the AC curve at a point to the left of lowest average cost, is not valid. It is also argued that the concept of an industry is ambiguous when products are differentiated, and that the empirical content of an equilibrium analysis of such an "industry" are correspondingly vague.

Finally, it can be argued that conditions of monopolistic competition can exist only when the initial decline in average cost is of limited magnitude. Thus the principle that firms will not operate at the point of lowest average cost, once long-run adjustments have been completed, is of little significance, since the difference between price and the point of lowest average cost will be slight. Accordingly, the purely competitive analysis is regarded as applicable, even though the demand curves of the firms are not perfectly elastic.

It may be admitted that these criticisms have some merit. Few markets are completely free of oligopolistic influence, and established reputations undoubtedly are a frequent bar to complete elimination of excess profits. However, monopolistic competition has some interest as a limiting case in which interdependence is relatively weak and entry of new firms is relatively easy. Moreover, the fact that some criticisms of *existing* monopolistic competition analysis are valid does not mean that

[6] Possible examples in manufacturing include the women's cloak and suit industry, with 3,178 firms in 1954, no one having as much as 1 percent of the market, and the commercial printing industry, in which the largest firm has only 1.5 percent of the total business of the industry.

we should forthwith condemn all *conceivable* models of this type. Here as in most other areas of economic analysis, further research, analytical and empirical, is in order.

SELECTED REFERENCES

CHAMBERLIN, E. H. *The Theory of Monopolistic Competition.* 7th ed. Cambridge: Harvard University Press, 1956. Originally published in 1933, this was the pioneer contribution to the development of the analysis of monopolistic competition.

COHEN, K. J., AND CYERT, R. M. *Theory of the Firm,* chap. xi. Englewood Cliffs, N.J.: Prentice-Hall, 1965.

"The Theory of Monopolistic Competition after Thirty Years," series of papers in the *Proceedings of the American Economic Association* for 1963, pp. 28–57.

QUESTIONS

1. What are the assumptions upon which the model of monopolistic competition is based?
2. In what sense is monopolistic competition a hybrid of monopoly and pure competition?
3. Suppose that you are considering the purchase of each of the following items, the prices charged by various sellers being the same. What considerations would influence your choice of the particular seller or brand?
   a) A new car—make of car.
   b) Shoes—make of shoe.
   c) Gasoline in your home area—dealer and brand.
   d) Gasoline while on a trip—dealer and brand.
   e) A motel while on a trip.
   f) A restaurant in your home area.
   g) An airline for a trip to Europe.
4. Contrast the nature of the average revenue function in monopolistic competition with those in (*a*) monopoly, (*b*) pure competition.
5. In a market period in which the seller in monopolistic competition cannot adjust rate of purchases or output, will he be more willing to reduce prices if his sales lag behind his output or to raise prices if his sales outrun his output? Explain.
6. In setting price in a short-run period, on what bases may the firm estimate the typical "industry" price?
7. Why are fixed costs not likely to be significant portions of total costs in monopolistic competition?
8. Explain the meaning of the *DD* curve on Figure 10–2.
9. Suppose that, in the short run, a firm in monopolistic competition has set price at the level at which MC = MR, the latter dependent upon his

original estimate of the demand function for his product. Why may he find that the price thus set does not maximize profits, and thus he must readjust price? Explain, and indicate the process of adjusting.

10. Explain the "tangency" case in monopolistic competition.

11. Why cannot the firms in monopolistic competition be operating at the point of lowest long-run average cost, if all excess profits have been eliminated? Illustrate with a graph.

12. What leads to excessive entry of new firms in some markets of monopolistic competition?

13. Why may some firms in monopolistic competition continue to earn excess profits for long periods even though new firms may easily start up?

14. Explain the effect of selling activities upon prices in monopolistic competition.

15. Indicate some of the major criticisms advanced against the model of monopolistic competition, on both analytical and empirical grounds.

<table>
<tr><td>*Chapter*
11</td><td># NONPURELY COMPETITIVE
MARKETS: OLIGOPOLY</td></tr>
</table>

Oligopoly is characterized by mutual interdependence among firms, each seller shaping his policy in terms of the policies of the other firms in the industry, and taking into consideration the effects which his own policies may have upon the policies of competitors. Oligopoly is likely to occur whenever the number of firms in an industry is so small that any change in output or price by one firm materially affects the sales of competing firms. In this situation, it is almost inevitable that competitors will react directly to changes initiated by other firms; each seller may therefore be expected to take these reactions into consideration in determining its own policy. For example, if a service station operator considers reducing prices in order to increase sales, he is almost always aware that his competitors are likely to reduce also, and he will take this reaction into consideration in deciding whether or not to make the price reduction.

Conditions of oligopoly occur throughout the American economy. Many manufacturing industries are dominated by a few firms operating in typical oligopoly situations. Tin-can production is dominated by two firms, copper refining and automobile production by three, cigarette and rubber production by four. These are merely representative examples. In retailing, in any particular market, there is usually only a limited number of stores; while there may be five hundred drugstores in a large city, considerations of convenience usually limit any particular group of consumers to a relatively small group of stores.

What is responsible for the widespread occurrence of oligopoly? Primarily, it is a result of the relationship between technological conditions of production and potential sales volumes. Reasonably low cost of production of many products cannot be obtained unless a firm is producing a large volume of output; if this constitutes a substantial percentage of total potential sales in a market, the number of firms will be small.[1] Automobile and steel production are good examples. Even

[1] See J. S. Bain, *Industrial Organization* (New York: Wiley, 1959), chap. iv.

though bakeries or theaters require relatively small volumes of business for low cost, only the largest cities can provide a sufficient number of customers to allow numerous competing firms.

Decreases in the number of firms in an industry may also result from the desire of firms to consolidate to lessen the severity of competitive pressures, or to control larger business empires.

Classification of Oligopoly Markets

Pure versus Differentiated Oligopoly.   Situations of oligopoly can be classed into two groups on the basis of the presence or absence of differentiation. If the products of various firms are identical, the term *pure oligopoly* is applied. This model is approximated in some of the capital goods industries, such as cement production. Mutual interdependence will be greater when products are identical than when they are differentiated, since any price change by one firm is certain to produce substantial effects upon the sales of competitors and cause them to alter their policies.

On the other hand, in *differentiated oligopoly,* in which products are not homogeneous, price changes will have a less direct effect upon competitors because of the partial isolation of the market for each firm. The stronger the differentiation, the weaker will be the feeling of mutual interdependence. Differentiated oligopoly is characteristic of a very large portion of the total economy, including most manufactured consumer goods, and retailing in most areas. Even many of the capital goods industries have only a few firms and some differentiation of product. The degree of differentiation and the strength of feelings of mutual interdependence vary widely among industries, however, a fact which greatly complicates the development of a model for price and output analysis.

Collusion versus Spontaneous Coordination.   Oligopoly situations may also be classified on the basis of whether mutual interdependence manifests itself in outright *collusion* or merely in *spontaneous coordination* of the policies of firms through recognition by each firm of the effects of its actions upon those of its competitors.

Collusion involves direct negotiation and agreements among competitors (of necessity informal in countries such as the United States). Such collusion increases the stability of oligopoly, since otherwise firms may base their actions upon mistaken estimates of their competitors' behavior.

The coverage of agreements made with collusion may vary widely. Agreements may extend to price only, or to both price and output. In other cases, merely the method of price determination is agreed upon, such as the rule of following prices set by one firm, or the use of certain pricing methods which will produce substantial price uniformity. Acceptance by firms of standard cost accounting procedures for allocation of overhead among various products, for example, will normally reduce price differences.

Frequently, however, oligopoly involves *spontaneous coordination* rather than outright agreement. Each firm simply takes into consideration the expected responses of competitors to its own actions and determines its policies accordingly. With each firm following similar practices, price and output levels will eventually adjust to figures which are acceptable to all firms. Spontaneous coördination may involve the independent adoption by various firms of pricing practices comparable to those agreed upon in situations of collusion, or the implicit acceptance of one firm as a price leader, or the adoption of methods of price setting—such as the markup system common in retailing—that lessen effective price competition.

Complete versus Partial Oligopoly. Oligopoly is described as *complete* if the interdependence among the firms is sufficiently strong that the profits of the firms as a group are maximized, *partial* if this optimum is not obtained. As explained later, complete oligopoly is in all likelihood rarely attained, varying degrees of partial oligopoly being the typical situation. But analysis of the former is important, since it represents the ultimate ideal from the standpoint of the oligopolist.

The wide variety of possible situations, and thus of possible assumptions, in oligopoly makes analysis of price and output determination difficult. A broad theory, with assumptions so general as to cover all possible oligopoly situations, can offer little for the analysis of particular situations. To develop separate theories based on all possible assumptions is an impossible task. At present, it is possible only to consider those cases which appear to be of primary importance. Additional empirical work on behavior in oligopoly is necessary to determine which situations are of sufficient importance to warrant further attention, and what kinds of models are likely to be most fruitful.

The complexities and diversities of oligopoly make it necessary to break the analysis of price and output determination in such markets into several segments. As a convenient starting point, we shall deal first with complete oligopoly, and subsequently with major forms of partial oligopoly. We shall assume initially that the product is differentiated; pure oligopoly will be considered later.

COMPLETE OLIGOPOLY

Oligopoly may be designated complete when relationships among the firms are sufficiently close to permit maximization of the joint profits of the firms, considered as a group. This condition may result from spontaneous coordination of the policies of the various firms or, more probably, from outright cooperation among officials of the firms. This model does not differ fundamentally from that of complete monopoly, except that there is more than one firm, and costs are certain to be different.

Maximization of joint profit requires the determination of price on the basis of the total demand schedule for the product and the sum of the marginal cost schedules of the various firms, as shown in Figure 11–1. With outright agreements—necessarily secret because of the antitrust laws—firms will attempt by collective action to estimate demand and cost schedules, and set optimum price and output figures accordingly. If prices are set by one firm and followed by all others, the price setter will act on the basis of total schedules rather than his own situation, and other firms will abide by the decision. When collusive action is absent, maximum joint profits can be obtained only if each firm, acting independently, correctly estimates the price that is optimal from the standpoint of the group.

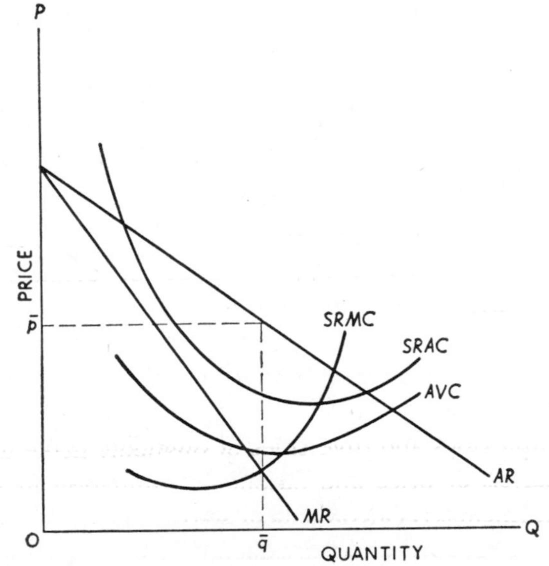

FIGURE 11–1

SHORT-RUN ADJUSTMENT OF PRICE AND OUTPUT

The manner in which total profits are shared by the firms in the industry depends in part upon relative costs and sales of the various firms. Firms with low costs and those with large sales volumes will of course obtain the largest profits. Sales, in turn, will depend in large measure upon consumer preferences for various brands. With outright collusion, firms may agree upon market shares under cartel arrangements, and thus upon the division of profits. The division of total profits will depend upon the relative bargaining strength of the firms, influenced by relative financial strength, ability to inflict damages on other firms if an agreement is not reached, ability to withstand similar action on the part of other firms, relative costs, consumer preferences, and bargaining skill.

Obstacles to the Attainment of Maximum Joint Profits

There are many obstacles to actual maximization of joint profits and the attainment of complete oligopoly. The basic difficulty lies in the unwillingness of firms to surrender all freedom of action, and the desire of each to increase its own share of total sales and profits.

First, the maximum-joint-profit price will be optimal for each firm as well as for firms as a group only if cost and demand schedules are the same for all the firms. If this is not true (and it is surely unlikely), those firms which will be worse off at the joint-profit-optimum figure must be compensated by other firms or frightened into compliance by threats of punitive action, or they will not accept the overall optimum figure. In some instances it would be necessary to close down high-cost firms to attain the optimum, but these firms may resist such a policy. In the absence of adequate compensation or other means of obtaining compliance, the best that can be obtained is a compromise, a level of profits tolerable to all the firms, but not the joint-profit optimum.

Second, not only is it difficult to determine the exact nature of the demand curve, but different firms will have different opinions and compromises are inevitable. The view that total demand curves are highly inelastic appears to be widespread in business circles, a bias which might lead to prices higher than the joint-profit optimum.

Third, profit maximization may also be checked at times by strategical moves by one firm designed to force other firms to take certain actions, or to discourage them from carrying out policies detrimental to the interests of the given firm (see below, page 239). Thus, action may be taken to drive rivals out of business completely, or to test their strength and bargaining power.

Fourth, attainment of maximum group profits may be rendered

difficult by the inability of firms to agree upon product changes, advertising policies, and new techniques. Typically, it would appear that agreements relate only to price, and with spontaneous coordination, firms are likely to be much more conscious of competitors' reactions to price changes than to changes in other variables that affect profits. Agreements on nonprice elements is particularly difficult because the future strength of various firms in these elements cannot be discounted satisfactorily to the present. Each firm is certain that it will be able to outdo the other firms on selling activities, and therefore is unwilling to reach an agreement about them. Firms are highly conscious that price changes lead to changes by competitors; hence agreements, explicit or implicit, on prices may appear highly desirable. But firms apparently believe that they will be able to do better than competitors on new methods, products, and advertising procedures.

A fifth deterrent to the setting of maximum-profit prices is the fear that such prices will stimulate the growth of new firms. Although most industries in which oligopoly is present are characterized by significant barriers to free entry by new firms (e.g., large volume of output necessary for low cost, and established reputations of existing firms), newcomers may nevertheless seek to enter. High prices and excess profits not only provide great incentive to entry but also make such entry easier. High prices ease the problem of covering heavy initial costs of operations, and good profit prospects facilitate the raising of money capital. As a consequence, existing firms may deliberately hold prices below the short-run maximum-profit level, preferring instead a "reasonable" profit that will continue longer because less encouragement will be given to prospective entrants.

Finally, difficulties in obtaining coordinated action discourage firms from making frequent price changes in the light of changing conditions. Continuous maximization of joint profits is clearly out of the question, however, if prices are not altered.

PARTIAL OLIGOPOLY

While complete oligopoly may be regarded as the ultimate goal of a group of oligopolists, it is not the typical behavior pattern; partial oligopoly—situations in which joint profits are not maximized—is the general rule. Spontaneous coordination is probably more common in partial oligopoly than outright agreements. Firms set their own prices on the basis of estimates of their own demand schedules, taking into consideration possible reactions on the part of their competitors and their own cost schedules. The primary difference between price setting by oligopolists and by other firms is the attention given to possible reactions by competitors, which reduce the elasticity of demand below what it would otherwise be. If competitors tend to follow price changes, shifting of customers among firms in response to price changes will be reduced, and demand elasticity will be controlled primarily by the elasticity of total demand for the product. As oligopoly develops in an industry, prices may be expected to rise as the demand schedules of firms become less elastic. As in other competitive situations, <u>maximum profit for the firm is determined by the level of operation at which marginal cost is equal to marginal revenue</u>.

Although the mutual interdependence which characterizes oligopoly may have a tendency to make demand schedules more inelastic, it also creates great uncertainty about their nature, since a firm can rarely be sure of the exact response of its competitors. Even if a firm suspects that changes in its price will lead to reactions by competitors, it cannot know the extent of the reactions. A small price reduction may cause a large increase in sales if competitors do not reduce, but only a slight increase if competitors meet or exceed the cut. Under such circumstances, the firm is in a sense confronted not by one demand curve, but by an infinity of potential curves, the appropriate one in a particular instance depending upon the exact (but unknown) reactions of competitors. However, the firm must act; it must set some price and must accept one of the potential demand curves as the most probable. But the uncertainty is itself a major influence upon the policy of the firm, and encourages firms to develop techniques of pricing which minimize the danger of following policies based upon mistaken estimates of the reactions of competitors. <u>Uncertainty also encourages firms to minimize the frequency of price changes because of possible dangers</u> arising out of changes in the status quo.

What means does a firm have to increase knowledge of its demand schedule? One is to <u>study actual sales</u> data over a period of time during which different prices have been changed. Such a study must be made with great care, since other determinants of sales—consumer incomes and preferences, prices of substitutes, weather conditions, etc.—are constantly changing. Isolation of the effects of price changes from the effects of other changes is very difficult, but careful analysis may yield some useful information. Study of sales volumes of competitors charging different prices (when obtainable) and analysis of the nature of the market to facilitate an estimate of elasticity of total demand may also be of assistance. Many large firms devote considerable effort to <u>market</u>

research, either by their own personnel or by independent firms specializing in this work. Market research today, however, is devoted primarily to such problems as estimating sales potentials in particular areas, determining new uses and outlets for a product, discovering consumer reaction to various quality changes, checking on the effectiveness of advertising and other selling campaigns, and estimating the probable response of a firm's sales to changes in national income. Little attention has been given specifically to the problem of determining price-sales relationships, primarily because of the great difficulties involved. But the information obtained and techniques employed in present market research are valuable in providing further information about price-sales relationships.

Another approach is experimentation with price changes. But firms must use this procedure with great care. Other determinants of sales may change during the period. But far more serious is the danger that if the change proves unprofitable, the firm may be unable to return to the old price and recover its original sales volume. Competitors may meet reductions, or even exceed them, and may not follow the change back to the earlier level. Consumer resistance to the return to the old figure may be encountered; buyers may consider that the low price is the "satisfactory" one and may shift to other brands or products when the firm attempts to raise it. Experimental price increases are less dangerous than decreases, since they are unlikely to produce undesirable reactions on the part of competitors. But they may drive customers permanently into the arms of competing firms. A final difficulty with experimentation is that the entire effect of the price change may not be manifest for a substantial period. Buyers may not shift away immediately when prices are raised, but many may do so over a longer period. Reductions may cause temporary sales increases as buyers stock up in anticipation of the return of prices to the original level. In general, because of these problems, most firms consider experimentation with price changes extremely hazardous. Seldom will they deliberately experiment, but will make changes only when they are reasonably certain that the new prices will be more profitable than the old.

The Case of the Kinked Demand Curve

It has been suggested—more on the basis of commonsense observations than on careful empirical study—that oligopoly demand curves will frequently contain a sharp bend or kink at the level of the existing price. This kink, as illustrated in Figure 11–2, is produced by the greater tendency of competitors to follow price reductions than

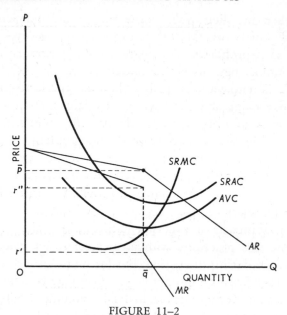

FIGURE 11–2

price increases. A reduction takes business away from other firms and forces them to cut prices in order to protect their sales, while an increase does not necessitate a readjustment, since other firms gain customers if one increases its price. At the point of the kink the MR curve is discontinuous, and thus, in a sense, marginal revenue is not defined. But at higher and lower levels of output the figure is defined, being as great as or greater than r'' for lower levels, and equal to or less than r' at higher levels of output (Figure 11–2).

The point of maximum profit for the firm is almost of necessity at the output level ($\bar{q}$ in Figure 11–2) at which the sharp change in elasticity occurs. It is likely that marginal cost will not equal marginal revenue at a lower volume of output because the MR curve is so nearly horizontal in this output range. At output levels to the right of the kink, the MR curve drops—perhaps to a negative figure—and almost certainly will lie below the MC curve. The optimum price ($\bar{p}$ in Figure 11–2) is indicated by the point at which the AR curve changes slope. It is likely to be obvious to the firm that any other price would be unprofitable, since increases would cause great losses in revenues, while reductions would yield little additional business. The more standardized the product, the sharper the kink, since customers will shift more readily and thus competitors will react more quickly and precisely.

One important consequence of the kink in the demand curve is that the firm may be slow to adjust price in response to cost changes. Because of the discontinuity in the MR curve, the MC curve can move up or down over a substantial range without affecting the equilibrium level of output. However, if a cost increase affects all firms in an industry, it may bring about a movement in the level of the kink. If all firms readjust price by the amount of the cost increase in the belief that all other firms will do so as well, the level of the kink will be raised by the amount of the cost increase, and price will rise by the same amount. Such a reaction is especially likely to occur in response to a cost increase that affects all firms uniformly, such as an excise tax. Each firm adds the tax to the selling price, yet loses relatively few sales because other firms follow exactly the same policy. This reaction is illustrated in Figure 11–3. As a result of the cost increase, the kink moves from the point *k* to the point *k'*—upward because of the cost increase, leftward because sales will be less at the higher price, and the position of the AR curve will change accordingly. Essentially, the firms move closer to the maximum joint-profit level, such a shift being impossible prior to the cost increase, given the degree of mutual interdependence.

While the kinked demand curve is useful for explaining reactions

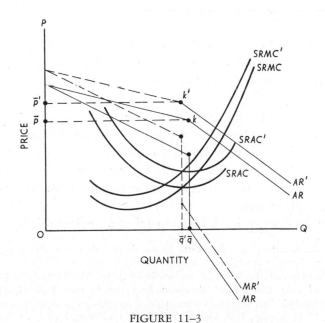

FIGURE 11–3

Adjustment of Price in Response to a Cost Increase Affecting All Firms, Kinked Demand Curve

of the sellers to various changes in the situation, the analysis of the case, in itself, contributes little to the explanation of existing price and output levels because it throws no light on the determinants of the height of the existing kink in the curve. In Figure 11–3, why does the kink occur at k and not at some other point? There appears to be no general principle to explain this level; appeal must be made to historical price trends and to particular techniques used by the firms in setting prices, as noted in subsequent sections.

Approaches to Pricing: Price Leadership

Firms may lessen the significance of oligopolistic uncertainty by making no independent price changes, but instead adopting and following prices set by other firms, or maintaining a fixed differential above or below other prices. If this policy is so widespread in an industry that all firms follow the prices set by one firm, *price leadership* is said to occur. Or some firms may follow independent price policies, while others follow the price set by one or more of these firms. The policy of following the leader, of course, causes nonleaders to set price on the basis of demand conditions alone without reference to cost; the relationship between price and average cost at the volume sold by the firm determines profits. If profits so determined are not satisfactory, the firm may seek to increase sales by advertising and other selling activities.

Price leadership is most likely to develop when one firm produces a large portion of total output, the remainder being distributed over several relatively small firms. Almost inevitably, the large firm comes to dominate pricing, the small firms perhaps being in a position to sell as much as they wish at the price set by the "dominant" firm. For maximum profits, the large firm will set its price on the basis of its own cost schedule and the total demand schedule for the product less the expected amounts to be sold by other firms. Price may approach the maximum profit figure, unless deliberately kept lower to discourage growth of smaller firms.[2]

In other cases, price leadership takes a "barometric" form. One

---

[2] In some industries once dominated by one large firm, the smaller firms gradually grew in size to the point at which the domination was broken. One of the best discussions of price leadership is to be found in the article by J. W. Markham, "The Nature and Significance of Price Leadership," *American Economic Review*, Vol. 41 (December, 1951), pp. 891–905. Extensive discussion of price leadership is also to be found in the study by A. D. H. Kaplan, J. B. Dirlam, and R. F. Lanzillotti, *Pricing in Big Business* (Washington, D.C.: Brookings, 1958).

firm in a group of firms of more or less comparable size comes to play the role of price leader, not because of its dominant position in the market, but because other firms regard its actions as a suitable barometer of changing market conditions and are willing to follow its policies in the belief that competitive disturbances are minimized by so doing. But the actual powers of a barometric price leader are greatly restricted by its realization that other firms will follow only within reasonable limits. Hence, if the firm is to retain its leadership position, it must consider the effects of its actions upon the profit positions of other firms. As long as the existing price is acceptable, it will be reluctant to make any changes which are not clearly advantageous to other firms, such as an increase in price by the amount of a new excise tax.

Price Following or Imitative Pricing

In an industry with price leaders, inevitably the other firms are followers. But, even in industries without price leaders, there are frequently firms which deliberately adopt no independent pricing policy, merely adapting to the prices of others. Such a policy avoids the necessity and cost of calculating prices, avoids any danger of upsetting competitive conditions, and allows the firm to concentrate on nonprice competition. A recent case study suggests several major examples of firms traditionally following such a policy: Gulf Oil, National Steel, and to a considerable degree, Kroger.[3]

Price following in some instances involves the selection of a price higher or lower than the typical figure in the industry. Hence a firm stressing high quality and prestige may price at some percentage in excess of the typical industry figure. Cut-rate firms may deliberately set prices below the market. Thus, independent gasoline retailers frequently follow a policy of selling at from 2 to 3 cents less than the price of major stations.

The Cost-Plus, Average Cost, or Markup Approach

Empirical study suggests that the most common approach to pricing is the use of an estimated figure of average cost as the primary basis. Average cost, in turn, is ascertained by adding to direct cost a markup that includes the rate of profit regarded as normal or attainable by the firm. This approach is often called the cost-plus or target return technique. Average cost so calculated may be set as the price, or

[3] Kaplan, Dirlam, and Lanzillotti, *op. cit.*

adjustments may be made in the light of estimates of demand and other factors.

Calculation of Price. There are several basic steps in the operation of the markup approach to pricing. First, the firm ascertains the direct separable cost per unit of output for which the product is responsible, primarily labor and materials cost. These costs are usually assumed to vary proportionately with output, so that the amount per unit is the same regardless of the volume of output. Second, when, as is typical, the firm is producing more than one product, it must allocate among the various products the *common costs,* i.e., costs incurred for the production of more than one product, no one of the products being responsible for any particular portion of the total. Thus, the costs of machinery used to process several different products must be allocated among products on the basis of some formula, such as machine-hours, specified by cost accounting techniques. Indirect labor costs—those of labor not directly engaged in physical production—are often allocated on the basis of hours of direct labor cost per unit of various products. Finally, there is added a markup, usually expressed as a percentage, to cover common costs not specifically allocated and a return on investment. In this process of calculation, two major questions arise: (1) What volume of output shall be used as the basis for determining per unit cost for those costs which do not vary, in total, in relation to output; and (2) what rate of profit should be included in the markup?

While a few firms apparently use estimated actual volume of output to determine cost per unit, most employ a so-called "standard" or "normal" output figure, which is a certain proportion of capacity, usually between two thirds and three quarters. This figure is preferred to an estimate of output for several reasons. The need to make an estimate of the actual volume is avoided. Price stability is encouraged, and there is less danger of upsetting relationships with other firms. Finally, the actual volume figure would lead to price increases when sales fall, a practice most businessmen regard as contrary to common sense.

The rate of profit that is included in cost calculations depends upon the attitude of officials of the firm as to the rate which is attainable and appears to them to be the optimum in terms of long-range profit possibilities. A number of firms have set up, on the basis of experience over the years, a *target return* figure which, on the average, they believe that they can earn. The following table indicates the reported goals of several major companies:

Company	Target Return on Investment Figure (after Taxes)	Actual Return on Investment, Average, 1947–55, after Taxes
Alcoa	10%	13.8%
General Electric	20	21.4
General Motors	20	26.0
International Harvester	10	8.9
Sears Roebuck	10–15	5.4
U.S. Steel	8	10.3

Source: R. F. Lanzillotti, "Pricing Objectives in Large Companies," *American Economic Review* Vol. 48 (December, 1958), pp. 924–26.

The rate of profit earned will of course differ from the target rate whenever actual sales volume differs from the standard volume used in calculating markup.

Customary Markups and Retail Pricing. Some firms, particularly retailers, use customary markup figures, which are rarely recalculated. Under usual retail pricing techniques, the markup percentage, applied to the purchase price of goods sold, is set sufficiently high to cover all common costs, called overhead in retailing, such as clerk hire, heat, light, rent, and the like, plus expected profit. In some fields of retailing, a uniform markup percentage is used on all items, but more typically, there will be variations. Items requiring refrigeration may be subject to a higher markup to cover the additional separable costs for which they are responsible. Prices on other goods will be adjusted to bring them to certain price lines at which the goods are traditionally sold; for example, neckties may be carried only at $2.00, $2.50, and $3.00. Other articles, such as electrical appliances and women's clothing, are typically priced at figures ending in 95 cents, in the belief that these have significant psychological advantages. The retailer has no control over prices on some goods, since the manufacturer establishes the resale price. In recent years, however, as a result of the rise of discount houses and the lessened role of state legislation sanctioning maintained prices, substantial shading of manufacturers' suggested prices has become common. Finally, demand considerations may force a retailer to vary his standard markup; some staple goods have come to bear markups typically smaller than the average.

While customary markups are widespread in retailing, some firms recalculate markups at frequent intervals by dividing total overhead, including expected profit, by expected sales to determine the desired margin, and then converting this to a markup percentage applied to purchase price of goods sold.

Rigid versus Flexible Markups. In a few industries, firms typically set prices at figures calculated by the average cost approach. But more commonly markups are flexible; that is, average costs serve as a point of departure in price setting, but do not determine the actual price. Thus the firm considers demand conditions as well as cost. If average cost is higher than the prices charged by other firms, the seller must consider whether or not he can charge more than competitors; if not, he will readjust downward. If, on the other hand, average cost is less than the prices other firms are charging, it may be advisable to increase price since competitors may otherwise reduce their figures, and all will be worse off. Or if demand appears to be very inelastic, price increases may be in order. Retailers not infrequently apply higher than usual markups to luxury food items; and automobile manufacturers apparently load expensive cars with a greater share of overhead than cheaper cars, the buyers of which are more price-conscious.

The Advantages of the Average Cost Approach

The widespread use of the average cost approach to pricing indicates that it must offer significant advantages. One obvious merit is simplicity; when firms have thousands of products, some workable rule-of-thumb pricing technique is imperative. Second, as long as the method is widely employed, it leads to uniformity of pricing and lessens the danger of price wars and breakdown of oligopolistic stability. Especially when markups are customary and uniform among firms, and materials, labor, and other direct costs are comparable, firms will set similar figures. Third, the approach lessens the dangers created by the existence of common costs for the maintenance of satisfactory prices. Unless firms distribute common costs among products in some standard fashion, different firms will arrive at substantially different prices on similar lines. But because of market competition, prices on each product will tend to gravitate to the lowest figure set by any firm. If some firms employ marginal cost pricing, therefore, no firm may be able to cover total common costs, for marginal costs for any particular line may appear to be very low because most of the costs, being common in nature, will continue whether the particular product is produced or not.

Consider, for example, a case in which a firm has considerable excess plant capacity capable of producing a variety of products, with a large portion of the costs being common. Further increases in output of goods now produced are unprofitable, because price reductions would be necessary on all units, and marginal revenue would be correspondingly slight. But if a new line of goods is taken on, a low price can be set on this good without affecting the revenue from other goods, and the utilization of plant capacity will be improved. However, the effect of this policy of firms whose primary business is in the new line may be disastrous, and retaliation will occur. For instance, if a radio manufacturer, in order to utilize excess plant capacity, commences to produce electric ranges and sells them at prices lower than the current prices charged by other firms, range manufacturers may follow the same policy with radios, and firms in both industries will suffer losses. Accordingly, firms in each industry will hesitate to start such practices. In an effort to discourage this type of competition, trade associations may encourage the use of policies which minimize marginal cost considerations.

Use of the average cost approach to price setting is also furthered by a belief on the part of businessmen that this method is "reasonable" and "fair." The notion that all commodities should bear their "share" of overhead, and that prices should be set at a figure which includes a "fair" profit, is widely accepted in the business community, although there are many exceptions.

Average Cost Pricing and Profit Maximization

The extent to which average cost pricing constitutes a departure from the assumption of profit maximization has been the subject of much controversy. It is obvious that any method of pricing that involves the addition of a certain percentage to variable costs can hardly maximize profits except by sheer accident. It is also inevitable that the manner in which overhead is distributed over products will be different if firms approach price determination on the basis of estimates of marginal revenues and marginal costs. Nevertheless, given the circumstances of oligopoly, the average cost method, properly employed, may allow firms to come closer to maximum profit than any other pricing system. There are several reasons.

In the first place, as noted earlier, the average cost technique is an effective means of stabilizing competition and lessening the uncertainty characteristic of oligopolistic markets. Second, as long as demand elements are taken into consideration, price may not differ too greatly from the figure which would be selected on the basis of marginal considerations. Adjustments made in average cost estimates in setting actual price bring demand aspects into the picture and thus lead to a price more closely approximating the maximum profit level.

Third, once various firms in an industry have set prices on an average cost basis, the price so set may actually seem to yield maximum profits—equality between marginal revenue and marginal cost—for any given firm because the kink in each firm's demand curve will be at this level. The price at this level may not yield maximum profit for the firms as a group, and may be substantially different from the price firms would set if price determination were initially approached via estimates of marginal revenue and marginal cost. But given prevailing competitive relationships and the inability to maximize joint profits, the price arrived at by average cost methods may represent a relative if not an absolute optimum.

While the use of average cost pricing may in general be consistent with profit maximization in oligopolistic industries, excessive reliance on average cost figures may cause firms to sacrifice profits, particularly if relatively small price reductions will lead to large increases in sales. As indicated above, most business firms consider these factors in setting prices rather than using average cost techniques alone, but some may overemphasize the significance of average cost.

The Significance of Average Cost Pricing

From the standpoint of resource allocation and reactions to demand and cost changes, the use of the average cost pricing technique has considerable significance:

1. *Effect on Prices.* In the first place, the use of this technique results in a different allocation of common cost among various products than would occur with the direct use of marginal techniques, and thus in different prices and outputs of particular goods.

2. *The Effect on Price of an Increase in Demand.* With the establishment of prices on the basis of an estimate of marginal cost and revenue schedules, an increase in demand will usually lead to price increases, as illustrated in Figure 11–4. When the revenue curve shifts from AR to AR', equilibrium price rises from $\bar{p}$ to $\bar{p}'$. But when the average cost approach is used, the decline or constancy of average cost consequent to increased sales will lessen the likelihood of price increases and in some instances actually lead to price reductions. Reductions would be more common if average cost were calculated on the basis of estimated sales instead of normal sales. Likewise, when demand falls, strict adherence to average cost price, with actual sales used as a basis for calculating average cost, will bring about price increases. But the use of the standard output basis lessens this tendency.

3. *Reaction of Price to an Increase in Cost.* With marginal cost pricing, price will never (except under unlikely assumptions) be raised

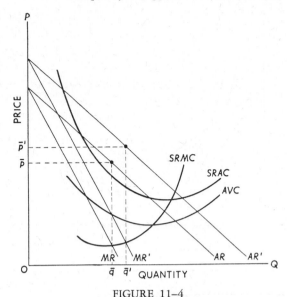

FIGURE 11–4

REACTION OF EQUILIBRIUM PRICE TO AN INCREASE IN DEMAND

immediately by the full amount of a cost increase. A firm will readjust output until marginal revenue and marginal cost are again equal, thus raising marginal revenue by the amount of the increase in marginal cost.[4] Thus price will be raised by a smaller amount, as shown on Figure 11–5. Price rises from $\bar{p}$ to $\bar{p}'$, while the amount of the cost increase is the vertical distance between AC and AC'. When price is set on the basis of average cost, however, firms are likely to raise price immediately by the full amount of the cost increase. Suppose, for example, that the wages paid by all firms in an industry increase. Average cost is raised by the amount of the wage increase per unit of output; accordingly, price is likely to be raised by the same amount. If all firms follow the same policy, all will be better off (unless they have already attained maximum joint profits) than they would have been had they raised by a smaller amount. If the total demand for the product is at all elastic, the firms will not cover average cost despite the increase (assuming average profit before the wage rise), but will more closely approach doing so than if they raised price by a smaller amount. Some departure of firms from the industry will still be necessary to restore average profits. It should be noted that such a price

[4] If, as in Figure 11–5, marginal cost is not constant in the particular range of output, marginal revenue will rise by less than or more than the amount of increase in marginal cost once adjustments are complete. But this modification does not affect the basic relationship between changes in marginal revenue and average revenue noted in the paragraph.

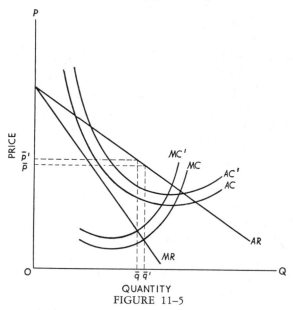

FIGURE 11–5

RESPONSE OF EQUILIBRIUM PRICE TO AN INCREASE IN COST, MARGINAL
APPROACH TO PRICING

increase would have been profitable even in the absence of the wage
increase. But, given the competitive situation, no one firm could raise
because there was no assurance that others would follow. When a cost
increase occurs in all firms, however, each is likely to feel that the others
will raise prices if it does, and the increase will take place accordingly.

Introductory Pricing

For established products, the task of determining prices involves
merely the question of desirable change from existing levels. But when
entirely new products are placed on the market, the problem is more
complicated, and the policies followed vary widely. Some firms merely
apply their standard pricing techniques. Others set relatively high
prices, in an effort either to recover very quickly the costs incidental to
the development of the new product or to take advantage of the
temporary lack of competition. Drug manufacturers have, from all
indications, tended to price new products relatively high in order to
recover heavy research costs in a short period of time and, in so doing,
have incurred substantial public criticism. Other firms have followed
the opposite policy, pricing at less than average cost (which is typically
high until volume becomes substantial) in an effort to stimulate
widespread use of the new products.

Adjustment of Product to Price

In some lines, there is a definite policy of selecting a price and then adjusting quality and thus cost to allow profitable production at the price selected (provided volume is adequate). The classic example is the 5-cent candy bar, which many firms retained for long periods, despite rising costs, by reducing the size. Some firms vary the size from year to year in conformity with varying prices of cocoa and other elements. But in other fields as well, the phenomenon is encountered. Producers of household electrical appliances and farm implements have frequently followed the rule of selecting a price at which they believe a product will sell in profitable amounts, and then adjusting the quality of the product to obtain a cost figure which will allow an adequate profit.

Strategical Moves in Oligopoly

In some respects a situation of partial oligopoly resembles a military campaign or a poker game. Certain actions may be taken not because they are advantageous in themselves, but because they improve the position of the oligopolist relative to his competitors and may ultimately result in an improved financial position. Deliberate price cutting, in itself unprofitable, may be undertaken either to drive competitors out or to scare them sufficiently to discourage them from undertaking actions contrary to the interests of other firms. On the other hand, the desire for security and the ability to hold out against aggressive action on the part of competitors may lead a firm to take action which is itself contrary to profit maximization. Thus, a firm may expand in order to increase the absolute size of its financial resources, or to insure supplies of materials or market outlets during periods of competitive struggles, even though these actions are not in themselves profitable.

Some students of oligopoly have suggested that the entire approach to oligopoly price and output policy should be recast in terms of the behavior of participants in a strategic game, replacing the analysis based upon the assumption of profit maximization. This point of view, first developed in the work of J. von Neumann and O. Morgenstern entitled *The Theory of Games and Economic Behavior*,[5] stresses the tendency of various parties in such circumstances to combine in order to get the best of the opponent. In terms of this approach, there is a set of alternative solutions (with respect to price and output levels, for exam-

[5] Rev. ed.; Princeton: Princeton University Press, 1947.

ple), the actual one attained in a particular case depending upon the specific policies followed.[6] Or, the firm may seek to ascertain the competitors' most likely countermoves to one's own policies, and formulate alternative defense measures.

The chief contributions of this line of thought are a novel terminology and a more precise characterization of alternative possible oligopoly situations. It has done little or nothing to improve our ability to predict patterns of behavior in concrete oligopoly situations, largely because it has not led (as originally expected) to an acceptable general solution to the problem of describing "rational behavior" under conditions of limited information. As of the present time, indeed, there is no reason to suppose that the "theory of games" approach to oligopoly is in all respects superior to that of traditional economic theory; some specialists would even argue that, in most respects, it is inferior.[7]

Other Objectives of Oligopolists

Other students of oligopoly pricing have argued that the profit-maximization goal is not in accord with the objectives of management of large-scale widely owned businesses. W. J. Baumol has stressed the importance of the goal of maximizing sales—that is, gross revenue from sales—provided that the profit level is regarded as adequate at the maximum sales figure.[8] Thus output is extended until MR is zero, instead of equal to MC, and selling activities are extended to the point at which they will bring no further increases in gross revenue. Thus in Figure 11–6 the point of operation is $\bar{q}$. Baumol defends this thesis on several grounds: management regards total sales and thus the share of the market as the prime measure of its success; and salaries of management are more closely related to gross sales than to profits. Adherence to this goal is strengthened by emphasis on "satisfactory" or "fair" profit instead of maximum profit.[9]

[6] See the article by L. Hurwicz, "What Has Happened to the Theory of Games," *Proceedings of the American Economic Association,* May, 1953, pp. 398–405.

[7] Compare E. G. Bennion, *Elementary Mathematics of Linear Programming and Game Theory* (East Lansing: Bureau of Business and Economic Research, Michigan State University, 1960), pp. 135–36. For a treatment of oligopoly problems from a game-theory point of view, see M. Shubik, *Strategy and Market Structure* (New York: Wiley, 1959).

[8] See "The Theory of Oligopoly," *Economica,* Vol. 25 (August, 1950), pp. 1871–98.

[9] See W. C. Pardridge, "Sales or Profit Maximization in Management Capitalism," *Western Economic Journal,* Vol. 2 (Spring, 1964), pp. 134–41, for a criticism of the Baumol arguments.

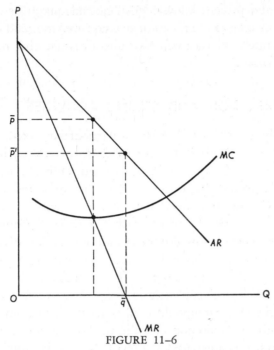

FIGURE 11–6

EQUILIBRIUM OUTPUT, GOAL OF MAXIMUM SALES REVENUE

Other writers, such as Oliver Williamson, have stressed the importance of the personal goals of the corporation management.[10] In widely held corporations, management has certain "expense preferences"—types of expenditures which yield benefits to management over and above those yielded to the firm, and thus will be carried beyond the profit-maximizing level. Additional expenditures for staff constitute a major example; each subordinate executive seeks to increase the staff working under him, since doing so increases his own salary, prestige, and security. This is, of course, the phenomenon frequently attributed to government agencies. It is also argued that management at all levels seeks to increase "emoluments"—various supplements to management salaries, which obviously yield direct benefits to the recipients. Management likewise regards the amount of funds available for investment use at their discretion as important. Emphasis on these considerations will lead to differences in price and output policy compared to those based on the profit-maximizing goal.

The significance of these nonprofit-maximizing goals is an empiri-

[10] See, O. E. Williamson, "Managerial Discretion and Business Behavior," *American Economic Review*, Vol. 53 (December, 1963), pp. 1032–57.

cal question, and present knowledge is not adequate for a satisfactory answer. Further empirical studies of decision making, and development of more elaborate models of behavior under diverse and multiple goals, are clearly required.[11]

PRODUCT VARIATION AND SELLING ACTIVITIES

Oligopoly conditions provide a particularly fertile ground for product variation, advertising, and other forms of selling activities. Price tends to stablize at a certain figure; and while the firm is anxious to increase sales in order to lower average cost, price reductions are not profitable because of the danger that other firms will also reduce prices. Firms turn to various forms of selling activities primarily because reactions on the part of competitors are likely to be less disastrous to the firm than reactions to price reductions. Time will be required for the competitors to follow suit, whereas they can meet price cuts almost instantly. By the time competitors have discovered the success of nonprice policies and attempted to duplicate them, customers may be so well attached that they do not return to the competing firms. Moreover, there is always a chance that competitors will be unable to devise equally satisfactory selling methods. A price cut is a definite, conspicuous act which competitors can match or exceed if they wish. Sales activities are less obvious in their effects upon competitors. Furthermore, the widespread attitude on the part of businessmen that price cutting is unethical encourages the use of selling activities instead of price adjustments. Legislative action, such as that sanctioning resale price maintenance and placing restrictions upon selling below "cost," may also direct competition into nonprice lines.

Mutual Interdependence in Selling Activities

While interdependence is less significant with selling activities than with price changes, it is not necessarily absent. There is a wide range of possible relationships among oligopolists in the field of product policy and selling activities. At one extreme, there may be perfect collusion, the firms agreeing implicitly or explicitly to select those products and selling policies which maximize profits for the group. There is substantial evidence, however, that complete collusion on product and sales activities is rare. From all indications, firms are

[11] Note the Cohen and Cyert, Cyert and March, and Simon references at the end of the chapter.

much less willing to agree on these matters than upon price, and more willing to follow completely independent policies, partly because of the belief that the firm can carry on these activities more effectively than competitors, partly because the results of failure to agree appear to be less disastrous, as noted earlier.

The absence of complete collusion on product and selling activities almost certainly results in a higher level of selling activities than would occur with such collusion. Each firm attempts to increase its share of the market at the expense of other firms. Since competitors follow the same policy, much of the activity will cancel out, and none of the firms will gain anticipated sales volumes. All firms would be better off if all would cut the volume of advertising, yet no one firm can do so independently.

On the other hand, to the extent that firms take into consideration any effects that changes in their own selling activities will have upon the policies of competitors, the level of selling activities will be reduced below that which would otherwise be attained. If a firm believes that initiation of an extensive selling campaign will induce its competitors to follow suit, it will be inhibited from taking any action at all.

If competitors follow increases in selling activities but not decreases, retreat from a high level of selling activities will be very difficult.

The Significance of Selling Activities

The success of selling activities among oligopolists is a major influence on the sharing of the total market among the competing firms. The largest shares may go to firms which do the best selling job, rather than to those which attain the lowest cost in manufacturing. The firms that fail may be those which make mistakes in the adjustment of product (such as introducing too revolutionary changes in style) or fall behind in selling activities. Furthermore, the tendency of firms in oligopoly situations to stress selling activities as a means of increasing sales may lead to a higher level of selling activities than would be carried on in other competitive conditions, and average cost (including selling cost) will be higher. On the other hand, to the extent that firms take into consideration the effects which their selling activities have upon the sales policies of their competitors, the overall level of selling activities may be less than if the market were one of monopolistic competition. Moreover, successful selling activity may concentrate the total business in the hands of a smaller number of firms, and allow operation nearer the point of lowest average cost. Thus the price of the product could be lower than it would be if no selling activities were carried on (but not lower than the purely competitive price).

PRICE DISCRIMINATION

Price discrimination is necessary, in all likelihood, for maximum joint profits. However, it is not possible unless the various firms follow uniform pricing policies, because prices in the high-price markets would be pulled down to those in the lower-price markets. Firms must either agree on the prices to be charged in the various markets or spontaneously follow uniform practices. Because of the difficulties of obtaining complete cooperation, effective discrimination is less likely to occur than with monopoly.

Some of the most significant instances of price discrimination in the United States have arisen from devices designed to lessen price competition rather than from a pricing policy introduced to adjust prices in terms of demand elasticities in various markets. The most important of these devices has been the basing point system, under which the price of the product in each locality was calculated by adding to the price at the basing point the freight from the basing point to the locality, regardless of the actual origin of the goods. For many years steel prices in all parts of the country were determined by adding to the Pittsburgh price the freight from Pittsburgh, regardless of the actual origin of the steel. A Chicago buyer obtaining steel from a Gary mill would pay the Pittsburgh base price plus freight from Pittsburgh, although the steel was shipped only from Gary. In later years, several basing points were used instead of one. The single-point system provided a uniform price in each area for all firms, regardless of the location of the plant, and served as a device to lessen price competition. Ultimately, Supreme Court decisions interpreting the antitrust laws brought an end to most basing point techniques. The use of a uniform price for the entire country, followed frequently in industries in which freight is a relatively unimportant item, also facilitates the avoidance of price differences and price cutting, but is not interfered with under the antitrust laws.

LONG-RUN ADJUSTMENTS

In oligopoly, just as in other types of market situations, equilibrium price and output will be different in the long run than at any particular time, partly because of internal adjustments designed to attain the optimum-sized plant in terms of the market situation, and partly through a change in the number of firms in the industry.

Long-Run Cost Adjustments

Over a long-run period, firms will adjust their plants to the sizes which are most satisfactory in terms of current and expected demand situations. Thus, LRMC, including plant as well as current operating costs, will become a primary determinant of output and price policies. Just as with monopoly, long-run adjustment requires equality of MR with both LRMC and SRMC with the plant which is the optimum under the circumstances.

Tendencies toward the Elimination of Excess Profits

The existence of mutual interdependence is no guarantee, in itself, of excess profits. Even if the firms in an industry succeed in maximizing joint profits, the rate of profit may not be greater than average. The extent to which excess profits disappear depends upon the ease with which new firms can enter the industry. When entry is easy, newcomers will be attracted by excess profits. They may break down existing pricing institutions and agreements, as they cut prices in order to establish themselves in the industry. Older firms may reduce prices to avoid excessive losses in sales, and the general level of prices will approach average cost more closely. If the demand curves of firms are kinked, the action of newcomers in setting lower prices will lower the level of the kink for all firms.

On the other hand, new firms may follow the same pricing policies as existing firms, either initially or after a period of price cutting. As a consequence, equality of price and average cost, at least for some firms, will be attained through an increase in average cost rather than a decline in price. The increased number of firms results in a division of total business among a larger number of firms and so in smaller sales volume for each. If loss of sales forces a firm to operate at a higher point on its AC curve, excess profits may be eliminated without a reduction in price.

Figure 11–7 illustrates the elimination of excess profits through the entry of new firms; the *AR* curve moves to the left as new firms enter, until excess profits are eliminated and *AR* is tangent to *LRAC* at a price of $\bar{p}'$. Figure 11–8 illustrates a completed adjustment with a kinked demand curve. If the curve is kinked, the chances of a price reduction as new firms enter is particularly slight. So long as the new firms follow the prices of the old, none will find a price reduction (or increase) desirable;

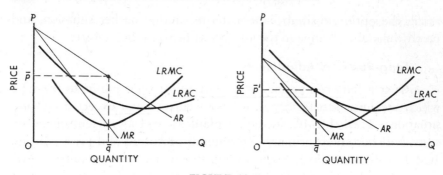

FIGURE 11-7

ADJUSTMENT OF PRICE TOWARD AVERAGE COST, FREE ENTRY

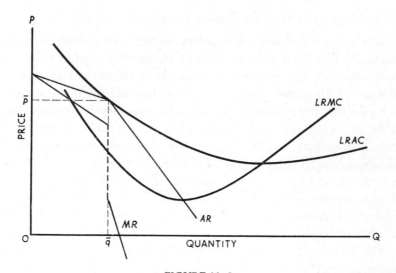

FIGURE 11-8

ADJUSTMENT OF PRICE TOWARD AVERAGE COST, KINKED DEMAND CURVE
AND FREE ENTRY

thus the point of the kink will gradually move to the left, but will stay at the same horizontal level, until it is just tangent to *LRAC*. The use of average cost pricing techniques also increases the likelihood that excess profits will be eliminated without a price cut. The loss in sales to new firms raises average cost (if it is calculated on the basis of actual sales), and discourages price reductions.

Excess profits may sometimes be avoided deliberately by existing firms, being sacrificed for greater long-run security. If excess profits are earned and new firms enter, there is always a danger that too many will commence operations, with consequent losses (for a period) for many of the firms. To avoid this danger, existing firms may deliberately set

prices to yield only a more or less average rate of return, and price may
be only slightly above or equal to lowest average cost.

Entry Restriction

To the extent that entry is relatively free, empirical studies of actual
levels of operation of firms should indicate that firms are typically operating on the downward-sloping portions of their LRAC curves, as explained in the previous section. But a study by Bain of twenty major and
long-established manufacturing industries reveals that, except for a marginal fringe, the firms have reached a scale of plant and firm size great

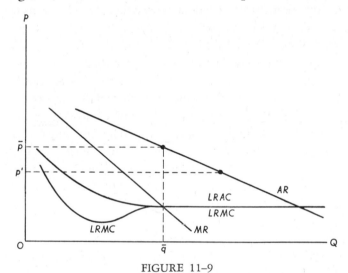

FIGURE 11–9

LONG-RUN EQUILIBRIUM, ENTRY RESTRICTION

enough to allow lowest cost of operation and, in fact, in a number of
instances were well beyond the minimum necessary for low cost.[12] In
graphical terms, their positions appear as shown in Figure 11–9. The
maximum-profit price is represented by $\bar{p}$. Typically, the rate of profit
was higher than the figure regarded as an average rate of return for the
economy as a whole.

This phenomenon can be explained in two ways. First, the firms
may deliberately hold prices below the maximum-profit point (illustrated by p' in Figure 11–9) as a means of discouraging newcomers
from entering, or because of general acceptance of the idea of a "fair"
profit rather than the maximum one. This attitude undoubtedly plays
some role. Second, restriction of entry may prevent an increase in the

[12] See J. S. Bain, *Barriers to New Competition* (Cambridge: Harvard University
Press, 1956).

number of firms. The profit rate in these industries suggests that this explanation is the primary one.

The Bain study examined entry barriers and found three to be of primary importance:

1. Economies of large-scale production, which make operation on a small scale during the early years of a new firm extremely unprofitable. A firm cannot build up a large market overnight; in the interim, cost per unit will be so high that losses will be heavy. Recognition of this feature discourages new firms from entering.

2. Product differentiation and established reputations, which make the development of an adequate market by new firms very slow and, particularly when coupled with the first restriction noted, may make entry almost impossible. Bain concludes that, on the whole, differentiation is more significant as a barrier than economies of large-scale production. Among the major features of differentiation noted are durability and complexity of product, which makes consumer appraisal of new brands difficult, and leads to reliance on established reputation. A second is dealer relationships; exclusive dealerships and the reluctance of retailers to carry a large number of lines seriously impede the development of a new market. Finally, conspicuous consumption, the desire to be seen using the "popular" make or brand, plays some role.

3. The absolute magnitude of money capital required. The ability to obtain money capital depends primarily upon a satisfactory credit standing. New firms without an established credit position often have great difficulty obtaining necessary capital, even in periods when loan funds are generally plentiful. New businesses must be developed primarily with the capital of the promoters plus reinvested earnings; thus, persons lacking adequate resources of their own find the establishment of a business extremely difficult, regardless of profit prospects and their own management abilities. This type of restriction is particularly serious for lines of production which require heavy initial capital investment, such as steel.

In addition, there are certain absolute restrictions to entry, found by Bain to be of little significance in the industries which he studied, but undoubtedly of greater importance in other sectors of the economy. These include:

a) Limited raw material supplies. When necessary specialized resources, such as ores of a certain type, are to be found only in limited areas and existing firms control the entire supply, it is impossible for new firms to commence operation. Entry into nickel production and diamond mining, for example, is severely restricted by this consideration.

b) <u>Legal restrictions</u>. Governmental activity may restrict entry of new firms. Patent rights may interfere with the ability of new firms to develop competing products. Trademarks protect various differentiation devices. Tariffs interfere with the entry of foreign competition into domestic markets. Cities may limit the numbers of certain types of enterprises (taverns, for example) or prevent peddlers from operating, frequently under the terms of the so-called "Green River ordinance." Licensing requirements for various trades are often used to restrict numbers. The most severe legal restrictions are applied to public utilities; new firms are not permitted to enter without approval of regulatory agencies. In general, sanction will not be given unless substantial proof can be presented that the service of existing firms is inadequate.

Some of these legal restrictions are established in the interests of general welfare. Control of entry into public utility industries is necessary to prevent excess plant capacity and higher rates, for example. But many of the restrictions, such as most tariffs and many licensing requirements, result from the political activity of interested groups.

Common Costs and the Level of Average Cost

When a firm is producing several products and some of the costs are common, there is no determinate average cost for each product, that is, no average cost figure which price must cover in the long run and to which price will equal if there is completely free entry. The enterprise, as a whole, must cover common as well as separable costs; and <u>with free entry, total receipts will equal total costs for all products, including common costs and a necessary profit</u>. Furthermore, each particular product must sell for a price which covers its average separable costs, or the firm will cease producing it. But there is <u>no necessary way in which common costs must be shared among the various products</u>. In practice, some articles may carry more than a proportionate share of overhead and others less; but it is advantageous for the firm to continue to produce items contributing relatively little to common cost, provided they make some contribution. The actual distribution of common costs among the various articles will depend primarily upon the techniques employed by firms in allocating common costs, the nature of consumer demands for the various products, and the extent of competition in various markets.

Elimination of Losses

<u>Mutual interdependence</u> among the various firms in an industry does not insure that all firms can earn even an average rate of profit,

since the number of firms may be so great relative to demand that at each possible output level average cost exceeds the price which can be obtained. There are two possible adjustments when losses are incurred. If price and output are not at the level at which joint profits are maximized, increased cooperation on the part of firms may produce a sufficient increase in price to cover average cost. The NRA period of the 1930's was characterized by extensive activity of this sort, when for a short period such coöperative action was not illegal. In the absence of greater coöperation, however, restoration of price to the average cost level necessitates the departure of some firms from the field. These are most likely to be the ones that fall behind in the race for customers because of poor selling efforts. They may, however, be firms whose equipment wears out first or whose owners are most pessimistic about the future. As some firms leave the field, the increased sales volumes of remaining firms will allow them to cover cost (assuming that their average cost declines as they increase sales). Prices may not rise at all, as they would under similar circumstances in pure competition, the losses being eliminated entirely by the decline in average cost.

Nonuniformity of Price

With differentiation, the prices of the various sellers are not likely to be uniform, even after long-run adjustments. Differentiation often involves deliberate quality differences, designed to appeal to different income levels. As a consequence, both cost schedules and the height of demand schedules will differ. Even with outright price agreements, price differentials are almost essential if low-quality-product firms are to remain in business. In other situations, firms without established reputations must maintain lower prices if they are to continue to sell. Most of these sources of differences are not eliminated by the passage of time. Even though all firms in an industry are making a normal rate of profit, prices charged may vary substantially from one firm to another.

PURE OLIGOPOLY

The analysis in preceding sections rests upon the assumption that products are differentiated. Oligopoly may also be accompanied by *standardization* of product, a situation designated as *pure oligopoly*. This is most closely approximated in markets for capital equipment, building materials, etc., which are purchased by expert buyers to meet specific uses in production. Markets for lumber, cement, brick, railroad equipment, industrial machinery, steel, copper, and aluminum provide examples. Rarely, however, is differentiation completely absent, primarily because of differences in service rendered in conjunction with sales, the personal relation between officials of various companies, and the efforts of salesmen.

With standardized product, realization of mutual interdependence and tendency toward outright cooperation are greatly strengthened. With no differentiation, prices must be uniform, or the high-price firms will sell nothing. Accordingly, independent price determination on the part of each firm, no attention being paid to competitors' actions, would be suicidal, with price fluctuations and frequent periods of losses as firms sought to increase sales by price reductions. Hence, some type of coordinated action is imperative—much more so than with differentiation, in which each firm has an established clientele and quality differences lessen the severity of price competition. The forms which coordinated action may take are, in general, the same with standardized products as with differentiation. Price leadership or outright agreements are most likely, since the use of standard pricing techniques may not give the necessary degree of uniformity. Price agreements are of course illegal, but they nevertheless exist, their secret nature preventing effective enforcement of the antitrust laws. Occasionally, upon the advent of a newcomer into an industry or in a period of severe depression, when firms are anxious to increase sales, established pricing institutions break down, and a period of price competition ensues. But such action is not frequent.

The same considerations of price and output determination apply to pure oligopoly as to differentiated oligopoly, apart from the greater necessity of maintaining price uniformity. The greater degree of cooperation may insure closer attainment of maximum joint profits, and of temporary excess profits. Lack of differentiation makes the entry of new firms easier, but in many capital equipment industries the heavy capital investment and large volume of output necessary for low-cost operation constitute formidable obstacles to the free flow of firms into the field.

MONOPSONY AND OLIGOPSONY

Up to this point in our analysis, the assumption has been made that the number of buyers is large, and that sellers have no preferences for dealing with some purchasers instead of others.

There are, however, situations in which these assumptions are not realized, individual buyers being able to exert influence on price. There are three possible cases:

1. Monopsony: a single buyer, the counterpart of monopoly. Examples are rare, except for purchases by the government of various specialized defense items.

2. Oligopsony, characterized by a sufficiently small number of buyers that each is aware that he can influence price, and thus there is mutual interdependence among them. Thus, for example, an oil refining company may buy so much of the crude oil in a particular market area that it is aware that it can influence market price, and that changes which it makes in the prices offered for crude oil will affect the prices offered by other firms. Oligopsony may take the form of collusion among buyers or spontaneous coordination.

3. Monopsonistic competition, characterized by large numbers of buyers, but with preferences on the part of the sellers for dealing with particular buyers. This situation does not appear to be empirically significant.

Monopsonistic influences may develop in an industry characterized by a homogeneous product and a large number of sellers. Such a market is essentially one of pure competition from the standpoint of the sellers, since no one seller can influence price, but price determination is actually dominated by buyers. Examples of this situation are found in the market for crude oil, in which a few refineries buy a standardized product from many small producers, and in wholesale markets for tobacco and sugar beets. More commonly, however, oligopsony elements exist in conjunction with differentiation and oligopoly on the sellers' side. Such situations are found in many capital goods markets; specialized machinery is produced by a few firms and is used by only a few buyers. Labor markets are frequently influenced on the sellers' side by labor union action, and thus coordinated control of supply, and on the buyers' side by a few dominant employers. While oligopsony is not commonly found in final markets for consumption goods, it occasionally exists in wholesale markets for such goods. Three large automobile manufacturers buy approximately half the annual output of tires, which are in turn produced by a small number of firms. Large department stores, mail-order houses, and chain stores frequently dominate wholesale markets for consumption goods.

Monopsony and Large Numbers of Sellers

Suppose that in a certain market there is a single firm buying from a large number of small producers whose products are identical. The

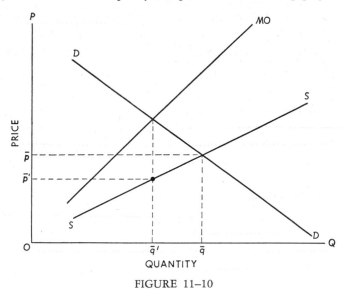

FIGURE 11–10

<small>EQUILIBRIUM PRICE AND OUTPUT, MONOPSONY</small>

buyer has a certain demand for the product, as indicated by the curve *DD* in Figure 11–10. If he acted without regard to the effects of his purchases upon price, he would extend purchases to the level at which his demand and the market supply (*SS*) were equal—$\bar{q}$ in Figure 11–10. But he will, of course, recognize that the quantity of his purchases will affect price. Each additional unit bought will cost him not only the price paid for it, but also the additional sum on the units he could otherwise have bought more cheaply. Therefore, his marginal outlay on the commodity—the additional amount he pays as a result of the purchase of another unit—exceeds the price. In Figure 11–10 the marginal outlay is represented by the curve *MO*. In order to maximize his profit, the buyer must extend purchases to the point of equality of marginal outlay and demand. He will thus buy a smaller quantity ($\bar{q}'$ in Figure 11–10) than he would if he ignored the effect of his purchases upon demand, and the market price ($\bar{p}'$) will be lower than it would be if the market were purely competitive ($\bar{p}$).

From a long-run standpoint, the effect of monopsony power upon price will depend upon cost conditions. No amount of monopsony power will allow a buyer to continue to obtain a product for less than average cost, year after year, because production will fall. If the industry is one of increasing cost, price will remain permanently lower than the purely competitive figure because of smaller purchases and output. However, if the supplying industry is one of constant cost, price will be the same as if the market were purely competitive, since average cost, which price must cover, is the same regardless of output. The long-run supply curve is a horizontal line, and thus marginal outlay and price paid are identical.

Oligopsony with Large Numbers of Sellers

Oligopsony occurs if there is more than one buyer, but so few that each is aware that his buying policies affects those of other firms. Buyers will take the initiative in setting price, provided that there are numerous sellers.

If there is little interdependence and quantities purchased by any one firm have only a slight effect on price, the various firms may bid up price toward the purely competitive level. On the other hand, if mutual interdependence is complete, firms may succeed in setting the same purchase price as a monopsonist. If the actual situation lies between these extremes, generalizations about price levels are difficult, just as with partial oligopoly. The greater the degree of mutual interdependence, the greater the extent of deviation of the supply price of the good from the marginal outlay of each firm, and thus the closer will the price approach the monopsony figure. In less precise terms, buyers seek to pay the minimum sum for the quantities they desire; but these quantities, in turn, are dependent upon the price which must be paid. If the buyers are business firms, the picture is complicated by the fact that the price the firm must pay for purchases affects its costs of production and thus the amount of its product that can be sold. Firms will seek to determine a purchase price which will allow maximum profit, taking into consideration the supply which they can obtain at this price, their costs at this price, and their selling prices and sales. The supply of agricultural products depends upon the size of the current crop: if the crop is large, a low price can be set; if the crop is small, the price is likely to be higher. When the supply is relatively limited, there is a tendency for oligopsony power to disappear as buyers bid against one another to obtain an increased share of the limited quantities available.

Regardless of the power over market prices possessed by oligopsonists, they cannot ignore the costs of production of suppliers of the goods purchased. In any particular year, very low prices may not affect total supply. But over a period of time, prices must cover the average costs of producers at the equilibrium output level if the supply is to be forthcoming. If the industry producing the product is one of increasing costs, the smaller volume of purchases will hold the price permanently below the purely competitive equilibrium. If, however, the industry is operating in constant cost conditions, there will be no permanent effect on price.

Bilateral Monopoly and Bilateral Oligopoly

In the two preceding situations, it has been assumed that the number of sellers was large. But monopsony or oligopsony on the buyers' side may be accompanied by monopoly or oligopoly on the sellers' side. Such cases are known as bilateral monopoly and bilateral oligopoly. If both oligopsony and oligopoly are complete, firms may succeed in setting a price which will maximize the gains of both buyers and sellers, and split the gains on the basis of bargaining. But it is perhaps more likely that differences in bargaining strength will result in a figure relatively more advantageous to the stronger party than the maximum joint-gain figure. No matter how strong the buyers are, they cannot keep price below the average cost of the sellers, or their supply will disappear. With prices above the optimum, sales of the product produced by the buyers will drop sufficiently to cut profits all along the line. But subject to these limits—which may be far apart—the actual price will depend upon bargaining, and no further generalization is possible. The theory of games, discussed on page 239, has been of some use in analyzing the strategies that might be followed by oligopolists and oligopsonists in dealing with each other. But there are no settled questions in this area of theory.

SELECTED REFERENCES

BAIN, J. S. *Barriers to New Competition.* Cambridge: Harvard University Press, 1956.
>   The most compete study, largely empirical, of barriers to entry.

BAUMOL, W. J. *Business Behavior, Value and Growth.* New York: Wiley, 1959.
>   The maximization of sales thesis.

COHEN, K. J., AND CYERT, R. M. *Theory of the Firm,* chaps. xii, xvi, xvii. Englewood Cliffs, N.J.: Prentice-Hall, 1965.
>   An excellent presentation of the classical theory of duopoly and oligopoly, and new approaches to oligopoly decision making.

COLBERG, M. R.; FORBUSH, D. R.; AND WHITAKER, R. G. *Business Economics,* chap. vi. 3d ed. Homewood, Ill.: Irwin, 1964.
>   Case illustrations.

CYERT, R. M., AND MARCH, J. R. *Behavioral Theory of the Firm.* Englewood Cliffs, N.J.: Prentice-Hall, 1963.
>   New approaches to theory of the firm.

FELLNER, W. J. *Competition among the Few.* New York: Knopf, 1949.
The basic work in contemporary oligopoly theory.

HAYNES, W. W. *Managerial Economics,* chap. x, xii. Homewood, Ill.: Dorsey, 1963.
Case illustrations of various approaches to pricing.

SIMON, H. A. "New Developments in the Theory of the Firm," *Proceedings of the American Economic Association for 1961,* pp. 1–15.

QUESTIONS

1. How would you explain the importance of oligopoly in the contemporary American economy?
2. Distinguish pure and differentiated oligopoly; collusion and spontaneous coordination; complete and partial oligopoly.
3. Explain the requirements for establishing price and output at the maximum-joint-profit level.
4. Explain the major obstacles to the attainment of maximum joint profit.
5. Why is the interdependence of firms apparently much less with selling activities than price?
6. What is the general influence of the development of a feeling of interdependence upon the elasticity of demand for the product of the firm?
7. Explain the kinked demand curve model, and indicate why the optimum price point is at the level of the kink.
8. Distinguish between dominant-firm and barometric price leadership, and contrast the relative influence over price of firms in each of these situations.
9. Explain the average cost approach to pricing.
10. What are the advantages to the firm of the average cost approach to pricing? Why may this approach bring about a price such that $MR = MC$ for the firms, even though joint profits are not maximized?
11. There is considerable empirical evidence as well as casual observation that firms will typically increase prices by the amount of an increase in excise or sales taxes. Does this reaction suggest the use of an average cost or an MC-MR approach to pricing? Explain.
12. What is the significance of the use of the average cost approach to pricing for the reactions of firms to increases in demand?
13. Explain strategical pricing policy.
14. Explain the Baumol hypothesis of the goal of maximizing sales revenue and its significance for price-output policy.
15. Explain the Williamson "managerial discretion" hypothesis.
16. What was the purpose of the basing point system of price discrimination?
17. Suppose that entry into an oligopoly field is relatively easy. Explain the process by which excess profits will tend to be eliminated.
18. Some writers maintain that free entry and oligopoly are inconsistent: if entry is free, oligopoly relationships will break down. Explain.

19. Explain briefly the major barriers to free entry.
20. What would appear to be the primary barriers to entry into the following industries in the United States?
    a) Farm machinery production
    b) Cement production
    c) Bus operation
    d) Soft drink production
    e) Quicksilver mining
    f) Beer manufacture
21. What is the significance of the absence of differentiation for oligopoly policy?
22. Explain and illustrate the effect of monopsony upon price in a market in which there are numerous sellers.
23. Why would a monopsonist be unable to depress price over a long-run period in a constant cost industry with large numbers of sellers?
24. Why is it impossible to establish generalizations about price-output levels under conditions of bilateral oligopoly?

PART III

Factor Price Determination

INTRODUCTION TO THE
THEORY OF FACTOR PRICES
AND INCOME DISTRIBUTION

Much of the analysis of the pricing of consumption goods is also applicable to the pricing of factors. However, because factor units are acquired by business firms for use in production rather than by individuals for the satisfaction of personal wants, the determinants of factor demand are different from those of demand for consumption goods. To be sure, the demand for factor inputs is derived indirectly from the demand for commodity outputs by households; but the links connecting product demand with factor demands may be satisfied by using a wide variety of different combinations of factor inputs and production technologies. With the exception of capital goods, moreover, the determinants of factor supply are significantly different from those of consumption goods, because factor units (other than capital goods) are supplied by individuals rather than business firms.

This chapter will analyze the demand for factor inputs and develop some general principles of price determination that are broadly relevant for all kinds of factors. The application of these principles to particular types of factors—labor, land, capital goods, entrepreneurship, and money capital—will be examined in subsequent chapters.

Factor Prices and the Distribution of Income

In a market economy, the prices paid by producers for factor units constitute the primary source of income available to individuals for purchasing the output of industry. Accordingly, an explanation of factor prices not only completes the analysis of the functioning of the price system and the resource allocation mechanism but also provides an understanding of the forces that underlie the distribution of total income among various groups of factor owners. Wages, for example, are costs from the standpoint of producers, but are incomes for the workers and provide them the means to buy consumption goods. Wage levels, therefore, not only affect costs, prices, and relative outputs of various goods, but also determine the share of national income received by workers.

However, the explanation of factor pricing does not provide a complete description of the manner in which individuals share in the national income. It tells us little, for example, about the manner in which property resources are distributed among individuals and thus about the way in which property incomes are shared by individuals. Likewise, it tells us nothing about nonmarket income transfers. Many persons share in the national income through the receipt of old-age pensions, aid to dependent children, federal scholarships, and other transfer payments even though they supply no factor units for use in production. Others lose portions of their incomes through tax payments, or voluntarily relinquish funds by making gifts to charitable organizations, etc. Description of the forces governing such transfers lies beyond the scope of the present volume. The analysis of factor pricing as we shall present it is designed to provide a basic framework for explaining those aspects of income distribution that are market determined.

FACTOR DEMAND

Under the assumption that the goal of the business firm is to maximize profits, factor demand is determined by the desire of the firm to produce any given quantity of output at minimum total cost, and to choose that level of output at which total revenue exceeds total cost by the greatest margin. Thus there is a close relation between the theory of demand for individual factor inputs and the theory of production and cost developed in Chapters 6 and 7; and also a close relation between the demand for factors as a whole and the theory of output and price determination developed in Chapters 8–11. The discussion that follows is, indeed, an elaboration of certain topics and points of view that have already been presented (sometimes in rather different guise) in earlier parts of our analysis.

The Basic Rule of Optimum Factor Use by the Firm

The kernel of the theory of factor demand is contained in the general principle that *a firm will find it profitable to hire any factor unit that "pays for itself."* More precisely, it will be profitable for a firm to hire a factor unit if the addition to total cost resulting from its acquisition will be equaled *either* by an equivalent increase in total revenue *or* by an equivalent decrease in total outlay on other factor inputs. The precise meaning of the terms "addition to total cost" and "increase in total revenue" relating to the hiring of factor inputs depends on the character of the markets in which factor inputs and commodity outputs are traded, and also the nature of the production function of the firm. In order to develop the implications of the principle stated above, therefore, we must first study the nature and significance of these background conditions.

Average and Marginal Outlay

The costs that a firm seeks to minimize in producing a given level of output depend partly on the quantity purchased of each variable factor input, partly on the unit price or *average outlay* (AO) that the firm expects to pay for various kinds of factors. If we use the letters $v_1, \ldots, v_i, \ldots, v_n$ to represent quantities of relevant inputs, and $w_1 \ldots, w_i \ldots, w_n$ to represent expected prices of these same inputs, total (variable) outlay (O) corresponding to any given set of values of the price and input variables is defined by

$$O = w_1v_1 + w_2v_2 + \cdots + w_iv_i + \cdots + w_nv_n .$$

The input quantities in this equation are, of course, decision variables for the firm—ones over which the firm has control—but the values of the average outlay (price) variables will depend on numerous influences over which the firm has little or no control. In particular, if the input of factor i is purchased in a purely competitive market, then w_i will normally be regarded by the firm as a fixed parameter—equal to the prevailing market price of the factor. If the factor is purchased in a nonpurely competitive market, however, the value of w_i may depend partly on the quantity of the factor input that is purchased by the firm, partly on the price at which the factor is currently selling, etc.

In the first (purely competitive) case, the addition to total cost or *marginal outlay* (MO) associated with a unit increase in purchases of a variable input will be equal to the market price of the factor; that is to say, marginal outlay will be equal to average outlay: $MO = AO$. Thus the "supply curve of the factor as seen by the firm"—i.e., the firm's *average outlay curve*—will be represented by a horizontal line such as $AO (= MO = w)$ in Figure 12–1; and the same line will also represent the firm's *marginal outlay curve*.

In the second case, marginal outlay on a factor will differ from average outlay. If the firm is a monopsonistic buyer of the factor, for example, AO will be an increasing function of quantity purchased, as illustrated by the curve AO^* in Figure 12–1, and the corresponding MO

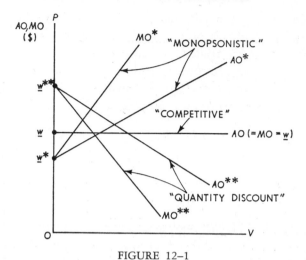

FIGURE 12–1

"Competitive," "Monopsonistic," and "Quantity Discount"
Average and Marginal Outlay Curves

curve (MO^* in the figure) will lie above AO^* at every positive level of factor purchases. Alternatively, if the firm receives quantity discounts, calculated, for example, as a fixed percentage of same base price w^{**}, AO will be a decreasing function of quantity purchased (AO^{**} in Figure 12–1), and the corresponding MO curve (MO^{**}) will lie below the AO curve.

As will become clear later, nonpurely competitive conditions in factor markets create serious problems for the definition of factor demand functions. For the sake of simplicity and convenience in the argument that follows, therefore, we shall proceed temporarily on the assumption that AO curves are represented by horizontal lines, with identity of average outlay (factor price) and marginal outlay. However, in order that our statement of general principles may be considered applicable to all cases, competitive or otherwise, we shall use the phrase "marginal outlay" rather than "average outlay" to refer to the expected addition to total cost resulting from the acquisition of one additional unit of a given factor input. Conclusions strictly valid *only* for the case of purely competitive factor markets will be so indicated explicitly.

Average and Marginal Revenue Product

As in Chapter 6, we will assume that the output of the firm is a given function of the variable factor inputs it uses:

$$x = f(v_1, \ldots, v_i, \ldots, v_n) .$$

Hence the total revenue which the firm can expect to realize from using any given set of factor inputs is indicated by the total revenue product relation

$$px = pf(v_1, \ldots, v_i, \ldots, v_n) .$$

The *average revenue product* (ARP) of any given factor input, say v_i, is then defined by

$$\text{ARP}_i = \frac{px}{v_i} ;$$

i.e., total revenue product divided by the number of units of the factor unit being utilized (e.g., dollar value of steel output per man-hour). This relation may be represented graphically (see Figure 12–3, p. 270)

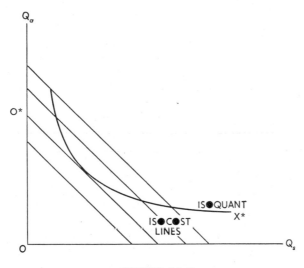

FIGURE 12–2

by a curve of the same form as the average (physical) product curve described in Figure 6–1 (the vertical coordinates of the ARP curve at any given level of input are those of the AP curve multiplied by the appropriate value of AR).

The addition to total revenue that the firm can expect to realize by purchasing and using an additional unit of any particular factor input is simply the marginal physical product (MPP) of the input—as defined by the production function—multiplied by marginal revenue—as defined by the firm's AR curve. In general, of course, AR will vary with the amount of product offered for sale and so MR will differ from AR. For except in the case of pure competition, we must distinguish between the price at which a firm expects to sell an additional unit of product and the prevailing price. In every instance, however, the addition to total revenue which will be of concern to the firm when it is considering buying an *additional* unit of any factor input is described by the formula

$$MRP = MPP \cdot MR .$$

For convenient reference, we shall call this concept the *marginal revenue product* (MRP) of the factor input. It should be noted that the MRP of one factor need not and, except in unusual circumstances, will not be equal to the MRP of another. Where we have to consider more than one MRP in the discussion that follows, therefore we shall use appropriate subscripts to distinguish among different magnitudes; e.g., the MRP of factor "1" will be symbolized by MRP_1, the MRP of factor "2" by MRP_2, etc.

Cost Minimization and the Demand for Factor Inputs

As indicated earlier, a necessary condition for a firm to maximize profit is that it produce any given quantity of output with a least-cost combination of factor inputs. The implications of this condition for the theory of factor demand may be indicated most conveniently in terms of the isoquant and iso-outlay diagram in Figure 12–2, which shows the production possibilities and cost alternatives that are open to a firm for a given output (viz., $x = x^*$). As indicated in Chapter 6, the least-cost combination of factor inputs which can be used to produce the given output is defined by the tangency of the iso-outlay curve O^* with the production isoquant x^*.[1] At such a point of tangency, the marginal rate of factor substitution is equal to the (negative) slope of the iso-outlay curve; i.e.,

$$\frac{dv_2}{dv_1} = -\left(\frac{MO_1}{MO_2}\right).$$

But along the given isoquant, we know that any potential change in output associated with a change in input 2 of dv_2 is just offset by a simultaneous variation of dv_1 in input 1 so that total output does not in

---

[1] The iso-outlay curves O, O', O'', etc., are necessarily straight lines only if both factor inputs are purchased in competitive markets (i.e., if marginal outlay is identically equal to average outlay for both inputs). If one or both markets are not purely competitive, the iso-outlay curves will normally be convex or concave to the origin. Quite generally, however, the slope of an iso-outlay curve at any point is measured by the ratio of the MO of one factor to the MO of the other at that point.

fact alter. The potential changes in output involved in this experiment are simply the respective MPPs of the two factor inputs. Thus, along the given isoquant we have

$$dv_2 \text{MPP}_2 + dv_1 \text{MPP}_1 = 0 ,$$

or, rearranging terms,

$$\frac{dv_2}{dv_1} = -\left(\frac{\text{MPP}_1}{\text{MPP}_2}\right) ;$$

i.e., the marginal rate of factor substitution at any point along the production isoquant x^* is equal to the ratio of the MPPs of the factor inputs (with a minus sign prefixed). At the point of tangency between the iso-outlay curve and the isoquant, therefore, we have

$$\frac{\text{MO}_1}{\text{MO}_2} = \frac{\text{MPP}_1}{\text{MPP}_2} ,$$

or, again rearranging terms,

$$\frac{\text{MO}_1}{\text{MPP}_1} = \frac{\text{MO}_2}{\text{MPP}_2} = C^* ,$$

where C^* is the common value of the two ratios. Now C^* is the marginal outlay on any factor input divided by the increase in total product associated with the use of the input, and this is the same as what we have earlier called marginal (production) cost. For example, if the cost of hiring one additional worker to chop wood is $10 per day, and if his services lead to an increase in output of one-half cord of chopped wood per day, then the marginal cost of production of one cord of wood is $20. We therefore conclude that *at any least-cost combination of inputs, the marginal outlay of the firm on any factor unit must be equal to the MPP of the input multiplied by marginal cost;* i.e.,

$$\text{MO}_i = C^* \text{MPP}_i \qquad (i = 1, \ldots , n) .$$

Alternatively, we may say that *total cost will be a minimum for a given level of output if and only if the marginal productivity of a dollar's worth of any one factor input is the same as the marginal productivity of a dollar's worth of any other factor input;*[2]

$$\frac{\text{MPP}_1}{\text{MO}_1} = \frac{\text{MPP}_2}{\text{MO}_2} = \frac{\text{MPP}_n}{\text{MO}_n} = \frac{1}{C^*} .$$

[2] Note the similarity between this condition and the requirement in the theory of consumer demand (Chapter 5) that the marginal utility of a dollar's worth of one commodity be equal to the marginal utility of a dollar's worth of any other commodity.

It is the last condition that underlies our earlier statement that it will be profitable for a firm to hire a factor unit if the additional cost resulting from its acquisition can be offset by an equivalent reduction in total outlay on other factor inputs. The same condition tells us that it will be profitable to hire (or fire) any factor up to the point where marginal outlay on the factor is equal to its MPP multiplied by MC. But we know from earlier chapters that to *maximize profit* a business firm must not only combine factor inputs in such a way as to produce any given output at minimum cost, but it must also choose a level of output at which marginal cost is equal to marginal revenue. So we arrive finally at the general rule that it will pay a firm to continue hiring any (or all) inputs up to the point where marginal outlay on the factor is equal to its marginal physical productivity multiplied by marginal revenue; i.e., where $MO_i = MPP_i \cdot$, $MC = MPP_i \cdot MR$.

Given the equilibrium condition $MO_i = MPP_i \cdot MR$ it is a short step to the definition of factor demand functions. For the right-hand term of this condition is the marginal revenue product of a factor (MRP_i) as defined earlier; and the value of the left-hand term corresponding to any particular quantity of an input is given by the MO curve for the input. So we have only to describe the relation between the quantity of an input purchased and its MRP in order to determine the equilibrium input of the factor corresponding to any given MO curve.

The Behavior of Marginal Revenue Product in the Short Run

In a short-run period, plant capacity is given and so the MRP of a factor may be expected to rise initially and then fall, on the basis of the theory of production outlined in Chapter 6. In terms of the assumptions made in the development of that theory, which, as indicated, appear to be appropriate in many circumstances, MRP rises as units of a factor are first added, because of more efficient utilization of both fixed and variable factor units, and thus MRP will rise unless the price reductions necessary to sell the additional output in nonpurely competitive markets outweigh the effect of the rising physical product.

Beyond a certain point, however, and perhaps a fairly early stage in the adding of units of the factor, MRP will diminish. There are several forces responsible for this behavior, the relative importance of the various forces depending upon the nature of the production process and the type of market in which the firm is selling:

1. If the factor being added is substituted for other factors, a decreasing marginal rate of substitution between this factor and others

will eventually be encountered; accordingly, beyond this point the contribution of the additional factor units to net revenue consisting of reductions in costs of other factors will diminish.

2. If the additional factor units are used to increase output, MPP will eventually diminish for reasons explained in Chapter 6. Since some factors are fixed in quantity in the short-run period, the addition of further units of other factors will eventually encounter the operation of the Law of Diminishing Returns. A very rapid decline in MPP may occur if the fixed factors are of such a nature that output cannot be increased significantly once all units have been brought into operation.

3. In nonpurely competitive market conditions, the price of the product must be reduced as greater quantities of output are placed on the market; thus, as additional factor units are added, MRP will decline, even if MPP remains constant. If MPP is declining, MRP will decline at an even faster rate than MPP. The magnitude of the price reduction necessary to sell the increased output depends upon the elasticity of the firm's AR curve.

Behavior of Marginal Revenue Product over a Longer Period

When we consider a period of time sufficiently long to allow the firm to adjust the quantities of all factors employed, the MRP of each factor will be substantially different from the period in which some factors are fixed in quantity, primarily because MPP will behave in a different manner. In general, however, in a long-run period as well as in a period in which plant capacity is given, MRP will initially increase and then diminish. The increase results from economies of large-scale production; the use of more efficient types of capital equipment and increased specialization entail an increase in the MPP of the factor. Eventually, however, just as in the short run, but at a different level of output, MRP is likely to commence to fall. In part, the decline is due to the fall in MPP which occurs once decreasing returns to scale (due to problems of large-scale management) are encountered. In addition, just as in the short-run period, the diminishing marginal rate of substitution between this factor and others, the tendency of costs of other factors to rise as more units are acquired, and the necessity to reduce the price of the product to sell more units (except in purely competitive conditions) cause MRP to fall.

The Demand Schedule for a Factor by an Individual Firm

It is now possible to complete the explanation of the determination of equilibrium purchases of a factor by an individual firm; i.e., to show what quantity of an input will be purchased by a profit-maximizing business firm corresponding to any given (short-run or long-run) MO curve.

On the basis of the immediately preceding discussion, we may suppose that the relation between the input of a factor and its MRP takes a form such as that illustrated by the curve *MRP* in Figure 12–4.

Included in the same figure is the corresponding average revenue product curve, *ARP*. For reasons already indicated, these relations are similar in form to the AP and MP curves described in Chapter 6 (Figure 6–1); the ordinates of each are, in fact, simply the ordinates of

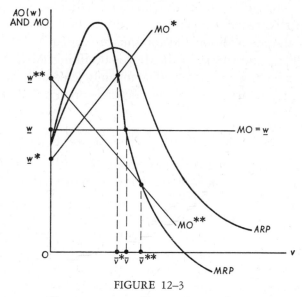

FIGURE 12–3

EQUILIBRIUM PURCHASES OF A FACTOR INPUT CORRESPONDING TO
ALTERNATIVE MARGINAL OUTLAY CURVES

the earlier curves multiplied by appropriate value magnitudes (average revenue in the case of the ARP curve, marginal revenue in the case of the MRP curve).

Three alternative MO functions are shown in Fig. 12–2 (page 265). Applying the rule that units of the factor will be hired up to the point where MO = MRP, we conclude that $\bar{v}$ units will be hired (in equilibrium) if the relevant marginal outlay curve is $MO = w$; $\bar{v}^*$ units will be hired if the outlay curve is MO^*, and $\bar{v}^{**}$ units will be hired if the outlay curve is MO^{**}.

The effect of monopsonistic conditions in the factor market (marginal outlay curve MO^*) is apparently to reduce equilibrium purchases below the level that would obtain under conditions of pure competition;

similarly, the effect of quantity discounts (MO curve w^{**}) is to increase equilibrium purchases as compared with the competitive level.

Assuming that equilibrium purchases of a factor corresponding to any given MO curve are uniquely determined by the MRP curve of the factor, we can derive a demand schedule (or function) for each factor by varying the values of the parameters in order to determine the MO curve. The demand curve for a factor purchased in a purely competitive market, for example, will be identical to the portion of the MRP curve that lies on or below the ARP curve (see Figure 12–4), since in this

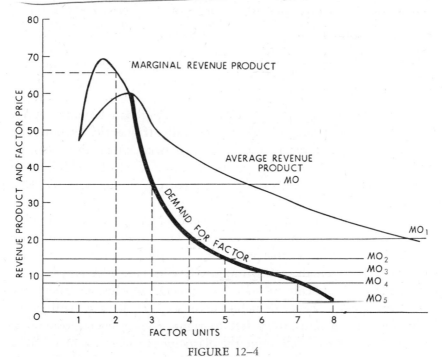

FIGURE 12–4

MARGINAL REVENUE PRODUCT AND THE DEMAND FOR A FACTOR

case the position and form of the MO curve are determined by a single parameter, namely, the market price of the factor. Only the lower portion of the MRP curve is relevant under competitive conditions because at factor prices above the highest point on the ARP curve $AR = MO = MRP > ARP$, and profits are not maximized since the factor amounts involved cost more, per unit, (OA) than their yield in average revenue (ARP). At any price above the maximum point on the ARP curve, therefore, equilibrium purchases of the factor input are zero. A factor demand schedule corresponding to the MRP and ARP curves shown in Figure 12–4 is presented in Table 12–1.

TABLE 12–1

SCHEDULE OF AVERAGE AND MARGINAL REVENUE PRODUCT OF A FACTOR AND
DEMAND SCHEDULE OF THE FIRM FOR THE FACTOR

	REVENUE SCHEDULE			FACTOR DEMAND SCHEDULE	
Units of Factor	Average Revenue Product of Factor	Marginal Revenue Product of Factor		Price of Factor	Quantity of Factor Demanded
1.....................	$47.50	$47.50		$50.00	0
2.....................	59.50	71.50		35.00	3
3.....................	51.33	35.00		20.00	4
4.....................	43.50	20.00		14.90	5
5.....................	37.78	14.90		10.75	6
6.....................	33.27	10.75		7.72	7
7.....................	29.62	7.72		3.00	8
8.....................	26.29	3.00			

The demand schedule for a factor that is purchased in a nonpurely competitive market cannot be defined so easily. If quantity discounts are available, we might regard the base price from which discounts are calculated as a parameter, changes in the value of which yield different MO curves and so permit us to define a corresponding factor demand function.

A firm's demand for any factor input depends partly on the kind of market in which the input is purchased (the MO curve), partly on production possibilities (the production function), partly on the kind of market in which the firm's product is sold (the MR curve). It is correspondingly difficult to state any precise conclusions about the nature of "typical" factor demand curves except that they will invariably slope downwards from left to right. Some general comments about the factors that determine the elasticity of a firm's demand for a factor can be made, however, on the basis of earlier analysis. Elasticity of demand will be influenced by:

1. The rate of decline in the marginal rate of substitution between a given factor and all others; i.e., the degree of curvature of production isoquants. For example, if steel and aluminum are good substitutes for each other in the production of a certain product, the demand by the producer for either metal is likely to be fairly elastic. Any change in relative factor prices will cause substantial substitution of one metal for the other (i.e., a significant shift in the point of tangency between the iso-outlay curve and the equilibrium isoquant curve), and so a substantial increase in purchases of the metal whose price has fallen.

2. The rate of decline in MPP when additional units of a factor

are added to increase output. If the rate of decline is small, and additional factor units add almost as much as previous units to total physical product, small factor price declines will generate substantial increases in the quantity of the factor used (provided that the demand for the product is relatively elastic). If MPP drops sharply, additional factor units will contribute so little that they will not be added unless the factor price falls drastically. As previously indicated, the rate of decline in MPP is less over a longer period, when all factors can be adjusted, than in a shorter interval of time, in which some of the factors are fixed in quantity.

3. The elasticity of the demand schedule for the product of the firm. The smaller the reduction in price necessary to sell additional units of output the greater will be the impact of factor price reductions on the sales of the product and thus upon use of the factor. The elasticity of the demand schedule of a merchant for merchandise is controlled almost entirely by the elasticity of the demand schedule. Substitution of this factor for others by the merchant is virtually impossible and few important economies or diseconomies in the operation of the store are likely to result from a change in the volume of one product handled. Some variations in the rate of purchases compared to the rate of sales may result from the adjustment of inventory in anticipation of price changes, but these are of temporary significance only.

Changes in Factor Demand

Shifts in the demand schedules of business firms for a factor arise from changes in the parameters of the schedules. Major causes of change include:

1. Technological change which increases the substitutability of the factor with others or increases the MPP of the factor. New types of machinery which increase output per man-hour and per dollar of capital invested may raise the marginal product of both labor and capital goods.

2. Changes in the prices of other factors. An increase in the price of one factor will increase the demand for a factor which is easily substituted for it. Where two factors are not readily substitutable, the effect of an increase in the price of the other factor depends upon the relative strength of two opposite reactions. The higher price encourages substitution and an increase in the use of the first factor; the higher cost of the other factor encourages output reduction, which reduces the demand for all factors used by the firm. When factors are complementary, a rise in the price of one will reduce the demand for the other.

Total Demand for a Factor[3]

The total demand for a factor can be precisely defined only if the factor is purchased in a purely competitive market. If so, the demand may be defined as the sum of the demand schedules of all producers employing the factor. However, at factor prices other than the prevailing level, the total quantity demanded may be different than it would appear to be on the basis of the existing individual schedules. That is, if the factor price changes, the quantity of the factor which each producer finds it profitable to employ at the new price may not be the same as the quantity that he would have employed at the new level had the change affected only the prices which he paid, and not those of other firms. Suppose, for example, that the prevailing wage for a certain type of worker is $14 a day. If it falls to $12 a day for one firm, but remains at $14 a day for competitors, the firm may increase its labor force 10 percent, as the lower labor cost allows it to reduce price and increase output. But if the wage rate falls to $12 a day for all of the firms in the industry, the firm may increase the labor force by only 2 percent.

On the whole, the total demand is likely to be much less elastic than that for the typical individual firm. In the first place, when all firms adjust output in response to a factor price change, the demand schedules for the products of the firms will be affected. If wages fall, for example, and each firm hires more men and increases output, the demand schedules for the products of each of the firms will fall because the prices of competitors are lowered. Thus, greater price reductions than those anticipated will be necessary to sell the additional output, schedules of MRP will be lower, and fewer additional men will be hired. If pure competition prevails in the market for the output, price will fall as soon as additional production comes on the market.

Second, the adjustment of output and factor purchases by all firms in response to a factor price change will alter the prices of other factors and thereby modify MRP schedules to a greater extent than would an adjustment by one firm alone. For example, a reduction in the price of a certain raw material A may cause substantial replacement of other materials by A. As a consequence, the prices of the other materials may fall and lessen the substitution and the net increase in the use of factor A. Reduced factor prices will cause increases in output, which will necessitate greater use of other factors and raise their prices. Thus the

---

[3] Attention is again called to use of the term *factor* in reference to a particular type of homogenous factor unit, such as labor of a certain variety, not to broad factor groups, such as labor of all types.

output increase and the quantity of the factors used will be less than anticipated.

Third, increased factor employment in one industry due to a decline in factor price may be offset by consequent decreases in the use of the factor in other industries. Reduced wages in the brick industry, for example, might increase employment in that industry. However, the decline in brick prices resulting from the lower wages may increase the use of brick relative to that of lumber and reduce the demand for labor in the lumber industry.

Finally, change in factor prices may, by altering the pattern of income distribution, affect total spending in the economy, and thus total factor demand. This consideration is an element in macroeconomic theory, and so will not be considered further here.

The Marginal Revenue Product Principle and Business Policy

The principle that business firms adjust the quantity of each factor purchased to the level at which MO = MRP follows as a matter of logical necessity from the assumption that business firms are seeking to maximize profit. Actually, as previously indicated, this statement is merely a more precise way of expressing the rule that "a man will be hired only if he will pay for himself." But actual attainment of the principle is obviously not always realized.

In the first place, as noted in earlier chapters, other motives besides profit maximization influence business decisions, and their pursuit may lead to departure from the MO = MRP rule. If firms temporarily determine output and price on the basis of "satisfactory" rather than maximum profits, for example, output may be greater than the level at which MC = MR and the number of factor units acquired will be greater. The desire to avoid taking action which will appear to aggravate a depression may cause a firm to continue to employ more men than the optimum number, if finances of the firm permit. Or unprofitable expansions, involving the adding of factor units beyond the MO = MRP figure, may be undertaken in an effort to build a greater business empire.

An analysis of producer demand built upon the assumption of profit maximization, although not entirely adequate because of the exceptions noted, is nevertheless more satisfactory in the present state of knowledge than one built upon any other assumption. Actual attainment of the goal of profit maximization is obviously difficult. The determination of MRP with any degree of accuracy is an extremely difficult task. Often it is not even easy to determine the MPP of an additional factor unit, as for example, of workers not directly involved in physical production. The firm's revenue schedule, knowledge of which is essential for determination of MRP, can at best only be estimated. The various determinants of marginal outlay and marginal revenue product, such as the prices of other factors, techniques of production, and demand schedules, are constantly changing. As a consequence of these difficulties, all a producer can hope to do is to approximate the MO = MRP rule.[4]

FACTOR SUPPLY

For a general theory of factor pricing, generalizations about factor supply must be very broad because of differences in the influences that affect supplies of particular factors.

A sharp distinction must be made between the determinants of the supply of capital goods, on the one hand, and other factor inputs and money capital, on the other. Since capital goods are produced by business firms, the determinants of output and supply are the same as those of consumption goods, as explained in preceding chapters. Costs of production thus play the dominant role. One difference, however, should be noted: Durable capital goods last over a period of time and once they have been produced, the quantity available is independent of cost of production. But over a period of time, cost is relevant, and plays an important role in the pricing of new capital goods coming on the market.

The other factors are not produced by business firms on a profit-making basis; hence, cost of production (at least in the usual sense) has no relevance for supply. The supply depends on the number of units of the particular type of factor in existence at any time, and on the willingness of factor owners to allow their factor units to be used in production.

The nature of the supply schedule of the various types of factors will be considered in the next several chapters. One general statement, however, may be useful. Decisions with regard to the supply of factor

[4] For many years, controversy has occurred over the usefulness of the marginal productivity analysis. See, for example, the attacks on the principle by R. A. Lester, "Shortcomings of Marginal Analysis for Wage-Employment Problems," *American Economic Review,* Vol. 36 (March, 1946), pp. 62–82; and the defense by F. Machlup, "Marginal Analysis and Empirical Research," *American Economic Review,* Vol. 36 (September, 1946), pp. 519–54. Note also H. M. Oliver, Jr., "Marginal Theory and Business Behavior," *American Economic Review,* Vol. 37 (June, 1947), pp. 375–83; and R. A. Gordon, "Short Period Price Determination in Theory and Practice," *American Economic Review,* Vol. 38 (June, 1948), pp. 265–88.

units are made by the owners of these units, and the owners may have
the option of advantageously utilizing the units to satisfy their own
wants. Thus a worker has the option of reserving his time for leisure
instead of making it available for use in production, and a holder of
money capital may gain the advantage of liquidity by holding the
money. Thus there is the possibility of a "backward bending" supply
curve; that is to say, above certain price levels owners may prefer to
hold additional factor units to meet their own personal preferences for
them, since those units being made available will provide income which
is regarded as adequate. At lower prices for the factor units, larger
quantities would be supplied in order to obtain as much money income
from the factor units as possible. Thus the supply curve may appear as
shown in Figure 12–5.

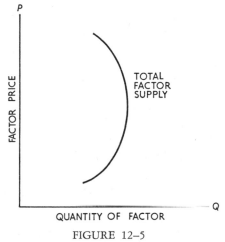

FIGURE 12–5

BACKWARD BENDING FACTOR SUPPLY CURVE

FACTOR PRICE DETERMINATION

Given the demand and supply schedules of each type of factor, the
price of each factor will adjust to the level at which the quantity of the
factor supplied is equal to the quantity demanded, under the assumption
of pure competition in the factor markets. Given the determinants of
supply of each factor, at each possible price for the factor there are a
certain number of factor units available for use. At each factor price,
likewise, there is a certain quantity of the factor demanded, namely, the
number which allows equality of MRP and MO for each firm
employing the particular type of factor. The actual price must adjust to

the level at which the quantity demanded equals the quantity supplied, since at any higher level more units are available than firms wish to use, while at lower levels the factor price would be less than MRP for some firms, and the firms would seek to add more units. At the equilibrium figure the factor price must equal MRP for each firm, or the firms will seek either to obtain more factor units or to lessen the number they have, upsetting the equilibrium and causing a change in the factor price.

In other words, equality of MRP and MO is attained because each firm adjusts the quantity of each factor employed until MRP is equal to the price paid for the factor. Once equality of supply and demand of the factor is attained, as it must be in a purely competitive market, the actual price of the factor will equal the MRP of the factor for each firm, with the available number of factor units employed. This explanation of factor price determination is known as the Marginal Productivity Theory of Distribution (of income).[5]

In equilibrium, the MRP of each factor will be the same in each use to which the factor is put, apart from the effects of imperfections arising out of difficulties in the calculation of MRP. Likewise, the ratios among the prices of various factors will be equal to marginal rates of substitution among them in all uses, since only this relationship allows the use of optimum factor combinations, and is attained once each firm adjusts the quantity of each factor to the level at which the MRP = MO.

Deviations from Pure Competition

Markets for factors are characterized by substantial deviations from conditions of pure competition. Probably the least deviation occurs in markets for money capital on a long-term basis, since both the numbers of lenders and the numbers of borrowers are large, the units are standardized, and the market is highly organized. As a consequence, long-term bond interest rates adjust on essentially a purely competitive basis. Some rates on short-term money capital, however, are determined in nonpurely competitive markets, with rates dominated by the principal lenders.

The market for land is characterized by a large number of local markets, with a small number of buyers and sellers in each. The average lessor has only one or a few pieces of land to rent and participates in

---

[5] It was once argued that income distribution based upon marginal productivity was inherently "just" since each factor was paid according to its contribution to production. It is now recognized that such a conclusion was completely inappropriate. Justice in income distribution can be evaluated only in terms of a set of value judgments. See Chapter 21.

lease transactions only on relatively rare occasions. Direct bargaining is thus significant in land-rent determination; collusive action among buyers or sellers is rare, however, and total supply-demand relationships still play a role. The total land market is further broken up into small segments because many users prefer to buy land rather than rent it; accordingly, two distinct types of transactions occur. However, as will be explained later, land rents and land sale prices bear a definite relationship to each other.

Markets for labor services involve the greatest deviation from conditions of pure competition. Before the development of labor unions, wages were largely dictated by employers; a very large number of small suppliers (workers) were selling their services to a relatively small number of employers, who exercised monopsonistic domination over wage levels. This situation is still found in some labor markets today. But the development of labor unions has transformed many of the old monopsonistic markets into ones of bilateral oligopoly (oligopoly-oligopsony), in which wages are determined by direct bargaining between unions and employers or employer groups. As a consequence, explanation of wage levels on the basis of any general principles becomes difficult, as is always true with bilateral oligopoly. There is good reason to believe, however, that wage levels in such markets are different than they would be if set by supply and demand forces in a purely competitive market. Wages in nonunion industries are patterned to a large extent on union wage levels.

TWO OVERALL QUESTIONS OF FACTOR PRICING

The Adding-Up Problem: Euler's Theorem

An issue discussed at length in past decades was that of whether the entire revenue of producers from the sale of goods would be paid out to factor suppliers if the price paid for each factor unit were equal to the MRP of the factor, or whether there could be something "left over" as a source of exploitative return for the owners of the business. Or, to consider yet a third possibility, could total revenue from the sale of the product be inadequate to allow all factors suppliers to receive prices equal to MRP? A rule known as Euler's Theorem shows that with a linear and homogeneous production function, total physical product will be exactly equal to the sums of the MPPs of the various factors multiplied by the amounts of each factor used; i.e.,

$$x = v_1\mathrm{MPP}_1 + v_2\mathrm{MPP}_2 + \cdots + v_n\mathrm{MPP}_n .$$

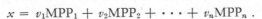

From this identity it appears that payment of each factor according to the competitive rule $MRP = MO = AO$ would imply a set of factor payments that precisely exhausted the total value product. For if we multiply both sides of Euler's identity by the market price of the product p, and set $p = MR$ and $MPP_i \cdot MR = MRP_i$, we obtain

$$\text{Total Revenue} = px = v_1 MRP_1 + v_2 MRP_2 + \cdots v_n MRP_n$$

So if AO on each input is equal to its MRP (i.e., if each input is hired up to the point where $MO_i = w_i = MRP_i$) we have

$$px = w_1 v_1 + w_2 v_2 + \cdots \& w_n v_n ,$$

and thus the desired "exhaustion of value product" identity.

If factor units were paid less than their MRPs, or if production functions displayed decreasing rather than constant returns to scale, then by similar reasoning it would appear that product would fail to be exhausted; a surplus would remain after all factors were remunerated and presumably this surplus would be appropriated by entrepreneurs as "rent on institutional advantage" or "gain from monopsonistic exploitation." Alternatively, if production functions displayed increasing returns to scale and factors were paid their MRPs, value product would appear to be more than exhausted; i.e., at every positive level of output, average product would be less than marginal product; hence MRP would exceed ARP and no firm could undertake production except at a loss.

Actually the problems posed by these considerations are of no practical significance. If demand conditions are sufficiently favorable, businesses can be earning large profits in a purely competitive industry even if MRPs are invariably greater than ARPs; for it is only in a state of competitive equilibrium that questions of revenue and cost can be settled by looking at given ARP and MRP curves. And in other than competitive conditions, disequilibrium situations (and so "excess" profits) may easily prevail in practice over indefinitely long intervals of time. It is neither useful nor meaningful, therefore, to attempt to "explain" observed distributive shares by reference to static production possibilities and static revenue and cost relationships. Profits, losses, and distributive shares can be analyzed satisfactorily only in terms of dynamic exit and entry considerations and related market demand and output conditions, following procedures such as those used in our earlier account (Chapters 8–11) of short- and long-run adjustments in various kinds of market situations.

Long-Run Trends in Labor's Share of Output and the Cobb-Douglas Production Function

Time-series data on the distribution of total real income in the United States between "labor" and "capital" indicate that the share of "labor" has been relatively constant over the past 75 years, accounting for some 70–85 percent of total real income (the precise figure depending on what is included in the category of "wage, salary, and other labor income"). Numerous efforts have been made to explain this phenomenon, most of them provocative, but none entirely satisfactory. Perhaps the most notable of these attempts was that of Paul H. Douglas and C. W. Cobb,[6] who conjectured that an explanation might be provided by assuming that the total output of the economy at any given date could be predicted by inserting appropriate values for "labor" (L) and "Capital" (C) into an aggregate production function of the form

$$Y = kL^a C^{(1-a)} ,$$

where Y denotes aggregate real income (product), k and a are given constants, and a is less than unity. This relation, now known as a "Cobb-Douglas production function," directly implies that the shares of labor and capital will be constant, namely a and $1 - a$. Moreover, when Cobb and Douglas first fitted their equation to aggregate time-series data, the points defined by the data clustered closely about the graph of the relation and implied a value for a (labor's share) of about .75 (i.e., 75 percent).

Like most early empirical studies, that of Cobb and Douglas did not stand up well to scrutiny by later investigators. Subsequent attempts to fit a Cobb-Douglas function to more refined time-series data suggested that the constant term should be regarded as an increasing function of historical time—a result that was quickly interpreted to indicate that "technical progress" occurred more or less steadily in the years following 1890.[7] Numerous studies are now under way that seek to identify more precisely the factors responsible for technical progress and to clarify various other ambiguities that are inherent in the use of aggregate production functions of any variety—e.g., how can one arrive at meaningful measures of "capital," "labor," and "aggregate output" in a world where the quantity and quality of all kinds of goods and

---

[6] See Paul Douglas, *The Theory of Wages* (New York: Macmillan, 1934).

[7] M. W. Reder, "Alternative Theories of Labor's Share," in *The Allocation of Economic Resources,* Essays in Honor of B. F. Haley (Stanford: Stanford University Press, 1959); R. M. Solow, "A Skeptical Note on the Constancy of Relative Shares," *American Economic Review,* Vol. 48 (September, 1958), pp. 618–31.

services are in a constant state of flux. If (as seems inevitable) all aggregate magnitudes have to be measured in dollar units, what significance can be attached to a "technological relation" among the various magnitudes such as the Cobb-Douglas production function entails? Results reported in investigations that have been completed up to this time provide little grounds to hope that either of these issues will be satisfactorily resolved.

SELECTED REFERENCES

BAUMOL, W. J. *Economic Theory and Operations Analysis,* chap. xvii. 2d ed. Englewood Cliffs, N.J.: Prentice-Hall, 1965.

COHEN, K. J., AND CYERT, R. M. *Theory of the Firm,* chap. xiii. Englewood Cliffs, N.J.: Prentice-Hall, 1965.

LIEBHAFSKY, H. H. *The Nature of Price Theory,* chap. xii. Homewood, Ill.: Dorsey, 1963.

MACHLUP, F. "Marginal Analysis and Empirical Research," *American Economic Review,* Vol. 36 (September, 1946), pp. 519–54.

QUESTIONS

1. Why is it necessary to have a separate treatment of factor pricing, distinct from the analysis applied to the pricing of products?
2. Why is the theory of factor pricing often called the theory of distribution?
3. Under what circumstances does marginal outlay on a factor exceed the price paid for the factor? Under what circumstances is it less than the latter?
4. Define marginal physical product; average revenue product; marginal revenue product.
5. Under what circumstances is:

   a) Marginal revenue product less than average revenue product?

   b) Marginal revenue product zero, yet average revenue product positive?
6. Complete the table below:

Units of Factor	Total Output	Marginal Physical Product	Price of Product	Total Revenue	Marginal Revenue Product	Average Revenue Product
1	40	......	$1.40	......	......	......
2	90	......	1.35	......	......	......
3	130	......	1.30	......	......	......
4	150	......	1.25	......	......	......
5	165	......	1.20	......	......	......
6	172	......	1.15	......	......	......
7	175	......	1.10	......	......	......

7. With a given plant, why does MRP decline as units of the factor are added, beyond a certain point? Why will the rate of decline be faster if the industry is one of nonpurely competitive conditions than if it is purely competitive (other conditions being the same)?

8. Construct a demand schedule for the factor for which the product data are given in Question 6, above.

9. Plot MRP and ARP data from Question 6, and join the points to represent the demand curve of the firm for the factor.

10. Why will a competitive firm increase the number of units of a factor used up to the point at which the MO on the factor is equal to the MRP, if it wishes to maximize profits?

11. If marginal outlay exceeds the factor price, will the firm acquire more or fewer units with a given schedule of productivity than if P = MO? Why?

12. Indicate the effect upon the elasticity of demand for a factor of:
    a) A reduction in the rate at which the marginal rate of substitution of this factor for other factors falls, due to technological changes.
    b) A rapid decline in marginal physical product beyond a certain point.
    c) Reduced elasticity of demand for the product of the firm, due to scarcity of substitutes.
    d) Increased scarcity of materials used in conjunction with the particular factor.

13. What will be the effect upon the demand for a factor of:
    a) Increased substitutability of this factor for others?
    b) A decline in demand for the product of the industry?
    c) Increased prices of other factors?

14. Why is the total demand for a factor likely to be less elastic than the demand for the factor by any one firm?

15. Why, in practice, may firms not actually in all cases add factor units up to the point at which the marginal revenue product of the factor is equal to marginal outlay on the factor?

16. Distinguish between the determinants of the supply of capital goods and those of other types of factors.

17. Explain the determination of the price of a certain type of factor, under the assumption of a purely competitive market for the factor.

18. Why, under competitive assumptions, must the equilibrium factor price equal the marginal revenue product of the factor?

19. How can the statement that the equilibrium factor price is equal to the marginal revenue product have precise meaning, when the marginal revenue product varies with the number of factor units employed?

20. It is sometimes maintained that the marginal productivity theory of distribution involves circular reasoning, by use of the following argument: "The marginal revenue product of a factor depends upon the number of factor units used. But in order to know how many factor units to acquire, the firm must know the factor price. Therefore the argument that the factor price depends upon the marginal revenue product involves circular reasoning and explains nothing." Evaluate this argument.

Chapter 13   THEORY OF WAGES

The largest share of national income and thus the largest element in the costs of business firms consists of wages and salaries—sums paid for the use of labor services. Department of Commerce figures show that in recent years, about 65 percent of national income in the United States has consisted of wages and salaries.[1] In addition, a large but unmeasurable portion of income reported as profits of unincorporated businesses is made up of implicit wages of farmers, shopkeepers, etc. Without question the combined figure of explicit and implicit wages exceeds 75 percent of total national income.

The explanation of wage determination involves an elaboration of the general theory of factor price determination to deal with the special characteristics of labor. Labor is distinguished by the direct human activity involved; the factor service consists of the work of human beings, and the payments made for the services directly constitute the incomes of the persons providing the services. In a nonslave economy the source of the service, namely, the worker, cannot be sold; only the individual worker (or more accurately, his household) can obtain the wage income. Because the factor service consists of work by the person, considerations of personal likes and dislikes for work are major determinants of supply schedules. Personal considerations also affect the nature of competition in the labor market.

Furthermore, because of the personal nature of labor service, other considerations in addition to wages are significant to the suppliers of labor service. The worker is concerned with the number of hours worked, the relative security of his income, working conditions, pensions, vacations, etc. Detailed analysis of these considerations is not possible in this book, but their importance must be stressed.

---

[1] The figure is about 70 percent if various supplements to wages and salaries are included.

Finally, the basic source of labor service—the population itself—is not "produced" for economic reasons; families do not raise children for the income which ultimately can be gained from their services. Trends in population and labor supply appear to be dependent primarily upon factors other than wage rates (provided they are high enough to allow persons to subsist).

WAGE DETERMINATION UNDER PURELY COMPETITIVE CONDITIONS

The most satisfactory way of approaching the explanation of wage determination is to start with the assumption of a purely competitive market. While the purely competitive model is of little significance in itself as far as present-day labor markets are concerned, it is useful as a background for later analysis of the other market forms.

The Determinants of the Aggregate Supply of Labor

Labor service differs from other factor services in two primary ways: workers are not produced on a profit-making basis, and the provision of labor services requires activity on the part of human beings. Thus personal preferences for working or not working, and for various circumstances of working, become significant influences on the supply function. Accordingly, the determinants of the overall supply of labor available to the economy at any particular time include:

1. The total population capable of working.

2. Institutional factors, such as education requirements, minimum age legislation, compulsory retirement, attitudes toward women working, and the like, which determine the size of the available labor force. For example, if two countries of equal population and age distribution are compared, one characterized by acceptability of wives working, the other, by a strict Moslem culture in which the wives do not engage in labor outside the home, the labor supply will be much greater in the former than in the latter.

3. Preferences for income and leisure. In a sense a person may be regarded as demanding a portion of his own labor supply, and thus he may offer to others less than the potential amount, since he prefers to reserve a portion of the potential quantity for his own enjoyment.

Given these considerations, what is the nature of the overall supply function of labor available to the economy? The question will be considered first from a strictly short-term point of view. Wage changes may lure additional labor hours into the labor market in one of two ways: (1) by causing existing workers to work more hours per week—by working longer work days, working on weekends, forgoing vacations, etc.—or (2) by luring into the labor market persons otherwise not working. These include persons able to subsist on nonlabor income or by dependency upon others—children, retired persons, wives, etc.

Granted that wage changes may have some effect on the quantity of labor available, what is the nature of the functional relationship? Will the quantity of labor supplied be greater at high wages than at low (as is true of the supply schedules of commodities), or vice versa? Rules which apply to commodities are not necessarily applicable to labor, because workers have another use for their time—namely, leisure, an alternative which is not usually relevant for suppliers of commodities.[2] The answer is by no means obvious, since there are two conflicting effects:

1. The substitution effect: when higher wages are offered, the sacrifice for forgoing labor to gain greater leisure will become greater, and thus there will be a tendency to substitute labor for leisure.

2. The income effect: at higher wage levels, the income from a given quantity of labor is greater, and thus the person may feel that he can afford more leisure.

Since these forces operate in opposite directions, it is not possible to say what the net effect is, and thus to define the nature of the supply schedule of labor. This is basically an empirical question which cannot be answered by deductive analysis. Yet it is a question of major interest, of concern for tax policy and other issues.

On the basis of such evidence as is available, several observations can be made:

1. Most households must obtain wage income in order to maintain desired living standards; therefore one member of the family will ordinarily enter the labor market regardless of the wage rate, within limits. This consideration is a force tending to make the schedule relatively inelastic.

2. Most persons, by the requirements of modern production, have relatively little control over hours worked. This is particularly true in manufacturing; requisites of efficiency in operation do not permit individual variance. This consideration also tends to produce inelasticity in the schedule.

3. Some variation, however, is possible through working of

[2] This consideration may also be relevant for the supply of goods produced by individuals operating their own small businesses.

overtime, moonlighting, and deferring retirement. Likewise other members of the household may enter or leave the labor market.

4. The portion of the schedule at relatively low-rate wage rates is likely to show a positive relationship, higher wages bringing forth additional labor hours. With wage rates very low, it may not appear worthwhile to work overtime; and other members of the family will not find it worthwhile to enter the labor market, expecially in view of the fact that doing so will often result in certain costs—for additional clothing, transportation, child care, etc.

5. The upper portion of the schedule is more likely to show a negative relationship; as wages reach relatively high levels, persons will feel that they can afford additional leisure, since they can do so and yet maintain a relatively high standard of consumption. Thus they will refuse overtime and take more time off, and wives will quit working.

6. The precise nature of the schedule is obviously affected by general cultural patterns and goals. If maximization of income is of paramount importance, higher wages will bring forth additional labor hours. If the primary goal is maintenance of a given standard of living, the reverse will be true; as wages rise, persons will work fewer hours in order to maintain the same living standard.

As a consequence of these considerations, it is widely argued that the supply curve of labor as a whole is backward sloping, as illustrated on Figure 13–1. As wages rise from very low levels, additional persons

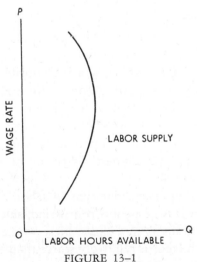

FIGURE 13–1

LABOR SUPPLY, CURVE NEGATIVELY
SLOPED IN PART

will be lured into the labor market and others will work longer hours. Once living standards have reached certain levels, further increases will result in "purchase" of greater leisure, and the labor hour supply will fall. This statement, however, must be regarded as an empirical observation based on rather limited evidence.

One approach to further enlightenment on the question is an historical analysis of the relationship between changes in wage levels and changes in the average workweek. One such study for the United States shows that as wages rose, the typical workweek declined. To the extent that this decline reflected the desires of the workers, as it presumably did, it shows that labor preferred to take a portion of its gain in greater leisure. In other words, the higher wages led to a reduced supply of labor hours, at least for the groups of workers and the time period covered by the studies (1900–1957). The elasticity was found to be .25.[3]

Too much weight cannot be attached to this conclusion, because of the impossibility of excluding other considerations, but at least the evidence suggests that the relationship may well be negative.

Supply of Labor of Particular Types

Labor is of course not a homogeneous commodity; the aggregate supply consists of a pattern of supplies of workers of various skills and training. The schedule for any particular type of labor—clerical workers, mechanics, carpenters, and so on—is typically more elastic than the overall supply because of the possibility of workers shifting from one occupation to another. Such transfer depends upon the degree of skill required, the number of persons now in other occupations who possess this skill, the extent to which seniority and pension rights restrict mobility, and the importance of prestige and other nonmonetary considerations in various types of employment. Another important consideration is the extent to which persons not normally in the labor force can enter the particular occupation. It is far easier, for example, for housewives to become domestic servants or store clerks than to become mechanics or plumbers.

The supply of any particular type of labor is more elastic over a period of time than it is in a short-run period, since additional persons can gain necessary training and skills. New workers will more readily enter fields in which labor is relatively scarce than existing workers will

[3] See the article by A. C. Harberger, "Taxation, Resource Allocation and Welfare," in *The Role of Direct and Indirect Taxes in the Federal Revenue System* (Princeton: Princeton University Press, 1964), pp. 45–50, for a summary.

retrain for these occupations. On the whole, however, regardless of the time period, the possibility of shifting occupations creates a positive relationship between the wage rate and the quantity of labor available. Thus if work-leisure considerations for a particular type of labor also produce a positive relationship, the combined effect of the two influences is certain to be positive. Higher wage rates will not only lure workers from other occupations, but will also induce additional persons to work, or additional workers to work longer hours. If, however, the work-leisure relationship produces a negative effect, the net influence will depend on the relative strength of the two conflicting forces.

Demand Considerations

The aggregate demand for labor is dependent upon the relationship between wage rates and the marginal revenue product (MRP) of labor, in the same fashion as the demand for any factor. The aggregate demand consists of a large number of demand schedules for particular types of labor. For each type, an employer will hire workers up to the point at which the MRP of the additional worker is equal to the marginal outlay on the worker, the latter figure being equal to the wage rate if the market for labor is purely competitive.

The elasticity of demand for each type of labor depends upon the rate of decline in MRP of the particular type of labor. The rate of decline, in turn, is controlled by the nature of the production function, the substitutability of labor for other factors, and the elasticity of demand for the product.

Elasticity will be less to the extent that:

1. The nature of production is such that once existing capital equipment is brought into use, additional workers will add little to physical output.
2. The demand for the product of the industry is relatively inelastic.
3. Employers cannot easily ascertain MRP of successive workers, and thus can only estimate the optimum number. Thus a change in the wage rate may not lead to any readjustment.

On the basis of these considerations, it is commonly argued that the demand for labor is very inelastic; i.e., that wage reductions will not significantly affect the number of jobs available. This is, however, an empirical generalization for which there is no conclusive evidence.

Over a longer period of time, the elasticity is obviously greater since the quantity of capital and other resources can be altered, as well as the nature of the capital equipment. The sharp decline in MRP in the short run resulting from the operation of the Law of Diminishing Returns can be avoided.

Purely Competitive Wage Levels

If labor markets were purely competitive, the wages of each type of labor would come to the level at which the demand for and supply of the particular type of labor were equal. Since the demand schedules are dependent upon MRP, each employer hiring workers up to the level at which MRP is equal to the wage rate, the equilibrium wage for each type of labor would be equal to the MRP of that type of labor, with the quantity of the particular type of labor available at this wage rate fully employed. If the wage level were temporarily higher, the number of workers available would exceed the number employers wished to hire at that wage rate; wages would decline as the unemployed workers sought to find jobs and offered to work for lower wages. If wages were temporarily below the equilibrium figure, employers would seek to hire more men than were available; they would compete against each other for additional workers and thus bid the wage up to the equilibrium figure.

The adjustment is illustrated on Figure 13–2. The analysis is applicable only under the following assumptions:

1. Pure competition in the labor market, and thus the absence of labor unions, on the one hand, and monopsonistic domination of wages by the employer, on the other.
2. Productivity of workers independent of the wage rates paid.
3. Positive sloping supply curve for labor.
4. Given general level of commodity prices; thus a change in money wages is accompanied by a similar change in real wages.
5. Given total demand for commodities, independent of wage rates paid.

The assumption of pure competition is, of course, not applicable in most labor markets as noted in subsequent sections. Failure of the second and third assumptions to be realized in particular cases makes possible more than one equilibrium position. If wage increases lead to greater productivity, for example, by allowing workers to maintain a better level of health and efficiency and raising morale, there may be a substantial range of equilibrium wage figures. Within this range an increase in wages will be accompanied by an increase in MRP, and the new equilibrium may be as stable as the old. If the supply is in part negatively sloped, there is also a possibility of several equilibrium levels. In graphical terms the supply curve and the demand curve may intersect at more than one point, as shown in Figure 13–3. The levels are stable, however, only if $S > D$ at wage rates higher than the equilibrium, and $S < D$ at lower wage rates.

The last two assumptions, of a given general price level and given

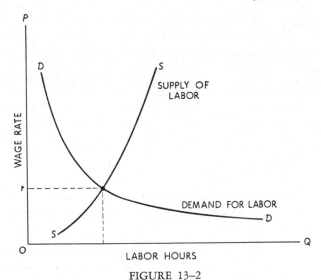

FIGURE 13–2

EQUILIBRIUM WAGE LEVEL FOR A PARTICULAR OCCUPATION,
PURELY COMPETITIVE LABOR MARKET

total demand for commodities, are not necessarily realistic, and will be considered in later sections.

Occupational Wage Differentials

As indicated by empirical observations, wages paid for different types of labor vary widely. The differentials at any time will depend on

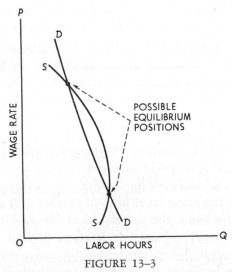

FIGURE 13–3

EQUILIBRIUM WAGE LEVELS, NEGATIVELY SLOPED SUPPLY CURVE FOR
LABOR

relative supply-demand conditions for various types of labor, and hence on relative MRP figures in various occupations, the strength of the tendency toward lessening of inequalities depending upon the mobility of labor. At any one time, wages will be relatively high in occupations in which supply is limited relative to demand and MRP is high. The inability of other persons to move into the occupation allows the high wage rate to continue for a period of time. Wages can never remain relatively high in a field in which immediate entry of large numbers of workers is possible.

Over a period of time, workers will tend to flow toward those occupations offering the greatest advantages relative to the costs of entering them, considering both monetary and nonmonetary factors. Certain occupations require longer periods of training than others, and wage levels must remain sufficiently high in them to induce persons to undertake the added training. Some occupations have greater nonmonetary advantages than others, such as prestige, comfort of work, regularity of employment, etc. Thus, at equal wage rates, workers would prefer these to other occupations, and differentials in money wages must remain in order to balance supplies of workers in various occupations with demand for them. Under the assumptions of pure competition and lack of market imperfections, relative wages will eventually adjust to the levels at which the wage differentials exactly compensate for the higher costs of training and the monetary values of nonwage differences, so long as entry into occupations is not restricted by lack of sufficient numbers of persons with requisite abilities to perform the work involved. If there are such restrictions, the scarcity of this type of worker will maintain a higher wage differential than would exist on the basis of different training costs, etc. If the assumptions of perfect knowledge and mobility are dropped, the precise adjustments will not be attained, and the adjustments will be slower, but the basic nature of the equilibrium position will be the same.

Geographical Wage Differences

Distinct from the occupational wage differentials are those among workers in given occupations in different areas. The labor market, for almost any type of labor, is not nationwide, but covers a limited region only. At any time the wage level in each market will depend on local supply-demand conditions, the geographical immobility of labor preventing any immediate regional equalization. Over a period of time, however, labor tends to flow to the high-wage areas, and real wages for a given occupation in various areas tend to be equalized, unless workers find nonmonetary advantages of living in certain areas, such as California. Money wages, however, will not be equalized when costs of living differ, as they frequently do, especially between rural and urban areas.

However, labor is by no means completely mobile, and differences which arise will continue for long periods. Moving is costly, and many persons are reluctant to move away from familiar areas to look for jobs which they are not certain they will obtain. Empirical studies show some trend toward equalization, but the process is very slow and erratic.[4]

Long Period Aggregate Supply of Labor

The discussion up to this point has been concerned with the supply of labor in a relatively short period of time, with a given population. However, in terms of a longer period of time, what is the significance for population and thus labor supply of various levels of real wages? Is there a functional relationship between changes in wages and changes in the total population, and thus of the supply of labor?

Such a functional relationship was developed by T. R. Malthus, whose *Principles of Population* was a major landmark in the development of economic theory. According to the well-known Malthusian doctrine of population, any increase in wages above subsistence level will lead to an immediate increase in population, since population is constantly held in check by famine, disease, and war arising out of inadequate food supply. As a consequence, wages are held down to a bare subsistence level—to the "cost of production" of labor.

Malthus wrote during the early nineteenth century, when conditions were such in many parts of the world as to give substantial empirical support to his doctrine.[5] However, in the succeeding century, as incomes rose, the birth rate fell; higher levels of education and changing standards of social behavior brought substantially smaller families. As persons came to realize the significance of large families for their economic well-being and gained knowledge of birth control methods, they had fewer children. However, in certain areas of the world the population never rose above extreme poverty levels, and the Malthusian rule has been applicable.

---

[4] R. J. Wonnacott, "Wage Levels and Employment Structure in United States Regions," *Journal of Political Economy*, Vol. 62 (August, 1964), pp. 414–17.

[5] Anyone who questions this should read Cecil Woodham-Smith's *The Great Hunger* (New York: Harper and Row, 1963), the story of the famine in Ireland in the mid 1840s.

Recent experience suggests that once a society has reached a relatively high level of income and education, still further increases in wages, coupled with high availability of jobs, lead to a higher rate of population growth. Persons marry earlier, and feel that they can afford larger families.[6] But certainly no close relationship has been established between wage rates and population growth.

NONPURELY COMPETITIVE INFLUENCES IN THE LABOR MARKET

Employer Domination

The analysis thus far in this chapter has been based upon the assumption of pure competition in the labor markets. Numerous empirical studies of labor relations, plus everyday observations, suggest the importance of nonpurely competitive forces. In some instances, to a greater degree in the past than at the present time, the employer has a superior bargaining position, and takes the initiative in setting the wage; the worker has the choice of working or not working at the figure set. Today, frequently unions have developed as bargaining organizations for the worker. While in a few instances the union may itself dictate the wage, the development of unions ordinarily results in the determination of the wage by bargaining between union and employer or employer group. This type of market is essentially one of bilateral oligopoly or, if there is but one union and one group of employers, bilateral monopoly.

Until unions developed in strength, wages were typically set by the employer, with individual employers exercising substantial influence over the actual wage level. Employer domination of wages was possible because the number of employers was much smaller than the number of workers; the workers were not highly mobile from one employer to another, and the bargaining position of the workers as individuals was inherently weaker than that of the employer. In each particular labor market—which, especially in the past, has been very limited in size— the number of employers is often so small that there is no effective competition among them for workers. In other markets, although the total number of employers is large, a few employers use so much of the total labor force that they are able to dominate the wage level. Apart from the difference in numbers, the tactical position of the employer is

---

[6] See R. A. Easterlin, "The Baby Boom in Perspective," *American Economic Review,* Vol. 51 (December, 1961), pp. 869–911.

superior to that of the individual worker. It is <u>much more important for</u> <u>a worker to obtain and hold a particular job than it is for the employer</u> <u>to hire a particular man.</u> Failure to obtain a job leaves the worker without income; as a consequence, he cannot wait for a more favorable bargain, as can the employer. <u>Labor service is perishable</u>; the labor service of one day cannot be stored and sold on another day, whereas the property of the employer will not deteriorate in comparable fashion. The employer will not find his own income and living standard impaired by failure to hire any particular man.

The Determinants of the Extent of Employer Dominance

The <u>influence which an employer can exert on wages</u> depends in part upon the <u>mobility of workers and in part upon the extent</u> of competition for workers by employers. If workers move freely from one firm to another, and if firms act independently in determining wage and employment policy, the control over wages by any one employer is small. But <u>in practice, the mobility of workers is severely limited</u>. Most workers are tied rather closely to a particular firm by various bonds, and will not move easily in response to wage differentials. These bonds include privileges based upon seniority in the present job, such as pension and continued-employment rights, reluctance of workers to leave one job until they find another, preference for living in a particular locality and working with friends, and use by employers of personnel and hiring policies which prevent effective competition between those seeking employment in the firm and those already employed. Most employees are not "job shoppers" as long as they find their present employment reasonably satisfactory.

The <u>control of particular employers over wage rates depends also</u> upon the extent to which <u>employers agree with one another upon wage</u> <u>policies,</u> or take into consideration the effects of their wage-employment policies upon those of other firms. When common action develops, either with or without outright agreement, the situation becomes one of <u>oligopsony.</u> Thus, <u>two cases of employer-dominated wage determination</u> must be distinguished: that in which <u>each employer acts independently</u> but <u>immobility gives him some control over the wage level, and that of</u> <u>mutual interdependence.</u> Each case will be considered in turn.

Labor Immobility and Monopsonistic Competition

<u>Lack of mobility of workers among firms indicates preference</u> on <u>the part of employees for working for particular firms.</u> If <u>employees</u> <u>act independ</u>ently, the situation is therefore one of <u>monopsonistic com-</u>

petition. The basic feature is recognition by the employer that the wage he must pay depends upon the number of workers hired; that is, the supply schedule of labor is not perfectly elastic. The less the mobility of workers, the less elastic the schedule will be.

Since additional workers (at least beyond a certain point) can be obtained only by offering a higher wage, the marginal outlay exceeds the wage paid. In Figure 13–4 the marginal outlay curve (*MO*) is

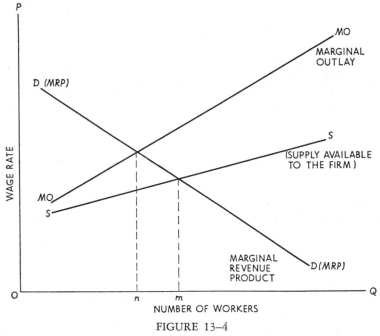

FIGURE 13–4

DETERMINATION BY AN EMPLOYER OF THE OPTIMUM. NUMBER OF WORKERS, MONOPSONY IN THE LABOR MARKET

above the supply curve of labor (*SS*). The employer, in adding workers up to the point at which MO = MRP, will not reach the point at which the *wage* is equal to MRP. At each wage rate, he will hire a smaller number of workers than he would if the supply schedule of labor were perfectly elastic. For example, in Figure 13–4, he will hire *On* workers in equilibrium, rather than *Om*. Since the same considerations apply to all employers in the market, the total demand for a particular type of labor at each wage rate will be less than it would be if the labor market were purely competitive, and thus the actual wage will be lower.

It must be emphasized that the supply price—the amount the employer must pay to get a given number of workers—depends primarily upon the exact degree of immobility of labor or, in other words, upon the alternative opportunities of workers. Two extreme cases may be noted. If there is but one employer in a certain market (perhaps in an isolated mining town) and workers cannot move, the necessary wage would be an extremely low figure—one just high enough to induce the workers to seek employment instead of starving to death. At the other extreme is the case in which workers are highly (but not perfectly) mobile among employers; the supply schedule will be highly elastic, and competition among the employers for labor will bring the wage level close to the purely competitive figure, even though the initiative in the setting of the wage figure rests with the employer. Between these extremes, there is a wide variety of possible cases, differing on the basis of the exact degree of elasticity of labor supply among firms.

Oligopsony

The second case of employer wage domination is that in which employers are conscious of wage interdependence; each firm realizes that changes in the wage it pays will result in changes on the part of other firms. Whenever the number of firms in a particular labor market is small, oligopsony attitudes are likely to be common. In this situation, either by outright collusion or merely by independent but coordinate actions, firms will not bid workers away from other firms by wage increases, since they recognize that the increases will be followed, and they will gain few additional workers. Under such circumstances, there is no tendency for wages or even marginal outlay on labor to adjust to equality with MRP, since each firm stops hiring workers short of the point at which this equality is attained. The actual level will be in large measure a product of historical accident, coupled with the factor of current labor mobility to and from employment in the particular field. If wages are set by outright collusion, the formal principles of setting will be comparable to those of the firm in monopsonistic competition acting independently, as analyzed above; but the MO curve will be that confronting the firms as a group, and thus will be controlled by the mobility of labor into and out of the particular labor market, and will be much less elastic than the curve confronting a particular firm. The degree of elasticity will determine the extent to which the wage level will be less than the purely competitive figure.

However, in practice, employers may voluntarily pay considerably higher wages than the minimum figure necessary to obtain the optimum number of employees. In the first place, many employers believe that the quality of the workers they can obtain and the productivity of their labor force will be affected by the wage level. Higher than necessary wages will be paid to attract particularly qualified workers, to maintain employee morale and efficiency at high levels, and to minimize costly labor turnover. Secondly, there is the possibility that purely noneconomic considerations, such as the ideas of the employer about the minimum wage necessary for a decent living standard and the prestige value of paying "good" wages, may lead an employer to pay more than the minimum. Some employers have been influenced by the principle that a high level of wages increases consumption and the general level of business activity. In depressions, many firms are reluctant to cut wages because of public censure for aggravating the decline in incomes. An even stronger force is the fear that the payment of lower wages will lead to unionization. Thus, wage levels in unionized fields exercise great influence on nonunion wage levels. Finally, in some instances, minimum wage laws are relevant.

LABOR UNIONS AND WAGE DETERMINATION

Typically, wages are no longer set by the employer but are determined through negotiations between unions representing the workers and employers or groups of employers. The significance of negotiated wages extends beyond the industries in which such methods are used, since wage rates in nonunion fields are greatly influenced by union scales.

Employer Policies

Deductive analysis of wage determination under conditions of bargaining between union and employer is not rewarding, as is true in any circumstances in which the outcome depends upon bargaining. All that can be done is to outline employer and union policies and note some of the factors influencing the results. With the present state of knowledge, no simple, clear-cut analytical tools can be developed.

The employer, of course, seeks to pay no more than necessary to obtain the optimum number of men, just as in circumstances in which unions are absent. However, his specific policies are affected by the existence of the union, and moves of strategy become highly significant. For example, he may not grant an increase he regards as reasonable simply because he feels that the union will then demand still more; on the other hand he may give more than is logical in terms of the direct economics of the situation in order to keep in power relatively "friendly" union officials. He may offer higher wages in order to persuade the union to drop demands for a union shop, featherbedding, or various fringe benefits. The employer's concessions will likewise be influenced by his estimate of the ability of the union to make a strike effective, and the effect of a strike upon his business, by his current profit situation; by his notion of what is "reasonable," and by his estimate of the effect of a wage increase upon his ability to raise prices, and the consequence of a price rise upon sales and profits.

Union Wage Policies

Analysis of union wage policy is far more difficult than the analysis of employer policy; primarily because the union itself is not a seller of labor but essentially a political institution representing the workers and having aims of its own distinct from those of its members. An important union aim is union survival and growth. As a consequence, it is difficult to apply the "maximizing" approach—which has been used in the analysis of all economic behavior thus far—to the policies of unions; there is no clearly defined single magnitude which unions are seeking to maximize.[7]

The most obvious assumption which may be made about union goals is that of maximization of the total wage bill, that is, the total amount of wages received by all union members. This is comparable to the profit-maximization assumption applied to business firms, and would be clearly acceptable if the unions were actually selling labor service. But of course, this is not the case. Attainment of the wage-bill maximization goal is likely to cause unemployment of some members of the union, and thus may be regarded as unacceptable, in light of the interests of those losing their jobs. On the other hand, the union may be so dominated by presently employed members that it disregards the interests of unemployed members and seeks a maximum wage bill for those now employed. For example, in a particular situation of unemployment, it is possible that a wage cut might allow reemployment of those out of work and increase total wage payments. But since the incomes of presently employed members would fall, they may refuse to accept the cut.

Pursuit of any of these goals (maximum total wage bill, maximum wage bill for presently employed members or jobs for all

[7] The "maximization" approach to union policy is presented by J. T. Dunlop, *Wage Determination under Trade Unions* (New York: Macmillan, 1944). For a criticism of this approach, see A. M. Ross, *Trade Union Wage Policy* (Berkeley: University of California Press, 1948).

members) requires that the union consider the effects of its wage policies upon the volume of employment available for its members. There is evidence that in some instances unions clearly consider the relationship between the wage and job opportunities, especially when employers are subject to strong competition in the product market and when the industry is not completely organized.[8] However, there is also evidence that unions, especially in periods of full employment, assume that the numbers of employees hired by the firms are determined largely by technological requirements and are independent of the wage rate, at least so long as the wage does not force liquidation of the firm—a possibility often regarded as very remote. If unions determine their policies under the assuption of a perfectly inelastic demand schedule for labor, the goals of wage-bill maximization are meaningless, since, if the demand schedule for labor is regarded as being perfectly inelastic, there is no total finite figure of a maximum wage bill. Essentially, the union is simply pursuing the goal of attaining a daily wage as high as possible. The oft-quoted goal of union leaders with respect to wages— "higher and higher, without limit"—is perhaps the most realistic single statement, although an incomplete one, about union wage aims. Unfortunately, recognition of this fact further complicates wage analysis, since in terms of this assumption the labor "maximum" is not a finite measurable magnitude.

The actual wage demands which unions make depend not only upon the goals they seek to attain, but also upon the tactics which union officials believe to be most satisfactory for this purpose. These tactics, in turn, are influenced by the desire of the union officials to insure the survival and expansion of the union, and the protection of their own positions.

Union Wage Demands. In determining precise demands, union officials are likely to have in mind two sets of figures—the one for which they are actually fighting and their initial asking figure. The former, which is the really significant figure, is influenced greatly by increases being obtained by other unions. If a 15-cent hourly increase is being accepted by other unions, union officials may feel it necessary to obtain this amount to prevent members from becoming dissatisfied with the existing union, or at least its management. As a consequence, a few wage bargains in major industries—steel and automobile production, for example—are likely to set the pattern for wage increases throughout the economy. Apart from increases obtained currently by other

[8] See G. P. Shultz and C. A. Myers, "Union Wage Decisions and Employment," *American Economic Review.* Vol. 40 (June, 1950), pp. 362–80.

unions, the officials will be influenced by their estimate of membership sentiment. The forces molding this sentiment are difficult to analyze. Cost-of-living changes and wage changes of preceding years play a part. Estimates of the employers' willingness to meet demands and their ability—as determined by their present profit position and the possibility of raising prices without serious losses in sales—also influence union wage goals. Finally, unions must balance wage goals with other union aims, such as dues checkoff, union shop, pension systems, working rules, etc.; smaller wage increases may be accepted in order to obtain concessions on these matters.

The initial demands of a union almost inevitably exceed the expected gains; the amount of the difference depends primarily upon the union's estimate of sound bargaining tactics. Most unions prefer to avoid fantastic demands which are obviously far in excess of anything that can be obtained. On the other hand, they usually ask for more than they expect to get. The possibility that a dispute over wages may ultimately be settled by arbitration increases the need for padding original demands, since arbitrators are likely to produce a compromise award.

There remains the question of the minimum figure the union will accept. There are essentially two minima, the figure below which the union will not go without calling a strike, and the figure believed essential for union survival. The minimum without a strike is likely to be the actual demand figure (not the initial inflated demand) if the union feels that it has sufficient strength to carry a strike through effectively. If the union is doubtful about the effectiveness of a strike, it may accept a lower figure than the expected amount. However, it will not go below the amount regarded as essential to the continued maintenance of the union organization. Estimates by union officials of the figure below which they will not go without a strike are influenced greatly by the figures which they believe the employer will grant, either with or without a strike. If they are certain that the employer will not exceed a certain figure even in the event of a strike, it is foolish to strike. The absolute minimum the union will accept is essentially the figure below which the union would disintegrate, its members drifting to other employments. If, regardless of the pressure applied to the employer through a strike, he will not accede to a wage equal to this amount, either the union will break up and the employer will set the wage, or the firm will liquidate and workers will be forced to seek employment elsewhere. But the concept of the absolute minimum is seldom of practical significance.

In summary, union wage demands—both the initial "asking" figure and the far more significant "expected" figure, as well as the minimum figure which the union will accept—must be recognized as the product of a variety of complex factors rather than simply as the figure estimated to maximize the total wage bill or any other precise sum. Frequently, under a widely accepted union assumption that employment is not affected by the wage level, unions seek constantly to drive the money wage figure higher, their demands in particular cases being influenced mainly by such considerations as increases being obtained by other unions, estimates of employers' profits and of the figures which the employers are willing to pay, the existence of pay differentials regarded as unwarranted, estimates of union membership sentiment, etc. Wage reductions are often fought to the bitter end, except in rare cases in which it is obvious that they are essential to prevent liquidation of the firm. In most situations, wage demands are weighed against the desire for other concessions relating to working rules, maintenance of union membership, and similar considerations.

The Actual Money Wage Level

Given the union and employer wage policies in a particular situation, the actual wage level will be determined by the relative bargaining strength of the two groups and their skill at the bargaining table. If the figure the employer is willing to pay is close to the figure the union is determined to get, an agreement will be reached quickly. If the union is too weak to make a strike effective, the wage is likely not to be far above the employer's minimum figure, regardless of the union's initial demands. If the union's strike minimum is above the maximum figure to which the employer will go in negotiations, a strike is inevitable; the eventual outcome depends upon the effectiveness of the strike and the employer's ability to withstand it and maintain financial solvency. The union's strength in a strike depends upon the completeness of its membership, the ability to keep nonunion men from working and to get other unions to respect its picket lines, the adequacy of reserves to support the members, and the existence of public relief for the strikers.

The Effects of Unions upon Money Wage Levels

What is the net effect of labor unions upon the structure and level of money wages? This is not an easy question to answer. To the extent that development of labor unions offsets monopsonistic influences of employers over wage levels, or gains for labor a relative bargaining advantage compared to the equal-advantage purely competitive situation, it would be expected that the money wages of the workers affected would be greater than they would otherwise be. If unions alter the flow of labor into various fields in any way, the altered supply-demand conditions may have further effects upon wage levels. Most empirical studies of the effects of unions upon wages have used the technique of comparing wage increases in unionized fields with those in nonunion fields. Such studies have shown that on the whole, in recent decades, there has been little tendency for union wages to rise more rapidly than nonunion wages, and some studies have even shown the reverse tendency. There appears to be a greater tendency for unions to affect the relative wage levels to the advantage of union members in depressions than in prosperity periods. However, in expansionary periods, some very aggressive unions force increases in excess of those obtained in other fields.[9]

Another technique involves comparison of union and nonunion wage rates in the same field. One of the most recent studies, by D. E. Kaun, shows a somewhat higher wage level for union than nonunion workers in 18 out of 21 observations.[10]

The basic limitation to these approaches to the study of the effects of union activity upon wage levels is their inability to take into consideration the effects which wage changes in unionized fields have upon wage levels in nonunion fields. The question of primary interest is: To what extent does union activity cause wage levels to differ from those which would exist if the unions were not present? No satisfactory answer can be given to this question by studying relative wage trends or levels in union and nonunion labor markets unless the effects of the union wage levels upon the nonunion levels can be eliminated, and this cannot be done. Employers in nonunionized fields are greatly influenced in their wage policies by union wages, not only because of the possibility of loss of labor supply in a period of labor shortages if they do not meet union levels, but also because of the desire to deter

---

[9] A series of papers in the *Proceedings of the American Economic Association,* May, 1954, discusses at length the question of the effects of unions on wage levels, and provides additional references on the subject. See also the book by H. M. Levinson, *Unionism, Wage Trends, and Income Distribution, 1914–1947* (Ann Arbor: University of Michigan Press, 1951); and the article by P. E. Sultan, "Unionism and Wage Rates, 1929–51," *Review of Economics and Statistics,* Vol. 36 (February, 1954), pp. 67–73. British experience is reviewed in the study by K. G. J. C. Knowles and D. J. Robertson, "Differences between the Wages of Skilled and Unskilled Workers, 1880–1950," *Bulletin of the Oxford Institute of Statistics,* 1951.

[10] "Union-Nonunion Wage Differentials Revisited," *Journal of Political Economy,* Vol. 72 (August, 1964), pp. 403–13; H. G. Lewis, *Unionism and Relative Wages in the United States: An Empirical Inquiry* (Chicago: University of Chicago Press, 1963).

unionization of their workers. As noted in a subsequent section, in periods in which demand for labor tends to outrun supply at existing wage rates, the existence of unions may actually slow down wage increases below those which would be attained with purely competitive labor markets, and perhaps in some cases even below those which would occur if labor markets were monopsonistic.

It is, therefore, difficult to generalize about the actual effect of unions on money wage levels. In terms of the general theory of price determination, it is to be expected that unions may raise money wages in those cases in which they eliminate monopsonistic wage domination, and perhaps may push wages above the competitive figure if they gain sufficient bargaining power. Much more empirical work is necessary before more positive conclusions can be reached.

Labor Unions and Wage Differentials

The development of unions undoubtedly has some effect upon wage differentials among firms, occupations, and geographical areas.

Interfirm Wage Differences. In the first place, widespread unionization tends to reduce interfirm wage differentials in a given occupation. These differentials, which would not exist if competition were perfect, are products of employer domination of the labor market, facilitated by relative immobility of labor. Unions almost always seek to eliminate these differentials which, if continued, would threaten the security of the union itself. Workers in low-wage plants will insist that the union eliminate the differentials, and high-wage employers may encourage the union to adopt a uniform wage policy. If industry-wide bargaining develops, a uniform wage policy is almost inevitable. The elimination of the differentials may merely destroy the excess profits of firms which had been able to hold wages to particularly low levels in the absence of unionization. In other cases, however, the low-wage firms were ones whose other costs were high, owing to inefficiencies in production or selling activities, poor management, or poor location. If the wage increase stimulates the firms to greater efficiency, the workers as well as the employers and society gain. If poor management or poor location is responsible, however, the high-cost firms may liquidate if they are forced to pay the uniform wage rate. If workers can shift easily to other plants, there is little loss; the sales of the other firms will increase, and society will benefit from the elimination of the less efficient firms. In other instances, however, unions encounter a serious problem: A uniform wage rate will compel liquidation of a firm with a substantial number of employees who cannot easily transfer to other jobs. Should the firm be allowed to continue to operate at a lower wage? The employees of the plant, if certain that higher wages will actually mean liquidation, will almost always favor retention of a differential. National union officials are likely to take the opposite point of view, because pressure will develop from other firms for lower wages. Sometimes one point of view will prevail, sometimes another.

If some firms in the industry become unionized and others do not, the development of the unions may actually increase, rather than decrease, the differentials. But this effect may be less common than might be expected. Nonunion employers may fear that their plants will be organized if they do not meet union wage levels, while the existence of nonunion firms in the industry may lessen the extent to which the union will seek to and be able to drive up wages in the unionized plants. There is some evidence, however, that on the average, nonunion firms pay lower wages than union firms in the same industry.

Occupational Wage Differentials.   For reasons indicated earlier in the chapter, the significance of union activity for occupational wage differences is difficult to assess. To the extent that unions are stronger in some occupations than others, it would be expected that differentials otherwise existing would be modified. However, union wage levels affect nonunion levels, and the empirical evidence is meager and somewhat conflicting. It does suggest, however, that unions have less significance for wage differentials than might be expected. But it is almost inevitable that particularly strong and aggressive unions may, at least for a time, raise the wages of the members of the group relative to those of persons in other occupations.

Likewise a union may be able to limit the number of men available for employment in an industry, and prevent the competition of nonemployed persons with those who have jobs. If unions obtain closed shop agreements and limit membership, the artificial control over supply will interfere with the flow of workers into the occupation and thus maintain greater differentials than would otherwise exist. Even if a union accepts all persons wishing to enter, it can ordinarily prevent newcomers from offering to work for lower wages. But this latter practice is apparently not common even in the absence of unions, and thus the presence of unions may have little real significance.

Geographical Wage Differences.   The development of widespread unionization would tend to lessen geographical wage differences. Wage differentials not offset by other differences such as variations in the cost of living create dissatisfaction among union members and injure the competitive position of high-wage firms. The higher wage figures often represent a goal which unions seek to attain in lower wage areas. For example, Canadian unions constantly refer to higher wage levels in the United States as goals for their own wage rates. The tendency toward industry-wide bargaining is likely to increase the elimination of geographical wage differences. In some instances, unions may actually seek to obtain uniform money wages despite cost-of-living differences, and may thereby increase real wage differences.

When unions are stronger in some areas than in others, the existence of unions may actually increase wage differentials over what they would otherwise be. Low wage levels in small towns often reflect a difference in the degree of unionization.

Unions and Economic Stability

In the last several decades, substantial attention has been directed to the question of the effects of union activity upon economic stability. On the one hand, it has been charged that unions have aggravated inflation during the period after World War II and are likely to do so in the future; on the other hand, during the depression of the thirties the unions were charged with increasing unemployment and checking recovery by holding wages artificially high. Both arguments have been hotly contested.[11] While these are basically macroeconomic questions, brief mention is warranted.

Unions and Inflation. The question of the significance of unions for inflation is closely related to the question of the significance of general wage increases upon the economy. It has been argued widely since World War II that unions exert a constant upward pressure upon prices, and make impossible the maintenance of a stable price level with full employment.[12] According to this argument, the insistence of unions on continuously higher money wages raises costs and total spending, and leads to a continuously increasing general price level, to the extent that the annual money wage increase exceeds the increase in productivity of labor. By this same line of reasoning, much of the inflation of the postwar years can be attributed to union activity.

This point of view has been seriously questioned by other writers, in part on the basis of the evidence, noted above, that nonunion wages have risen in much the same fashion in recent years as union wages. It is

[11] See W. G. Bowen, *The Wage-Price Issue* (Princeton: Princeton University Press, 1960), for an analysis of the question. See also J. M. Clark, *The Wage-Price Issue* (New York: American Bankers Association, 1960).

[12] One of the most detailed presentations of this point of view is to be found in the book by C. E. Lindblom, *Unions and Capitalism* (New Haven: Yale University Press, 1949).

argued, furthermore, that the existence of unions actually retards increases in wages in inflationary periods, primarily because union contracts run for lengthy periods, and increases cannot occur during the course of a contract. It is also maintained that employers may be reluctant to give increases they might otherwise offer, in order to take advantage of the concession of the increase in subsequent bargaining. Finally, the opponents of the union-induced-inflation argument maintain that price increases are due to excessive total expenditures on consumption and investment, and that wage increases are merely consequences of the excessive demand for all factors, and would occur regardless of the existence of unions.[13]

The present state of knowledge does not permit satisfactory conclusions on this issue of labor unions and inflation. From a theoretical standpoint, it is obviously possible for widespread, union-forced money wage increases to cause inflation, provided necessary adjustments in expenditures and money supply take place. The argument that wage increases *cannot* cause inflation is untenable.[14] But whether unions have in the past aggravated inflation or lessened it is an empirical question on which available evidence is inconclusive. Whether such effects will be encountered in the future depends in large measure upon the policies followed by unions. But from the present state of knowledge, it does not appear that reasonably full employment, price stability, and labor unions are necessarily incompatible.

Unions and Unemployment. During the depression years of the thirties, it was commonly argued that labor unions caused continuing unemployment because they held wages at artificially high levels, and prevented them from falling sufficiently to restore equality of the supply of and demand for labor. Superficially, this argument appears to have merit; in a sense, unemployment is a surplus of supply of labor over demand, and it would appear that a reduction in the wage rate would eliminate this surplus. Actually, however, more careful examination of the argument suggests serious limitations.

In the first place, wages fell relatively slightly in nonunion fields

---

[13] The argument that unions are not the source of inflation appears in the writings of M. Friedman, "Some Comments on the Significance of Labor Unions," in D. M. Wright (ed.), *The Impact of the Union* (New York: Harcourt, Brace, 1951; A. E. Rees, "Wage Levels under Conditions of Long-Run Full Employment," *Proceedings of the American Economic Association,* May, 1953, pp. 451–57; and W. A. Morton, "Trade Unionism, Full Employment, and Inflation," *American Economic Review,* Vol. 40 (March, 1950), pp. 13–39.

[14] The position that inflation can appropriately be attributed only to monetary considerations is held by several well-known economists. This argument is largely a terminological one, and its usefulness can be seriously questioned.

during the depression of the thirties; thus, it cannot be demonstrated that unions were artificially holding up the wage level. It must be granted, however, that had there been no unions at all in the economy, the decline in wages might have been greater.

Secondly, it is doubtful that declines in money wages during depression periods have much effect on real wages and therefore on the level of employment. Money wage reductions tend to produce price reductions, and essentially a general downward movement of national income in dollar terms; the decline in itself tends to depress business still more, especially if there is an expectation that the decline will continue. Only indirectly, through the effects of the price level decline upon the rate of interest, the costs of new equipment, the desirability of substituting manpower for capital goods, and the consumption-savings ratio, can any stimulus to increased employment be expected.

It is no doubt true that in certain particular instances, groups of workers can preserve their jobs by accepting wage reductions, especially when failure to do so will cause liquidation of the business. In other cases, certain marginal types of work, such as various aspects of plant maintenance, may be continued only if wages are sufficiently low. But it cannot be argued that the general level of employment is likely to be reduced as a result of the success of unions in holding up wages in depressions, because of the general tendency in such periods for prices to follow wage changes.

THE REAL INCOME OF LABOR

Recognition of the close relationship between money wages and prices, and particularly of the tendency of prices to change as wages change, brings the discussion back to the original point of departure: What determines the share of labor's real income, given the existing competitive conditions in the labor market? Does union activity, to the extent that it does affect money wage levels, actually alter the level of real wages and the share of labor in total national income?

The level of real wages, in total, depends in part on the total level of real income and in part upon the manner in which this total is shared between labor and other factor owners. The level of real national income depends upon the volume and quality of factors available, the techniques of production used, and the extent to which available resources are fully utilized. Increases in national product, in real terms, arise primarily from the development of new methods of production and the introduction of new types of capital equipment and increases in the skill of workers. Realization of this fact emphasizes the undesirable effects of policies sometimes followed by unions designed to restrict output or check the introduction of new methods of production. Such policies may aid a few individual workers, but they obviously injure workers as a group, as well as other members of society, by restricting the growth of national income. Society cannot become richer by producing less.

Given the level of real national income, the real income of the labor group is determined by the share of the total which labor receives. If all labor markets were purely competitive, the real wage of each type of labor would depend upon the MRP of the particular type of labor, and the overall share of labor in national income would depend upon the relationship between the MRP of labor and that of other factors. With monopsony in the labor markets, the real share of labor would be reduced somewhat below this level. The development of unions allows the elimination of this monopsonistic "exploitation" of labor, and thus tends to restore real wages and the share of labor in national income to the levels which would prevail with pure competition in the labor market. However, can unions do more than this, so far as wages are concerned, and raise labor's share above the purely competitive figure? This can occur, from a long-run standpoint, only if excess profits have been made possible by restriction of entry of new firms into certain industries. It is also possible for short periods of time when union strength is sufficient to force wages up to the point at which all costs are not covered by various business firms. But eventual liquidation of some firms will occur, and destroy the temporary gains to labor. Beyond these possibilities, the real wage level cannot be forced above the figure determined by the marginal productivity of labor; any increases in money wages beyond this point are accompanied by price changes, with no effect on the real wage level.

In recent decades the strength of unionization has greatly increased in the United States, yet the percentage of total national income which consists of wages and salaries has changed very little, as is noted in Chapter 12, and illustrated in Figure 13–5 on the following page. In depression years, the percentage of income which consisted of wages and salaries rose somewhat as profits were severely squeezed. The greatest relative increase in labor's share occurred after 1952, in a period in which relative union strength grew much less than in other years in the period. The behavior of the ratio of wages and salaries to national income has been approximately the same in Great Britain as in the United States, as shown in Figure 13–5, despite the fact that British

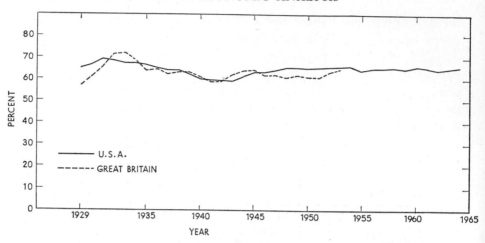

FIGURE 13–5

WAGES AND SALARIES AS A PERCENTAGE OF NATIONAL INCOME,
GREAT BRITAIN AND THE UNITED STATES, 1929–64

Sources: Great Britain: *Economic Journal,* Vol. 62 (June 1952), p. 277. United States: "National Income, 1954," *Supplement to Survey of Current Business,* July, 1954, pp. 162–63; and *Survey of Current Business,* August, 1965, pp. 28–38.

industry in much more highly organized. A study by Phelps-Brown of wage trends in France, Germany, Sweden, Great Britain, and the United States between 1860 and 1939 showed a high degree of uniformity of trends in real wages in the five countries, despite great differences in degree of unionization and changes in union strength over the period.[15] Studies referred to earlier in the chapter with respect to relative wage changes in union and nonunion fields serve further to confirm the point of view that unions actually have had less influence on real wage levels than might be expected.

In conclusion however, it should be noted that unions may bring very important advantages to labor even if they have relatively little effect on real wages, beyond eliminating the effects of monopsonistic influences. They may result in improved working conditions, hours of work more closely in line with the wishes of the workers, and greater job security; perhaps more importantly, they restore to the workers a prestige and a status which the unequal bargaining position of individual workers denies them in the absence of organization.

SELECTED REFERENCES

BOWEN, W. G. *The Wage-Price Issue.* Princeton: Princeton University Press, 1960.

[15] See E. H. Phelps-Brown, "The Course of Wage-Rates in Five Countries, 1860–1939," *Oxford Economic Papers,* Vol. 2 (June, 1950), pp. 226–96.

CARTTER, A. M. *Theory of Wages and Employment.* Homewood, Ill.: Irwin, 1959.

DUNLOP, J. T. *The Theory of Wage Determination.* London: Macmillan, 1957.

———. *Wage Determination under Trade Unions.* New York: Macmillan, 1944.
> An analysis of union wage policy and the significance of union activity for wage levels.

LEVINSON, H. M. *Unionism, Wage Trends, and Income Distribution.* Ann Arbor: University of Michigan Press, 1951.

LEWIS, H. G., *Unionism and Relative Wages in the United States: An Empirical Inquiry.* Chicago: University of Chicago Press, 1963.
> An empirical study of effects of unions on wage trends.

ROSS, A. M. *Trade Union Wage Policy.* Berkeley: University of California Press, 1948.
> An analysis of the factors controlling union wage policy.

TAYLOR, G. W., AND PIERSON, F. *New Concepts in Wage Theory.* New York: McGraw-Hill, 1957.

> See also footnote references to the discussion of the effects of unions upon wage levels and inflationary trends.

QUESTIONS

1. Indicate the major determinants of the supply of labor.
2. Explain the two conflicting considerations which influence the nature of the supply function of labor.
3. What is meant by a "backward bending" supply curve? Under what circumstances will the supply curve of labor be of this nature?
4. Why is the supply of labor believed to be relatively inelastic?
5. Indicate the significance of cultural patterns for the nature of the supply schedule of labor.
6. Empirical evidence shows that as real incomes rose over the years, the typical workweek declined. What significance does this evidence have for the nature of the supply of labor?
7. What additional considerations influence the supply of any particular type of labor?
8. What are the major influences upon the elasticity of demand for labor?
9. Explain the level to which wages would come in a purely competitive labor market.
10. Why is the purely competitive model of wage determination of limited significance?
11. Indicate the major sources of wage differentials, assuming pure competition in the labor market.
12. What is the nature of the long-run supply schedule of labor, in terms of the Malthusian theory of population?

13. Why did the Malthusian theory prove not to be applicable to the western world?

14. Evidence in recent years suggests that continued high levels of real income have led to an increase in the birth rate. How can this be reconciled with the failure of the Malthusian theory to operate in the last century?

15. Why, in the absence of unions, do labor markets tend to be monopsonistic?

16. What effect does the limited mobility of labor have upon the elasticity of the supply schedule of labor available to a particular firm?

17. Illustrate on a graph the supply curves of labor available to a particular firm (*a*) when labor is perfectly mobile and (*b*) when labor is highly immobile.

18. Why, in an employer-dominated labor market, does immobility of labor result in a lower wage level? Illustrate graphically.

19. What effect does the presence of oligopsony in the labor markets have upon wage levels? Explain.

20. Why may employers deliberately pay higher wages than the minimum figures necessary to obtain the optimum number of men?

21. What factors influence the wage figure the employer is willing to offer, when the workers are unionized? The maximum he is willing to pay?

22. Why are farmers typically much more hostile to the formation of unions among their workers than are manufacturers?

23. Indicate the various alternative assumptions with respect to the wage goals sought by unions.

24. Why cannot the maximization assumption in its usual form be applied to labor unions?

25. What forces influence the minimum figure a union will accept? The amount which it initially demands in a particular case?

26. Why are generalizations about the actual levels to which wages come in unionized fields difficult to make?

27. Why is it difficult to determine the actual effects which unions have had upon money wage levels?

28. What conclusions are reached by empirical studies made of relative wage trends in unionized and nonunionized fields?

29. On what basis was it frequently argued during the thirties that the unions were responsible for continued unemployment? What are the objections to this argument?

30. Why do general wage reductions probably have little effect in eliminating unemployment?

31. Discuss the conflicting points of view in the argument that labor unions have been responsible for much of the inflation of the last decade.

32. Under what circumstances can union activity actually improve the real living standard of the workers? Even if union activity does not raise the level of real wages, what other advantages may it convey to labor?

33. What are the primary determinants of the level of real wages at any particular time?

34. Does the empirical evidence indicate that the rapid development of union strength in recent decades has affected significantly the share of labor in total national income? Explain.

35. Under what circumstances does the development of unions lessen wage differentials within an occupation? Between occupations? Under what circumstances does it increase occupational differences?

36. What is the effect of the development of unions upon geographical wage differences?

Chapter 14

CAPITAL INVESTMENT AND CAPITAL BUDGETING

Durable capital goods constitute a major type of input in modern production.[1] They differ from the "basic" factors, labor and land, by virtue of the fact that they have been produced by business firms. The use of such capital goods in production involves the introduction of the time element: other resources are used to produce capital goods, rather than being directly employed to produce consumption goods to satisfy personal wants. Thus a period of time elapses from the moment of use of the other factors until goods are available for want satisfaction. Some time elapses, of course, in virtually any production process; goods are held for a time after production until the moment of consumption. But the time consideration becomes much more significant with the use of durable capital goods. In this analysis of investment in capital goods, we are concerned only with those which constitute an element in GNP; thus nondurable goods which are produced and used up in the production process during the period, such as raw materials, fuel, and consumables, and thus are intermediate goods rather than final products, are excluded from the discussion, since the general theory of factor demand and factor pricing is applicable to them without special qualifications.

The fact that durable capital goods are used over a period of years introduces several complications into the analysis, which arise to a much more limited extent with other factors in a nonslave economy:

1. Money capital is necessary to pay for the capital goods prior to the sale of the products made with them. Some money capital is required, of course, in any type of production since time elapses from the moment of payment for factor units until the sale of the product. But with the use of capital goods in production this time lag becomes much more significant. As will be explained in the next chapter, money

[1] For a recent analysis of the theory of capital, see Donald Dewey, *Modern Capital Theory* (New York: Columbia University Press, 1965).

314

capital commands a price in the form of interest; this interest must be taken into consideration in determining the profitability of additional investment in capital goods.

2. Since the capital goods will be used over a period of years, there is much greater risk that the expected returns will not be attained than there is with factors used on a current basis. All production requires prediction of the future, but predictions of sales and prices a week or month from now obviously have a much greater likelihood of realization than ones for five or ten or twenty years.[2] The risk of nonrealization of expected gains must be taken into consideration in the decisions to purchase capital goods.

Sources of Productivity of Capital Goods

Use of additional capital goods may be advantageous, and thus give rise to positive MRP, in several possible ways. In order to isolate the various influences, the discussion of the first three is based on the assumption of given technology.

1. Replacement of existing capital goods: a large portion of gross investment each year is designed to replace existing capital goods which have either worn out physically or have become economically obsolete. Calculation of the profitability of replacement investment is essentially the same as that of new investment, except for the need for considering the relative gain from continued use of the old equipment compared to the gain from new equipment. Thus, for example, relative maintenance expenses of new and old equipment must be included in the calculation. It is important to note that the original cost of the existing equipment is not a relevant factor in the decision to retain or replace it; once money capital has been "sunk" in a particular piece of equipment, it can be recovered (other than through the usually nominal salvage value) only through productivity in use.

2. Capital widening, that is, increase in the total stock of capital goods in use without change in capital intensity: a transport enterprise which has ten trucks adds another five of the same capacity. Purchases of additional capital goods for widening, that is, to allow the handling of additional output, are dependent primarily upon the rate of change in sales. Once the capacity of existing equipment is reached and sales continue to increase, purchase of additional equipment may be advantageous to handle the greater volume.

3. Capital deepening; the introduction of additional capital goods

---

[2] The potential life of some types of capital goods is almost infinite—a railroad tunnel through solid rock, for example. Buildings may be used for hundreds of years.

to allow more intensive use of capital relative to labor for a given volume of output. Such a change may be made advantageous by an increase in wages paid by a firm, with costs of new capital equipment unchanged.

4. Embodiment of technological change: each type of capital purchase thus far noted may be advantageous even though the state of technology remains unchanged. Actually, however, a large part of investment in new capital goods is a product of technological change; in modern terminology, the new capital goods embody the technological change. Some embodying investments are made for replacement purposes; new techniques may be introduced at the time replacement is made anyway, or it may result in replacement well ahead of the original retirement schedule. Substantial embodying investment is made, however, for the introduction of new products, to permit greater sales made possible by improved quality or lower cost consequent to the technological change, or because of other dynamic forces.

Determinants of Investment

The demand for capital goods is directly determined by the investment decisions of business firms. The same basic rule applies to capital goods as to other factor units: their purchase will be extended to the point at which the marginal gain—MRP—is just equal to the marginal outlay. But the time and risk considerations noted above create complications for the ascertainment of this optimum, and lead to the use of a variety of techniques of decision making in this realm. Three approaches warrant consideration:

1. *Direct calculation of marginal efficiency* of additional capital goods, often known as the *internal rate of return*. This may be defined as the rate of return at which the discounted present value of the future net returns is exactly equal to the cost of the capital equipment. For a simple example, suppose that a piece of machinery costing $5,000 is expected to last five years. If in each of the years the MRP is $1,500, the internal rate of return is 22.2 percent, the figure which when applied to the various MRPs will yield a discounted present value of $5,000. This figure in effect shows the net gain from the investment, discounting the MRP figure for each of the various years of use back to the present. Obviously those projects which promise the highest internal rate of return will be the most advantageous. It will be profitable, assuming the availability of money capital, to undertake all investments which yield an internal rate of return in excess of the interest which must be paid or forgone on money capital, since any

investment which yields more than the interest rate will add more to the firm's revenue than to its cost. Basically this technique will give satisfactory results, but there are certain situations, noted below, in which it will be less satisfactory than other approaches.

2. *Discounted present value.* The principal alternative involves calculation of the discounted present value of the future returns from the use of the capital equipment with the use of a given interest rate figure, equal to the current rate at which funds can be obtained. Any investment which will yield a discounted present value in excess of the cost of the investment is advantageous. Under usual circumstances this approach will give the same answer as the internal rate of return method; any investment which will show an internal rate of return in excess of the interest rate will show a discounted present value in excess of original cost (with, of course, the same interest rate figure).

There are at least two situations, however, in which the two methods will not give the same answer. First, projects with highly irregular expected returns may, at certain interest rates, appear profitable with one method and not the other. Secondly, when the firm cannot obtain all of the money capital required to extend investment to the level at which the internal rate of return is equal to the interest rate, and thus investment must be rationed to a certain dollar figure, the methods may give different answers for the ascertainment of the best projects. If the rationing were necessitated by some other reason than shortage of money capital, clearly the discounted present value method is preferable since it indicates the largest potential gain. But if capital shortage is the cause, this is not necessarily true, since the interest rate used in discounting future returns is not the true measure of opportunity cost of money capital to the firm, and some version of the internal rate of return method must be used.

3. *Rule-of-thumb approaches.* The problems of ascertainment of the internal rate and discounted present value and the uncertainty about the future yield lead many firms to use simplified approaches. One is the payout period rule. The firm calculates the number of years necessary to pay off the capital investment involved from the earnings (before subtraction of depreciation); priority is given to those projects with the shortest payoff period, and projects will not be undertaken with a payout period in excess of a specified number of years—five or ten, for example. This method is obviously a very crude one; it ignores completely the yield from the investment in the years beyond the payout period, which may be very significant, and it ignores the time distribution of the earnings within the payout period. An investment

which yields most of its net return in the early years of use is obviously more profitable than one which yields equivalent return in later years.

Other firms place primary stress on the urgency or estimated necessity for continued operation of the firm or attainment of some specific goal, such as integration of raw materials supplies. This criterion is clearly suitable in some instances; if a mile of railroad track is washed out, it must be replaced if the line is to continue in operation. But excessive reliance on this method can result in piecemeal replacement of extensive capital equipment not warranted by profit considerations, and the method as applied to expansion is based on mere guesswork.

Risk Considerations

We have considered thus far only the time dimension and not the risk dimension in investment decisions. Any investment in capital goods involves risk; conditions may turn out to be substantially less favorable than anticipated, and not only may the expected return not be gained, but the capital sum invested in the equipment may be lost. A new business may find that sales are much less than anticipated, and an existing business may miscalculate the gain from a particular investment. Dynamic forces in the economy are difficult to predict; technological change may render the equipment obsolete far ahead of the expected time, or shifts in consumer preferences or development of additional competition may result in lower returns. History provides many examples; a classic one is the investment of over $1 billion in electric interurban railways, which were rendered obsolete by the motor vehicle long before the investment was recovered.

On the other hand, of course, investment may turn out to be much more profitable than anticipated. Sales may be greater, or the actual economic life may prove to be much longer.[3] It must be recognized, however, that forces of competition tend to set a limit on returns higher than expected, since such returns lead to development of new firms.

That risk is created by capital investment is obvious; how to adjust for it in calculation of profitability of investment is quite another matter. The simplest method is to apply a risk discount factor to the expected return, reducing the latter accordingly. The obviously greater

---

[3] While no one would seriously anticipate the economic life of any transportation equipment at more than 25 years or so, the Grand Trunk Railway car ferries Huron and Lansdowne are now in their 91st year of operation between Detroit and Windsor (the hull of the Lansdowne is 81 years old). A locomotive built in 1864 and shipped around Cape Horn for use on early California lines continued in regular service until 1950 on the Stockton Terminal and Eastern, a total of 86 years.

risk of the later years is taken into consideration by the greater impact of the discount factor for these years. While the discount approach adjusts for the risk consideration, it suffers from a major limitation: there is no basis upon which to select the discount percentage other than sheer intuition. Obviously the risk consideration differs with various types of industries: electric power generation or telephone service on the one hand, and silver mining or restaurant operation on the other, are good examples of extremes. Furthermore, the attitudes of various persons toward risk differ significantly, on the basis of their general point of view toward the future. The sources of funds and the financial situation of the enterprise obviously affect the risk. As noted below the risk is greater if funds are borrowed than if earnings are reinvested; they are much greater, for investment of a given magnitude, for a small company with little reserve than for a large enterprise with substantial reserve capital.

Various attempts have been made to simplify or improve the risk discounting adjustment. These take several forms:

1. Use of a cutoff date or finite horizon. Potential returns beyond a certain date are not taken into consideration, on the grounds that the degree of risk is so high that any prediction would be useless. This technique is not scientific, of course, and could produce misleading results in instances in which it is reasonable to assume that there will be some use beyond the cutoff date.

2. The Shackle approach, involving what may be called potential surprise, instead of application of a uniform risk discount rate. To take a simple example, suppose that the person believes that there are equal chances of 4, 5, and 6 percent internal returns on a particular investment, and no chance of any other return. If so there is no risk discount adjustment to be made. Where there is danger of "surprise" an equivalent return figure for the investment which would be riskless may be estimated; the difference indicates the appropriate risk discount in the particular case.

3. Probability adjustments. A firm faces alternative investment possibilities, with varying degrees of probability of occurrence for various returns, the probabilities projected from previous experience or estimated. These various alternatives will show different estimated returns. For various of the alternatives, the most-certain-return projects are those offering lowest potential yield; the least certain are those offering the potentiality of very high return (as is also true, for example, of certain types of gambling). The situation is illustrated by indifference curves in Figure 14–1. The firm must make its decision in

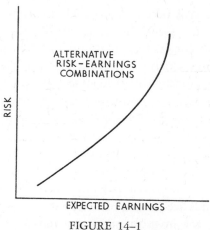

FIGURE 14–1

RISK-EARNINGS POSSIBILITIES

terms of relative preferences for the various alternatives, if it is to maximize gain. But, of course, in many instances, probability cannot be projected with any degree of certainty from past experience; intuition and sheer guesswork will determine the relative certainty of various adjustments. Nevertheless, this approach should give more satisfactory results than the risk-discount method, since it stresses varying return-risk situations.

Some assistance in improving the quality of estimation of the risk of the various alternative investments may be given by selecting those factors in the situation which appear to be particularly critical (e.g., prices of raw materials), and estimating the returns with various figures for these criteria. At some level of raw materials prices, for example, the investment will be completely useless, since production cannot be carried on profitably. Some estimate of the likelihood of such a level of raw materials prices occurring, therefore, will increase the quality of the predictions.

The Cost and Availability of Money Capital

As noted above, the crucial comparison to be made in capital budgeting, if profits are to be maximized, is that of the internal rate of return and the cost of money capital. The cost figure—and thus the optimum level of investment for the firm—is influenced by the source of the money capital. There are three major sources:

1. Borrowing of money, the direct cost being the interest which must be paid on the money. The borrowing of money gives rise, of course, to an additional risk not incurred with the other methods of

financing, that of bankruptcy and loss of control of the company in the event the investment proves to be so unsuccessful that interest and repayment obligations cannot be met. The owners run the risk of losing their entire investment, not merely the additional investment.

2. Sale of stock. No contractual obligations to pay interest or repay principal are incurred, but the earnings—on the old investment as well as the new—are shared with the owners of the new stock; the cost, therefore may be considered to be the current yield figure on the additional stock issue. If new issues of stock paying $5 annual dividend can be sold at $100, the yield is 5 percent. While no risk of bankruptcy is incurred, there is danger of loss of control of the enterprise if a sufficient amount of additional stock is issued.

3. Reinvested earnings or plowback. The most important source of investment funds consists of money accumulated internally from profits, together with accumulated earned depreciation charges. The cost of the use of such funds is the opportunity cost of not using them for other investments—in securities of other corporations, for example. Since the borrowing rate exceeds the lending rate because of transactions costs, this opportunity cost figure is lower than the cost to the firm of acquiring funds from outside sources. In addition, no secondary costs of greater danger of bankruptcy or loss of control are created; the only secondary cost is the loss of liquidity, which could endanger the financial stability of the company in the event of losses, and which precludes the investment of the funds in more advantageous pursuits which arise during the period.

The cost element of the money capital for the additional investment, will, therefore, differ with the source of the funds, and with the general credit standing of the particular company, which affects the rate at which funds may be obtained from the outside. Actual choice of the methods of financing will depend upon relative costs and availability of funds from the various avenues together with attitudes toward risk and dilution of control. Many firms as a matter of policy will expand only when internal funds are available for this purpose. Others—particularly small enterprises—cannot raise funds by any other means, at least beyond a certain point. Thus the availability of various sources of funds will affect the total volume of investment.

The Functional Relationship between the Amount of Money Capital Used and the Cost

In a perfect market, with no uncertainty, a firm could presumably obtain any desired sum (within the range of such a market) at a given percent cost. But in practice market imperfections and uncertainty create a positive functional relationship. At a given time, as additional funds are obtained, a higher interest rate must be paid on borrowed capital (beyond a certain point) or higher return given to new stockholders; the risks created by additional borrowing or stock financing are increased, as well as the liquidity losses of the use of internal capital. Thus the marginal cost of additional investment, which is the relevant cost figure, will rise.

One of the most significant peculiarities of the acquisition of money capital is the prevalence of capital rationing: that is, a firm may be unable to raise funds at all beyond a certain point. A firm has a limited amount of internal funds. Lenders, chary of the eggs-in-one-basket danger, frequently will be unwilling to lend beyond a certain amount to a particular firm. Similarly, it may be difficult or impossible to sell stock beyond a certain amount; in fact, very small firms cannot do so at all. Many firms will stop short of the absolute maximum they can obtain from the outside; if they follow such a policy, the significance is the same as if they could not raise the money at all.

When the quantity of money capital available limits the firm to a volume of investment less than the optimum in terms of the relationship of the rate of return and the cost of money capital, the investment decision becomes one of the selection of the investment projects which offer the greatest potential return. More specifically the capital available becomes one of the constraints of the problem, and the goal becomes that of maximizing the return from this amount of capital, taking risk into consideration. Together with other common constraints, the problem is one which can be solved rather simply by linear programming techniques, as discussed in Chapter 19. Whether the choice proves to be the correct one or not depends upon the accuracy of prediction of the returns.

Total Investment

The chapter to this point has been concerned with the investment decisions of particular firms. The pattern of such decisions determines the total volume of investment in the economy, given the following constraints:

    a) The prices or supply schedules of capital goods.
    b) The supply schedules of money capital at various interest rates.
    c) The anticipated profitability of various investments.
    d) The anticipated risk of these investments.
    e) The level of national income.

Constraints (*c*) and (*d*) have been discussed in this chapter; constraint (*e*) is an element of macroeconomics. The determination of the interest rate is discussed in the next chapter. Constraint (*a*) warrants further consideration.

The Prices of Capital Goods

There is a negative functional relationship between the prices of capital goods and the demand for them, as there is for any type of factor unit. Subject to the special qualifications involved in calculation of MRP, as noted previously in the chapter, and the influence of possible capital rationing, the same considerations apply to the demand for capital goods as to the demand for other factor units. Higher prices of certain types of capital goods, other elements being given, will cause firms to substitute alternate forms of capital equipment and to use more labor intensive methods, and total investment will thus be less. However, in terms of the economy as a whole, it is important to note that it is difficult for capital goods prices to rise relative to wage rates, since the latter are the primary cost elements in the production of capital goods.

Since capital goods are produced by business firms on a profit-making basis, the same considerations apply to output, supply and pricing policies as those relevant for consumption goods. Many capital equipment industries are characterized by relatively tight oligopoly, with close implicit or explicit cooperation as a consequence of limited differentiation. But there are no basic differences in pricing policies.

Changes in the Demand for Capital Goods

There are several dynamic forces which affect the demand for capital goods, and thus the volume of investment.

Changes in Factor Supplies. An increase in the quantities of other factors available will tend to increase the demand for capital goods. Discovery of new natural resources will lead to purchase of capital goods by firms exploiting the new resources or using products made from them. Growth in population makes available an increased supply of labor, and requires the use of more capital equipment if the least-cost combination of factors is to be maintained, provided the increase in population does not adversely affect the supply of money capital available for investment. This qualification is particularly significant in underdeveloped countries in which families use so much of their incomes for consumption purposes that little money capital is available for investment.[4] In highly developed countries, in periods in which there is a tendency for persons to seek to save more than the current rate of investment, the effect of population growth in increasing the percentage of income consumed will stimulate investment by increasing sales of consumption goods, apart from the encouragement given to investment by the effect of population growth upon labor supply.

Changes in the Supply of Money Capital. The demand for capital goods and the demand for money capital are complementary to one another, since increased use of capital goods requires additional use of money capital. Accordingly, an increase in the supply of money capital, which tends to lower the interest rate and make money capital more readily available, increases the demand for capital goods. This result will be attained, however, only if developments which increase the supply of money capital do not simultaneously reduce MRP of capital goods.

Increases in National Income Due to Lessened Unemployment of Resources. As national income rises from depression levels through reemployment of idle factor units, additional investment will be profitable because the increasing sales of products will increase MRP of capital equipment. When recovery first commences, the effect upon MRP may be slight, because firms have substantial idle capacity. But once the capacity of existing equipment is approached, sharp increases in investment are to be expected.

However, net investment due to a rise in national income will continue only so long as the increase in output (or expectations thereof, noted below) continues. As full employment is approached, the rate of increase in national income must slacken; and once full employment is attained, the rate of increase is limited to the rate permitted by increases in factor supplies and technological change. As a consequence, the volume of net investment must fall below the high levels possible during the period in which idle resources are being reemployed. Reinvestment will, of course, remain at higher levels because the total stock of capital goods is greater.

Technological Change. From a long-range point of view, the most important dynamic force influencing the volume of investment is technological change—the development of new *products* and *methods* of production. The development of new *products* will almost always temporarily produce new investment, although over a period of time investment for the production of goods for which the new products are

---

[4] If additional money capital is created by bank or governmental action under such circumstances, inflation will result.

substituted is likely to fall. If the new articles require relatively large amounts of capital goods in their production—as, for example, automobiles—substantial net investment will occur during the period of their development, and annual reinvestment will remain at a permanently higher level. The significance for capital investment of a few major new products during the last century has been tremendous. The automobile, for example, has led to great investment in factories producing automobiles and their parts and accessories (such as tires), in the oil-refining industry, in service stations, and in highways. The net effect has probably been offset only to a minor extent by consequent reduction in investment in the production of horse-drawn vehicles and in the railroad industry.

The development of new *methods* of production has significant effects upon the volume of investment. Over the last several centuries, most inventions have necessitated the use of relatively more capital equipment, compared to the amounts of labor and natural resources. In general, inventions have provided means of accomplishing with capital goods tasks formerly directly performed by labor. There have been exceptions; some technological developments have been capital-saving, in the sense that they allow certain tasks to be performed economically with less capital investment (per unit of output). The replacement of streetcars by buses in local transit service provides an example. But the general pattern of technological change has required the use of progressively more capital goods and thus has made possible continuous net investment, except in years of sharp decline in national product. Not only have new techniques increased investment in the industries directly concerned; but often, by freeing labor and natural resources, they have made possible increases in output and investment in other industries. Some developments have lessened the cost of producing capital goods and have increased the relative advantages of capital compared to other factors. Net investment resulting from technological change will continue only so long as the development of new products and methods continues. While the introduction of a series of new techniques will permanently increase the volume of capital goods in use and the annual volume of reinvestment, it will give rise to continuing new investment only as long as the new techniques are being introduced.

Changes in Expectations. Since capital equipment acquired in a certain period will be used over succeeding periods of time, changes in expectations about the future will affect the estimated MRP and the demand for capital goods. In a period of depression, the development of increased optimism about the future, even if based upon no tangible changes in the current profit situation, could in itself stimulate recovery. Regardless of the initial cause of a recovery movement, once it does get under way, the tendency for expectations of businessmen to improve and a general feeling of optimism to develop are likely to increase the volume of investment to a much higher level than would be justified on the basis of current sales. Changes in expectations about future technological changes can also alter present estimates of MRP of additional capital goods.

The Payments for Capital Goods and Factor Incomes

The sums paid by business firms for new capital equipment do not in themselves constitute factor income payments, since the equipment has been produced by business firms; the payments serve to cover the costs, explicit and implicit, of the equipment-producing firms. The amounts involved are paid out by the equipment producers in the form of factor incomes to the persons supplying factor units to them in the same manner as amounts paid for consumption goods.

The amounts paid for capital goods by business firms constitute costs from a long-range point of view, since the sums must be covered if operation is to be carried on indefinitely. The costs of capital equipment acquired in any one year, however, cannot appropriately be regarded as costs for which the output of the year is wholly responsible, since the equipment will be used to produce output over a period of years. Accordingly, under usual practice, the purchase price of the equipment is depreciated over the period of years of expected life, a formula being used to allocate a share of the total cost to each year. The allocation is inevitably somewhat arbitrary, since there is no way of ascertaining in any one year what the actual decline in value of the equipment for that year is, or how long the equipment can actually remain in use.

These annual depreciation charges, the form which the cost of the capital equipment takes, are, of course, not incomes; they are merely the charges which reflect the decline in the value of the capital equipment and thus represent the recovery for the firm of the money capital invested in the equipment. The sums involved are available for the repayment of loans, for replacement of old equipment, for expansion, or for increases in liquid balances or security holdings.

Hence the amounts paid for the capital equipment, in themselves, do not give rise to a distinctive form of income, distinguishable from that which would arise if capital equipment were not used. The distinctive return which arises from the use of capital equipment can be discovered only by considering the money capital which is required to obtain the equipment.

REFERENCES

BAUMOL, W. J. *Economic Theory and Operations Analysis,* chap. xix. 2d ed. Englewood Cliffs, N.J.: Prentice-Hall, 1965.
>   One of the best summary statements of capital budgeting.
BIERMAN, H., AND SMIDT, S. *The Capital Budgeting Decision.* New York: Macmillan, 1960.
>   A review of investment decision making.
DEWEY, DONALD. *Modern Capital Theory.* New York: Columbia University Press, 1965. A recent summary of capital theory.
LUTZ, F. A., AND HAGUE, D. C. (eds.). *The Theory of Capital.* London: Macmillan, 1961.
>   A collection of papers on capital theory.
————, AND LUTZ, V. *The Theory of Investment of the Firm.* Princeton: Princeton University Press, 1951.
>   A high-level analytical study of investment.
SOLOMON, E. *The Management of Corporate Capital.* New York: Free Press of Glencoe, 1959.

QUESTIONS

1. What consideration distinguishes capital goods from other factors?
2. Indicate the complications created for the theory of factor pricing by the fact that durable capital goods are used over a period of years.
3. Distinguish between capital widening and capital deepening.
4. What is meant by embodiment of technological change? What role does technological change play in investment decisions?
5. Distinguish between the internal rate of return and discounted present value methods of calculation of the profitability of additional investment.
6. Define the internal rate of return.
7. Under what circumstances will the two methods of calculation noted in Question 5 give identical results? Under what circumstances will they not do so? Which method is preferable in these instances?
8. Why do many firms turn to "rule-of-thumb" methods for investment decision making?
9. What is the payout period rule? What are its limitations?
10. Under what circumstances is use of the "urgency of investment rule" warranted? What is the danger in its use?
11. Indicate the various approaches to the introduction of risk into investment decision making, and the limitations of these approaches.

12. Indicate the nature of the cost of money capital, under the borrowing, sale of stock, and plowback methods of financing investment.

13. Why are firms more likely to undertake marginal investment projects if they have their own funds for the purpose than if they must borrow the money or sell additional stock?

14. What is capital rationing? Why does it arise? What significance does it have for investment decision making?

15. Indicate the major determinants of the total demand for capital goods.

16. What is the nature of the functional relationship between the price of capital goods and the quantity demanded? Why?

17. Note the major causes of changes in the demand for capital goods.

18. Why are payments for capital goods not in themselves factor payments? Do earned depreciation charges constitute factor incomes? Explain.

Chapter 15   THE THEORY OF INTEREST

Requirements for money capital to acquire capital equipment and to make other factor payments prior to the sale of the products were explained in the previous chapter. This chapter is devoted to the question of the determination of the interest rate—the price paid for the use of money capital. This charge is a cost to business firms, and an income to its recipients. If money capital is borrowed by a business firm, interest charges take a contractual form; if it is supplied by the owners of a firm, either from their personal wealth or through retention of earned depreciation charges or profits, interest is an implicit cost. In addition to interest paid by business firms for the use of money capital, interest is also paid by individual consumers and by governments for the use of borrowed money.

The Nature of Interest

So far as the production process is concerned, interest arises because of the lapse of time from the moment at which payments are made for factor units until the goods produced with these units are sold. Money to pay for the factor units must be available prior to the time at which it is received from the sale of the products. Even if no durable capital goods are used in production, some money capital is required to pay for labor, materials, and the like prior to the sale of the product. But the primary need for money arises from the use of capital goods, which are used in production over a period of years. If the use of such goods allows the firm to earn an MRP greater than the cost of the equipment, business firms are able to pay for the use of money capital to acquire the equipment.

Payment of interest is necessary to induce those persons who have money capital to turn it over to those who wish to use it. A person who currently has wealth in liquid form—that is, in the form of money, including demand deposits—has three general alternatives: he can

329

spend it on consumption;[1] he can hold it in liquid form; or he can make it available for use by business firms (including governments). Alternatively, the interest may be regarded as a payment to induce people to save instead of consume, or as a payment to forgo liquidity and make wealth available for use in production. Traditionally, in classical economics, interest was regarded as a payment to induce persons to save rather than spend on consumption. It is recognized today, following the work of Keynes and others, that it is more appropriate for analytical purposes to regard interest as compensation for forgoing liquidity—that is, for making money available to others rather than holding it idle. The act of saving does not in itself enable a person to obtain interest; he must make his money available for use, and thus forgo liquidity in order to do so. But nevertheless decisions with regard to consumption and savings obviously have significance for interest rate determination, and must not be ignored.

DECISIONS AFFECTING THE INTEREST RATE

Since interest is the price paid for the use of money capital, its determinants, in a purely competitive market, are the demand and supply schedules of money capital; in nonpurely competitive conditions the interest rate is influenced by the precise nature of competition and by the policies followed by those exercising influence on the market. Before the demand and supply schedules are explained, however, it is desirable to consider decision making with regard to the allocation of income between savings and consumption, and with regard to the holding of wealth in liquid form or making it available for use in production.

Allocation of Income between Consumption and Saving

Recipients of income have two alternatives for the use of their income: They may use it for the purchase of consumption goods, or they may save it. Savings are defined as the excess of income over consumption. The income allocation which a person makes between consumption and savings is dependent upon his relative *time preference* for the use of the income, that is, preference for use of the income at present rather than at some time in the future. For all persons, time preference is positive on at least a portion of income; that is, they prefer

---

[1] He may also lend it to other persons for consumption purposes. If he does, the effect, from the standpoint of the economy, is the same as if he had spent it on consumption himself.

to allocate a portion for immediate use. But for many persons, time preference for a portion is negative; that is, they prefer to retain a portion of the income for future use rather than spend it currently. There are several reasons: to build a reserve for emergency purposes, to accumulate for old age, to provide for one's heirs or for some particular use in the future, such as education of children, purchase of a home, establishment of a business, etc.

On the basis of the relative importance attached to these considerations, on the one hand, and the desire for current consumption, on the other, each family allocates its income between the two uses. Individuals will differ widely in the allocation made, depending on the amount of wealth already accumulated, the number of dependents, expectations regarding future income, foresight in planning for the future, availability of desired goods, expectations of price changes, and the extent of current windfall capital gains and losses (such as changes in the value of securities). The level of family income may be a major consideration, as is the intensity of desire for present consumption.

The final factor which may influence the choice is the rate of return which may be obtained if the income is saved and loaned. It was long argued that there was a significant functional relationship between the interest rate and the level of saving. Today, however, it is generally believed that the relationship is not strong. This is, of course, an empirical question, but several elements in the picture suggest that the interest rate has little significance. It is obvious that most savings are made for reasons completely unrelated to the rate of return. In addition, many families cannot possibly save larger amounts because of the pressing needs of current consumption. Some savers, seeking a given annual return in dollar terms from their savings, will save more rather than less if the interest rate falls. For many families, saving is largely a matter of habit, and the margin is not calculated at all closely.

The actual sum of savings made during a period, that is, the excess of income over consumption expenditures, may be called *ex post* or realized savings. This sum may differ from *ex ante* or planned savings, the amounts which persons planned to save at the beginning of the period. The two sums will be identical if all expectations are realized, with regard to incomes, prices, and other circumstances. But they are not necessarily realized. For example, suppose that persons on the average commence to save a higher percentage of their incomes than they did in previous periods. If all incomes remain the same, and prices and other determinants are unchanged, people will succeed in saving, *ex post,* the larger sum. But the general increase in the propensity to save may reduce production and incomes because of the lessened purchase of consumption goods, and so the actual sum of savings during the period may be much less than the anticipated sum. The attempt to save more may thus reduce the actual sum saved, which is the source of money capital. While some individuals succeed in saving larger amounts, this is more than offset by reduced saving on the part of others—those whose incomes fall because other persons spend less on consumption.

The division of national income between consumption and savings is affected not only by the decisions of individuals in allocating disposable income between consumption and savings, but also by decisions of corporate management with regard to retention of profits. These decisions are influenced by a number of factors, such as the estimate of need for additional reserves, the desire for funds for expansion, and the demands of stockholders for dividends. The influence of the current interest rate on the decisions would appear to be slight.

Liquidity Decisions

Savings do not automatically become available for use. Only if the individuals and business firms that accumulate liquid wealth are willing to use it in their own enterprises or make it available to others is the supply of money capital actually increased by the additional savings. Thus the factors influencing decisions with regard to liquidity are of prime importance for the supply of money capital.

There are several reasons why persons wish to hold portions of their personal wealth in monetary form:

1. *Transactions Motive.* Persons must have on hand at any time a certain amount of money for the conduct of day-to-day transactions. Income and outgo of individuals and business firms do not balance exactly in any short period of time. A person may receive a weekly paycheck and spend the money gradually during the following week. Accordingly, he will have on hand during the week the portion of the money not yet spent; he cannot conveniently lend out half the amount of the check on Saturday and obtain the money back on Tuesday. A person will also usually seek to have some margin left over at the end of the week, since he cannot calculate his exact expenditures in advance. The average amount that a person has on hand depends on the size of his income, the interval of receipt of the income, and the extent to which he pays in cash. Business firms likewise must keep substantial cash balances to meet current payments. In some enterprises (many

types of farming, for example) the entire annual receipts will be received in a very short period of time. Financial institutions must keep a substantial portion of their assets in the form of money, since they are under obligation to meet the demands of customers at any time and on short notice.

The total amount of money required in the economy for transactions purposes is significantly affected by the level of national income. As employment and output or the general price level (or both) rise, the total volume of money needed for transactions will rise. Individuals will be receiving greater money incomes and therefore holding greater average cash balances; business firms will require more money to handle the larger volume of transactions.

Balances kept for transactions purposes may be called *active* balances, as distinguished from *inactive* balances held because of other motives.

2. *Precautionary Motives.* In addition to amounts needed to meet routine and foreseen expenditures, individuals and business firms typically keep additional sums of money to provide protection in the event of emergency. The expenses of a business may rise sharply, or revenues may fall. Failure to have sufficient money or other highly liquid assets may cause forced liquidation. An individual may suddenly experience loss of income—due, for example, to illness—or unexpected expenses; failure to have adequate funds may cause expensive borrowing, loss of a home, or resort to charity. One misfortune, both for an individual and for a business firm, may lead to another. Illness, for example, by reducing income and raising expenses, will necessitate emergency borrowing and thus impair a person's credit standing, as well as his ability to meet other emergencies. The holding of money for precautionary purposes is made particularly necessary by the credit-rationing policies of financial institutions. Regardless of credit standing, persons are usually unable to borrow in excess of a certain sum at current interest rates.

3. *Convenience Motive.* The making of loans and the reconversion of loans into money are sources of cost and inconvenience. Any type of loan, even that of making a savings deposit, results in a certain amount of nuisance and loss of time. The purchase of securities necessitates the payment of brokers' fees. Persons with relatively small amounts of savings will frequently hold them in monetary form, either indefinitely or until they accumulate a sufficient amount to warrant purchase of securities. Typically, the small saver is interested much

more in the preservation of the capital sum of his savings than in any possible return; the easiest and simplest way to keep small amounts is in the form of money.

The existence of savings accounts, which in the United States, at least, are not classified as money since the deposits cannot be used directly for making payments,[2] greatly lessens the amounts of cash and demand deposits which individuals hold for both convenience and precautionary motives, since savings accounts offer most of the advantages of money itself from the standpoint of these motives, yet earn interest. However, the placing of funds in these accounts does not automatically make them available as money capital. Bank lending policy determines their availability.

4. *Speculative Motive.* Whenever persons expect security prices to fall and thus interest rates to rise, they will prefer to keep their wealth in monetary form at present, in order to be able to purchase securities at lower prices in the future. If they lend now, they will be unable to realize from the benefits of an increase in interest rates until maturity of the securities purchased; and if they wish to reconvert their wealth to liquid form prior to maturity, they will suffer a capital loss. When persons expect security prices to rise, they will wish to lend out larger portions of their wealth at the present time than they otherwise would.

The Significance of the Interest Rate for Liquidity Decisions

To what extent is the desire for liquidity influenced by the rate of interest? It is generally assumed that the functional relationship between the interest rate and liquidity is much more significant than that between the interest rate and the savings-consumption ratio. Interest is a direct compensation for forgoing liquidity, whereas it is not a compensation for saving, as such. At low rates the amount received for incurring the inconvenience and danger from loss of liquidity and for taking the risk of decline in the value of the securities and of nonrepayment of the principal is relatively small; as a consequence, persons are likely to seek to keep substantial portions of their wealth in liquid form. At high rates the sacrifices of income caused by holding wealth in liquid form are great, and persons will be more willing to reduce their cash balances and suffer the consequences of loss of liquidity. If a person can receive only $10 a year from lending out $1,000, he is likely to regard this sum as inadequate for the inconven-

---

[2] In Canada, savings deposits must be regarded as a portion of the money supply, since checks may be drawn upon them.

ience and risk of capital loss, and loss of liquidity. If he can receive $60 a year on a loan with the same degree of risk, he is much more likely to consider the return as adequate to compensate for sacrificing the advantages of liquidity. When interest rates rise, even balances held for transactions purposes will be reduced.

Furthermore, when interest rates are relatively low, there is greater likelihood that persons will anticipate an increase in rates than they will when rates are already at high levels, and thus greater amounts will be held because of the speculative motive. Lenders of money—just like sellers of wheat—become accustomed to certain rates as being "standard"; if the actual rate rises above this figure, expectations that the rate will decline are likely to be stronger than they are when the rate is low. This principle is not necessarily valid in all cases. In some instances a decline in rates may lead investors to believe that further declines are likely. It is widely believed, however, that the principle is a significant determinant of the nature of the demand schedule. It is commonly argued that the portion of money held for speculative purposes is much more responsive to interest rate changes than that held for other motives.

Finally, when interest rates are low, the current selling prices of securities are relatively high; for example, if the interest rate level drops from 6 percent to 4 percent, bonds issued at 6 percent will sell well above par. Thus the total value of a given quantity of securities held will become greater. To the extent that wealth holders seek to maintain a balance between the current value of security holdings and the amount of their liquid balances, a relatively high figure for the former will encourage them to hold relatively larger sums of money than they would at higher interest rates.

Money Creation

Money capital may be forthcoming not only from accumulated liquid wealth but also from money creation: the issuance of additional cash by the government, or the creation of additional demand deposits via the banking system. If, for example, the central banking system purchases government securities in the open market, commercial bank reserves will rise, and the banking system can increase its loans by several times the amount of the increase in reserves, under the fractional reserve system.

The extent to which new money is being created in any period depends upon bank lending policy, upon central banking policy, and upon governmental action in creating new cash. Bank lending policy, in turn, is dependent upon the extent of excess reserves in the banking system, upon the demand for new loans, and upon the reserve ratios regarded by the bankers as adequate. The expectations of bankers about future business conditions also influence their lending policies.

Central banking policy is controlled by the general philosophy of use of the interest rate as a weapon of economic stability, and the current estimates of the needs for particular types of action. Governmental policy on direct creation of new money is dictated by political considerations which are beyond the scope of the present discussion; the policy will merely be considered as a "given" in any particular situation.

What significance will the level of the interest rate have upon the volume of new money being created? So far as banks are concerned, the higher the interest earned, the greater is the compensation for incurring the risks which arise from depletion of reserves. Beyond a certain limit, however, the supply of additional bank credit (in the absence of central-bank policy to increase bank reserves) is extremely inelastic, since banks cannot exceed their reserve limits and, in the United States, are reluctant to obtain additional reserves by borrowing from the Federal Reserve System.

The significance of the interest rate for the rate of expansion of bank deposits depends in large measure upon central-bank policy. If the central banking system wishes to hold the interest rate stable at a certain level, it will take measures to increase the supply of money, primarily through open-market operations, whenever the rate commences to rise, and to decrease it if the rate starts to fall. Commitment to a policy of a stable interest rate makes the total supply of money capital perfectly elastic at the interest rate which the central bank wishes to preserve. A policy of allowing flexible but reasonably stable rates will give some—but not perfect—elasticity to the supply.

DETERMINATION OF THE INTEREST RATE

It is now possible to consider the nature of the supply schedule of money capital—the quantities of money capital available for use at various rates of interest—and the demand schedule for money capital. Several incidental issues must be noted before the main thread of the argument is developed:

1. Treatment of money capital from internal sources. The total amount of money capital held internally by business firms from accumulated undistributed profits, earned depreciation charges, or other

sources, will be regarded as a part of the total supply of money capital, and the use of portions of this sum by the firms as a portion of the total demand.

2. Money capital available through the sale of stock, also regarded as a portion of the total money capital supply.

3. Amounts borrowed for consumption purposes, regarded as an element in total consumption of the economy, and thus a deduction from savings, rather than as an element in the demand for money capital.

4. Government borrowing, treated as a form of borrowing for production use even though a portion is obtained for essentially consumption purposes.

The Supply of Money Capital

The supply of money capital may be defined as the schedule of amounts of money available to business firms at various interest rate levels, in a given period of time. Initially we shall assume a given level of national income; this assumption will subsequently be modified. The supply schedule of money capital, therefore, is dependent upon the following primary determinants:

a) The propensity to save: the total volume of new savings made during the period, including undistributed profits of corporations, at various interest rate levels. As noted it is assumed that the schedule is perfectly inelastic.

b) The liquidity preference schedule: the total amount of money capital offered at various rate levels. It is assumed, for reasons noted above, that a significant positive functional relationship exists.

c) The schedule of the amounts of new money created by the government and the banking system at various interest rate levels, with a positive functional relationship.

Given the nature of these determinants, and the assumptions relating to the nature of the schedules, there will be a positive functional relationship between the interest rate and the supply of money capital:

1. Higher interest rates will provide greater inducement to forgo liquidity preference.

2. The higher the interest rate, the less the amount which will be held in liquid balances for speculative purposes.

3. The higher the interest rate, the more willing will be the banks to create additional money, and, assuming full employment and the acceptance of the goal of stability by the central banking system, the

more money creation which will be made possible by central-bank action.

In addition, if higher interest rates do increase the preference to save, so that the assumption of a perfectly inelastic savings schedule is involved, additional money capital will be available at higher interest rates from this source as well.

Two possible types of supply schedules are illustrated in Figures 15–1 and 15–2. Figure 15–1 is based on the assumption that the

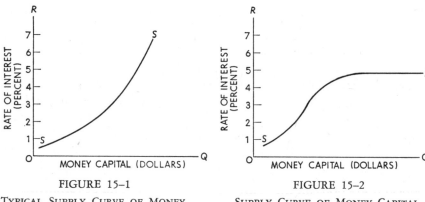

FIGURE 15–1

TYPICAL SUPPLY CURVE OF MONEY
CAPITAL

FIGURE 15–2

SUPPLY CURVE OF MONEY CAPITAL,
MAXIMUM RATE OF 5 PERCENT
PERMITTED BY CENTRAL BANK

central banking system will permit the interest rate level to rise; Figure 15–2 is based upon the assumption that the rate will not be permitted to exceed a certain figure.

The Demand for Money Capital

The demand for money capital consists of the total amounts of money capital which will be invested during the period by business firms (and governmental units), at various interest rate levels. The demand for money for consumption use is excluded from the picture, for purposes of simplicity, and regarded as a reduction in potential supply. The determinants of the demand by business firms have been indicated in the preceding chapter. Some of the money will be required for additional working capital—for payment of current costs in advance of sales, as total output rises. But most money capital will be required for investment in capital goods. At each interest rate level, the quantity demanded will be the amount which will allow the firm to obtain the optimum level of investment, as defined in the previous chapter. The schedule undoubtedly has some interest elasticity, particularly for the longer-range investments, for which the discounting feature assumes particular significance. Nevertheless, it is widely believed that the interest elasticity is not great, that a large portion of investment made in any period is so profitable that it will be undertaken despite substantial increases in the interest rate, whereas most of the potential additional investment is of such low profitability that it would not be undertaken even if the interest rate were substantially lower. The nature of the elasticity of investment is an empirical question, which cannot be answered by deductive analysis.

As noted, it is assumed initially that the level of national income is given, thus eliminating any induced investment—that arising out of increases in national income. This assumption will be altered later in the chapter.

Government borrowing, which has become an important segment of the total, appears to have limited interest elasticity. State and local borrowing is undertaken in part for commercial enterprises, and is thus subject to the same considerations as business borrowing. Even that undertaken for noncommercial projects, such as schools, is affected to some extent by the interest rate, in view of the legal, economic, and political restrictions on the ability of the states and local governments to raise tax revenue to pay interest. Federal borrowing would appear to have little or no interest elasticity.

The Equilibrium Interest Rate Level

Under the assumption of pure competition in the markets for money capital, the interest rate must come to the level at which the total demand for money capital is equal to the total supply available. Figure 15–3 indicates the determination of the basic equilibrium rate, i. This equilibrium rate of interest will be maintained so long as the determinants remain unchanged. If the interest rate is higher than i, the total supply of money capital will exceed the demand, and suppliers will lower the rate; if the actual interest rate is lower than i, the demand will exceed the supply, and the rate will be bid up by borrowers.

This analysis is based upon the assumption of pure competition in the money capital markets; exceptions to this assumption will be noted later in the chapter.

Additional Requirements for Interest Rate Stability

For the interest rate level thus determined to be a stable equilibrium figure, two additional requirements must be met:

    1. Changes which are occurring in the total supply of money (not

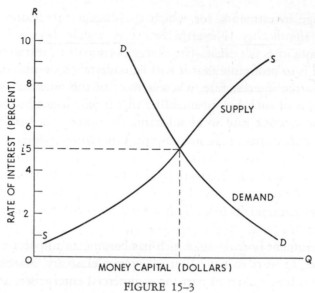

FIGURE 15–3

THE EQUILIBRIUM RATE OF INTEREST

money capital, but money as such) in the economy must equal the change which is occurring in the demand for money to hold (not the demand for money capital) for the various liquidity motives, or, in other words, the total demand for liquid balances must equal the amount of money existing in the economy.

2. The level of national income must be consistent with the interest rate.

The Demand for Liquidity Balances. There exists, in any period of time, a certain quantity of money—cash and demand deposits—in the economy. Each dollar of this money must be held by someone. The amounts persons wish to keep in cash balances depend in part upon the interest rate, as noted; given the other determinants of liquidity, the lower the interest rate the greater is the sum which persons wish to hold. Suppose that the current interest rate level is such that persons wish to hold less money than there is in the economy. They will offer a portion to borrowers, and the supply of money capital will be larger than it would otherwise be by this amount. Thus the interest rate will be somewhat lower. But persons will not continue to reduce their liquid balances; eventually this element in the supply of money capital will come to an end as persons attain the desired level of liquid balances. When this occurs, the supply of money capital will fall, and interest rates will rise. Eventually an equilibrium will be reached at which the supply and demand for money capital are equal, and there is no net attempt being made to increase or reduce liquid balances.

Another way of stating this requirement is in terms of the relationship between the net increase in money in the economy and the additional amounts which individuals and firms are desirous of adding to their cash balances. On the one hand, all new money which enters the economy must enter the cash balances of some persons or firms; on the other hand, they cannot hold additional sums unless a greater amount of money is available. Unless the additions to money supply are equal to the sums which persons wish to add to their balances, the supply of money capital will not remain constant. If, for example, persons are attempting to add greater amounts to their balances than the amount of inflow of new money, there will be a temporary excess of demand for money capital over supply, which will come to an end once the interest rate has moved up to the point at which persons will no longer be attempting to do the impossible—hold more money than there is. It is important to keep in mind that the desire of persons to hold greater amounts of their wealth in monetary form does not increase the total amount of money available for such purposes. Attempts to hold greater amounts than are available lessen the supply of money capital, and drive up the interest rate to the figure at which persons will cease trying to hold excessive amounts.

The Level of National Income. The preceding analysis has been based upon the assumption of a given level of national income. Thus induced investment as a source of additional demand for money capital was not considered, nor the significance of the level of national income for the total volume of savings and the total demand for money for liquidity purposes. Thus the picture was incomplete. The introduction of national income changes greatly complicates the analysis, and leads us into the realm of macroeconomic analysis, which is beyond the scope of this book. But brief summary reference to the question must be made.

The problem is complicated because of the interrelationship of the interest rate, the level of national income, and the volumes of savings and investment. On the one hand, changes in the interest rate will alter the level of national income; the assumption of a given level of national income with varying rates of interest is unrealistic. On the one hand, changes in the interest rate, to the extent to which they affect the level of investment, will alter aggregate demand, and thus the overall level of employment and national income. On the other hand, changes in national income will also affect the volume of savings and the demand for money for liquidity purposes; the higher the level of national income, the greater will be the need for money for transactions purposes, for example. Stability of the economy requires equality of planned savings and planned investment; and the second, and perhaps the first, are influenced by the level of the interest rate.

Thus the rate of interest and national income must adjust to levels which are mutually consistent with one another; a temporary equilibrium figure for one is not stable unless it is consistent with a stable equilibrium figure for the other. The demand schedule for money capital must take into consideration investment generated by a change in income and the effects of a higher income level on the demand for money capital; the supply schedule must recognize differences in levels of saving at various levels of national income.

Let us consider an example of the mutual adjustment of interest and national income. Suppose, for example, that the basic interest rate is currently, with national income of $400 billion, 5 percent. With this interest figure, given the other determinants of national income, let us assume that national income adjusts to the $450 billion level. But at this level the demand for money capital may be such, relative to supply, that the interest rate rises to 6 percent. This rate may be incompatible with the maintenance of national income at $450 billion, because investment is curtailed. Thus, national income and the interest rate must adjust until they reach levels which are consistent with each other. When these levels are reached, the interest rate will not interfere with stability of national income, and the latter will be consistent with the interest rate.

This interrelationship can be demonstrated graphically by a method based upon the work of J. R. Hicks. In Figure 15–4, national income is measured on the horizontal axis, and the interest rate on the vertical axis. The *LL* curve shows the interest rate which will prevail at each level of national income, given the determinants of the rate, that is, the various factors influencing the supply of and demand for money at the various income levels. The curve slopes upward from left to right beyond a certain point, unless central-bank credit policies insure a perfectly elastic supply of money capital, because the higher levels of national income will require larger amounts of money for transactions purposes. The left-hand portion is believed to be more or less horizontal, because once the interest rate falls below a certain level, any additional amount of money freed through the reduced volume of transactions will merely enter idle balances rather than the active supply of money capital.

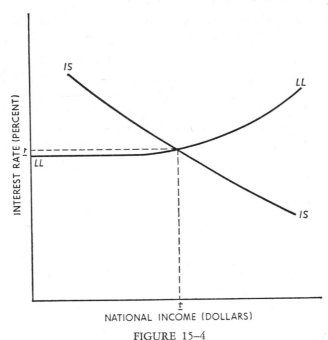

FIGURE 15–4

<small>SIMULTANEOUS ADJUSTMENT OF THE INTEREST RATE AND NATIONAL INCOME</small>

The *IS* curve, on the other hand, indicates, for each level of national income, the interest rate figure which is consistent with the stability of the particular level of national income, that is, the rate which will allow equality of planned savings and planned investment. If, as national income rises, planned investment tends to lag behind planned savings at a given interest rate, the curve will slope downward from left to right, a lower rate being necessary at the higher levels of national income to raise investment up to the planned savings level. The actual location of the curve depends upon the consumption function and the behavior of MRP of capital goods as investment increases. If investment is relatively unresponsive to interest rate changes, as is often assumed, the *IS* curve will be very steep and may cut below the horizontal axis at a fairly low level of national income.

The point at which the *LL* and *IS* curves cross is the point at which the interest rate and the level of national income are mutually consistent with each other. In Figure 15–4 the equilibrium interest rate figure is *r*, and the equilibrium level of national income is *t*. At any higher level of national income, with the determinants as given, the interest rate would be raised by the need for additional funds for transactions purposes to a figure too high to permit equality of planned investment with planned savings. At any lower level of national income, the interest rate would be too low; the stimulation to investment would raise the level of national income.[3]

This analysis is significant only if (1) the rate of interest is free to move, rather than being maintained at a certain level by central-bank action, and (2) the interest rate does exercise some influence on the volume of investment. If the interest rate is maintained at a given level, LL will be a horizontal line (as is illustrated in Figure 15–5) and the

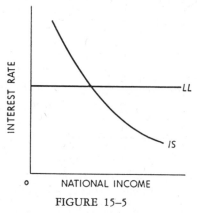

FIGURE 15–5

PERFECTLY ELASTIC SUPPLY OF
MONEY CAPITAL

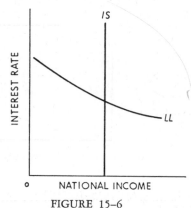

FIGURE 15–6

INVESTMENT INDEPENDENT OF THE
INTEREST RATE

actual rate is thus independent of the level of national income. If investment (and savings) is not affected by the rate of interest, IS is a vertical line, and the actual level of national income is not affected by the height of the interest rate (as shown in Figure 15–6).

The analysis does not introduce the possibility of variations in the general price level. To do so adds further complications to the analysis and thus is reserved for more advanced studies.[4]

Equilibrium Relationships of the Interest Rate

In equilibrium, the interest rate will equal:

1. The net rate of return on capital goods, since each producer will adjust the volume of his investment to the point of equality of these two magnitudes.

2. The marginal rate of liquidity preference for each individual

[3] See J. R. Hicks, "Mr. Keynes and the Classics: A Suggested Interpretation," *Econometrica*, Vol. 5 (April, 1937), pp. 147–59, reprinted in W. Fellner and B. F. Haley (eds.), *Readings in the Theory of Income Distribution* (Philadelphia: Blakiston, 1946).

[4] See D. Patinkin, *Money, Interest and Prices* (2d ed., New York: Harper and Row, 1965).

and business firm; that is, for each, the rate of interest will just balance the gains from keeping the marginal dollars of personal wealth in liquid form.

3. The marginal rate of time preference of those persons, if any, whose allocations of income between consumption and savings are influenced by the interest rate. These persons will adjust their level of savings to the point at which the marginal gain from the use of an additional dollar for present instead of future consumption is just equal to the interest rate obtainable. This adjustment probably has little significance for the adjustment of the overall level of savings, for reasons indicated earlier in the chapter.

In practice, deviations from pure and perfect competition will interfere somewhat with the attainment of these relationships; these include absence of pure competition in the money capital or capital goods markets and the difficulties of ascertaining MRP. Capital rationing will have the same effect.

The Structure of Interest Rates

The analysis up to this point has assumed purely competitive conditions in the market for money capital and has been concerned only with the basic interest rate level, ignoring variations in rates among various parts of the market. While a detailed examination of these questions is beyond the scope of this book, a few observations can be made.

The basic interest rate, which may be called the pure interest rate, is that on loans of minimum risk and maximum liquidity, or, in the terminology of some writers, on a purely riskless investment. But various types of loans will have varying degrees of risk and liquidity; real estate mortgages, for example, are much less liquid than General Motors stock or government bonds. Variations in rates reflect the consensus of investors about relative risk and relative liquidity.

The various parts of the money capital market vary widely in the extent of departure from pure competition, and also in the degree of market imperfection. The various segments will be noted briefly.

Long-Term Corporate and Government Bonds. The bond market is one approximating pure competition, and with a high degree of perfection. Thus the interest rate in this market can be analyzed in terms of supply and demand forces. It should be noted that the current interest rate, the rate which must be paid for new borrowing in this market, is indicated by the yield on existing bonds. For example, a 6 percent bond issued in perpetuity and selling for $200 would be yielding 3 percent, the figure which the company would need to pay on new bonds which it issued of comparable risk and liquidity. When bonds are issued for limited periods, as they are in the United States, in calculation of yield (called yield to maturity) consideration must be given to the capital gain or loss which will be incurred between the present time and the maturity of the bonds, but the principle is the same.

Market adjustments of the bond interest rate can be analyzed most satisfactorily in terms of the total demand for bonds, old and new, and the total supply offered for sale at various price levels. The general level of bond prices must adjust to the figure at which the quantity available for sale is just equal to the quantity which persons wish to purchase. If bond prices are higher than this level, and thus the interest rate is lower than the equilibrium figure, the quantity offered on the market will exceed the quantity demanded. If the bond prices are temporarily below the equilibrium level, the quantity of bonds people wish to buy will exceed the quantity offered for sale, and bond prices will rise, with a consequent decline in interest rates.

Stock Financing. The cost of stock financing is likewise indicated by the current yield on the stock, which indicates the rate at which the firm will share earnings with the holders of any new stock which it issues. The yield, given the current rate of dividends, is determined by the selling price of the stock, which in turn depends upon the supply of and the demand for the existing stock of the company. When the total quantity demanded and quantity supplied are equal, the quantity of new money capital used to buy stock will equal the total of new stock being issued during the period. Since bond and stock purchases represent alternative uses of money capital on the part of lenders and alternative sources on the part of business firms, the relative rates of return will adjust in terms of relative advantages. However, since the rates of dividend payments on stock are not fixed, stock prices will fluctuate in response to actual and expected changes in the rate of dividends, and the flow of money capital into this field will be greatly influenced by expectations of changes in stock prices. Thus a constant ratio between stock and bond yields will not be maintained.

Funds from Internal Sources. The most important segment of the money capital market for business expansion is in a sense no market at all; it consists of the utilization for the acquisition of capital goods of funds obtained by the firm in its internal operations, particularly from earned depreciation charges and retained earnings. In this "market," supply and demand are merely opposite sides of the same coin, and no contractual interest rate is determined. However, the firm has the alternatives of placing the internal funds in the bond or stock market by buying securities in other companies, holding them in liquid form, or using them for expansion. Given the returns from the purchase of bonds or stock and the advantages of holding the funds in liquid form, the firm will seek to obtain a balance between these returns and the gain from using the funds to finance expansion of the enterprise. Thus, investment of the funds in new capital equipment for the firm will be extended to the point at which MRP of the capital goods is just equal to the interest returns obtainable from lending the money to others and the marginal gains from funds held in liquid form, with differences in risk taken into consideration.

Short-Term Commercial Loans. Short-term loans to business firms are made primarily by commercial banks, although in New York some market transactions in commercial paper occur. Because of the domination of this type of lending by a relatively few large banks, they are able to set rates in a market of differentiated oligopoly. In setting rates, the banks are influenced primarily by the state of their reserves, which, in turn, depend upon the rate of expansion of loans in the preceding period and upon central-bank policy. When reserves are relatively low, banks will raise their rates and curtail the volume of loans which they are making.[5] Short-term loans to governments are made in more highly competitive markets, and rates are less subject to bank domination.

Because of the significance of bank reserves for short-term rates, these rates are particularly subject to control by the central banking system.

Long-Term Mortgage Loans. Smaller business firms, including farmers, are not able to raise money by the sale of securities. As a consequence long-term funds normally must be obtained on a real estate mortgage basis. Likewise, large sums are borrowed annually on a mortgage basis by individuals for the purchase or building of homes. Mortgage loans are made primarily by banks and by insurance and building and loan companies, in a market which is by no means purely competitive. In general, the policies followed by these institutions are similar to those of the commercial banks in setting short-term rates. However, the rates are less mobile, often being unchanged for long periods. When bank reserves run low, banks simply refuse to make

[5] To a large extent, banks adjust the volume of loans to the amount which they can safely lend by refusing to grant loans when their reserves are depleted rather than by interest rate adjustments. The latter are made, however, to a limited degree.

further loans rather than raise interest rates significantly. The rates for home purchases and farm improvements are greatly influenced by direct governmental action through the setting of maximum figures eligible for FHA and veterans' loan guaranty and through the farm lending program.

Interrelationships among Interest Rates in Various Segments of the Money Capital Market

Interest rates in particular segments of the overall market for loanable funds are directly dependent upon the nature of the supply and demand conditions in the various parts of the market, and competitive conditions. But the general pattern of rates which develops must equate the overall supply of and demand for money capital (apart from possible modifications from this rule caused by deviations from pure competition), and the rates in the various segments must be mutually consistent with one another. Each market segment receives a certain portion of the total supply of money capital at various interest rates, and a certain portion of the total demand. The relative supply, compared to the total, depends upon the preferences of the owners of liquid wealth for the different forms of outlets for their money, and relative rates of return. Relative risk is a major factor shaping preferences. An increase in the rate of interest on bonds, for example, will encourage persons to purchase more bonds and less stock. Increased fear about future economic conditions, on the other hand, will shift buyers from stock to bonds.

The relative demands for money capital in the various segments of the market depend upon the nature of the sources of funds, the personal preferences of borrowers, and relative rates. For example, low bond rates will encourage the use of this method of finance instead of the sale of stock, while inability to sell bonds at reasonable rates will cause firms to turn to real estate mortgage markets. The strong preference on the part of many firms for the use of internal funds may cause them to limit their demand for money capital to the sums they have available from this source, and not seek outside funds. For firms which are willing to sell additional bonds or stock, the amount of internal funds which they have, relative to the volume of profitable investment, will influence the extent to which they will turn to outside sources.

The general pattern of rates will adjust to the structure which will allow equilibrium of supply and demand in each of the segments of the market. The rate differences will be such that there will be no net shifting of lenders or borrowers from one market to the other; and they will reflect the relative advantages, from the standpoint of both lenders and borrowers, of the various channels. Some deviation from this pattern results from the absence of purely competitive conditions in some instances and the inability of certain borrowers to shift from one market to another. Hence, interest rates on personal loans are relatively high, not only because of the relatively great risk, but also because many of the borrowers have no other source of funds, and the field is dominated by a relatively few firms.

Changes in the General Level of Interest Rates

The basic overall interest rate level will change in response to variations in supply of and demand for money capital. Some of the major causes of shifts in these determinants can be noted briefly.

1. *A Change in the Willingness to Part with Cash Balances.* If persons seek to hold a smaller portion of their wealth in liquid form (but maintain the same consumption-savings ratio), the supply of money capital will increase, and the interest rate will tend to fall. This fall will, of course, reduce the willingness to part with liquid balances and restore the equilibrium at a somewhat lower rate level.

2. *A Change in the Supply of Money.* Change in policy relating to creation of new money, either directly by government or central banking action or through expansion of bank loans and deposits, will alter the funds available for loans and affect the interest rate. If the central banking system wishes to lower the interest rate, it will purchase securities in the open market, thus raising security prices and lowering the rate of interest. In addition, the policy increases the reserves of the member banks and places them in a position to make additional loans. If they do so, the supply of money capital is increased, and the rate of interest falls still further.

However, this policy can succeed only if individuals and banks are willing to loan on the basis of the additional money which they receive. If all of the additional money is absorbed in cash balances, there will be no net increase in money capital, and the rate will not fall. Apparently there are certain levels below which the interest rate cannot be driven, because of the tendency, at very low rates, for persons to absorb in liquid balances any additional money made available.

3. *Changes in the Volume of Investment.* A change in MRP of capital will alter the volume of investment and thus the demand for money capital. This increase in demand will in itself tend to raise the rate of interest, unless the supply of money capital is perfectly elastic because of central-bank policies. However, the increase in investment

will raise the level of national income (at least in monetary terms, if not in real terms), and the actual volume of savings and supply of money capital will rise. When equilibrium of national income and the interest rate is again established, the rate of planned savings and the rate of investment will again be equal, since such equality is required for stability of national income. Any difference between the old and the new interest rates cannot be attributed directly to a change in the relationship between investment and savings, but to the effects of the rise in national income upon the amount of money in the economy and the amount required for liquidity purposes. Unless the supply of money is perfectly elastic, the higher level of national income will necessitate a somewhat higher interest rate because of the larger sums required for transactions purposes.

4. *A Change in the Propensity to Save.* An increased desire to save, not accompanied by an equivalent and simultaneous increase in investment, will tend to reduce the interest rate by depressing the level of national income and lowering the amount of money needed for transactions purposes. It might appear that the increased desire to save would have a direct and immediate effect on the interest rate by increasing the supply of money capital relative to the demand for it. But this will not occur; the increase in planned savings will not manifest itself in an increase in the actual supply of money capital unless the volume of national income is maintained. This cannot occur unless investment rises simultaneously with savings—in which event there is no surplus of money capital at the old interest rate level! The only source of the relative increase in the supply of loanable funds is the freeing of money from liquid balances as national income falls.

Functions of the Interest Rate

The major functions which interest performs in the operation of the economy may be summarized briefly. In the first place, and of greatest importance, the interest rate insures that the flow of current savings is made available for investment in capital goods, instead of seeking to go into liquid balances. In other words the interest rate insures equilibrium of the supply of money capital with the demand for it, by inducing persons to make available their liquid wealth for business expansion and other purposes instead of retaining it in liquid form.

In the second place, the interest rate rations the total available amount of money capital among various possible uses, to those which offer the greatest prospect of return. This rationing device does not always function perfectly, of course, primarily because some firms will undertake expansions with internally acquired capital which would not meet the tests of the market rate.

Thirdly, the rate establishes equilibrium between the amount of money (not money capital, but money in existence) in the economy and the amounts which persons wish to hold in cash balances.

Fourthly, in full-employment periods, the interest rate is one factor which assists in restricting the total volume of investment to the volume of planned savings and thereby aids in checking inflation. This function was once regarded as the chief task of the interest rate. But the volume of investment does not appear to be highly responsive to changes in interest rates, especially because of the importance of internal funds for financing of expansion, and the volume of savings is clearly unresponsive to the rate. The rate is still regarded, however, as a useful tool for dampening mild inflationary pressures.

In periods of unemployment the effect of the interest rate in limiting the volume of investment is detrimental to the recovery of the economy. However, this effect is easily exaggerated, since the volume of investment appears to be extremely unresponsive to interest reductions in such periods.

SELECTED REFERENCES

CONARD, J. W.   *Introduction to the Theory of Interest.*   Berkeley: University of California Press, 1959.
    A thorough review of the development of interest theory, and various alternative modern approaches.

CULBERTSON, J. M.   "The Term Structure of Interest Rates," *Quarterly Journal of Economics,* Vol. 71 (November, 1957), pp. 485–517.

HANSEN, A. H.   *A Guide to Keynes,* chaps. vi, vii.   New York: McGraw-Hill, 1953.
    A restatement of Keynesian and loanable funds theories.

HICKS, J. R.   "Mr. Keynes and the Classics: A Suggested Interpretation," *Econometrica,* Vol. 5 (April, 1937), pp. 147–59.   Reprinted in *Readings in the Theory of Income Distribution* (eds. W. FELLNER AND B. F. HALEY). Philadelphia: Blakiston, 1949.
    The best earlier presentation of the interrelation of interest, investment, and the level of national income.

JOHNSON, H. G. "Monetary Theory and Policy," *American Economic Review,* Vol. 52 (June, 1962), pp. 335–84.
    A review of the theory of interest and other aspects of monetary theory over recent years.

PATINKIN, D.   *Money, Interest and Prices.*   2d ed.   New York: Harper and Row, 1965.
    A significant contribution to the theory, at a relatively high level of analysis.

SHACKLE, G. L. S. "Recent Theories Concerning the Nature and Role of Interest," *Economic Journal,* Vol. 71 (June, 1961), pp. 209–54.
A review.

QUESTIONS

1. Why is the payment of interest necessary?
2. Why is the payment of interest more satisfactorily regarded as a payment for overcoming liquidity than as a payment for saving?
3. What is meant by liquidity preference? Time preference?
4. Why, for most persons, is time preference negative for a portion of their incomes?
5. What considerations influence a family's decisions regarding the allocation of income between consumption and saving?
6. Why is it believed today that the rate of interest has little significance for decisions to save or consume?
7. Distinguish between *ex post* and *ex ante* savings. When will the magnitudes be different?
8. Explain the nature of the transactions motive for savings. Explain the relationship between changes in national income, in both real and monetary terms, and the amounts held to satisfy the transactions motive.
9. What significance does the existence of savings accounts in the United States have upon the demand for money for convenience and precautionary purposes? Why?
10. Why are savings accounts regarded as a portion of the money supply in Canada but not in the United States?
11. Under what circumstances will persons hold wealth in liquid form for speculative reasons?
12. Why will persons tend to hold more money when interest rates are low than when they are high? Answer in terms of the various motives for liquidity.
13. What additional sources are there of money capital in addition to savings?
14. When will the supply of money in the economy be perfectly elastic? Illustrate on a graph.
15. Summarize the primary determinants of the supply of and demand for money capital, and the nature of the supply and demand schedules.
16. Explain the determination of the equilibrium rate of interest, assuming a given level of national income. Illustrate on a graph.
17. Suppose that persons seek to hold more money than there is in the economy. What will happen?
18. Explain the interrelationship between the equilibrium rate of interest and the equilibrium level of national income.
19. Explain the meaning of the *LL* and *IS* curves on Figure 15–4.

20. Why does the *IS* curve slope downward from left to right? Under what circumstances would it be a vertical line?

21. Why is the *LL* curve horizontal in its left portion, and then upward sloping? Under what circumstances would it be horizontal throughout?

22. Suppose that the *LL* curve is a horizontal line. What significance does the level of national income have for the interest rate?

23. To what magnitudes is the equilibrium interest rate equal?

24. Suppose that bonds of a company, issued in perpetuity, are paying 4 percent interest and selling at $150. What interest rate will the company have to pay on new bond issues of comparable maturity and risk?

25. In which parts of the money market are nonpurely competitive influences significant?

26. What are the primary forces influencing the relative interest rates on different types of loans?

27. Explain the effects of each of the following upon the interest rate level, and the process of adjustment:
    a) An increase in the overall propensity to save.
    b) An increase in the profitability of investment.
    c) An increase in the total money supply.
    d) Increased fear of the coming of a severe depression.
    e) Federal Reserve open-market buying.

28. What functions does the interest rate perform in the economy?

Chapter 16

RENTS AND QUASI RENTS

Attainment of the optimum factor combinations requires, in most instances, the use not only of labor and capital goods, but also of natural resources—goods provided directly by nature. Natural resources, or land, to use the more common although less descriptive term, differ from capital goods in that their existence is not dependent on human effort. Accordingly, the supply cannot be increased by deliberate action, although the usefulness of land for production purposes can be increased by various improvements—clearing, draining, introduction of irrigation facilities, etc.—which require labor, and constitute capital goods. Since, however, land available for use is limited relative to demand, a price must be paid for its use, a price which constitutes an income to the owners in a society in which natural resources are privately owned. This return, which is not a compensation necessary to overcome any real costs, is known as *land rent* or, more commonly, *rent*.

In the last century the theory of rent played a major role in economic analysis, and was the source of bitter controversies. In recent decades, however, there has been a tendency to relegate rent theory to a position of minor importance. The similarities between capital goods and natural resources have been stressed, as well as the difficulties of distinguishing clearly, in practice, between the two. By many modern writers, rent in the traditional sense is not regarded as a distinct functional return, the return from investments in land being treated simply as a form of return on money capital. At the same time, the concept of rent has frequently been extended to cover any return attributable to specific factor units which is not necessary to make the factor units available, either to the industry or to the economy as a whole. This concept will be considered at the end of the chapter.

This tendency to regard the return on land as merely a type of return on invested money capital obscures certain basic differences between the determination of the price paid for the use of land (which is provided by nature) and that paid for the use of capital goods (which are produced), and thus the cost elements arising from the two types of factors. While, in practice, land and capital cannot be clearly distinguished from one another, and, as noted below, in the short-run period capital goods take on certain of the characteristics of land, nevertheless separate attention to the determination of land rent is desirable. Whether this return is designated as a separate type of functional return or merely as a form of return on invested money capital is largely a matter of terminology.

Marginal Productivity Analysis Applied to Land

The basic marginal productivity analysis presented in Chapter 13 can be applied to land as well as to other factors. The demand for land of a particular type is dependent upon the MRP schedule of this type of land to various users of it; MRP falls beyond a certain point, as additional units are added. For most business firms the quantity of land in use is not easily adjustable in the short-run period; hence the demand may be relatively inelastic.

The nature of the supply schedule of land is conditioned by the basic characteristics of this factor; since land is fixed in quantity and cannot be increased by human activity, the potential supply to the economy is perfectly inelastic even over a long-run period. Relatively high prices paid for the use of land will of course stimulate the making of improvements for irrigation, drainage, etc., which will increase the output on given land; but these improvements are capital goods, and the higher output is attributable to them. Not only is the potential supply of land perfectly inelastic, but so will be the actual supply offered to users at positive prices, so long as the market is purely competitive. Since the owner of land gains nothing by holding it idle, it is better for him to get the going market return for it, regardless of how low this figure is, than to get nothing at all. In contrast, the holders of money capital gain the advantages of liquidity by holding their capital idle, and workers avoid the disutility of labor by not working. But there is no gain from holding land idle.[1]

Under the assumption of purely competitive markets for the use of land, the rent figure for any particular type of land would adjust to the level at which the demand for and the supply of this type of land were equal. At this level, rent would equal the MRP of the land. Because of

---

[1] There are rare exceptions, for short periods; some types of land will increase in productiveness if kept out of use for a few years.

the perfectly inelastic supply, changes in demand would produce sharp changes in rent; a substantial increase in population, for example, not offset by technological improvements in agricultural production, would result in significant increases in land rent, and thus in the share of national income going to the landowning class. It was this tendency in nineteenth-century England which led to such great interest in the theory of rent, as reflected in the writings of Adam Smith, Ricardo, and Malthus.

In the absence of imperfections in the land market, the adjustment on a supply-demand basis would be rapid. Actually, the land market is highly imperfect. A particular market is limited in area, with a relatively small number of tenants and lessors. Knowledge of market conditions may be very limited, and the bargaining position of the various parties may be unequal. The small number of buyers and sellers prevents the markets from being purely competitive in many cases; monopolistic restriction of supply may develop, or monopsonistic influences on price. The rent may be set by direct bargaining, with results difficult to predict by general analysis. If monopoly or semimonopoly elements develop, not all the available land may come into use; it may be advantageous for landowners to withhold a portion of land in order to mazimize revenue received. The fact that much land may be bought outright by owners, rather than rented, further segments the market and lessens its perfectness. When land is owned by users, rent payments cease to be contractual in nature and take an implicit form.

The basic difference between the determination of the cost of land use and the cost of the use of capital equipment from a long-run standpoint is that the former depends solely upon the potential yield of the land in alternative employments, since no cost of production is involved, whereas the cost of using capital equipment is dependent upon the cost of producing the equipment, plus the interest cost element. The supply of land is perfectly inelastic, while that of capital equipment depends upon the relationship between the yield from the equipment and the cost of production of the equipment, and is thus highly elastic over a period of time. The entire sum paid for the use of land constitutes an income to the recipients, while the amounts paid for the use of capital equipment serve, from a long-run standpoint, to cover the costs of the production of the equipment; only the interest constitutes income.

The Selling Price of Land

Land, like capital equipment, may be purchased outright by the business enterprises using it. The selling price is dependent upon the supply of and demand for the land at a particular time (assuming purely competitive conditions in this market). The price which the buyer is willing to pay for a particular piece of land and the price at which the present owner is willing to sell are determined by the current and prospective rent (explicit or implicit) which may be gained from the land. Specifically, the selling price will tend to equal the capitalized sum of the expected rental return, the return being capitalized at the interest rate obtainable on other investments of comparable risk. Suppose, for example, that the current interest rate on such loans is 5 percent. A parcel of land yielding, and expected to yield indefinitely, $600 a year in rent will sell for $12,000 if the market is perfect. If the buyer paid more for the land, he would be getting a return on his investment less than he could get from other investments. If, for example, he paid $20,000, he would be getting an annual return on his investment of only 3 percent; whereas if he had purchased bonds, he would have earned 5 percent. On the other hand, the present owner would not sell for less than $12,000, or he would be getting less return after making the sale than he is at present.

The markets for the sale of land, like those for its rental are highly imperfect because of the lack of an extensive market organization (comparable to the stock market, for example) and the relatively small numbers of buyers and sellers, each of whom may sell or buy land only at extremely infrequent intervals. Monopoly or monopsony conditions may be rare but the actual price may be determined in many cases by direct bargaining because the numbers of buyers and sellers are small. Neither party can be certain about the future yield, and estimates of this figure will differ. Furthermore, in some cases the relative bargaining positions of the buyer and the seller will be different. For example, the seller may be desperately in need of cash and be forced to let the land go for a very low figure. But, except in unusual cases, the buyer would not pay more than the sum representing the capitalization of his estimate of yield; the seller would not part with the land for a figure much less than the capitalized sum of his own estimate of yield.

Care must be taken not to apply the rule as given above to real estate containing both land and buildings, since the buildings are subject to depreciation. The selling price of existing buildings and other durable capital goods is affected by the yield, but the capitalization must be based upon the limited period of expected remaining useful life, not upon permanent life as in the case of land. Furthermore, reproduction cost is significant; in general, capital goods cannot sell for amounts in excess of the cost of building new ones, provided that the construction of new units is possible even though on a yield basis the value figure might exceed this amount.

The Differential Theory of Land Rent

The supply-demand analysis of land-rent determination, coördinate with the explanation of other factor prices, is not questioned on a logical basis. But for a long period an alternative approach, under which rent was explained in terms of differential returns on various grades of land, was regarded as a more satisfactory explanation of rent determination. This approach arose in part because of the wide variation in quality (and thus productivity) of different types of land, and in part from the fixed nature of the supply and the tendency, in many instances, for the producer—particularly the farmer—to regard his acreage as a permanent fixed factor, to which he adjusts quantities of other factors employed. This is not an unrealistic assumption from the standpoint of the firm in many countries in which, for reasons of law or custom, additional land cannot be purchased. From the standpoint of the entire economy, it is a realistic assumption in any country. This differential return approach to the theory of rent is often called the Ricardian rent theory, for the early nineteenth-century economist, David Ricardo, who popularized it.[2]

Land Rent with Land of Uniform Quality. The differential approach can be explained most simply by assuming initially that a new area of land, a previously unknown island, is discovered and settled. In this area, all land is equally fertile and equally well located. Further assumptions are made that only one commodity is produced and is sold in a purely competitive market. When the area is first settled and all the land is not yet in use, the price of the product will be equal to average capital and labor cost, with the firms operating at the point of lowest average cost. If the demand for the product increases so that the market price of the product rises temporarily above average cost, additional land will be brought into use as new firms enter production. Since the average cost for the new firms will be the same as that of the old, the supply will continue to increase until the price falls back to the original level. There is no competition among producers for land, since all are making optimum use of labor and capital on their existing land. If any one producer were not doing so, he could reach the level of lowest cost by taking up additional land. If a firm increases the amount of land being used beyond the amount which allows lowest average cost, the higher average cost will cause losses. As long as land is not scarce—as

---

[2] See David Ricardo. *Principles of Political Economy* (1817).

long as producers seek no more land than the amount which they can ✕
obtain by taking up idle land—there can be no rent. Price will equal
average and marginal capital and labor cost.

Eventually, however, if population increases sufficiently, the demand for the product will become so great that all land will be brought
into use. Further increases in demand for the product beyond this point
will raise the market price, and each firm will increase its output until
marginal cost is equal to the new price. This expansion will lower

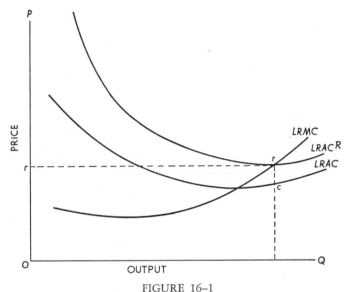

FIGURE 16–1

LAND RENT DETERMINATION, LAND OF UNIFORM QUALITY

market price somewhat. But so long as the demand is great enough that,
at the price equaling lowest average cost, the quantity demanded
exceeds the total amount that can be supplied at that price, the price
must remain above this figure (at *Or* in Figure 16–1). Thus a
differential arises between price and average capital-and-labor cost
(represented by the distance *cr* in Figure 16–1), which cannot be
eliminated by the entry of new firms, since all available land is now in
use. This differential between price and average cost arises because of
the scarcity of land, once the demand for the product becomes so great ✕
that the output cannot be produced on the available supply of land at
the lowest figure of average cost. In order to meet the high level of
demand, output must be produced at a figure of marginal cost (*Or* in
Figure 16–1) in excess of average cost. Price must be high enough to
cover this greater marginal cost figure, and thus exceeds average cost

(exclusive of rent). The amount of the differential between price (which equals marginal cost) and average cost (exclusive of rent) is the land rent per unit of output. On a given acreage of land, the total land rent will be the amount of rent per unit of output multiplied by the annual acreage yield on the acreage. With rent included in cost, the firm's long-run average cost curve in Figure 16–1 is $LRAC^R$.

Differences in Fertility and Location

The assumption made in the preceding section that all land is equally fertile and equally well located is of course an unrealistic one. Units of land in any area differ greatly in these respects.

The fertility differences of farm land are due largely to variations in the nature of the soil. With a given application of labor and capital, some types of soil will yield more output than others because of physical differences in content. Productivity is influenced also by temperature, rainfall, and other climatic factors, as well as by drainage and ease of cultivation. Productivity differences manifest themselves in differences in average cost figures (exclusive of rent) for the firms on various grades of land. On very fertile soil, well drained, with good rainfall and warm climate, the average capital and labor cost per unit of output will be low because of the high yield per dollar spent on these factors. The opposite will be true on poor land.

Location likewise will affect cost. The products of the various grades of land will be sold in the same market areas; firms using the more remote land and that served by poor and costly transportation facilities will have higher costs of marketing their products than those producing on better located land. Firms in poorer locations cannot sell at prices higher than those obtained by firms located close to market.

These differences do not modify the theory of rent significantly, but require some amplification of it. It will be assumed that land falls into certain definite grades, with successively higher cost schedules. In practice, land shades off gradually from the best to the poorest; but classification into grades, the assumption being made that producers on all parcels of land in particular grades have identical cost schedules, will simplify the explanation without lessening its significance.

As long as the demand for the product is small, only the very best land—Grade A land—will be used. The situation will be the same as in the initial stage of the first example above. Once the demand is great enough to bring all Grade A land into use and the demand still cannot be satisfied at the price equal to lowest average cost on Grade A land, price will remain above the Grade A lowest average cost figure. As demand increases, market price will eventually rise above lowest average cost on Grade B land, and units of this land will come into use. The increased market supply of the product will bring market price to the level of the lowest average cost on Grade B land. Price cannot fall below this figure, with the demand at assumed levels, or all Grade B land will go out of use, and the total supply of the good will be lower than the quantity demanded at the lower price level. On Grade A land, production will be carried to the point at which price is equal to marginal cost. On Grade A land, price will exceed the old average cost figure; the differential between price (which equals average cost on Grade B land, the marginal land) and average cost (exclusive of rent) on the Grade A land is the land rent. The firms on Grade A land will be operating at a level of output at which marginal cost is equal to price and thus at a level of output beyond that of the old low-cost figure.

If the demand for the product continues to increase, eventually all Grade B land will come into use; further demand increases will raise the market price until it covers lowest average cost on Grade C land, and the latter is brought into use. The price, which must now remain high enough to cover average cost on Grade C land if supply of and demand for the product are to be maintained at equality, will now exceed average cost on Grade B land, and rent will arise on the latter. Grade B land has ceased to be marginal land; Grade C, formerly submarginal, is now the marginal land. The rent on Grade A will be greater.

Typical cost curves for the firms on each of the three grades of land are illustrated in Figure 16–2. So long as only Grade A land must be used, price will remain at 50 cents. When demand has increased sufficiently to require the use of Grade B land to make supply and demand equal, the price must be 75 cents, or all Grade B land will drop out of use, and market demand will exceed market supply. Accordingly, a differential, a rent of approximately 24 cents per unit of output (nr in Figure 16–2) arises on Grade A land.[3] When demand increases still more, so that all B land is used and C land comes into cultivation, the price of the product must be $1.00. A rent of 24 cents per unit of output (ms) now exists on Grade B land, and of 48 cents per unit ($n'r'$) on the Grade A land. The rent per acre would be the rent per unit of output multiplied by the average yield per acre on the particular grade.

In summary, price at any time must equal average cost on the

---

[3] The figure is less than 25 cents, since average cost rises slightly as output is pushed beyond the point of lowest cost.

marginal land, the poorest (in the sense of highest cost) land which will be used in production. On better grades of land the average cost (exclusive of rent) is lower. The difference between this lower average cost figure and the marginal-land average cost figure is the amount of land rent on the better land.

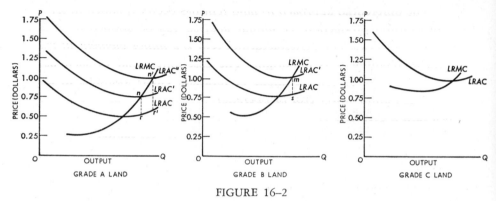

FIGURE 16–2

LAND RENT, LAND OF VARYING QUALITY

Once land rent has arisen, it constitutes a cost from the standpoint of the individual producer. If he leases his land, he will have to pay rent to his landlord; if he owns his land, his costs include the amount which he could make by leasing the land to someone else, since he must cover this sum (along with his other costs) if he is to remain in business. Land rent may be regarded as a differential return from the standpoint of the economy but is a cost from the standpoint of the individual producer.

The analysis above, for purposes of simplification, was based upon the assumption of the production of a single product. Actually, a variety of products will be grown in any area; and some land is more suited for one purpose, some for others. Each parcel of land will be used for the purpose in which it will yield maximum rent (apart from the effects of miscalculations by producers); the price of each product will equal average cost on marginal land, and the rent on better land will be a differential between this and the actual cost (exclusive of rent) on the better pieces of land. The rent yielded by the crop actually grown on each parcel of land in excess of the amount of rent which the land would yield in the next-best use is a differential rent from the standpoint of the particular industry, as well as that of the economy, but is a cost to the individual producer. The rent which the land would yield in the next-best use is a cost both to the individual firm and to the industry, but is not a cost from the standpoint of the economy as a whole.

Nonagricultural Production

The differential approach to land rent has been explained in terms of agricultural production. A similar analysis can be applied to other types of industries. For manufacturing, rent is a minor element in cost while in retailing it is important. The cost differential in such uses arises solely out of considerations of location. Good locations in any city, which allow lower cost of operation primarily because the rate of stock turn is greater than in stores on poorer sites, are limited relative to the demand for them. The more rapid turnover lowers capital cost, since a given amount of money capital can be invested in a greater total volume of goods during a certain period of time. Faster turnover lessens loss from spoilage and obsolescence. Good locations usually allow better utilization of personnel and greater effectiveness of advertising.

In locations marginal for retailing, no rent will be earned over and above that which the land would yield from nonretailing use. In better locations the average cost of operations (exclusive of rent) will be less. This differential is the additional rent arising out of the use of the land in retailing. Landowners will be able to extract this amount (plus, of course, the amount of rent that the land would yield in the next-best use) from retailers since the latter can pay this amount and still earn a normal return on their own investment.

The Merits of the Two Approaches to Rent Determination

The marginal productivity and the differential theories of land rent are merely alternative explanations of the same phenomenon, and are in no sense contradictory. Actually, the differential theory contributes very little toward a better understanding of the nature of rent, and the use of this explanation for the determination of rent while other factor prices are explained on a supply-demand basis suggests a basic difference between the rent on land and other factor prices which is not realistic. The marginal productivity analysis is adequate; the differential approach was presented in the preceding pages only because of the major role which it once enjoyed in economic theory.

Land Rent as a Distinct Functional Return

Should rent be regarded as a type of return distinct from other income, paid for the provision to business firms of units of natural resources for use in production? This point of view was long accepted in economic theory; but in recent decades, its appropriateness has been questioned. The unique characteristic of natural resources is the perfectly inelastic supply, from a long-range standpoint. But from a shortrun standpoint, other factor supplies, especially of certain types of capital goods, may also be perfectly inelastic, and the return therefore does not differ significantly from land rent. From the standpoint of the receiver of rent, the income is essentially a return on the money capital value represented by the selling price of the land and does not differ from the usual interest return. Because of these considerations, there has been a tendency in recent years to regard *land rent* as merely one form of return on money capital, or interest in the broad sense of the term. On the other hand, the term *rent* itself was first broadened to include short-period returns from the use of capital equipment, known as *quasi rents*, and was then extended still further by various writers to apply to all returns which are surpluses over and above the amounts necessary to retain factor units in the industry, or available to the economy as a whole. But rent in this broad sense is not regarded as a distinct functional return, but rather as a surplus element in all forms of factor income.

Quasi Rent

Over a long-run period, capital equipment must yield a sufficient amount to cover depreciation—that is, to maintain intact the money capital invested in it—and earn an average interest return (including the appropriate risk premium). If the equipment fails to do so, some units will not be replaced, and the return on the remaining equipment will rise. If the return is greater than this, additional equipment will be produced, and the return will fall. The depreciation element in the return is not an income, but merely return of money capital; the interest element is a functional return to the suppliers of money capital.

In a short period of time, however, the actual receipts obtained from the use of the equipment may differ substantially from the depreciation-plus-necessary-interest figure, the actual returns to the owners of the equipment being determined solely by conditions of yield of the equipment.[4] Furthermore, from the short-term point of view, in a sense the cost to the firm arising out of the use of the equipment is not the depreciation-plus-interest-on-investment figure, but the amount which the equipment could yield in the next-best employment. It is this amount which the firm sacrifices by continuing to use the equipment in the enterprise. If the actual return in the particular firm is greater than the return from the next-best use, the additional amount is a rent, from the standpoint of the firm, attributable to the capital equipment.

From the standpoint of the economy, the entire sum of the return from the use of existing capital equipment is similar to rent, since the equipment is available for use once it has been produced, whether any return is earned or not. If the equipment will yield more in this particular industry than in others, the differential is a rent from the standpoint of this industry, as well as the economy. Accordingly, the term *quasi rent* is often applied to the short-period return from the use of existing capital equipment. The similarity to land rent is strictly a temporary phenomenon, however, since over a period of time the return must cover the depreciation-plus-interest figure.

In any particular period the quasi rent figure may be less than or exceed the depreciation-plus-interest return on the capital equipment. If, for example, the demand for the product produced with the equipment falls, the return from the use of the equipment will decline below the long-run necessary return figure; the firm cannot sell the equipment or lease it out except on a reduced basis due to the lower return, and thus has no better alternative than continued use of the equipment—unless it can be used in another industry more advantageously. On the other hand if the demand for the product and the return on the equipment rise, the return will exceed the long-run figure in the interval until additional equipment of this type can be produced and placed in operation.

The Concept of Rent as a Generalized Surplus Return

There has been a tendency on the part of many economists to expand the concept of rent to include all payments for factor units (and implicit returns attributable to specific factor units owned by the firm) which are not cost elements from the standpoint of the industry or the entire economy because payment or earning of them is not necessary to make the factor units available to the industry or the economy. In large measure, these elements are costs from the standpoint of the individual

---

[4] Except as modified by the use of long-term leases of equipment.

firms, since the firms must make the payments to get the factor units away from other firms in the industry, except to the extent that particular factor units offer a greater yield in the one particular firm than in any other. But if the units are available to the industry whether payment is made or not because they have no use in other industries, the payments are rents from the standpoint of the industry as well as from the standpoint of the economy. If the units are not available to the industry without the making of payments, but are available to the economy as a whole whether they are made or not, the payments are costs from the standpoint of the industry, but rents from the standpoint of the economy.

Rents in this sense are not a distinct functional return, but are elements in other returns. Land rent is a rent, in this sense, in its entirety so far as the economy as a whole is concerned; and the excess earned in one industry over the amount which the land would yield in the next most advantageous use is a rent from the standpoint of that industry as well. From a short-run standpoint the returns arising out of the use of capital equipment are rents from the standpoint of the economy; and to the extent that the equipment is usable (or yields a higher return) in one particular industry only, the returns are rents (entirely or in part) from the standpoint of that industry as well. Over a longer period, however, the payments for the use of capital goods are true costs. Wages may consist in part of rents in this sense of the term; if, for example workers have skills which are of greater value in one industry than another, the additional amounts which the workers earn in the industry over and above the amounts which they could earn in other lines of work are rents from the standpoint of the industry.

Boulding has emphasized that whenever the supply of factor units is not perfectly elastic, a portion of the returns to the factor owners consists of rent, since the full amounts are not necessary to make all of the factor units available.[5] If the supply is not perfectly elastic, some factor units will be available at a return lower than the amount their owners actually receive; the differential between the actual return and the one necessary to make them available is a surplus, and thus a rent in this sense. The size of this differential will be different if rent is considered from the standpoint of the industry than it would be if viewed from the standpoint of the economy, since factor supplies are typically much more elastic from the standpoint of one industry than to

[5] See K. E. Boulding, "The Concept of Economic Surplus," *American Economic Review,* Vol. 35 (December, 1945), pp. 851–69.

the economy as a whole because of the possibility of shifting of factor units among various industries.

Summary

The price paid for the use of land, in the sense of factor units provided directly by nature and therefore nonreproducible, may be regarded as a separate type of return designated as land rent, or it may be regarded simply as an interest return on the money capital equivalent of the current sale value of the land. Regardless of the designation, the determination of the sum involved may be explained in terms of the usual marginal productivity approach applied to each type of land or, in traditional terms, as a differential between the average cost (exclusive of rent) on the particular type of land as compared to average cost on marginal land. These approaches are alternative methods of explanation; but there is no particular advantage in applying a method of analysis to land different from that applied to other factors.

The distinguishing feature of land is the fact that, since it is provided by nature and is not producible, the supply is perfectly inelastic, and the return is dependent solely upon the yield. But in a short-run period, specialized capital equipment is likewise perfectly inelastic in supply, and cost of production is not relevant once it has been produced. Thus, in a short period the return on capital goods is dependent solely upon the yield of the equipment in production, and is similar to land rent; it may be designated as *quasi rent*. But this is a short-period phenomenon only; since capital goods are produced and wear out, over a longer period the return is dependent upon the cost of production of the equipment, and must cover this cost plus an interest return on the money capital.

In recent years the term *rent* has been extended to cover all returns attributable to specific factors which are surpluses, in the sense that payment of them is not necessary to insure that the factor units will be available, either to an industry or to the economy as a whole. Rent in this sense is not a distinct functional return, but an element in all types of factor returns arising whenever factor supplies are not perfectly elastic.

SELECTED REFERENCES

BOULDING, K. E. "The Concept of Economic Surplus," *American Economic Review,* Vol. 35 (December, 1945), pp. 851–69.
     The concept of rent as a generalized surplus return.

MARSHALL, A. *Principles of Economics,* Book VI, chap. ix. 8th ed. London: Macmillan, 1920.

 The differential rent theory, and the concept of quasi rent.

WORCESTER, DEAN A. "A Reconsideration of the Theory of Rent," *American Economic Review,* Vol. 36 (June, 1946), pp. 258–77.

 A review of the various approaches to rent theory.

QUESTIONS

1. How does land differ from other types of factors?

2. What is the nature of the supply schedule of land from the standpoint of the economy? From the standpoint of a particular industry?

3. Why is the market for the renting of land highly imperfect?

4. A piece of land is yielding $650 a year rent and is expected to continue to do so in the future. What will be the approximate selling price of the land, assuming an interest rate of 4 percent on investments of comparable risk?

5. Why will the land not sell for more than the figure given in the answer to Question 4? For less?

6. Why will the sale price of a house not equal the capitalized sum of the figure for which it rents?

7. How, in general, does the Ricardian theory of rent differ in its approach from the marginal productivity theory?

8. Why can rent not arise when not all of the best land is in use?

9. Would rent arise if all land were equally fertile and well located, but limited in amount relative to demand?

10. Would land rent arise if the Law of Diminishing Returns did not operate?

11. Explain, in terms of the Ricardian rent theory, how the rent is determined on a particular piece of land.

12. In earlier chapters, land rent has been regarded as a cost. Yet, in the Ricardian rent analysis, rent is explained as a differential between rent and cost. Explain.

13. Stores in outlying areas sometimes advertise that they can sell more cheaply because they are outside the high-rent area. Is the lower rent which they pay responsible for the lower prices they charge, or is the rent lower because they must charge lower prices to attract customers? Explain.

14. Explain the term *quasi rent.*

15. Why, in a short-run period, are the determinants of the supply of capital goods similar to those of land?

16. Explain the concept of rent as any surplus return attributable to a specific factor.

17. How is it possible for a particular payment for factor units to be a cost from the standpoint of the firm, but a rent, in the broad sense of the term, from the standpont of the economy as a whole?

18. Why is a portion of the returns to a certain group of factor owners rent (in the broad sense of the term) rather than a true cost, unless the factor supply is perfectly elastic?

19. If the supply schedule of a particular factor to a certain industry is perfectly inelastic, what portion of the payment to the owners of the factor unit is rent?

20. On which types of land has land rent been increased by the development of the automobile? On which types has it been decreased?

Chapter 17

THE THEORY OF PROFITS

The preceding chapters have reviewed the manner in which contractual payments made to the owners of factors, or, in other words, the prices paid by business firms for the services of factor units, are determined. Demand schedules for the various types of factor units depend upon the schedules of marginal revenue product of the factors; supply schedules are dependent upon the particular circumstances affecting the availability of factor units, and differ widely among various types of factors. If markets are purely competitive, factor prices depend directly upon demand and supply relationships; if they are not, the actual figures will be affected by the exact nature of competition, the strength of monopoly and monopsony elements, and, in some instances, the actual bargaining policies followed. The same basic analysis has been applied to all types of factor units and to money capital; the differences in the determination of the prices of various factors can be traced to differences in supply determinants and competitive conditions. The marginal productivity analysis cannot be applied, however, to the residual income received by owners of businesses. The final step in the analysis of factor pricing and distribution is the explanation of the determination of this return, known as *profits*.

The first step in the analysis of profits is the clarification of the concept. The term is used in two distinct senses: (1) in the business or accounting sense, as the excess of receipts over all contractual costs and depreciation, and (2) in the sense of the excess over and above the implicit cost elements in business profits. Each will be considered in turn.

BUSINESS PROFITS AND IMPLICIT COSTS

As the term *profits* is used in accounting and in the business community generally, it refers to the sum available to a firm after all payments for factor unit services acquired on a contractual basis, other current obligations such as taxes, and depreciation charges have been covered. During a given interval of time, a firm obtains a certain sum from the sale of its products. During this period, it must make various contractual payments for labor services, materials, power, etc. It must meet rent and interest obligations. Since capital equipment owned declines in value during the period, a portion of the receipts, known as *depreciation charges,* must be regarded as merely a return of capital and must be charged against receipts as a cost. Taxes must be paid. The excess of the total receipts over these various payments and charges is regarded as the profit of the business firm. In a proprietorship, this sum is directly available for the personal use of the owners; in a corporation, it may be paid out to the stockholders in the form of dividends or may be retained in the business. Essentially, profits in this business sense comprise the total share of income which accrues to the business firm as such, and thus to its owners (although in a corporation the owners may not gain access to it).

Examination of business profits reveals that the sum of such profits is made up in large measure of implicit (that is, noncontractual) elements of other types of factor incomes, representing cost of factor units and money capital provided by the owners of the enterprise. These are true cost elements, as explained in earlier chapters, in the sense that they must be covered over a long-run period if the firm is to continue in operation. They differ from contractual costs only in that there is no formal, legal obligation for payment of the return. The cost elements take the form of forgone earnings from other possible uses of the factor units. Each of the major elements of implicit costs will be reviewed briefly.

Interest Return on the Money Capital of the Owners

In virtually all businesses, a portion of the money capital employed in the enterprise will have been supplied by the owners, directly in the partnership and proprietorship, and indirectly through the purchase of stock or through retention of earnings in the corporation. Since the owners forgo the advantages of liquidity or of a monetary return from the placing of the funds in other investments by placing the money in this business, a return on the money is an essential cost item from the standpoint of the business. The money would not have been invested in the business initially if a return had not been expected, and will not be retained in the business indefinitely if a return is not earned.

This necessary interest return on the money capital supplied by the owners may be broken down into two elements. The first is the pure interest return, the sum equal to the basic rate of interest on safest types of investments. The second element is a risk premium sufficient to compensate, on the average, for the greater risk of loss of the capital sum from investing it in the undertaking rather than placing it in high-grade securities.

What is the capital sum upon which the implicit interest rate must be earned? With unchanged technological conditions and prices, the sum would be the total amount which had been placed in the enterprise by the owners, directly or through retained earnings. But changes in prices and technology alter the amount of money capital required to purchase the equipment needed to produce a given output. Suppose, for example, that the general price level, including the price of capital equipment, rises. As the present equipment wears out, output can be maintained economically only if additional money capital is invested in the enterprise. Thus the necessary return must be earned on the sum required for *replacement* of the capital equipment, if continued operation is to be maintained, rather than on the sum originally invested. If general price declines or technological developments allow the replacement of the equipment at a lower cost than the original, it is not necessary that the owners earn a return on the larger original sum invested, but merely upon the new, lower amount required for replacement. The price and technological changes will essentially have destroyed, through capital losses, a portion of the money capital originally invested, but operation of the enterprise will continue so long as an average return is earned upon the smaller sum of money capital now required.

Implicit Wages

Especially in smaller firms, a portion of the business profits may consist of noncontractual wages for work performed in the enterprise by the owners. The typical farmer or small shopkeeper performs substantial amounts of ordinary labor service for which he rarely pays himself a formal wage. A large portion of the sum which he regards as his business profit is essentially an implicit wage, equal to the amount which he could obtain from hiring his services to other firms.

Closely related are implicit wages of management. In a small business, typically, the person or persons controlling the operation of the enterprise and making the management decisions do not compensate themselves directly for this activity. A portion of the business profit earned is a compensation for this work, equal to the amounts which these persons could earn as hired managers of other firms. In larger enterprises, likewise, a portion of business profits may represent wages of management of officials of the business, who are not paid as much as their actual contribution to the business. In this case, however, the sums do not accrue to the persons responsible for them, but to the owners, and therefore in a sense are not necessary cost elements, but a form of monopsonistic profits, discussed in a subsequent section. Were the markets perfect, these items would become explicit costs; they accrue to the owners rather than to the managers only because of imperfections in the market.

Implicit Rents

If rent is regarded as a distinct form of factor return arising out of the scarcity of nonreproducible assets, a portion of business profits may fall within the category of implicit rent. If the firm owns land or similar nonreproducible assets, a portion of the profits consists of the sum which this land would earn if rented out instead of being used in the business. Alternatively, an implicit interest return on the current monetary value of the property may be regarded as an implicit cost. The sums involved will be the same regardless of which approach is used.

THE PORTION OF BUSINESS PROFITS IN EXCESS OF IMPLICIT COSTS

Any excess of business profits over and above the various implicit costs was in the past regarded as a homogeneous return designated as pure or economic profit. More careful analysis of this return, however, has led to increased emphasis upon the diversity of the elements which comprise it. Only one segment of the excess may be regarded as a truly distinct return, with other segments, particularly those arising from monopoly or monopsony influences, constituting special forms of other types of factor returns, and thus in a sense implicit costs. These segments of profit will be considered first, with subsequent attention to the residual or pure profit.

Monopsony Profits

The first element in the excess of business profits over the implicit costs noted above is that arising from monopsonistic influences in the factor markets. When a particular firm is able to pay factor owners less than the competitive factor income figure, the owners of the firm essentially receive a portion of the factor income attributable to these factor units, and thus in a sense "exploit" the other factor owners. For example, if one coal mine is able to hire workers more cheaply than other mines, the firm can earn a higher than average rate of business profit; the excess consists simply of the wage differential which the owners of the firm have been able to appropriate for their own use because of market imperfections. Only when markets are imperfect— when factor owners lack adequate knowledge of other possibilities, or factor units are immobile—or competition among various firms for factor units is not complete can monopsonistic profits be earned. It should be noted that if all firms in the industry gain similar advantage, the profits will tend to disappear. Only a differential advantage on the part of particular firms enables them to earn profit from this source.

Firms may be particularly likely to obtain monopsony profits from failure to pay top management personnel the full contribution which they make to the enterprise. The market for such personnel is highly imperfect, and firms may succeed for a considerable period of time in compensating successful managers at a lower rate than the actual contributions of these persons, and the amounts which the persons could obtain from other firms if they sought employment with them and their abilities were known.

Monopsony profits, while constituting an excess over implicit cost elements as defined in the preceding section, tend to capitalize in the same manner as monopoly profits, and thus are distinguishable from pure profit. Capitalization will be discussed in the following section.

Monopoly Profits

When a firm is protected from entry of new firms, it will be able to earn profits over and above the implicit cost elements, provided average revenue is, in any range of output, above average cost. This higher return protected by entry restriction is known as monopoly profit, although the market situation may be one of oligopoly or monopolistic competition, or complete monoply as previously defined.

Popular thinking attributes a large portion of "excess" profit to monopoly positions, and some economists have regarded monopoly as the primary source of pure profit. However, closer examination of monopoly profits suggests that they differ in several respects from the pure profits noted below, and should be distinguished from the latter.

Imputation of Monopoly Profits. In the first place, unlike pure profits, monopoly profits are frequently imputable—or, in other words, attributable—to certain factor units or property rights. Suppose, for example, that entry into a field is restricted because the firms possess patent rights or well-established trademarks. The excess rate of profits which continues because of the inability of new firms to enter the industry is clearly attributable to the patent right or trademark. The firm could lease this to other firms for an equivalent return, and thus the return is in a sense an opportunity cost to the firm as the owner and user of the patent, instead of being a true profit. The amount involved is essentially a rent, in the broad sense of the term, since the asset—the patent right—is not reproducible for the period in which it is valid, and other firms cannot find substitutes. The return is not a necessary cost from the standpoint of the industry, if the patent has no value outside of the industry, since it would have no rental value if it were freely available to all firms.

Capitalization of Monopoly Profits. When restriction of entry is due to the large volume of business necessary for low cost and heavy capital requirements, the monopoly profits are less clearly attributable to particular factors. However, the higher rate of profits tends to capitalize if it is expected to continue, the sale value of the enterprise increasing by the capitalized sum of the monopoly return. Thus, not only will new purchasers of the firm, or of stock in it, receive only an average rate of earnings on their money capital, but the existing owners, who could dispose of the firm or their interest in it at the higher price figure, are in a sense only earning a normal return on the money capital represented by the sale price. The monopoly profit is therefore very similar to rent in the broad sense of that term and from the standpoint of the firm itself has some characteristics of a true imputed cost.

An example will serve to illustrate the capitalization of monopoly profits. Suppose that a firm established with an investment of $50,000 succeeds in building up a strongly attached reputation which competitors cannot duplicate, and earns annual business profits of $20,000, year after year. If the firm is offered for sale, it may bring as much as $400,000; if investors regard 5 percent as an appropriate return on investments with the particular degree of risk involved, and expect the profits to continue indefinitely. Hence the new purchasers would earn only 5 percent on their money capital, and the monopoly returns appear to have vanished, having become an implicit cost. Actually, however, the return is greatly in excess of the sum necessary to insure continued operation of the firm; if entry barriers are broken and profits fall, the enterprise will continue to operate on a permanent basis, so long as the business profits are as much as $2,500—representing 5 percent return on replacement cost.

Monopoly Profits Distinguished from Other Returns. As indicated, monopoly profits have certain characteristics of rent and interest returns, since in large measure they are imputable to particular factor units and they tend to capitalize. Thus, they resemble implicit costs from the standpoint of individual firms. However, they may be distinguished from true implicit costs in several ways. In the first place, they are not necessary to ration economically scarce resources among competing units; most entry-restricting elements are artificial barriers to the establishment of new firms, rather than true scarcity factors. Patent rights could be used by all firms in an industry if the law permitted, and brand names could be shared. Even when limited raw material resources restrict new firms, the restriction is a product of the ownership by the existing firms of the available resources. Furthermore, the monopoly receipts are not necessary to maintain output of the industry. If the earnings of the firms drop to an average-return level through the breaking of the barriers to entry, no firm will leave the industry. Finally, the existence of monopoly profits gives rise to constant striving on the part of the other firms to break the entry-restricting barriers and enter production in the field. Therefore, while monopoly profits must be distinguished from pure profits, they must also be distinguished from true implicit costs even though they resemble the latter, and must be regarded either as a special form of return or as a major but distinct species of the general category of rents.

Innovations as a Source of Pure Profits

A third source of an excess of business profits over and above usual implicit costs is the undertaking of *innovations*—of deliberate changes in production and demand functions—by business firms. Some economists, of whom the most famous was Joseph Schumpeter, have regarded pure profits as solely the result of innovations.[1] They may be classed into two groups: those affecting production and those affecting the market. The first group includes all changes which alter techniques of physical production and distribution, and methods of organization and operation. If a firm is successful in introducing cost-reducing techniques, it will earn, at least temporarily, a higher rate of profit. The second type of innovation includes all changes which affect the consumer demand for the product, such as the introduction of new products, new styles, advertising techniques, etc.

Innovational profits cannot be attributed to particular factor units, as can most monopoly profits, and since they are not predictable with any degree of certainty, and those due to any one innovation cannot be

[1] See J. Schumpeter, *Theory of Economic Development* (Cambridge: Harvard University Press, 1934).

expected to continue, they cannot capitalize. They will continue only until other firms succeed in duplicating the innovations successfully. If the innovation proves difficult to duplicate, and other firms are restricted from entering the field, the continuing profits must be regarded as monopoly profits, and will capitalize. Any one firm can continue to make innovational profits, as such, only by continuing to introduce successful innovations.

Innovational profits, as a form of noncontractual residual income, accrue directly to the firm and ultimately to its owners. In the small firm, therefore, the persons responsible for the undertaking of the innovation in large measure reap the reward from it, and it is sometimes argued that innovational profits are essentially a form of managerial wage and not a distinct type of income. However, the complete unpredictability of the success of innovations and their noncontinuing character suggest that they should be regarded as a distinctive and essentially residual type of income, rather than a form of managerial wage. This approach is particularly appropriate for large corporations, in which the persons responsible for the innovations typically do not receive the gains from their success. The argument that their failure to do so constitutes merely a monopsonistic absorption by the owners of gains arising from the actions of the managers obscures the basic difference between innovational gains and other managerial returns.

Uncertainty as the Source of Pure Profits

Pure profits may arise not only from deliberate innovations, but also from essentially windfall sources, that is, from unexpected changes in revenues or costs, as, for example, from unanticipated shifts in consumer preferences, declines in raw material prices, etc. If the changes are favorable, they give rise to profits; if they are unfavorable, they give rise to negative profits, i.e., losses. If the concept of uncertainty is defined broadly, the outcome of innovations may be regarded as one case of uncertainty; thus, uncertainty may be regarded as the sole source of pure profits. The tendency in recent years has been to explain profits in this way, following the classic work of Frank Knight.[2] In terms of this uncertainty thesis, pure profits may be defined as the difference between expected receipts and actual receipts during a given period, although, as noted in succeeding paragraphs, the term *expected* is subject to more than one interpretation.

Uncertainty arises in two major realms: in circumstances directly

---

[2] See F. H. Knight, *Risk, Uncertainty and Profit* (Boston: Houghton Mifflin, 1921). Knight's work has been extended in recent years in the work of J. Fred Weston; note the references to Weston's articles at the end of the chapter.

affecting the cost and revenue schedules of the firm, and in changes in the general environment, such as national income, government policies, etc., which indirectly affect cost and revenue schedules. A firm can never be certain about the behavior of sales, prices, and various cost items in the coming period; and pure profits are frequently earned because sales or prices rise, or costs fall, without offsetting unfavorable changes. Even if a firm undertakes a deliberate change—as, for example, by introducing a new technique or product—it cannot be certain of results. If expectations are exceeded, pure profits are earned. On the other hand, pure profits may arise as a result of changes extraneous to the immediate circumstances surrounding the firm, as, for example, changes in the weather, increases in governmental expenditures, tax reductions, changes in government regulatory policies, changes in tariffs, etc. When the changes are adverse, losses are suffered.

The Concept of Expected Returns. Clarification of the concept of pure profit requires interpretation of the term *expected* in the definition given above. If by this term is meant the prediction of the firm itself, any foreseen pure profits would not be pure profits at all—since the latter are defined as the difference between expected and realized receipts. If a firm undertakes an innovation in anticipation of a certain profit and actually attains this profit, the sum would not be pure profits, in terms of this interpretation of the term *expected,* but would be an implicit cost. The concept of profits will be a more useful one, however, if the term *expected* is interpreted to mean a forecast accepted with certainty, not only by the firm but by general opinion in the market. Returns expected in this sense will be reflected in factor prices and the selling or rental price of the firm as a whole, and capitalize in the same manner as monopoly profit, and thus should not be regarded as pure profit. But profits which the firm hopes to gain, but which are not accepted by the market as certain, are not capitalized, and, if realized, constitute pure profits, even though the firm may have anticipated them. Hence, gains from both innovational and windfall changes which are not market-anticipated constitute pure profits.

The Absence of Pure Profits and Monopoly Profits in Perfect Competition

For reasons outlined in earlier chapters, neither monopoly profits nor pure profits can exist in a static, perfectly competitive market situation. Under such circumstances, business profits will adjust to the level at which necessary implicit wage, interest, and rent costs are covered, the necessary interest return being based upon replacement cost of capital equipment. The purely competitive nature of such a market insures that inflow of new firms will eliminate any temporary excess returns; if the market is truly perfect, the adjustment will be instantaneous, and there will not even be temporary pure profits in the transitional period. If conditions are static, that is, if production and demand functions remain unchanged, there will be no uncertainty and no pure profits. Monopoly profits result from continued departure of market conditions from pure competition; pure profits are the result of change—of the operation of dynamic forces in the economy—which give rise to uncertainty.

PROFITS AS A FUNCTIONAL RETURN

The question whether pure profits should be regarded as a functional or a residual return has been significant in the general controversy in the field of profit theory. By *functional return* is meant a compensation for the performance of a specific function in production by the recipients of the return. By *residual return* is meant simply a sum which remains to certain factor owners after all costs have been covered, accruing to these persons because of existing institutional relationships rather than as a direct compensation for performing a function. It is obvious that the portions of business profits which consist of implicit wages, interest, and rent are true functional returns, accruing to factor owners for the provision of factor units made available to the business firm on a noncontractual basis. Monopoly profit, while functional in the narrow sense of the word because it becomes a type of opportunity cost to the firm, is not functional from the standpoint of the economy, since its receipt is not necessary for continued production of the output of the industry. The controversial question has related to the functional nature of pure profit.

It was common in the past to regard pure profits, when earned, as a distinct type of functional return, received by the entrepreneurs of the enterprise as compensation for undertaking innovations and bearing the primary risks of uncertainty. The entrepreneurs, as owners of the business, also receive the implicit cost returns and monopoly profit, if any. But the distinctive return to the entrepreneurs was considered to be the pure profit, a functional return for innovation and uncertainty bearing.

The usefulness of the functional concept of pure profits can be seriously questioned. In the modern large corporation the separation between ownership and management causes the pure profits to accrue largely to persons other than those who perform the entrepreneurial functions. In such enterprises the identity of the "entrepreneurs" and the profit receivers is lost. Furthermore, pure profits are not *caused* by uncertainty; they arise in conditions of uncertainty when realized conditions exceed expectations, and they can best be regarded as a residual income. Even in a small enterprise in which the entrepreneur and the profit receiver are identical, the pure profits can scarcely be regarded as a reward for the performance of the function of bearing uncertainty, since the act of doing so does not in itself insure pure profits, which arise only if conditions prove to be better than expected. Even when pure profits result from innovations, they can most satisfactorily be regarded as a residual income which accrues to the owners of the enterprise, rather than as a functional return for the work of introducing the innovations. Not only does the mere act of introducing innovations not necessarily lead to pure profits, but in many cases the persons who make the decisions to undertake the innovation are not the ones receiving the profit.

The Role of Profits in the Economy

The statement that profits can best be regarded as a residual return rather than a functional return does not imply that pure profits play no role in the functioning of the economy. In the first place the anticipation of making pure profits is an important lure which leads firms to undertake innovations of all types, and thus to maintain economic progress and investment necessary for full employment. While the pure profits actually realized cannot, particularly in the large corporation, be regarded as a functional reward for undertaking change, the possibility of making such profits is an important source of encouragement to the firms for making the innovations. Secondly, the making of pure profits constitutes a signal for the revision of behavior by the firm. Failure of expected and realized profits to coincide suggests the need for revision of estimates and policies.

Thirdly, the making of pure profits on the part of some firms leads other firms to readjust their policies. Both pure profits and monopoly profits constitute a stimulus to other firms to attempt to duplicate the policies of the successful firms which gave rise to these profits, or to attempt to develop other policies which will accomplish the same result profitwise. In a highly competitive field, firms dare not lag behind the more successful firms, or they will soon be suffering losses; the earning of pure profits by some firms constitutes a warning to other firms to adjust their policies if they are to avoid future losses. Likewise, the earning of high profits in a certain field leads additional firms to enter the industry and brings about a redistribution of allocation of resources in conformity with changes in consumer demand and other variables.

NEGATIVE PROFITS OR LOSSES

The preceding sections have been concerned with positive profits arising when actual results are better than expected results. But actual receipts may be less than anticipated, and, as a result, pure profits are negative; in other words, a loss, from an economic standpoint, is incurred. Economic profits are negative whenever the receipts are less than the sum of contractual obligations, depreciation charges, and implicit interest, wage, and rent costs. If receipts are so low that contractual obligations plus depreciation are not covered, the situation may be described as one of *business losses,* or losses in the accounting sense. If these items are covered, but all implicit costs are not covered, the firm is earning a business profit, but is suffering negative economic profits, or an economic loss.

Certain types of losses, if expected to continue, will tend to capitalize, reducing the sale value of the enterprise by the capitalized sum of the loss. It may be argued that the implicit cost element arising out of the investment is not the normal return on the replacement cost of the equipment, but one upon the current sale value. In other words, the quasi rent on the capital goods, not the interest return on their cost, is the appropriate element in cost. From a strictly short-run point of view, this argument has limited merit. But for purposes of analysis, it is preferable to define losses as the excess over receipts of all cost items which must be covered if the firm is to remain in business permanently. It is a loss in this sense which is significant in determining long-range policy of the firm and the flow of resources among various industries.

The Various Situations of Losses

It is important to distinguish between those loss situations in which firms will cease operations immediately and those in which they will continue to operate over a short-run period. In the first three states, business losses occur, while in the fourth, business profits are earned, but economic losses are incurred.

1. *Failure to Cover Explicit Variable Costs.* If the enterprise is not taking in enough in current receipts to meet those variable costs which are explicit in nature, continued operation is obviously undesirable unless an immediate improvement is expected, and is impossible

unless the firm or its owners have adequate reserve funds with which to meet the deficit.

2. *Coverage of Explicit Variable but Not Contractual Fixed Costs.* If receipts cover explicit variable costs, but not explicit fixed costs, of which interest is likely to be the most significant, the enterprise will go into bankruptcy, unless the reserves of the firm are adequate to meet the necessary payments, or the owners of the firm are able and willing to supply the necessary funds. Through reorganization in bankruptcy, the creditors become the new owners of the enterprise, and explicit interest costs are reduced or eliminated; the situation thus becomes one of (3) or (4), below.

3. *Coverage of Explicit Variable and Contractual Fixed Costs, but Not Depreciation Charges.* A firm may, before or after reorganization, be able to meet all contractual obligations involving both fixed and variable costs, but not depreciation. The firm can obviously continue operations as long as existing equipment can be used, but once the equipment wears out, it will lack funds for replacement and will be unable to obtain them unless the owners are willing to supply additional money capital. This they obviously will not do, unless an improvement in conditions is expected. Prior to the point at which substantial replacement of equipment is necessary, however, liquidation will be advantageous unless improvements are expected. If the depreciation charges reflect the actual decline in the current salable value of the capital assets during the period, failure to cover this sum warrants immediate liquidation. If the depreciation charges exceed the actual decline in the value of assets, liquidation is desirable if the actual earnings toward depreciation charges are less than the sum of the interest return on the salvage value plus the actual decline in the value of the assets.

4. *Coverage of Contractual Costs and Depreciation, but Failure to Earn All Implicit Costs.* A firm may have adequate receipts to meet all contractual factor payments and depreciation, but not enough to cover all implicit costs, the most important of which is likely to be a return on the money capital of the owners. Such a firm *can* continue operations indefinitely if the owners wish. But it will not be advantageous for the owners to permit continued operation once the point is reached at which the cash earnings (receipts in excess of direct operating expenses, taxes, and the decline in salvage value during the period) fall below the expected earnings which can be made on the salvage value if the enterprise is liquidated. In other words, the optimum time to liquidate occurs when the ratio of cash earnings, as defined in the previous

sentence, to disposable (salvage) value falls below the figure the firm regards as a necessary minimum, and there is inadequate expectation of improvement.[3]

Until this point is reached, however, it is advantageous for the owners of the firm to keep it in operation, even though they are not making an average return on their capital, since they cannot withdraw their capital from the enterprise. Once money capital has been invested in specialized capital equipment, only a small portion can be withdrawn quickly (the amount equal to the salvage value), and the rental value of the equipment (if rental is possible) will depend upon the earning capacity of the equipment, not its cost. So long as the owners make a return in excess of the salvage or rental value, there is nothing that they can do to improve their position until the equipment wears out.

In practice, many firms operate far too long from the standpoint of the interests of the owners.[4] This is a product of continuing overoptimism about the future, of the dislike of persons to discontinue an enterprise with which they have long been identified, and reluctance of the officials of the company to lose their positions. As a consequence, depreciation funds and such business profits as are made are utilized to maintain and repair equipment, and eventually, the equity of the stockholders is destroyed. There are many examples of small railroads, and particularly of the electric interurban lines, which operated for years beyond the point at which the best interests of the stockholders would have been served.[5]

Causes of Losses

The sources of negative economic profits are the reverse of the causes of positive economic profits. In general, losses may be attributed to uncertainty—to unanticipated events which adversely affect the cost or revenue schedules. These events may consist of general changes in the economy, such as a fall in national income or altered governmental policy; or they may be changes in the circumstances directly affecting the particular firm, such as an adverse shift in consumer preferences, rises in materials costs, etc. Or they may result from the successful introduction of innovations by competitors, or the failure of innovations

---

[3] One of the very few careful analyses of decision making relating to liquidation is that of G. Shillinglaw, "Profit Analysis for Abandonment Decisions," *Journal of Business,* Vol. 30 (January, 1957), pp. 17–19.

[4] For illustrations, see G. W. Hilton and J. F. Due, *The Electric Interurban Railways in America* (Stanford, Calif.: Stanford University Press, 1960), chaps. vii, viii.

[5] *Ibid.*

attempted by the firm itself to produce desired results. Or they may result from mistakes, such as the failure to obtain optimum factor combinations. Where the losses are due to obvious managerial errors, it may be argued that the source of the loss from the standpoint of the firm is overcompensation of management personnel (the opposite of monopsonistic exploitation). One frequent type of mistake is the establishment of new enterprises under circumstances in which profitable operation is impossible, promoters lacking adequate knowledge of revenue and cost schedules, or being overoptimistic.

Losses lead to readjustments, which may eliminate them; they constitute a warning to a firm to alter its policies to obtain greater efficiency, to develop innovations, etc. The changes made may prove to be successful, and profitable operation may be restored; in other cases the firm may be unable to escape the losses and thus must eventually liquidate. In large measure, continuing losses may be regarded as the penalty for failure to adapt to changing conditions.

SELECTED REFERENCES

DAVIS, R. M. "The Current State of Profit Theory," *American Economic Review,* Vol. 40 (June, 1952), pp. 245–64.
> A review of the controversy in the field of profit theory.

KEIRSTEAD, B. S. *An Essay in the Theory of Profits and Income Distribution.* London: Basil Blackwell, 1953.
> An integration of various approaches to profit theory.

KNIGHT, F. H. *Risk, Uncertainty and Profit.* Boston: Houghton Mifflin, 1921.
> One of the classic analyses of the functions of the entrepreneur, with emphasis on uncertainty as the source of profit.

SCHUMPETER, J. *Theory of Economic Development.* Cambridge: Harvard University Press, 1934.
> The innovations theory of profit.

TRIFFIN, R. *Monopolistic Competition and General Equilibrium Theory.* Cambridge: Harvard University Press, 1940.
> A stimulating discussion of various aspects of profit theory.

WESTON, J. F. "A Generalized Uncertainty Theory of Profits," *American Economic Review,* Vol. 40 (March, 1950), pp. 40–60.
> An extension of the Knight approach to profit theory.

———. "The Profit Concept and Theory: A Restatement," *Journal of Political Economy,* Vol. 44 (April, 1954), pp. 152–70.
> An extension of Weston's previous work, containing a very complete bibliography of recent writings on profit theory.

QUESTIONS

1. Why does a large portion of business profits consist of elements which are costs from an economic standpoint?

2. Upon what base should the necessary return on the owners' capital be figured?

3. A farmer obtains $8,500 from the sale of his crop; his expenses, including taxes, were $2,000. His farm would sell for $25,000. He could obtain a job in a local feed mill at $5,000 a year if he wished. Determine his business profits, the implicit cost elements in the business profits, and his pure profit, if any. Use a figure of 4 percent as an average rate of return.

4. What is the source of monopsony profits? Why will they not be attained if the monopsony powers extend to all firms in the industry?

5. Define monopoly profit. Why are monopoly profits, in a sense, implicit costs? Why are they not true costs from the standpoint of the economy?

6. Suppose that you buy the entire stock of a corporation that is earning and expected to earn monopoly profits. Will you make a higher than average rate of return on the money which you place in the enterprise? Explain.

7. Explain the meaning of the concept of innovations, and give examples. How do innovational profits differ from monopoly profits? From windfall profits?

8. Why are innovational profits not regarded as a managerial wage attributable to the persons responsible for the introduction of the innovations?

9. Distinguish between uncertainty and risk.

10. If profits arising out of uncertainty are foreseen by the market as a whole, are they actually pure profits if and when they are earned? Explain. Are they pure profits if they are anticipated by the particular firm only?

11. What condition is necessary for monopoly profits to continue?

12. Why would there be no monopoly or pure profits in a purely and perfectly competitive market?

13. Why are pure profits not considered to be a functional return?

14. Indicate the major roles which profits play in the economy.

15. Explain the various meanings of the term *losing money*.

16. Suppose that a particular firm is covering all variable costs and depreciation, but not an average return on investment. If the owners are seeking to maximize their gain, at what time will they discontinue operations? Explain.

17. Why do companies sometimes operate far beyond the optimum (from a profit standpoint) time of liquidation?

18. In several instances in the last three decades, sharp increases in scrap metals prices have led to the abandonment of railroads whose owners had intended to keep them in operation for a longer period. Explain.

19. Some railroad companies have continued to operate for many years despite

the fact that they have never earned an average return on the investment. Why?

20. Indicate the major causes of losses.

21. How would you explain the following:

   a) Losses, despite general business prosperity in the economy, of some textile producers in recent decades?

   b) Frequent failure of small restaurants?

   c) The losses of the New York subway system?

22. The following data (with some rounding of figures) on revenues and expenses of four railroads are taken from the 1963 *Transport Statistics* volume of the Interstate Commerce Commission. Complete the table, and indicate whether each company is (*a*) making excess profits, (*b*) making business profits but not covering all implicit costs, (*c*) failing to cover explicit variable costs, or (*d*) covering explicit variable costs but not contractual fixed costs. In cases (*c*) and (*d*), indicate the additional information which would be required to determine whether abandonment was likely or not in the near future.

   Assume, in answering this question, that the investment figure given reflects accurately the base upon which the average return should be figured, that an average return for this type of investment is 5 percent, that there are no implicit costs other than return on investment, and that depreciation, which is included in operating expenses, equals 6 percent of investment.

Corporation	Investment	Operating Revenues	Operating Expenses and Taxes	Operating Income	Interest	Business Profits	Implicit Costs	Pure Profits
Des Moines and Central Iowa....	$1,380,000	$655,000	$665,000	$-10,000	$3,000	...	...	...
Amador Central.........	85,000	189,000	122,000	67,000	0	...	...	...
Quincy Railroad...	107,000	53,000	51,000	2,000	0	...	...	...
Camino Placerville and Lake Tahoe..	330,000	77,000	76,000	1,000	6,000	...	...	...

PART IV

Concluding Perspectives

Chapter	GENERAL EQUILIBRIUM
18	

The analysis of the preceding chapters describes the determination of the prices and outputs of *particular* commodities and the income and employment of *particular* productive factors. As noted earlier, this portion of economic analysis is known as *partial equilibrium theory* because it deals with adjustments in isolated sectors of the economy and makes only incidental reference to interrelations among different sectors. It is also referred to as *neoclassical theory* because it is a relatively modern extension of techniques of analysis that were first developed by the English classical economists.

Partial equilibrium analysis is adequate for the study of a surprisingly wide range of practical problems, despite its somewhat restrictive assumptions. In the analysis of the effects of the levy of a new excise tax on tobacco, for example, the assumption that prices are given in all markets other than the market for tobacco is not too unrealistic. Similarly, the effects of a lower price of steel upon the construction industry, shipbuilding, and so forth, can be studied fairly effectively using partial equilibrium methods, even though the total effect on the economy as a whole cannot be regarded simply as the sum of the separate effects on individual industries.

To obtain an adequate picture of the functioning of the economic system as a whole, however, and to develop tools of analysis suitable for studying problems whose ramifications extend through several sectors of the economy, it is desirable to know something more about interrelationships among the outputs and prices of various commodities and the prices and inputs of various factors. The portion of economic theory that deals with these interrelations is known as *general equilibrium theory*. Although originally developed in the last century in the work of Leon Walras,[1] its impact upon the general body of economic theory has

[1] *Elements d'economie politique pure* (Lausanne, 1884), translated into English by William Jaffé and published as *Elements of Pure Economics* (Homewood, Ill.: Irwin, 1954). More recent presentations of general equilibrium theory are listed at the end of the chapter.

been slight until the last three decades, in which the earlier work has been revived and amplified. Certain major interrelationships in the economy will be noted briefly before the framework of general equilibrium analysis is presented.

Consumer Price Interdependencies

The analysis of price and output determination of commodities in earlier chapters was based upon the assumption that the prices of other goods were given, apart from minor reference to the direct effects upon the prices of other goods which might result from a change in the price of a particular good. But this type of modification reflects only a small portion of the possible interdependencies. A change in the price of any one consumption good inevitably alters the demand for and possibly the supply of other goods. For example, a rise in the price of butter will increase the demand for substitutes, such as oleomargarine, and lead to increases in the price and output of these goods if markets are purely competitive. If they are not, the effect may be solely upon output, with a possible decline in the price of substitutes. The prices of goods complementary to butter, such as bread, may fall because the demand for them will fall if butter becomes more expensive. Changes in the outputs of these other goods will affect factor supplies available for the production of bread, and thus its cost of production and supply, while shifts in the prices of other goods will in turn affect the demand for bread. The changes in prices and outputs of substitute and complementary goods will in turn affect the prices and outputs of other commodities.

Thus, complete adjustment in the prices of all goods can occur only when the various prices and outputs attain levels that are mutually consistent with one another. Given the basic determinants of consumption goods prices—namely, consumer incomes, consumer preferences, factor price schedules, production functions, and the nature of competition in various markets—such an equilibrium can be defined. But a shift in the determinants affecting any one good may have widespread repercussions upon the equilibrium prices and outputs of other goods, reactions that are ignored in partial equilibrium analysis.

The Relationship of the Prices of Consumption Goods and Factors

In the analysis of the pricing of consumption goods, factor price schedules were assumed to be given, while in the discussion of the determination of equilibrium factor prices, for the most part consumption goods prices were assumed to be given. Actually, of course, the two sets of equilibrium prices are <u>mutually dependen</u>t upon one another. For example, a major element in the cost of consumption goods is labor cost, and therefore the wage level is a significant influence on the prices of products. But the demand for labor, and thus wage rates, are dependent upon the marginal revenue product of various types of labor, which in turn depends upon consumer goods prices. No circular reasoning is involved in the analysis, as is sometimes claimed. Both wage (and other factor price) levels and commodity price levels must adjust to figures which are mutually consistent with one another, because until such a situation is reached, there will be a tendency for one set of prices or the other to shift.

THE FRAMEWORK OF GENERAL EQUILIBRIUM THEORY

General equilibrium theory presents an overall framework of the basic price and output interrelationships, including both commodities (produced goods) and factors, for the economy as a whole. Its purpose is to demonstrate mathematically that, given the basic determinants (factor supply schedules, consumer preferences, production functions, and forms of competition), the prices of all commodities and factors and the outputs of various commodities can adjust to levels which are mutually consistent with one another; that is to say, there exists in a market economy a consistent pattern of *equilibrium* prices, factor inputs, commodity outputs, and consumer purchases.

General equilibrium theory does not deal directly with questions concerning the process of attainment of an equilibrium position. To study problems of this kind, it is necessary to have additional information about the actual *changes over time* in demands and prices under conditions of disequilibrium. This is a problem in economic dynamics rather than economic statics and, as such, lies outside the scope of general equilibrium theory as ordinarily conceived. For most practical purposes, however, it is reasonable to assume that a market economy tends to adjust fairly rapidly to a position of equilibrium. If this assumption is made, it is legitimate to ignore the time required for adjustment. Under these circumstances, we may argue that <u>any given set of basic determinants (factor supply conditions, consumer preferences, and so forth</u>) determines a definite *equilibrium state* for the economy as a whole, and that changes in these determinants will therefore be associated with a widespread pattern of readjustment in the economy until a new equilibrium state is established. Another way of expressing the same idea is to say that any given position of general equilibrium (defined by given determinants) is *stable*. This statement means that a change in the conditions determining a given equilibrium ultimately will be followed by the reestablishment of a new equilibrium in which prices and outputs throughout the economy are once again mutually consistent with each other.

The mathematical explanation of general equilibrium is based upon the following parameters:

1. Consumer preferences.
2. Factor supplies, independent of factor prices.
3. Techniques of production, with fixed coefficients of production; that is, fixed proportions of various factors are required to produce a unit of output.
4. Purely competitive commodity and factor markets, and thus attainment of equality of price and average cost for each commodity, equality of supply and demand for each factor, and equality of supply and demand for each commodity.

For simplicity, it is assumed (1) that incomes are derived solely from the provision of factor units, and (2) all income is spent on consumption.

In the mathematical exposition the following symbols are employed:

$x_1, x_2, \ldots, x_n$	Indicate quantities of various commodities
$p_1, p_2, \ldots, p_n$	Indicate prices of the respective commodities
$y_1, y_2, \ldots, y_m$	Indicate the quantities of various factors available
$w_1, w_2, \ldots, w_m$	Indicate the prices of the respective factors
$\left.\begin{array}{l} a_{11}, a_{21}, \ldots, a_{n1} \\ a_{12}, a_{22}, \ldots, a_{n2} \\ a_{1m}, a_{2m}, \ldots, a_{nm} \end{array}\right\}$	Indicate the quantities of various factors necessary to produce a unit of a commodity
$MU_1, MU_2, \ldots, MU_n$	Designate the marginal utilities of various commodities to a consumer

The Demand Equations

On the demand side of the picture, there are two basic sets of equations:

(1) The budget equation, showing for each person the equality between his factor income (the price paid him per unit for each factor unit he supplies, times the number of such units he supplies) and his expenditure (which consists of the sum of the quantities of each good he purchases, multiplied by the prices of the goods):

$$y_1 w_1 + y_2 w_2 + \ldots + y_m w_m = x_1 + x_2 p_2 + \ldots + x_n p_n .$$

The symbol x_1 refers to the commodity in terms of which the values of all other commodities are expressed; its price, therefore, is unity (i.e., $p_1 = 1$).

(2) The allocation-of-consumption-expenditures equation, showing for each consumer the equality of the ratios of the marginal utilities of all commodities to their prices, under the assumption that all persons allocate theier incomes among various commodities in such a way as to maximize satisfaction:

$$\frac{MU_1}{p_1} = \frac{MU_2}{p_2}$$

$$= \frac{MU_3}{p_3}$$

$$\cdots\cdots$$

$$= \frac{MU_n}{p_n}$$

The number of equations of the second type for each consumer is one less than the number of commodities $(n - 1)$, since one commodity (commodity 1) serves as the unit of measurement of the prices of the others. However, if equation (1), above, is included, the number of equations is equal to the number of unknowns—the amounts of the various commodities—and the purchases of the various commodities by each consumer are in general determinate, given the prices of the goods, the factor prices, and the quantities of the factor units possessed. Since this conclusion is valid for every possible price level for each good, the demand schedule of the person for each good is determinate. The demand for each good is thus a function of the price of the good in question, the prices of all other consumption goods (although the influence of many of these is negligible), and the prices of the factors (given the amounts of the factor units supplied). The factor prices and quantities determine the person's income and total expenditures.

These demand functions may be expressed symbolically as follows:

$$x_1 = f_1(p_2, p_3, \ldots, p_n; w_1, w_2, \ldots, w_m)$$
$$x_2 = f_2(p_2, p_3, \ldots, p_n; w_1, w_2, \ldots, w_m)$$
$$\cdots\cdots\cdots\cdots\cdots\cdots\cdots\cdots\cdots$$
$$\cdots\cdots\cdots\cdots\cdots\cdots\cdots\cdots\cdots$$
$$x_i = f_i(p_2, p_3, \ldots, p_n; w_1, w_2, \ldots, w_m)$$
$$\cdots\cdots\cdots\cdots\cdots\cdots\cdots\cdots\cdots$$
$$\cdots\cdots\cdots\cdots\cdots\cdots\cdots\cdots\cdots$$
$$x_n = f_n(p_2, p_3, \ldots, p_n; w_1, w_2, \ldots, w_m) .$$

The equation $x_i = f_i(p_2, p_3, \ldots, p_n; w_1, w_2, \ldots, w_m)$ in this system of equations may be considered to represent the demand for a typical commodity. On this understanding, the entire system of equations may be rewritten in a more compact but equivalent form, as follows:

$$x_i = f_i(p_2, p_3, \ldots, p_n; w_1, w_2, \ldots, w_m) \qquad (i = 1, 2, \ldots, n).$$

The expression in parentheses following the equation itself indicates the various values of i in successive equations (e.g., 1, 2, . . . , n). Thus, if the parenthetical expression were $(i = 1, 2, 3)$, this would indicate that there were three commodities to be considered and so a system of equations containing three separate relations. Similarly, if there were five commodities in the economy $(n = 5)$, the parenthetical expression would be written (i $= 1, 2, \ldots, 5$), and thus there would be five demand equations in the system as a whole.

As indicated earlier, there is a separate system of demand equations for each consumer, and each system contains as many equations as there are commodities in the economy. The entire collection of demand equations, if written out in full (i.e., one equation for each commodity and for each consumer), would look very complicated and would occupy considerable space. But the basic idea is a simple one, namely, that the quantity of each good demanded by each consumer depends not only upon the price of the good, but also upon the prices of all other commodities, and upon factor prices, which determine the consumer's income. Given the quantities of the factors owned and the consumer preference schedules, the quantity of each good demanded by each consumer is therefore determinate.

The total demand for each commodity is the sum of the demands of individual consumers. Since the quantity demanded by each consumer is given by an equation, it is possible to arrive at total quantity demanded by summing the individual demand equations. For each commodity the total demand equations can be expressed as follows (capital letters being used to designate total quantities):

$$(1) \quad X_i = F_i(p_2, p_3, \ldots, p_n; w_1, w_2, \ldots, w_m) \qquad (i = 1, 2, \ldots, n).$$

Notice that we are making use of the shorthand expression described above. That is to say, the expression (1) represents a system of n equations rather than a single equation, since the subscript i is to be set equal to each of the values 1, 2, . . . , n (as indicated by the expression in parentheses). In other words, X_i represents the total quantity demanded of a typical commodity; but the entire set of total demands is represented by the collection of n symbols $X_1, X_2, \ldots,$

$X_i, \ldots, X_n$, and the numerical value of each of these variables is determined by a separate equation of the general form illustrated by the expression $X_i = F_i$ ($p_2, p_3, \ldots, p_n; w_1, w_2, \ldots, w_m$). There is one equation for each commodity, and thus a total of n such equations in the system of equations would be represented by the expression (1) above.

The Supply Equations

On the supply side of the picture, there are two basic sets of equations. The first relates price to cost of production; under the assumptions of a purely competitive market and fixed production coefficients, the price of each good is equal to the sum of the figures obtained by multiplying the price of each factor used to produce the commodity times the quantity of the factor required to produce a unit of the commodity:

$$(2) \quad p_i = a_{i1}w_1 + a_{i2}w_2 + \ldots + a_{im}w_m \quad\quad (i = 1, 2, \ldots, n).$$

As in the case of the set of equations (1), the present expression describes a system of n equations $(i = 1, 2, \ldots, n)$; i.e., there is one equation for each commodity, and therefore as many equations as there are commodities (n). In the case of commodity "1," which is the common denominator of value of the others, $p_1 = 1$.

Second, there are equations showing the equality of the total quantities of the factors used to produce the various consumption goods with the total quantities of these factors available, under the assumption of attainment of equality of factor supply and demand. Hence, for each factor the quantity available must equal the sum of the quantities of the factor used in the production, per unit, of each consumption good, multiplied by the number of units of output of the consumption good:

$$(3) \quad Y_j = a_{1j}X_1 + a_{2j}X_2 + \ldots + a_{nj}X_n \quad\quad (j = 1, 2, \ldots, m).$$

Here, we are using a different symbol, "j," to represent a typical factor input. The expression (3) represents a system of equations $(j = 1, 2, \ldots, m)$, for there is one such equation for each factor, and thus m equations in total.

Solution of the Demand and Supply Equations

In total, there are three sets of equations:

n equations (1) relating the quantities of various commodities demanded to commodity prices and factor prices (the latter, in conjunction with given factor quantities, determining incomes).

n equations (2) relating the prices of all commodities to the costs of producing them (quantities of factor units used multiplied by factor prices).

m equations (3) relating the supplies of various types of factors available to the total quantities of the factors used in the production of the various commodities.

The total number of equations equals twice the number of commodities plus the number of factors $(2n + m)$. The number of unknowns is equal to the number of commodities (n), the number of commodity prices $(n - 1$, since one commodity is used as the unit of measurement of the values of the others), plus the number of factors, or $2n + m - 1$. Thus the number of equations appears to be one more than the number of unknowns. But one of the equations in (3) can be eliminated, since, if the prices of all commodities are known as well as the quantities demanded of all except one commodity, the quantity demanded of the remaining commodity can be deduced by using the budget equations of individual consumers (for these show that the total expenditure on any one good is equal to total income minus total expenditure on all other goods). With this adjustment, the number of independent equations and the number of unknowns are the same $(2n + m - 1)$.

From a mathematical point of view, mere equality between the number of equations and unknowns does not guarantee that the equations are solvable for a unique set of equilibrium values of the unknowns.[2] As a general rule, however, this result is attained if the equations are linear in form (as is true of all the equations considered above except the demand equations (1). For a wide range of other actual forms of the equations presented, moreover, equality between the number of equations and unknowns is both a necessary and a sufficient condition for the existence of a unique equilibrium solution which is meaningful from an economic point of view (that is to say, a solution in which prices and quantities are all represented by positive numbers or, at worst, zeros). Without entering further into questions of this kind, which are mainly of mathematical, not of economic, interest, we shall assume that the equations in the general equilibrium system described above are of such a form that the system is determinate. This means that, for given consumer preferences, given supplies of factor units, and given production functions, and under the assumptions noted

---

[2] For concrete examples to illustrate this remark, see D. W. Bushaw and R. W. Clower, *Introduction to Mathematical Economics* (Homewood, Ill.: Irwin, 1957), pp. 200–202.

on page 392 (with respect to pure competition, etc.), the equilibrium prices of all commodities and factors (valued in terms of numeraire commodity "1") are determinate, as well as the equilibrium quantities of output of the various goods and the equilibrium allocation of factor units among the production of various goods. If the data on factor supplies, consumer preference schedules, and production coefficients were actually known, all equilibrium prices and outputs could be calculated. As a matter of fact, this information is not obtainable. On our present assumptions, however, there is one and only one set of commodity and factor prices and outputs of commodities in which the various elements are mutually consistent with one another. Hence, a state of general equilibrium may be said to be defined in principle, and the calculation of corresponding equilibrium values of prices and quantities is theoretically possible, were necessary information available.

Further Extensions

It is a relatively simple matter to extend the preceding analysis to apply to an economic system in which money serves as a medium of exchange, and also to an economy in which individuals hold other kinds of assets (bonds, stocks, capital goods, etc.).[3] Moreover, the assumption of pure competition, which underlies the whole of the preceding argument, can be replaced by the assumption of various forms of competition in all markets, and the analysis can thus be extended to monopolistic and oligopolistic markets. The analysis can also be generalized to consider spatially separated markets in which transportation and location variables are included among the unknowns of the general equilibrium system. Whatever the direction in which the argument is extended, however, the basic conclusions reached above would not be altered. The importance of these extensions—apart from their intrinsic theoretical interest—is that they may indicate the existence of often unrecognized interrelationships among economic quantities and so facilitate empirical research by providing a theoretical check on the consistency of observational data.

The Usefulness of General Equilibrium Theory

General equilibrium theory is of greatest value in stressing the interdependence of various portions of the economic system, which is

---

[3] The classic book on these questions is Don Patinkin's *Money, Interest and Prices* (2d ed.; New York: Harper and Row, 1965). The interested reader may also find it helpful to consult the October, 1960, issue of the *Review of Economic Studies,* which is devoted entirely to these and related problems.

easily lost from sight in partial equilibrium analysis. Failure to recognize this interdependence is responsible for many errors in popular reasoning on economic questions. For example, tariff policy is often considered only in terms of its effect upon output and employment in the particular industry protected, with no consideration of the effects of the tariff in reducing exports and thus output and employment in exporting industries. The analysis calls attention to the fact that changes in one portion of the economy may have widespread repercussions in other segments, and that commodity and factor prices are mutually interrelated; wage changes, for example, will almost inevitably affect output and prices.

Another reason for attaching significance to general equilibrium theory is its provision of a useful framework for the organization of empirical research. For effective study of concrete situations, it is essential to approach data with a coherent sense of perspective. Preliminary examination of the data may indicate that only a small portion of one's total stock of theoretical knowledge is relevant for further analysis; but much foolishness and many serious mistakes can be avoided if provisionally relevant theoretical knowledge is retained for use until an explicit reason, based on factual knowledge, can be given for ignoring it. Even though general equilibrium analysis does not itself lead to any directly useful conclusions, it is an extremely powerful instrument for the orderly arangement of ideas about the real economic world.

Limitations of General Equilibrium Theory

General equilibrium theory is subject to two major limitations. First, it is essentially static in nature, defining the overall equilibrium in terms of given determinants. While it offers a tool for studying the effect of changes in specific determinants, as illustrated in the following sections, it is of limited value for studying general trends of economic development. In recent years, increased effort has been given to the attempt to remedy this inadequacy by further analysis of the role of money and other assets, and by work on the dynamics of general equilibrium; but much more work is required along these lines before the analysis can become a truly useful tool for the study of dynamic situations.

The second limitation is a more practical one relating to the actual body of the theory as it stands, namely, the difficulty of estimating various magnitudes in a general equilibrium system so that the equations may be solved in quantitative term, and so that the theory may be used to predict precise quantitative results of various changes and policies. The tremendous complexity of the actual economic system and the inadequacy of data make this very difficult, although in the last decade various attempts have been made to do so with a simplified model, as explained in the next chapter.

CHANGES IN THE DETERMINANTS

Changes in any of the basic determinants of the system may have widespread repercussions in the system, as suggested in previous paragraphs, and will lead to the establishment of a new equilibrium pattern. The effects of several major sources of change will be considered briefly.

Changes in Consumer Preferences

Consumer preferences constantly change as styles and tastes and needs vary, partly as a result of deliberate efforts on the part of business firms, partly from autonomous causes. Increased relative preference for one good (A) relative to that for another good (B) increases the demand for the former and reduces the demand for the latter. Accordingly, firms will find it advantageous to increase the output of A, while the output of B will fall. Thus, some resources will be shifted from the production of B to the production of A. If all factors involved are equally productive in the production of either good, factor prices may not change. But this is unlikely; some factors will be more efficient in the production of A and others in the production of B. Hence the prices of factors best suited for the production of A will tend to rise, and those best suited for B will fall; as a consequence, the incomes of the owners of the former set of factors will rise, and those of the owners of the later group will fall. Over a longer period, factors will shift from one use to another more easily than in a shorter period.

Techniques of Production

New inventions produce continuous changes in available techniques of production. These changes alter production functions, the quantities of various factors required to produce a unit of output of particular commodities in the optimum fashion, and the prices of finished products. Consequently, the allocation of factors to the production of various commodities is affected, as well as the prices of commodities and factors (and the distribution of income). For example, suppose that a new technique is developed for the production of glass tableware which lessens the amount of manpower necessary per unit of output, but increases the amounts of certain chemicals required. The reduction in the cost and price of the glassware stimulates increased consumer use, and greater use by the producers of the various ingredients. The quantities of chemicals, silica, and other factors not affected by the technological change will increase; the quantity of labor used will decrease unless increased sales more than offset the substitution of chemicals for manpower. Suppliers of chemicals and other materials will receive increased incomes, at least temporarily, and owners of nonproducible specialized resources used in their production will gain permanently higher incomes. Workers replaced by the new processes will experience declines in wages, unless their skills can be transferred to other industries. The net effects upon factor prices and income distribution will be greatly affected by the ease of transfer of factor units from one line of production to another.

The increased use of glassware will also affect the sales of other products. Sales of direct substitutes, such as plastic dinnerware, will tend to fall, with consequent repercussions on output and factor prices. If the demand for the glassware is relatively inelastic, less money will be spent on the product; and purchases of other unrelated products will rise, with further repercussions on prices, outputs, and factor prices.

Technological changes which make new products available likewise produce modifications in the general equilibrium system. Such products alter consumer preference patterns, the output of substitute and complementary goods, and relative factor prices. The development of the automobile, for example, has had tremendous effects upon the economy. The demand for and output of complementary goods, such as highways, gasoline, tires, etc., have increased greatly, together with facilities to produce them. The demand for and output of substitutes, such as horses, buggies and wagons, streetcars and railway service, have declined. The pattern of location of retail stores and of dwellings has been greatly altered, as well as the nature and location of places of amusement and recreation. Incomes of owners of factors of particular importance in the production of automobiles and the other complementary goods have risen, while those of factor units used primarily to produce the substitutes, and not adaptable to other uses, have fallen. The owners of land containing oil have experienced great increases in their incomes, while owners of land primarily suited to the growing of hay for horses have experienced declines in incomes. The relative incomes of the owners of completely adaptable factors have not been affected by the change.

Changes in Factor Supplies

Changes in factor supplies, either in quantity or in quality, have much the same effects as technological developments. An increase in the quantities of one factor available compared to those of others will alter relative factor prices, optimum factor combinations, and prices and outputs of consumption goods. The prices of goods using relatively large amounts of the factor which has increased in supply will fall relative to those of other commodities, and consumption and output will increase. The price of the factor which has increased in supply will tend to fall, but the total share of income going to the owners of this factor may rise. For example, a growth in the supply of capital goods relative to the quantities of other factors will increase the prices paid for labor and the incomes of the workers, and increase the relative outputs of goods requiring relatively large amounts of capital goods for efficient production.

Changes in Competitive Relationships

Changes in competitive relationships will produce modifications in the equilibrium system. For example, if strong oligopoly replaces pure competition in a particular commodity market, the relative price of the article will rise, and consumption and output will fall. The demand for other commodities will rise if the demand for this commodity is elastic, and will fall if it is inelastic. The owners of firms producing this commodity will obtain greater incomes, as long as they are protected from the entry of new firms into the industry. The reduced employment of other factors in the industry will lead to readjustments in factor prices, and in costs, and thus outputs, of other industries. Changes in competitive relations in factor markets will alter relative factor and commodity prices and the relative outputs of various goods.

Theories of Change in the Determinants of General Equilibrium

In the preceding paragraphs, the types of readjustments which occur when the basic determinants of equilibrium change as a result of forces autonomous to the economic system have been indicated in a general way. Relatively little attention has been given to the question of whether or not a theory of change in the determinants, relating this change to certain forces within or external to the economy, can be developed. A few such attempts have been made. T. R. Malthus, for example, developed a long-term relationship between wage levels and population growth, of such a nature that growth in population and thus labor supply were limited to the rate of increase in subsistence available to the workers.[4] This theory was accepted and developed by various English classical writers subsequent to Ricardo.[5] Joseph Schumpeter attached great importance to the rate of change in the introduction of innovations as the primary factor determining the rate of economic development and hence the rate and pattern of change in the determinants of the equilibrium system.[6] One of the most complete theories of economic development was that of Karl Marx. His basic principle of economic change was the thesis that each form of economic system develops within itself internal inconsistencies, which manifest themselves primarily in struggles between various groups in the economy. These ultimately destroy the particular form of economic system, which gives way to a new form, which in turn develops its own internal inconsistencies.

In recent years, renewed attention has been given to the establishment of theories of economic change and development, particularly with respect to the causes and processes of change in the level of employment, and the determinants of the rate of long-term economic growth in both underdeveloped and more highly developed countries. For some time to come, however, this subject will probably continue to be one of the more highly underdeveloped areas of economic analysis. The problems involved are so complicated and the stock of established factual knowledge so slight that almost any theory can be considered to have some degree of plausibility. And as long as this is true, substantial progress in understanding concrete problems of economic growth is unlikely.

SELECTED REFERENCES

BUSHAW, D. W., AND CLOWER, R. W. *Introduction to Mathematical Economics,* chap. vii. Homewood, Ill.: Irwin, 1959.
　　A recent discussion of the dynamics of general equilibrium.

CASSEL, G. *Theory of Social Economy,* Book I, chap. iv. New York: Harcourt, Brace, 1932.
　　A simple presentation of the general equilibrium model.

COHEN, K. J., AND CYERT, R. M. *Theory of the Firm,* chap. ix. Englewood Cliffs, N.J.: Prentice-Hall, 1965.

---

[4] T. R. Malthus, *Essays on Population* (London, 1798).

[5] Note the summary in W. J. Baumol, *Economic Dynamics* (New York: Macmillan, 1951), chap. ii.

[6] J. Schumpeter, *Theory of Economic Development* (Cambridge: Harvard University Press, 1934).

HICKS, J. R.   *Value and Capital,* chaps. iv–viii.   Oxford: Oxford University Press, 1938.

A classic literary presentation of general equilibrium theory.

PATINKIN, DON.   *Money, Interest and Prices.*   2d ed.   New York: Harper and Row, 1965.

A general equilibrium theory of money, prices, interest, and employment.

PHELPS-BROWN, E. H.   *The Framework of the Pricing System.*   London: Chapman and Hall, 1936.

A more elaborate presentation of general equilibrium theory.

QUESTIONS

1. Distinguish between partial and general equilibrium theory.
2. Trace the probable effects of an improved variety of orange, which allows a great increase in yield per acre, upon:
    a) The price of apples (immediate and long run).
    b) The production of apples (immediate and short run).
    c) The income of the owners of land best suited for (1) the production of oranges, (2) the production of apples.
3. Trace some of the probable effects of the development of nylon, dacron, and orlon shirts upon the prices and outputs of other commodities, and factor prices.
4. When will a change in consumer preferences *permanently* alter factor prices?
5. Explain the budget equation and the allocation-of-consumer-expenditure equation, and explain how the usual demand function is derived from them.
6. What are the two basic general equilibrium equations, from the supply standpoint?
7. What does the "*i*"th equation represent?
8. Does equality of equations and unknowns insure a determinate system? Explain.
9. Is the general equilibrium system regarded as mathematically determinate? On what basis?
10. Note the various assumptions upon which the simplified general equilibrium system is based, and indicate the extent to which these may be modified.
11. What are the advantages and limitations of general equilibrium theory?
12. In what sense is the general equilibrium theory a static theory?
13. Trace the effects on the economy of an improved method of producing helicopters, which would allow the sale of them for $3,000 and would make them as safe as automobiles.
14. Trace through the effect of a shift in demand from oranges to apples.

Chapter
19

LINEAR PROGRAMMING

Few economic problems have simple precise solutions. In the first place, economic phenomena are inherently complicated. This is a result partly of the great variety of goods and services in a modern economy and the difficulty of describing the processes by which they are produced and distributed. That these processes are largely social rather than physical in nature makes an already arduous task even harder. To make matters worse, the technical and institutional framework of economic activity is subject to constant change. In these circumstances, it is not always possible to formulate economic problems in a clear and meaningful way, and it is hardly surprising that specific solutions can seldom be provided for those problems which can be so formulated. In the second place, economics is a relatively young science, and much research effort in economics has traditionally been devoted not to describing the world as it is but rather to prescribing how the world ought to be.

It is an open question whether economic problems will always be as intractable as they appear at present. In recent years, economists have become increasingly aware of the inadequacy of their discipline, and considerable effort has been spent devising ways and means of diminishing the gap between "theory" and "practice." This has included the development, largely since 1930, of a new branch of economics called *econometrics,* which is concerned with the empirical measurement of relations described in general economic theory and, even more recently, the formulation of certain simplified techniques of analysis, commonly referred to as *linear programming,* which are designed to make possible the specific numerical solution of problems which have previously been solvable only in vague qualitative terms. Both of these developments have made possible the use of complex electronic computers in economic research and so the effective handling of problems which, only a few years ago, would have been unmanageable from a computational point of view.

While it is still correct to say that economics as a scientific study is in its infancy, recent advances lend support to the belief that this may not always be so. The purpose of this chapter is to give a brief and necessarily incomplete summary of the basic ideas of linear programming. A similar treatment of econometrics is presented in the chapter that follows.

LINEAR PROGRAMMING AND ECONOMIC ANALYSIS

To appreciate the relation between linear programming and economic analysis, it is helpful to think of the term *programming* as being roughly synonymous with the term *planning*. Almost the whole of microeconomic price theory is concerned with programming in this sense, that is, with the planning behavior of individual consumers and business firms. This is true, in particular, of the consumer choosing among alternative combinations of commodities so as to maximize total satisfaction, the firm choosing among alternative combinations of factor inputs in order to minimize the total cost of any given level of total output, the firm choosing among alternative levels of output in an attempt to maximize total profit, and so forth.

In each of these examples, it should be noticed that nothing is said about the execution of plans. As a general rule, it is simply assumed that an optimal plan (that is, a plan which maximizes satisfaction, minimizes cost, maximizes profit, etc.), once decided upon, can be and is carried into effect. It should also be noticed that the relations in terms of which optimal plans are defined are normally represented geometrically by curves (indifference curves, isoquants, total profit curves, etc.), many of which are not straight lines—that is, by *relations which are nonlinear*. Therefore the planning aspects of microeconomic theory consist primarily of techniques which may be called *nonlinear programming*. The only formal difference between this kind of programming and what is now called linear programming is that in the latter discipline, various kinds of *linear* relations are substituted for the usually nonlinear relations of traditional theory. By this procedure it becomes possible to develop quantitative solutions to various problems.

Establishment of Linear Relations

The way in which linear relations are established varies from case to case and is therefore difficult to describe in general terms. The basic idea is simple, however, and is illustrated in Figure 19–1. If we start

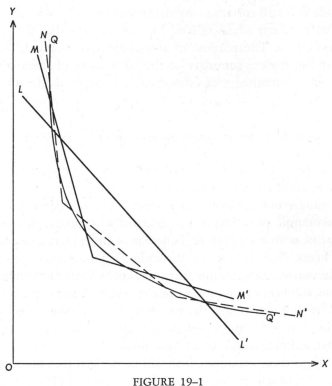

FIGURE 19–1

APPROXIMATION OF CURVE BY PIECEWISE LINEAR RELATIONS

with a curve (say, an isoquant) such as QQ', we may regard the straight line LL' as a rough approximation to QQ'. A better approximation is provided by the broken line MM', and an even better approximation by the dotted line NN', etc. Indeed, if we were to use an unlimited number of line segments, it is clear that the original isoquant QQ' might be approximated to any desired degree of accuracy by means of a "line" with an appropriately large number of "breaks." Or to use a more technical expression, the isoquant might be approximated by a *piecewise linear relation.* Thus, we might say that the difference between traditional programming problems and those considered in the modern linear programming literature is a result of the substitution of piecewise linear relations for the nonlinear relations of traditional theory. This is not the whole story; but as we shall see later, it is a significant part of the explanation of the outward differences between linear programming and programming of the kind described in traditional price theory.

Scope of Linear Programming

The first explicit use of linear programming techniques occurred in connection with the planning activities of the United States Air Force during the period immediately following World War II, and involved problems similar to those confronting a large business firm.[1] As often happens, however, the development of novel tools of analysis suggested applications in other fields that were quite different from those to which the tools were initially intended to apply.

Broadly speaking, linear programming is concerned with the solution of practical and theoretical problems in which some quantity (profit, income, the value of national product, aggregate transportation cost, travel time, etc.) is to be maximized or minimized, subject to the condition that various technical, institutional, and financial restraints are also satisfied. The subject thus includes, as one case, the types of problems in traditional theory that involve rational choice among a set of alternative possible plans. But it includes much more than this; many problems which at first sight do not look like planning problems at all can be treated *as if* they were planning problems, and so may be formulated and solved with the same kinds of techniques as those used to solve the planning problems of individual households or firms. For example, linear programming has been applied with considerable success to broad questions of economic development, interregional trade, general equilibrium analysis, and welfare economics.

LINEAR PROGRAMMING: SOME EXAMPLES

Some specific examples of linear programming problems will help clarify the nature of the methods that are used and their relation to the methods of general economic analysis. For the sake of simplicity, the examples presented below are drawn mainly from the realm of business practice, but it should be emphasized that the range of problems that can be handled with these and closely related techniques is much wider than the examples might suggest.

The Selection of an Optimal Diet

A cattle producer seeks to fatten steers for market in the most economical way while meeting various nutritional requirements to

[1] Full details are given in the fundamental paper of G. B. Dantzig, "Maximization of a Linear Function of Variables Subject to Linear Inequalities," *Activity Analysis of Production and Allocation* (T. C. Koopmans, ed.) (New York: Wiley, 1951), pp. 339–47.

insure high quality of the final product. The cattleman has a choice among various mixtures of two foods, hay and cottonseed cake. Both foods contain a certain quantity of one or more of four nutrients (protein, minerals, vitamins, and calories), so the use of a sufficient quantity of one or both foods will guarantee the satisfaction of any given set of nutritional requirements. Confronted with fixed prices for each of the two foods, the problem of the farmer is to choose a *feasible diet* (i.e., a diet satisfying certain minimal nutrition requirements) which minimizes the total cost of feeding a steer.

The essentials of the problem are illustrated in Figure 19–2. Any combination of hay and cottonseed cake represented by a point on or to the right of the line P is assumed to satisfy the *minimum* protein requirement (the slope of the line reflects the relative proportions of protein in the two foods); all other points represent food combinations that fail to satisfy this requirement. Similarly, the *minimum* mineral requirement is satisfied by diets corresponding to points on or to the right of the line M; this requirement is not satisfied by points to the left

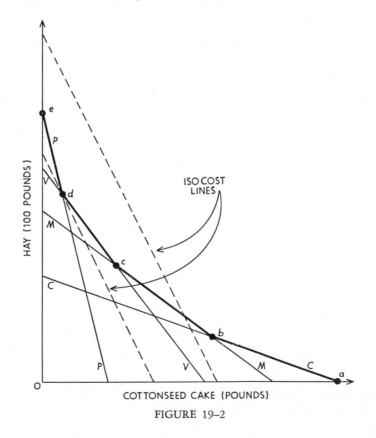

FIGURE 19–2

of the line *M*. Finally, the *minimum* vitamin requirement is satisfied by points on or to the right of the line *V*, and the *minimum* calory requirement is satisfied by points on or to the right of the line *C*. Neither requirement is satisfied at points that lie to the left of both of the lines *V* and *C*. All points on or to the right of the heavy line *abcde* thus represent combinations of cottonseed cake and hay which satisfy all four of the minimum nutrition requirements simultaneously. Any point to the left of the heavy line, however, clearly represents a combination of foods that fails to satisfy one or more of these same minimum requirements. The heavy line thus represents what might be called the lower boundary of *feasible* diets. This boundary is, indeed, a piecewise linear relation of the sort described earlier, and represents a kind of production isoquant in which "nutrition" is the "output" produced. Diets represented by points to the right of this boundary are, in a sense, wasteful of nutrients; more food is contained in such diets than is strictly necessary for fattening purposes. Diets represented by points on the boundary, on the other hand, are just large enough, in the nutrient-producing sense, to insure that cattle are fattened in an appropriate way.

Now, suppose that the unit cost of cottonseed cake and the unit cost of hay are known and constant, regardless of quantity purchased. The various diets that can be purchased for any given level of total cost can be represented graphically by points on an isocost line of the kind shown in Figure 19–2. The cattle producer's problem is to choose a combination of foods on the boundary of feasible diet combinations, line *abcde*, for which total cost is as small as possible. In the present example, such a combination is represented by the point *d* in Figure 19–2, since any other point on the boundary *abcde* will lie on a higher isocost line.

There is a clear analogy between this problem and that of a firm choosing a combination of factor inputs so as to minimize total cost for a given level of output (see Chapter 6); indeed, the main difference is that the present boundary of feasible diets is kinked, whereas the boundary of feasible input combinations in ordinary theory is represented by a smooth isoquant. But there is a considerable gap between principle and practice in the two problems. Whereas existing computational techniques can be used to obtain an explicit numerical answer to the linear programming problem even in cases involving as many as fifty foods and eighty nutrients, the analogous problem as posed in ordinary economic theory is ordinarily solvable only in principle. The difference between the two cases lies in the more specialized character of the assumptions underlying the linear programming problem. This would be of no practical advantage if the special assumptions were flatly inconsistent with practical experience, but the truth is that these restrictions are in fair accord with factual knowledge in a surprisingly large number of instances.

Choosing an Efficient Production Process

The manager of a grain warehouse must arrange for the loading and unloading of a certain number of boxcars each month. Two technically efficient processes are available for this purpose, one involving the use of a motor-driven conveyer belt, the other involving the use of motor-driven grain shovels. The major expenses associated with both processes are fuel and labor costs, but fifty tons of grain per hour can be loaded or unloaded by the conveyor process using three gallons of fuel and one man-hour of labor, whereas two man-hours of labor and one gallon of fuel are required to perform the same task with the shovel process.

The essential characteristics of the two processes are illustrated in Figure 19–3 by the lines OC and OS and the related production isoquants, showing, for each process taken separately, the various combinations of fuel and labor that are required to move either 50 or 100 tons of wheat per hour. If both processes can be used simultaneously, however, certain fuel-labor combinations other than those illustrated can be used to move a given amount of grain. If the conveyor

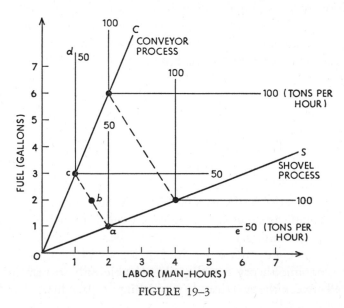

FIGURE 19–3

process is used to move 25 out of a required 50 tons an hour, for example, the remaining 25 tons must be moved by the shovel process. The total fuel requirement would then be two gallons (1½ gallons for the conveyor process and one-half gallon for the shovel process), and the total labor requirement would be 1½ man-hours (half a man-hour for the conveyor process and one man-hour for the shovel process). This combination is represented in Figure 19–3 by the point *b* on the dotted line joining points *a* and *c*. All mixtures of the two processes that would result in the moving of 50 tons of grain per hour are represented by points on this dotted line. Where a mixture of processes is possible, therefore, the production "isoquant" for grain movements of 50 tons per hour is represented by the broken line *eabcd,* and fuel-labor combinations which will permit loading of other quantities of grain can of course be represented by isoquants of the same form. The curve for 100 tons per hour is illustrated on the same figure.

If the warehouse manager is interested in minimizing the total cost of any required grain-moving operation, it is clear that the choice between the two processes (or a combination of the two) will depend on the relative costs of fuel and labor. The present problem is precisely the same as that of the cost-minimizing firm considered in Chapter 6, except that the number of available "processes" is limited to two. The production isoquants of the warehouse problem would have three "kinks" rather than two if three different processes were available, ten "kinks" if ten processes were available, 500 "kinks" if 500 processes were available, and so forth. The corresponding problem described in Chapter 6 may thus be regarded as the limiting case in which the number of available processes is infinite, making the kinks in the isoquant so close together that it appears as a smooth curve. As in the case of the diet problem considered earlier, the merit of the linear programming statement of the problem is that it permits extremely complicated practical problems to be formulated and solved in situations where the more general approach of traditional economic theory could not provide specific answers.

Selection of an Efficient Shipping Schedule

A manufacturer of aluminum sheets operates three separate plants, one in Chicago, one in Detroit, and one in Seattle. The sheets are sold in 20 different markets, located in various parts of the United States and Canada, to buyers who place a high value on prompt delivery. The manufacturer's total output capacity, taking the three plants together, is sufficient to meet any reasonable level of demand, but it is not always possible to satisfy demand in a given area by sending sheets from a plant in the same general locality. In any case, shipping costs do not depend simply on distance and weight, but also vary with the region. Given the demand in each market, therefore, the manufacturer has to determine what quantity of steel to ship from each of the three plants to each of the 20 markets in order to meet the given demands and, at the same time, minimize total shipping cost.

This problem is much too complicated to be represented in diagrammatic form. Like the two previous examples, however, it can be formulated and solved very easily using linear programming techniques.

That the correct solution to a problem of this sort is not easy to attain by nonmathematical techniques may be indicated by a simple example involving two factories and three markets. The relevant information is presented schematically in Figure 19–4. The letter S refers to capacity outputs (in tons); the letter D, to market demands (in tons); and the letter C, to shipping costs (in dollars).

At first sight it appears that the cheapest way to supply the requirements of the three markets is to allocate factory shipments in accordance with absolute shipping costs. If this procedure is followed, four units of output will be shipped from factory A to market I at a total cost of $12, and the remaining four units of output available from factory A will be shipped to market II at a total cost of $24. The total cost of shipping the output of factory A to markets I and II will thus be $36. In order to fulfill the remaining requirements of markets II and

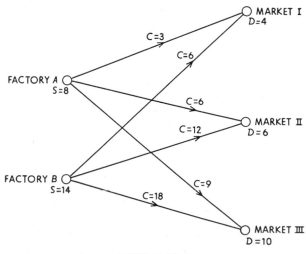

FIGURE 19–4

III, it will be necessary to ship two units of output from factory B to market II at a total cost of $24, and to ship ten units of output from factory B to market III at a total cost of $180. The total cost of distributing the output of factory B to markets II and III (two units of output remaining unsold) will thus be $204. With the total cost of distributing output from factory A ($36) added to this figure, overall shipping costs are $240.

To see that this is not the cheapest way of supplying the requirements of the three markets, we only need to notice that a transfer of one unit of the output of factory A from market I to market III will add $6 to total shipping costs ($9 per unit shipped instead of $3); but if one unit of output of factory B is simultaneously transferred from market III to market I, this will *reduce* total shipping costs by $12 ($6 per unit shipped instead of $18). With both transfers together, $6 can be saved for each unit of output of factory A that is transferred from market I to market III. Since a similar saving will be associated with every such transfer, total shipping costs can be reduced by $24 if the requirements of market I are met entirely by factory B, while a portion of the requirements of market III (namely, four units out of a total requirement of ten units) is met by shipments from factory A. If this rearrangement of shipments is carried out, total shipping costs will be reduced from $240 to $216.

But this is not the end of the matter, for total shipping costs can be reduced even more if another portion of the requirements of market III is met by shipments from factory A (shipments from factory A to market II being replaced by shipments from factory B to market II). The reasons for this is that $9 in shipping cost is saved on each unit of output sent from factory A rather than factory B to market III, whereas only $6 is added to shipping cost for each unit of output that is sent to market II from factory B instead of factory A ($12 per unit from factory B as compared with $6 per unit from factory A). Total shipping cost will therefore be reduced $3 for each unit of output of factory A that is transferred from market II to market III. A total of four units of output can be transferred in this way (factory A produces only eight units in total, and four of these units are already sent to market III). If this transfer is carried out, therefore, total shipping costs will be reduced by $12, from a previous level of $216 to a new level of $204.

This procedure leads to a pattern of shipments that is optimal from the standpoint of minimizing total shipping cost. The final result involves the shipment of the entire output of factory A (eight units) to market III at a total cost of $72. The requirements of markets I and II are then met by shipments from factory B: Four units of output are shipped to market I at a total cost of $24, and six units of output are sent to market II at a total cost of $72. Finally, two units of output are shipped from factory B to market III at a total cost of $36. Total shipping costs are then $204 ($72 + $24 + $72 + $36). This figure cannot be reduced by any rearrangement of shipments without violating the requirement that demand be satisfied in all markets (total demand must, of course, be less than or equal to total supply, or no optimal shipping pattern is possible; but there is no requirement that supply from both factories be exhausted in shipments to the three markets).

The optimal shipping pattern is represented more concisely in Table 19–1, the amount shipped from factory A to market II being

TABLE 19–1

OPTIMUM SHIPPING PATTERN

Factory	Market I	Market II	Market III
A....................0		0	8
B....................4		6	2

shown by the entry "0," from factory B to market II by the entry "6," and so forth. The surprising thing is that the optimal shipping schedule is one in which the cheapest route (from factory A to market I) is *not* used, while the most expensive route (from factory B to market II) is used.

This example is sufficiently simple to permit the optimal solution to be determined by trial-and-error methods. Even the addition of one additional factory or market would make the problem much more difficult to solve by this procedure. Problems vastly more complicated can be formulated and solved in a completely routine fashion, however, by linear programming methods. The essence of the linear programming method lies in the *systematic* comparison of alternative shipping patterns in terms of cost criteria. Instead of relying on commonsense calculations, the linear programming technique involves the application of specific rules which guarantee that an optimal shipping pattern will be discovered after a finite number of comparisons. By contrast, the trial-and-error method followed above, while it may lead to an optimal solution in a few steps in simplified situations, may entail an endless and unsuccessful search for an optimal shipping pattern if the problem is at all complicated. Whereas trial-and-error methods may take hours or even weeks of calculation, linear programming techniques permit the use of electronic computers which can provide an answer to extremely complex problems in just a few seconds.

THE TECHNIQUE OF LINEAR PROGRAMMING

The general principles of linear programming are best described by restating one of the preceding examples in mathematical form.

The diet problem is particularly appropriate for this purpose. We may begin by representing quantities of cottonseed cake and hay, respectively, by the symbols x_1 and x_2, and the corresponding dollar prices of these goods by p_1 and p_2. The total dollar cost of any given combination of the two goods is then given by the expression

$$(1) \; C = p_1 x_1 + p_2 x_2 , \qquad •$$

where C represents the number of dollars spent. This is called a *linear equation* in the variables x_1 and x_2 because, for any constant value of the variable C, the expression $C = p_1 x_1 + p_2 x_2$ is represented geometrically by a straight line, as illustrated by the isocost lines in Figure 19–2.

The problem of the cattle producer is not simply to choose values of x_1 and x_2, that is, quantities of cottonseed cake and hay, that make C as small as possible. In the first place, the producer's range of choice is limited by the requirement that purchases of cottonseed cake and hay be nonnegative, since negative purchases are impossible. This condition is expressed mathematically by writing the expressions

$$(2) \; x_1 \geqq 0 , \qquad x_2 \geqq 0 .$$

That is x_1 and x_2 must be equal to or in excess of zero. Geometrically, these conditions require that points representing feasible diets lie to the right of the "hay axis" and above the "cottonseed cake axis" in Figure 19–2. The conditions are called *inequalities* because they require that certain numbers (namely, x_1 and x_2) be *different from rather than equal to* a certain given constant (namely, zero). More precisely, the two inequalities are called *linear inequalities* because in the limiting case $x_1 = 0$, $x_2 = 0$ for which the conditions are barely satisfied, the relations $x_1 = 0$ and $x_2 = 0$ are represented geometrically by straight lines (namely, the lines corresponding to the "hay axis" and "cottonseed cake axis," respectively).

In the second place, the producer's range of choice is limited by certain nutrition requirements as well as the requirement that total cost be minimized. Specifically, we may suppose that the minimum quantity of protein required is represented by a number b_1, the minimum quantity of minerals by a number b_2, the minimum quantity of vitamins by b_3, and the minimum quantity of calories by b_4. Similarly, we may suppose that the quantity of protein contained in a unit quantity of cottonseed cake is represented by a given number a_{11}, the quantity of protein contained in a unit quantity of hay by a number a_{12}, the quantity of minerals contained in a unit of cottonseed cake by a number a_{21}, and so on (there are eight of these numbers in total, since there are two foods and each food contains some quantity, perhaps zero, of each of the four nutrients). The various nutrition requirements may then be expressed mathematically by writing the four linear inequalities

$$(3) \quad \begin{cases} a_{11}x_1 + a_{12}x_2 \geqq b_1 & \text{(protein requirement)} \\ a_{21}x_1 + a_{22}x_2 \geqq b_2 & \text{(mineral requirement)} \\ a_{31}x_1 + a_{32}x_2 \geqq b_3 & \text{(vitamin requirement)} \\ a_{41}x_1 + a_{42}x_2 \geqq b_4 & \text{(calory requirement)} \end{cases}$$

Taken in combination, the inequalities (3) define the lower boundary of feasible diets described by the heavy line *abcde* in Figure 19–2 (relevant portions of this figure are reproduced below as Figure 19–5). More specifically, each separate inequality in (3) *directly* represents an *area* on or to the right of one of the dashed lines in Figure 19–5. Taken as a group, therefore, the four inequalities in (3) *indirectly* describe an area of Figure 19–5 within which points representing feasible diets *do not lie* i.e., the area to the *left* of the heavy line *abcde* in Figure 19–5. The upper boundary of this area of nonfeasible diets, i.e., the line *abcde* itself, is therefore the *lower* boundary of *feasible* diets.

The term *linear inequality* is used to describe each of the relations in (3) because, in the special case in which x_1 and x_2 have values for which the requirements are barely satisfied, that is, values such that the four equations

$$a_{i1}x_1 + a_{i2}x_2 = b_i \quad (i = 1, 2, 3, 4)$$

are satisfied, the equations describing this situation are presented geometrically by straight lines. In less formal terms, each of the inequalities in (3) describes an area in Figure 19–5 that lies on or to the right of one of the dashed lines; the inequalities are referred to as linear inequalities because the area described by any single inequality is bounded on the left by a straight line.

The diet problem may now be stated as that of choosing a pair of numbers x_1, x_2, that minimizes the value of the linear equation

$$C = p_1x_1 + p_2x_2 ,$$

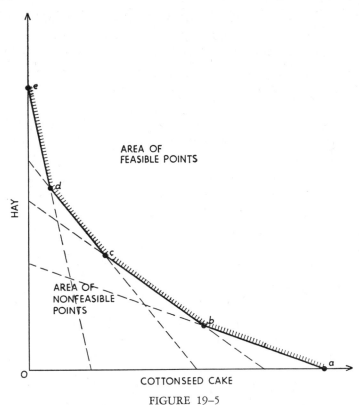

FIGURE 19–5

<small>AREAS OF FEASIBLE AND NONFEASIBLE DIETS DEFINED BY LINEAR INEQUALITIES</small>

subject to the condition that the same numbers x_1, x_2, also satisfy the set of six linear inequalities (2) and (3).

The solution of the problem (already presented graphically in Figure 19–2) will clearly depend on the values of the constants that appear in the statement of the problem, that is, on the values of the numbers $a_{11}, a_{12}, \ldots, a_{41}, a_{42}, b_1, b_2, b_3, b_4, p_1$, and p_2. That is to say, the numbers $\bar{x}_1$, $\bar{x}_2$ representing an *optimal diet* will depend on the form and position of the boundary of feasible diets and on the slope of the isocost line, which is to say that $\bar{x}_1$ and $\bar{x}_2$ will depend on the nutritional content of the two foods, minimal nutrition requirements, and the money prices of the foods purchased. As a general rule, an unlimited number of possible pairs of positive numbers x_1 and x_2 will satisfy the nutrition requirements (i.e., the linear inequalities [3]); but only one such pair will also satisfy the requirement that total cost be minimized. It is this *particular* pair of numbers that is denoted by $\bar{x}_1, \bar{x}_2$, and referred to as an *optimal diet*. Other diets that satisfy (2) and (3) are also *feasible* (nonfeasible diets are simply excluded from consideration); but the *optimal diet* is that particular feasible diet which makes the value of C in an equation (1) smaller than any alternative feasible diet.[2]

More Complex Problems

The simple diet problem is probably easier to solve graphically than by using computer techniques. But suppose that we wished to consider a similar problem involving, say, ten foods and fifteen nutritional elements; that is, suppose that the problem required choosing positive or zero values of the ten variables $x_1, x_2, \ldots, x_{10}$ so as to minimize the value of a linear equation

$$C = p_1 x_1 + p_2 x_2 + \cdots + p_{10} x_{10} ,$$

subject to fifteen linear inequalities of the same form as those given in (3), above. All of the examples given previously and, indeed, all other linear programming problems, can be expressed in essentially this way. An electronic computer would have no more difficulty with this problem than with one involving only two variables and three inequalities; but no such statement could be applied to a human being armed with pencil and paper! We cannot even visualize geometrically a problem that involves more than three basic variables.

The technique of linear programming involves much more, of course, than the mere feeding of information into hungry computers. The most interesting and important problems of linear programming are not mathematical or computational in character but are concerned instead with the task of interpreting concrete situations in such a way as to make them amenable to linear programming analysis. As a general rule, problems of planning that arise in actual practice do not lend themselves directly to treatment by linear programming techniques. First, it is seldom an easy matter to define a specific objective. A business firm, for example, may wish to maximize its long-run profit and, at the same time, maximize short-run payments to stockholders, but these two goals may not be consistent with one another. Similarly a state government wishing to maximize the "welfare" of its citizens must choose among a wide array of alternative indicators of "welfare" (aggregate income, per capita income, leisure, property values, etc.). Second, even if a specific objective is defined, it may be difficult to discover the restraints which are operative in a particular situation, that

[2] If the slope of the isocost line is the same as the slope of one of the lines in terms of which the boundary of feasible diets is defined, an infinite number of different diets will minimize total cost. But this is a special case.

is to say, what legal, social, financial, and other conditions should be taken into account in pursuing the given objective. Third, even if a specific objective is defined and a given set of restraints is known to apply, the restraints may not be directly expressible as linear inequalities. In actual practice, *precise* linearity of relevant restraints is more likely to be the exception than the rule. Finally, if linearity assumptions appear reasonable, it is always a major task to estimate relevant values of the various constant coefficients that enter into a linear programming problem (e.g., prices, nutrition requirements, capacity limitations, final demands, etc.). Once a problem is formulated, the task of finding an answer, or discovering whether an answer is possible, is largely a matter of routine computation which may be done with any one of several standard techniques (the so-called *simplex method* is perhaps the one most frequently used at the present time). But the task of formulation is another matter altogether. Vast ingenuity and intellectual boldness are prime characteristics of the successful linear programming expert.

INPUT-OUTPUT ANALYSIS AND OTHER APPLICATIONS

Before this chapter is concluded it is desirable to describe briefly some applications of linear programming to problems outside the range of individual business practice. Two major areas of application will be considered: input-output analysis and interindustry economics. Linear programming techniques have also been used to deal with problems in general equilibrium theory and in theoretical welfare economics. But the latter applications involve little more than the substitution of linear for nonlinear production functions and similar features of traditional theory. This has sometimes led to interesting results, but not to anything of sufficient novelty to merit separate treatment in this book.

The Theoretical Structure of Input-Output Analysis

The theoretical framework of input-output analysis is an area of economics which is largely the creation of the Harvard economist Wassily Leontief. The original purpose of the analysis was to present the essence of general equilibrium theory in a simplified form suitable for empirical study. In terms of techniques however, input-output analysis is a special case of modern linear programming. In every linear programming problem, two steps can be distinguished. First, a set of feasible plans has to be selected, that is to say, a set of plans which satisfy certain given nutrition, capacity, or other requirements. Second from the possibly very large set of feasible plans, a particular plan (of at least a more limited set of plans) has to be selected which minimizes or maximizes some quantity such as cost, output, etc. From the standpoint of technique, input-output analysis is the special case of linear programming in which the set of feasible plans, to be determined in the first step of a linear programming problem, *contains only a single plan.* This means that the second step does not need to be carried out; there is no problem of choosing among alternative feasible plans because there is only one feasible plan. The reasons for this will be explained more fully below. In terms of scope, input-output analysis is concerned with the entire economy, while much linear programming deals with problems of more restricted range.

The account which follows refers mainly to the foundations of the original version of input-output analysis. Recent developments by Leontief and his co-workers, as well as by other persons, are too varied and complex to be summarized here.[3]

As indicated above, the first stage in the development of input-output analysis involves little more than a simplification of traditional general equilibrium theory: specifically, the replacement of traditionally nonlinear relations by corresponding linear equations. The economy is initially divided into a relatively small number of segments, each including industries producing closely related products (from the standpoint of factor inputs). Equations are then introduced relating the output of each industry to the outputs of the industries using the product of this industry, and to final, autonomous demand.

In order to make the system manageable, several simplifying assumptions are made:

1. Given coefficients of production. That is to say, fixed quantities of various factors are necessary to produce a unit of output of a commodity.
2. Linear production functions. Thus a certain percentage change in the output of one product entails the same percentage change in the inputs of the various factors used to produce it.
3. Given factor supplies, consumer demands, and prices. Prices are not variables in the system, which is concerned solely with output adjustments.

Given these assumptions, the output of each sector depends directly upon the outputs of all sectors which utilize its product, and

---

[3] A good elementary account of some of the developments is presented in R. Dorfman, P. Samuelson, and R. Solow, *Linear Programming and Economic Analysis* (New York: McGraw-Hill, 1958), chap. ix.

upon final consumer and government demands. The assumed linear nature of the equations insures that, for example, an increase of 10 percent in the output of all industries using steel will result in an increase of 10 percent in steel input, and thus in a 10 percent increase in the output of steel, provided, of course, that the maximum output of steel possible with existing capacity is not exceeded. Since there is one equation for each sector product relating its output to the outputs of other sectors, there is the same number of equations as there are unknowns (the outputs of each sector), and the system is mathematically solvable under appropriate conditions. If available factor supplies and final consumer demands, as well as the production functions, are known, it is thus possible, to determine the equilibrium outputs of all sectors. As a rule, various possible levels of output of the various sectors will be mutually consistent with one another; but only one set of activity levels will be consistent with the actual factor supplies and consumer demands existing at a certain time.

Empirical Content

The second and more difficult step in input-output analysis is to give empirical content to the theoretical framework by determining actual magnitudes in the various equations. A substantial amount of work of this type has been done in the last decade, partly by government agencies or under government auspices, and partly by nongovernmental research organizations. The task is a tremendous one, partly because of inadequacy of data; but much progress has been made. As the elements in the equations are given magnitudes, it becomes possible to trace the quantitative effects upon various sectors of changes in the determinants, such as consumer demand, factor supplies, or governmental purchases. Particular use has been made of the analysis in estimating the reductions in output of civilian goods which would be necessary to allow a given output of military equipment in case of war, and the extent of production for military purposes which would be possible with a maximum feasible reduction in output of goods for civilian use.

Limitations to the Analysis

Despite its contributions, input-output analysis as it now stands is subject to serious limitations. The basic problem is that of the development of equations which are simple enough to be manageable, yet sufficiently refined to reflect to an adequate extent the actual behavior of the economy. The assumption of linear equations, relating outputs of one industry to outputs of others in a unique fashion, is obviously somewhat unrealistic. Increases in output do not in many cases require proportionate increases in input, mainly because of indivisibilities of various factors. The assumption of fixed production coefficients precludes the possibility of factor substitution. Even in a short-run period, some substitutions may be possible; and over a longer period the opportunities for substitution are likely to be relatively great. As a result, it is possible to maintain outputs of some goods at higher levels than would be possible on the basis of given production coefficients when materials currently used in the production of these products are diverted in part to other uses. For example, during World War II, it was possible to maintain production of office filing cabinets by making them from wood when steel supplies were diverted to war production. Theoretically, of course, the equations could be redesigned to introduce the possibility of factor substitutions, but to do so would tremendously complicate the task of establishing the magnitudes in the equations.

The assumption of fixed relationships between outputs of various sectors likewise precludes the possibility of increases or decreases in inventories; as a consequence, changes in inventories which actually occur as production levels change will prevent the attainment of the exact results anticipated on the basis of the analysis. The time factor—the lag between inputs and outputs—is also ignored. This is of little consequence in the continuous flow of a static situation, but is significant when changes in rates of output occur. The fact that different firms in a sector will employ diverse production techniques is also a complicating factor, since changes in outputs by various firms will have different effects upon the inputs of particular factors. Finally, the treatment of investment demand is a troublesome one. It is obvious that inputs of capital goods are not related in a proportionate fashion to changes in outputs of products. Some attempts have been made to develop a relationship between investment input and the *rate of change* in the outputs of the products, but this task is by no means simple. More commonly, input-output analysis has been based upon the assumption that investment is an autonomous variable, a procedure which simplifies the system but lessens the significance of its results.

Actual progress in the development of the analysis is of course retarded by lack of adequate knowledge about consumer demand and production technology. Information about both of these is necessary for satisfactory determination of actual magnitudes in the system.

Interindustry Economics

When substantial changes occur in patterns of production, as in periods of rapid technological change or economic growth, neither traditional price theory nor standard linear programming or input-output analysis is adequate for analyzing and resolving the many practical problems that arise. On the one hand, a detailed knowledge is needed of the structure of the economic system and of alternative production patterns; on the other hand, a technique of analysis is required which lends itself to concrete interpretation. The term *interindustry economics* or *activity analysis* is used to describe a broad collection of theoretical tools representing a judicious blend of linear programming, input-output, and general equilibrium theory, which have some of the desired properties. Strictly speaking, interindustry analysis is simply an elaborate kind of general programming technique, not necessarily linear or nonlinear. It differs from ordinary linear programming and input-output analysis only as regards matters of degree, not matters of substance. But the difference in the degree of complexity is such that a broader term is required to describe what is involved; hence the expression *interindustry economics* or *activity analysis.*

The main use of interindustry studies is to facilitate the formulation of programs of action by governments and large business firms. For this purpose, it is essential to begin with a fairly detailed knowledge of interrelations among various industries and among various geographical sectors of the economy. Then, for some appropriately defined goal or set of goals, a tentative selection among alternative courses of action is made. Since this analysis is extremely intricate and involves the estimation of a large number of empirical quantities, it is peculiarly subject to error. It is therefore important to review the effects of any measures that are actually put into operation, to evaluate the accuracy of the predictions which led initially to the recommendation of these measures, and to develop revised programs of action in the light of realized results.

Interindustry techniques have been used successfully in certain large-scale prediction problems (for example, to predict changing patterns of interregional trade among various sectors of the United States economy), and also in the formulation of plans and priorities for economic development programs in such countries as Italy, the Argentine, Colombia, India, Liberia, and Japan.

Much remains to be accomplished on the theoretical as well as the empirical level before a clear appraisal of the power of these techniques will be possible. Already, however, the work of such persons as Hollis Chenery of Harvard and L. H. Moses of Northwestern[4] demonstrates that this approach to applied economics can be extremely fruitful. One of its more significant aspects is that it sheds considerable light upon the factual realism of ordinary economic theory. As the approach is developed further and applied to broader areas of the economy, it is to be expected that the currently extensive cloud of factual ignorance surrounding conventional economic theory will be gradually diminished.

SELECTED REFERENCES

BAUMOL, W. J. "Activity Analysis in One Lesson," *American Economic Review,* Vol. 48 (December, 1958), pp. 837–73.

A balanced and clear presentation of linear programming and related topics, emphasizing theoretical applications.

BENNION, E. G. *Elementary Mathematics of Linear Programming and Game Theory.* East Lansing: Bureau of Business and Economic Research, Michigan State University, 1960.

A mastery exposition of the mathematical essentials of linear programming.

CHARNES, A.; COOPER, W. W.; AND HENDERSON, A. *An Introduction to Linear Programming.* New York: Wiley, 1953.

CHENERY, H. B., AND CLARK, P. G. *Interindustry Economics.* New York: Wiley, 1959.

A comprehensive survey of the theory and application of interindustry techniques.

DORFMAN, R. "The Nature and Significance of Input-Output," *Review of Economics and Statistics,* Vol. 36 (May, 1954), pp. 121–33.

An excellent brief review of the nature and development of input-output analysis.

——, SAMUELSON, P.; AND SOLOW, R. *Linear Programming and Economic Analysis.* New York: McGraw-Hill, 1958.

An almost encyclopedic account of linear programming, sometimes elementary, sometimes advanced; destined to be a classic in the field.

GALE, DAVID. *The Theory of Linear Economic Models.* New York: McGraw-Hill, 1960.

---

[4] Extensive references to Chenery's work are given in H. B. Chenery and P. G. Clark, *Interindustry Economics* (New York: Wiley, 1959). Professor Moses' most recent and impressive contribution to interindustry economics is "A General Equilibrium Model of Production, Interregional Trade, and Location of Industry," *Review of Economics and Statistics,* Vol. 42 (November, 1960), pp. 373–97.

    A relatively advanced account of the theory of linear economic models and of the mathematical tools required for professional work in this area.

HICKS, J. R. "Linear Theory," *Economic Journal,* Vol. 70 (December, 1960), pp. 671–709.
    A review of linear programming by a leading British economist.

LEONTIEF, W. W. *The Structure of the American Economy, 1919–1939.* New York: Oxford University Press, 1951.
    The basic conceptual and empirical framework of input-output analysis.

QUESTIONS

1. Describe in commonsense terms the relations between linear programming and standard economic analysis.

2. What is a "piecewise" linear relation? Is a straight line a piecewise linear relation? The perimeter of a triangle? The perimeter of a circle?

3. Linear programming is described by one writer as "a problem-solving technique intended to provide specific numerical answers to practical questions about the best way to accomplish a given objective." Is this a fair description of linear programming? Discuss.

4. A certain Siamese cat will eat either milk or cat food. In order to remain sleek and fit, the cat requires a minimum of 20 units of protein and 30 units of fat per day. A quart of milk costs 25 cents and contains 40 units of protein and 70 units of fat. A can of cat food costs 15 cents and contains 15 units of protein and 40 units of fat. If the owner of the cat wishes to minimize daily feeding cost, what mixture of milk and cat food should be given to the beast? (Provide an approximate solution to the problem, using geometrical techniques).

5. Given the following information about transportation costs per ton, output capacities, and market of demands, what pattern of shipments will minimize the total cost of transporting goods from factory to market? (Hint: The optimal shipping pattern entails a total cost of $390).

| | Factory | | |
Market	A	B	Market Demand
I.	$ 5	$10	20
II.	$10	$ 6	10
III.	$20	$15	14 \
Capacity	25	19	44

6. Considered geometrically, the inequalities $y \leqq x$, $y \geqq 0$, $x \geqq 0$ represents a certain area in the xy plane. Describe the area in words. Are all of these inequalities linear?

7. What is meant by a feasible solution to a linear programming problem? How does a feasible solution differ from an optimal solution?

8. Consider the linear inequality $3x_1 \; 4x_2 \leqq 6$. Is this inequality satisfied when $x_1 = 1$ and $x_2 = 1$? When $x_1 = 1$ and $x_2 = \frac{1}{2}$? Draw a graph to illustrate the meaning of the inequality.

9. Give a geometrical example of a nonlinear inequality. (Hint: What is meant by the phrase "the collection of goods A is preferred to the collection of goods B in connection with the theory of consumer preference"?)

10. What are some of the practical difficulties that are likely to arise in any attempt to formulate a concrete problem in linear programming terms?

11. Explain the nature of input-output analysis.

12. Input-output analysis is described in the text as a special kind of linear programming problem. In what sense is this statement true? To the extent that the statement is true, does it mean that input-output analysis is somehow inferior to linear programming? Discuss.

13. How do the equations of input-output analysis differ from those of general equilibrium theory?

14. Are prices or quantities, or both, variables in input-output analysis? Explain.

15. What are the major limitations to input-output analysis?

16. Describe some of the general characteristics of interindustry analysis.

17. What are some of the more important applications of interindustry analysis?

Chapter 20　ECONOMETRICS

Econometrics may be described as "the branch of economics in which economic theory and statistical methods are fused in the analysis of numerical and institutional data."[1] Interpreted broadly, this description suggests that there is no difference between econometrics and empirically oriented economic analysis. Indeed, the literal meaning of the word *econometrics* is "economic measurement," and this is the main task of all empirical research in economics.

As a matter of practice, however, the word *econometrics* is ordinarily used to refer only to empirical research that is concerned with the measurement of data involved in economic relationships which have been formulated in explicitly mathematical terms. From this point of view, econometrics is best regarded as an applied branch of mathematical economics. Any economic relationship that can be expressed as a mathematical equation may thus be considered a potential object of econometric study. Such relationships include supply and demand schedules, production functions, equations and inequalities used in linear programming problems, and so forth. However, econometrics does not include (at least at the present time) relations involving social and psychological data; some phenomena simply do not lend themselves to explicit mathematical treatment.

To state the matter another way, we may say that econometrics is concerned with the empirical measurement of economic relations that are sufficiently simple to be expressible in mathematical form. The potential scope of econometrics, thus conceived, is relatively broad. At the present time, it obviously cannot provide all the answers to economic questions, or even most of them. However, econometrics is clearly a potentially promising approach to the study of economic phenomena. This chapter seeks to explain the nature of the econometric

[1] W. C. Hood and T. C. Koopmans (eds.), *Studies in Econometric Method* (New York: Wiley, 1953), p. xv.

approach, some of its basic concepts and methods, and its merits and weaknesses.

THE PURPOSE AND SCOPE OF ECONOMETRICS

The introductory section indicated the general nature of econometrics; this section will review the purpose and scope in greater detail, and the subsequent sections will be devoted to the general approach and the types of techniques employed.

The Nature and Purpose of Econometrics

A hypothetical example will help clarify the basic features and objectives of econometric study. Suppose that the government plans to initiate a crop-restriction program in order to raise farm prices and increase farm incomes. Historical data on average farm production and average market prices are available on an annual basis for a number of years. An examination of these data indicates that a particular volume of production sometimes sells at one level of price and sometimes at another. This historical knowledge, by itself, gives no indication of the extent to which changes in farm production result in changes in price. For the crop-restriction program to be successful, however, the government must estimate approximately a year in advance the probable level of prices that will be associated with any given level of production. For this, accurate quantitative estimates of the demand and supply schedules of various agricultural commodities are required.

For example, if the exact nature of the demand curve for wheat is known, it will be possible to predict the equilibrium price of wheat with a given level of production, that is, the price which will clear the market. If the size of the wheat crop in a particular year can be estimated on the basis of information from previous years about rainfall, prices, acreage planted, and similar factors, it will then be possible to predict the approximate price of wheat in the given year on the basis of historical knowledge.

The only way to discover the actual demand curve for wheat, however, is to study data of past years on wheat consumption, wheat prices, and similar magnitudes. Economic theory suggests that the demand curve is likely to be downward sloping; but it does not provide precise information about the shape of the demand curve or the factors which control its position. In other words, economic theory provides *qualitative* but not *quantitative* information about the demand curve. It is the task of econometrics to develop this quantitative information.

To obtain some idea of the quantitative properties of the demand curve, it is necessary to assume initially that the quantity of wheat demanded depends on certain measurable data such as the price of corn, the price of bread, national income, population, etc., as well as the price of wheat. Historical measures of these data may then be used to arrive at a provisional estimate of the extent to which each of the factors influences the quantity demanded of wheat. If some of the factors appear not to influence quantity demanded at all, they may be eliminated from the relation originally suggested by economic theory. If all of the factors studied do not suffice to provide a satisfactory explanation of observed variations in quantity demanded, certain additional data may have to be introduced into the relation suggested by economic theory in order to arrive at a satisfactory quantitative description of the demand curve for wheat.

Econometrics can seldom provide completely precise knowledge of economic relations by this procedure. While the results are only approximate at best, nevertheless they may provide sufficiently accurate quantitative content to the purely qualitative relationships of economic theory to permit quantitative rather than qualitative predictions. For example, while on the basis of economic theory alone, it is possible only to say that a 10 percent increase in wheat production will lead to a *lower* price of wheat, econometric analysis may make it possible to say that a 10 percent increase in wheat production will lead to a *decline of approximately 20 percent in the price of wheat*. From a practical point of view, there is a vast difference between the two statements.

Thus the first major task of econometrics is to provide quantitative content for the purely qualitative statements suggested by economic theory and by everyday experience. These quantitative relationships, in turn, to the extent to which they are accurate, permit the making of specific quantitative predictions of future events—the second major task of econometrics. The use of the quantitative relationships to make predictions provides the crucial test of the accuracy of these relationships; to the extent that the predictions are inaccurate, the quantitative measurement of the economic relationships has not been entirely satisfactory.

The Scope of Econometrics

Econometrics potentially includes within its scope all work in economics that is concerned with empirical data, that is, with the explanation of observed phenomena. As a matter of practice, however, the work is largely confined to certain problems of the type included in partial equilibrium theory and in income and employment theory. The first category includes estimation of supply and demand functions, forecasting of price in a single market, and estimation of cost curves and production functions. In the income theory field, attention has been given to forecasts of consumer demand at various levels of income and estimates of the demand for money. However, one large-scale econometric study has dealt with the overall behavior of the United States economy,[2] and similar attempts have been made to describe the working of the Canadian and other economic systems. The projects have not been entirely successful from a predictive point of view, but they have yielded much valuable factual knowledge. What is perhaps more important at this stage in the development of econometrics, they have indicated some areas in which further theoretical and empirical research will be needed if future projects are to be more fruitful.

CONCEPTS AND GENERAL APPROACH OF ECONOMETRICS

Since econometrics seeks to add quantitative content to the relationships of economic analysis, it must concern itself not only with questions of data collection and with the statements of theoretical analysis, but also with the interrelationships between them. Specifically, it must select data in terms of the requirements of the models of economic analysis, and at the same time adapt these models in such a fashion as to permit quantification of them with available data and techniques. These problems must be considered in greater detail.

Preliminary Research and Data Collection

Starting from a given collection of facts about a particular situation, the econometrician's first task is to decide what portion of the information already available is relevant to the task at hand and what further information is required. Neither task is simple.

Suppose that the econometrician is seeking to estimate the demand for a single commodity—corn, for example. For this purpose, it will be desirable to have as much information as possible about past production, consumption, and price; but no amount of statistics on corn alone will permit estimation of the demand for corn unless by remote chance the demand for corn is independent of all other aspects of economic activity. The problem may be clarified by an illustration, as shown in Figure 20–1. With quantities of corn consumed measured on the

[2] L. R. Klein and A. S. Goldberger, *An Econometric Model of the United States, 1929–1952* (Amsterdam: North-Holland Publishing Co., 1955).

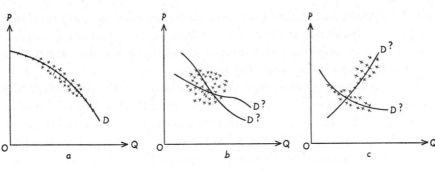

FIGURE 20–1

horizontal axis and the prices of corn on the vertical axis, a collection of historical quantity-price data may be represented by a *scatter diagram* in which each point corresponds to a single actual historical quantity-price observation. If the scatter diagram is of the nature indicated in Figure 20–1a, curve *D* might be regarded as a reasonable estimate of the demand curve for corn. If the scatter diagram is as represented by Figure 20–1b or Figure 20–1c, on the other hand, no single estimate of the demand curve would seem more logical than another; on the contrary, it is obvious that some factor other than price is influencing the consumption of corn, and further information must be sought.

Actually, however, the evidence provided by the scatter diagram of Figure 20–1a is just as ambiguous as that in the other two cases. Although the scatter of points appears to show an obvious demand curve, it could represent a *collection* of demand curves, each point being on a different curve, as illustrated in Figure 20–2. Indeed, if it were known that hog production had been increasing steadily for a number of years, the second interpretation of the scatter in Figure 20–1a might seem more plausible than the first; one would not expect the position of the demand curve to be unchanged, year after year, if the number of hogs was increasing.

The implication is that facts alone never speak for themselves, and

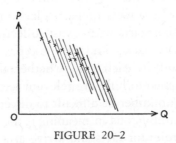

FIGURE 20–2

no interpretation of factual data can ever be regarded as final unless one knows the precise nature of the process by which the data are generated. In the case of economics, however, the nature of the data-generation process is seldom known with any precision.

To deal with a problem of the kind illustrated, the econometrician is therefore forced to undertake what might be called a "fishing expedition." He starts with certain basic facts, and then casts his net as widely as possible to discover whether other facts are available that might have a bearing on his interpretation of the original collection of data. In particular, he must obtain information about factors other than price that may influence the consumption of corn, such as prices in other markets, production and consumption of related commodities, consumer income, government purchasing programs, etc. The econometrician must also investigate the process by which the price of corn is determined, that is, he must acquire information about the production and marketing of corn. It may happen, for example, that the amount of corn supplied to the market comes partly from current production and partly from existing stocks. In this case the behavior of the market will depend partly on changes in stocks, and the data required to describe variations in price and consumption will be more difficult to obtain and more complicated to analyze than would otherwise be the case.

To add to the complications already mentioned, consumption, production, and price reactions observed during one period of time may be the result of events occurring at an earlier period. To take this possibility into account, it may be necessary to attach time references to factual data, that is, to work with scatter diagrams in which the various points are dated. This will almost inevitably increase the range of admissible interpretations of the data and so increase the difficulty of arriving at definite conclusions about the nature of the process by which the data are generated.

Theoretical Considerations

The role of economic theory in econometrics is the provision of a set of "hooks" upon which facts of particular kinds may be hung. In effect, the econometrician starts with a vast collection of hooks, most of them unencumbered by facts; and he proceeds from one hook to another, asking himself in each case whether the kinds of facts a particular hook is designed to hold are relevant to the problem at hand. If the hooks are few in number or difficult to discern (i.e., if the theory is narrow in scope or ambiguous in meaning), the econometrician may easily overlook some relevant facts and arrive at a poor solution to his problem. Alternatively, he may recognize the inadequacy of the theory and be forced to devote as much attention to a search for additional hooks as he devotes to looking for facts. The ideal situation is one in which the basic theory is relatively comprehensive and reasonably precise, but this is not always the case in practice.

Necessary Modifications in the Theoretical Analysis

Even if existing theory is adequate, the data actually available to the econometrician are not likely to conform exactly to the specifications suggested by the theory. Where the theory requires daily or weekly data on prices and quantities, for example, the econometrician may have to settle for quarterly or annual figures. Similarly, where the theory refers to data involving quantities with adjustments to equilibrium completed, the econometrician is forced to work with actual quantities, and these are not likely to reflect complete attainment of equilibrium. Difficulties of this kind cannot be overcome simply by ignoring them; the basic theory must be modified so that it can be used to interpret the data that are actually available.

Likewise, in the course of an econometric study, certain calculations often cannot be performed unless relations suggested by existing theory are first simplified. For example, as a practical matter, econometric work is usually confined to *linear relations* (represented geometrically by straight lines) rather than *nonlinear relations* (represented geometrically by curves other than straight lines). The precise form of a linear relation is determined simply by its *slope* relative to the axes on which the variables included in the relation are measured. The form of a nonlinear relation, on the other hand, can be specified only if much additional information is provided.

The importance of this consideration can be illustrated by consideration of the usual two-dimensional curve. If the "curve" in question is a straight line, one number (representing the slope of the curve relative to the X axis) suffices to determine the *form* of the relation, and another number (representing, for example, the point at which the line crosses the X axis) suffices to fix the *position* of the line. If the curve contains bends or kinks, however, as would be true if it were part of a circle, knowledge about the slope and position of one section of the curve would not indicate the nature of the curve in other sections. The use of linear relations in econometrics (more specifically, the use of *linear equations*) is almost a necessity under present circumstances. Furthermore, there is no need to use more complicated relations without first attempting to get along without them, and most curves can be approximated fairly well, within a limited range, by straight lines.

Other kinds of simplifications are also used in econometric work, as will be indicated in more detail below. It must be emphasized that these simplifications are introduced in order to avoid various practical difficulties. However, such simplifications involve the introduction of new and essentially untested hypotheses about the form of relations suggested by economic theory. An important task of econometric research, therefore, is to select simplifications that permit practical work but do not materially alter the character of the original theoretical model.

THE FORMULATION OF ECONOMETRIC MODELS

In current practice, most econometric analyses follow a standard pattern. The data relevant to a given problem are first divided into two classes: data that are to be interpreted by the theory and data that are to be taken as given. The variables of the theory are then divided into two corresponding categories, *endogenous* and *exogenous,* according to the same principle; and a series of theoretical *structural relations* or *structural equations* is established relating the various endogenous variables to one another and to the exogenous variables. The purpose of this procedure is to arrive at a system of relations (simultaneous equations) which can be used to determine the "unknown" values of the endogenous variables in terms of the "given" values of the exogenous variables.

A Typical Model

Thus a theory intended to describe price determination in a single market—say, the market for corn—could be represented by a system of three linear[3] *structural equations:*

[3] A linear equation is an expression of the general form

$$ax + by + cz + \cdots + dw + e = 0,$$

where the symbols $x, y, z, \ldots, w$ represent *variables* and the symbols $a, b, c, \ldots, d,$ and e represent given *constants* (called *coefficients* of the variables that appear in the equation). In words, a linear equation is a sum of one or more *terms,* each term consisting of a variable multiplied by a constant coefficient or of a constant standing alone, the entire expression being set equal to zero. Terms may, of course, be shifted from one side of the equal sign to the other, provided the sign of the term is reversed; i.e., terms appearing with a positive coefficient on the left-hand side of the equal sign must appear with a negative coefficient if they are shifted to the right-hand side of the equation. For example, $3x + 2y = 0$, and $3x = -2y$ represent the same linear equation; $3x^2 + 2y = 0$, and $3x + 2xy =$

$$d_c = \alpha_1 p_c + \beta_1 h \quad \text{(demand)}$$
$$(1)\ \ s_c = \alpha_2 p_c + \beta_2 r \quad \text{(supply)}$$
$$d_c = s_c \quad \text{(market clearance)}$$

In this system, d_c, s_c, and p_c are *endogenous variables* representing, respectively, the current demand, supply, and price of corn. The symbols h and r represent *exogenous variables* and describe, respectively, the current stock of hogs and annual rainfall. The symbols α_1, α_2, β_1, and β_2 represent given constants called *structural parameters*. The particular values assigned to these structural parameters determine the precise form of the structural relations of the system and so determine indirectly the equilibrium values of the endogenous variables d_c, s_c, and p_c corresponding to given values of the exogenous variables h and r.

A geometric interpretation of the system (1) is presented in Figure 20–3. The lines d_c^1, d_c^2, and d_c^3 represent three out of an indefinitely large number of possible positions of the demand "curve" corresponding to a *given value* of the structural parameter α_1 (which fixes the slope of each of the demand lines) and *three different values* h_1, h_2, and h_3

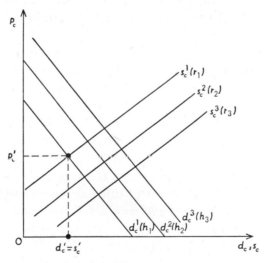

FIGURE 20–3

0, and $xy^2 + 3xy = 0$ represent *nonlinear* equations. Whether or not an equation is linear thus depends on the way in which the variables appear in any given term of the equation. If, *at most, one* variable appears in each term (multiplied by a coefficient), and if the variable appears *to the first power only,* then the equation is linear; otherwise, it is nonlinear.

The term *linear* is used because every linear equation in two variables is represented geometrically by a *line* in a two-dimensional space. A linear equation involving three variables is represented geometrically by a *plane* in a three-dimensional space, not by a line; but the term *linear* is still used to refer to the equation because the *algebraic form* of the relation is the same as in the two-variable case.

436 · INTERMEDIATE ECONOMIC ANALYSIS

of the exogenous variable h. The extent to which changes in the value of h alter the position of the demand relation depends on the magnitude of the structural parameter β_1; for example, if β_1 were twice as great, the demand lines illustrated in the figure would be more widely spaced. Similarly, the lines s_c^1, s_c^2, and s_c^3 represent three possible positions of the supply "curve" corresponding to a given value of the structural parameter α_2 (which fixes the slope of each supply relation) and three different values r_1, r_2, and r_3 of the exogenous variable r. The "shift effect" of changes in the variable r will depend, of course, on the magnitude of the structural parameter β_2. The line corresponding to the equation $d_c = s_c$ cannot be drawn explicitly in this graph because the variables d_c and s_c are not measured on separate axes. However, this market clearance condition will be satisfied at any intersection of a supply line and a demand line.

Suppose, for example, that h has the particular value h_1, while r has the particular value r_1 (i.e., suppose that h_1 and r_1 represent particular numbers such as 3 or 4). The corresponding demand and supply relations are represented by d_c^1 and s_c^1, respectively, and the equilibrium price is given by p_c^1 (a particular number, determined by the market clearance equation, $d_c^1 = d_s^1$). Different values of the exogenous variables r and h would determine different demand and supply lines, and so a different equilibrium price. Moreover, different values of the structural parameters α_1 and α_2 would result in demand and supply lines with different *slopes,* and thus a different equilibrium price. Finally, different values of the structural parameters β_1 and β_2 would determine different *positions* of the demand and supply lines, and so, once more, different equilibrium prices.

Thus, we see that the implications for price and quantity determination of the system of equations (1) differ depending on the particular values assigned to the exogenous variables h and r and the structural parameters α_1, α_2, β_1, and β_2. That is to say, the particular equilibrium values of the endogenous variables d_c, s_c, and p_c that satisfy the three equations in the system (1) will vary according to the internal structure of the system as determined by the particular values of the structural parameters α_1, α_2, β_1, and β_2, and the external factors affecting the system as determined by the particular values of the exogenous variables h and r.

Models and Structures

A general system of equations, such as (1), with the values of the structural parameters not specified exactly, is referred to as a *model.* If *specific* values are assigned to the parameters of the system, however, the system is known as a *structure* rather than a model. In other words, every model is an infinite class of different possible structures. The model is essentially *qualitative* in character; each structure represents a particular *quantitative* form of the model.

In this terminology the purpose of econometric study may be restated as follows. First, the study seeks to establish, with the aid of economic theory, a tentatively acceptable model, which is in purely qualitative terms. Next, on the basis of empirical data about past values of the endogenous and exogenous variables, it seeks to determine the particular quantitative structure contained within the model, that is, a set of values of the structural parameters of the model, which produces a set of values of the endogenous variables which accord with actual data of past experience. This structure can then be used for prediction of the magnitudes of endogenous variables in future periods, on the assumption that the parameters and exogenous variables for these future periods will be the same as in the past or will change in some specified way.

Shock Models

An obvious difficulty with this procedure is that no structure contained in a linear model (or for that matter, in any theoretical model) is likely to yield predictions that are completely accurate. Even with the most careful work and the most ingenious theories, errors are bound to occur because of imperfections in data, omission of relevant exogenous variables, and unforeseen changes in the behavioral and institutional character of the situation being studied.

To take some of these difficulties into account, and also to avoid working with models that are known in advance to provide a false picture of reality, it is standard econometric practice to introduce certain latent (unobservable) *shock variables* into every econometric model. The model described on page 435 by the system of relations (1), for example, would normally be written in the form

$$d_c = \alpha_1 p_c + \beta_1 h + u_1$$
$$s_c = \alpha_2 p_c + \beta_2 r + u_2$$
$$d_c = s_c + u_3 \, ,$$

the additional or shock variables u_1, u_2, and u_3 in each relation representing various unknown factors not otherwise taken into account in the model. Such a model is called a *shock model*.

With a model of this kind, together with certain assumptions about the nature of the shock variables u_1, the purpose of econometric study may be modified as that of determining the structure contained in the model which is *most nearly* in accord with known facts—i.e., to determine values of the structural parameters which lead to predicted values of the endogenous variables d_c, s_c, and p_c that differ as little as possible from their observed values.

The Complexity of the Models

The preceding discussion gives only a hint of the possible complexity and generality of econometric models. Systems may involve fifty or more equations, and consider not only current but also past (lagged) values of both endogenous and exogenous variables, and work with nonlinear as well as with linear relations. And this does not begin to exhaust the list of possible complications.

PROBLEMS OF ESTIMATION

While the collection of data and the construction of provisionally satisfactory theoretical models constitute more than half the battle in most econometric studies, the remaining task is not merely a matter of routine computation. This would very nearly be the case if models which provided perfectly accurate simulation of observed economic phenomena were feasible, for straightforward calculations would suffice to indicate whether a model did or did not provide a precise description of available empirical data.

In actual practice, however, there are major complications. First, available empirical data do not always provide enough information to permit the econometrician to say whether a chosen model is satisfactory; in order to carry out an analysis, it may be necessary to reformulate the model or to search out additional data. Second, even if available data appear to provide some information about the adequacy of a given theoretical model, the information provided may not be sufficiently detailed or exact to permit the econometrician to choose a single "best" structure from the set of structures contained within a given model. Third, there are various alternative methods of calculating numerical estimates of the structural parameters in any given model, and different methods do not always lead to the same results. The advantages and disadvantages of different methods of calculation are extremely difficult to determine on logical grounds. Each of these problems merits brief discussion.

The Identification Problem

A simplified example will illustrate the first of the problems of estimation mentioned above, i.e., situations in which available empirical data do not permit the econometrician to decide whether a chosen model is or is not worthwhile. Suppose that price in a given market is known to be determined by current supply and demand forces, in the sense that the market price always adjusts immediately to the level which is required to make quantity supplied equal to quantity demanded. But with available data on prices and quantities exchanged, it may not be possible to distinguish between supply and demand relations because the data on quantity exchanged represent both quantity supplied and quantity demanded at the equilibrium. This problem is called the *identification problem* because of the impossibility in such cases of separating the data for the various structural relations in the theoretical models, that is, to identify the data for a particular relationship.

The difficulty is most easily appreciated by considering the price-quantity data that relate to various demand and supply curves. Suppose, for example, that a shifting demand curve is combined with a fixed supply curve, as in Figure 20–4. This will yield a series of "observable" equilibrium points on the supply curve. But the *same* series of "observable" points could just as well have been generated by a shifting demand curve combined with a *shifting* supply curve, as illustrated in Figure 20–5.

From a given set of structural relations and given information

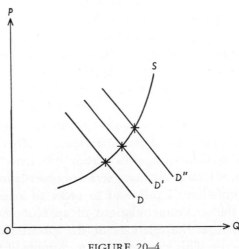

FIGURE 20–4

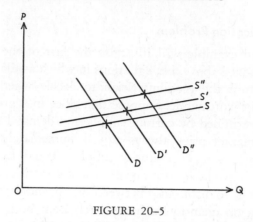

FIGURE 20–5

about shifts in these relations, it is possible to obtain precisely one set of "observable" points; but the reverse operation, that of obtaining a given set of structural relations and shifts from a given set of "observable" points, cannot be carried out in the absence of additional information. If it is known, for example, that the supply curve shifts from year to year according to the amount of rainfall, whereas the demand curve does not shift at all, it may be possible to *identify* the demand curve from observable price-quantity data. Similarly, if the demand curve shifts only in response to changes in income, and the supply curve shifts, as before, only in response to changes in rainfall, both the supply and the demand curves may be empirically identifiable.

There are various ways of adding extra information to a theoretical model in order to lessen identification problems. The structural parameters of the model may be assumed to lie within some particular range of possible values. Thus, some parameters may be assumed to have positive signs and others to have negative signs. Still other parameters may be assumed to have the value zero, that is, they may be assumed to be absent from some equations. Assumptions can also be made about the values of the shock variables in various structural equations. For example, it may be assumed that the average value of a shock variable in a long list of possible values is zero (implying that "errors" in one direction are approximately offset by "errors" in the opposite direction, at least in any long series of observations).

Whatever procedure is followed in order to achieve theoretical identifiability of the structural relations of an econometric model, it should be noticed that the relations of the model still may not be identifiable in practice. This will happen, for example, if the factors that *might* lead to shifts in structural relations *in fact* do not happen to vary significantly during the period for which empirical data are available. As an illustration, let us consider an attempt to analyze the effect of income changes on demand. Even if the supply curve is absolutely fixed, empirical data on price, quantity exchanged, and income will not provide an indication of the nature of the supply curve if, during the period of observation, income does not happen to vary. All observable price-quantity points will be the same, and will simply indicate the intersection of the given demand and supply curves.

The Problem of "Goodness of Fit"

The second type of problem described earlier—namely, one arising because empirical data are not sufficiently exact or detailed to indicate whether a particular theoretical model affords a good explanation of observed events—may be described as the problem of "goodness of fit."

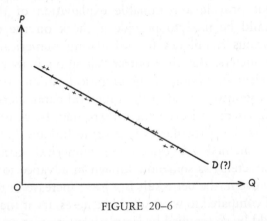

FIGURE 20–6

This class of problem may be illustrated with a supply-demand model in which the demand equation is identifiable. With a scatter diagram of the sort illustrated in Figure 20–6, there would be no difficulty about estimating the form of the demand relation. The data would indicate very clearly that a straight-line estimate of the demand curve is entirely appropriate. Matters would be very different, however, if on the same assumptions the scatter diagram was of the type shown in Figure 20–7. An embarrassingly large number of different demand relations would all seem to fit the data about equally well.

Unfortunately for econometrics, situations of the latter kind are not uncommon. The typical econometric model is too complicated, however, and the data available for estimating the relations of the model are too varied, to permit the investigator to discover by simple

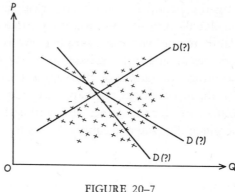

FIGURE 20–7

inspection whether a provisionally satisfactory model is likely to provide a "good" or a "bad" fit to the data. If it were possible to say, on the basis of casual inspection of empirical data, that a given structure did or did not provide a reasonable explanation of the data, such knowledge could be used to provide a check on the efficiency and validity of various techniques for calculating numerical estimates of structural parameters. But the contrary situation is more common in practice: No clear indication of the empirical validity of a theoretical model can be obtained until after the structural parameters in the model have been estimated; and even then, there may be considerable room for doubt unless the particular estimation technique that is used (i.e., the particular method for calculating numerical estimates of the structural parameters) is somehow known in advance to yield reliable results. In any event, the net result is a great increase in the amount of work required compared to what would be necessary if the usefulness of the model could be ascertained by simple inspection at an early stage in the process.

Choice of Estimation Techniques

In many situations, the econometrician faces a serious dilemma. Simple inspection of empirical data will not indicate whether a given model can be used to provide a satisfactory explanation of the data. To make any progress at all, the data must be processed by one of several possible methods so as to yield numerical estimates of the structural parameters in the given model. The values of the endogenous variables, calculated on the assumption that the structural parameters of the model are as estimated, may then be compared with observed values of the same variables to determine whether the theoretical predictions of the model are satisfactory.

If the results of this comparison are unsatisfactory, however, the econometrician may have difficulty deciding what factors are responsible for the failure. Are the data inaccurate? Is the model unsatisfactory? Or is the technique used to calculate estimates of the structural parameters in the model a poor one? The complexity of economic phenomena is such that reliable techniques of estimation are essential if econometric studies are to be fruitful; but reliable techniques of estimation are extremely difficult to establish because of the complexity of the models that must be used to describe economic phenomena.

Much of the difficulty springs from the fact that all of the estimation techniques that are currently used in econometrics are basically designed to apply to experimental data of the kind studied in physics, chemistry, and the biological sciences, where it is possible to maintain some degree of control over sources of error in the construction of models and the measurement of phenomena. Most of the data of economics, however, are nonexperimental in character. Economists have to take whatever factual information is provided by the everyday working of the economic system; they cannot ordinarily arrange experiments in which individuals, communities, or countries are subjected to controlled changes in external conditions and studied like bugs in a laboratory.

The problem would not be serious if different techniques of estimating structural parameters applied to the given data always yielded similar answers; but this is not the case. Neither would it be a serious problem if the theoretical models used in econometrics were known to be capable of simulating observed phenomena with a high degree of accuracy; but this is not true, either. As matters stand, the derivation of empirically significant estimates of structural parameters is perhaps the major unsettled problem of contemporary econometrics. Future progress may well depend as much upon the solution of this issue as upon the collection of better data and the construction of improved theoretical models.

CONCLUSION

Some of the more important limitations of contemporary econometric research have already been indicated in the preceding discussion. Most of these limitations—for example, those associated with the use of linear equations, the inability to perform controlled experiments, and the lack of accurate and complete statistical data—are not insurmountable. Other limitations—for example, those associated with estimation techniques—may well be of greater significance from a long-range point of view.

On the other hand, it is essential to recognize that econometric research is a unified activity in the sense that every aspect of such research has a direct bearing on every other aspect. Thus, improved data may lead to rapid improvement in estimation techniques, and improved estimation techniques may lead very shortly to the construction of theoretical models that can be used satisfactorily to describe nonexperimental data. Econometric research faces many serious and unsettled problems. At the same time, it is important to note that the *problems of econometric research are essentially the same as the problems of empirical economic research in general.* Every science has problems of this kind, many of them far from being completely resolved. In this regard, there is no reason to suppose that the problems of economics are any more serious than the problems of, say, nuclear physics or psychology; and the problems of economics are clearly much less serious than those of political science.

Scientific progress is a gradual phenomenon even in the best of circumstances. Economics in general, and econometrics in particular, have not displayed especially rapid rates of progress in the past; but neither has progress been slow. The fact that more and more professional economists are becoming interested in econometric research indicates that the present limitations of econometric work are not considered to be permanent. The same fact gives us reason to hope that the results of future econometric research will greatly expand our knowledge about the quantitative characteristics of the economic system. Perfectly accurate measurement of economic relations is perhaps an impossibility in any case; but even rather inaccurate measurement is infinitely better than no measurement at all.

SELECTED REFERENCES

BEACH, E. F. *Economic Models.* New York: Wiley, 1957.
    An interesting and useful elementary treatment of basic problems in economic theory and econometrics.

BRENNAN, M. J. *Preface to Econometrics.* 2d ed. Cincinnati: South-Western Publishing Co., 1965.
    A helpful introduction to quantitative methods in economics, including a survey of relevant mathematical and statistical materials.

HOOD, W. C., AND KOOPMANS, T. C. (eds.). *Studies in Econometric Method.* New York: Wiley, 1953.

An advanced treatise on econometrics, generally regarded as the standard reference source in this field.

JOHNSTON, J. *Econometric Methods.* New York: McGraw-Hill, 1963.
An extremely clear and relatively comprehensive treatment.

THEIL, H. *Economic Forecasts and Policy.* Amsterdam: North-Holland Publishing Co., 1958.
A classic account of the current state and future prospects of econometrics.

VALAVANIS, S. *Econometrics.* New York: McGraw-Hill, 1959.
A "bird's-eye view" of some of the central problems of econometrics, presented in a lively and readable fashion.

WOLD, H., AND JUREEN, L. *Demand Analysis,* Part I, pp. 1–80. New York: Wiley, 1953.
A fairly advanced account of econometrics and its problems, with a point of view somewhat different from that of other writers.

QUESTIONS

1. Distinguish between econometrics and statistics; between econometrics and mathematical economics.
2. In what way does econometrics differ from empirical economic research in general?
3. Describe the basic aims of econometrics.
4. What is the difference between a quantitative and a qualitative description of observed behavior? Illustrate your answer with some examples.
5. What is a scatter diagram?
6. Does the fact that all the points in a scatter diagram lie on or near a straight line indicate that the variables to which the diagram refers are linked by some simple "law"? Explain why or why not.
7. Using information from the *Survey of Current Business,* draw a scatter diagram to represent "observed" annual values of disposable income and personal consumption expenditure over the last ten years. Discuss your results.
8. Discuss the relation between economic theory and econometrics. How does this relation differ, if at all, from that between theoretical and experimental physics?
9. Econometric research involves many data problems. Describe three such problems.
10. What is meant by a linear relation? Why are such relations so often used in econometrics?
11. What is the difference between a variable and a constant? Between an exogenous variable and an endogenous variable? Between a variable and the value of a variable?
12. What is a structural equation? A structural parameter?
13. Represent graphically the system of equations

$$d = -2p + a$$
$$s = 3p + b,$$

using various alternative values of the parameters a and b (i.e., let $a = 20$ and 25, and let $b = 5$ and 6). What are the equilibrium values of market price p corresponding to each of the four different possible assumptions about the joint values of a and b?

14. In what sense can an econometric model be regarded as a class of structures?

15. What is a shock variable? What purpose do shock variables serve in econometric research?

16. What criteria would you use to distinguish between "good" and "bad" econometric models?

17. Describe in general terms what is involved in the problem of identification.

18. Is it possible for a structural equation in an econometric model to be identifiable in principle, yet not be identifiable in practice? Explain.

19. Describe and discuss some of the limitations of contemporary econometric research.

Chapter 21

WELFARE ECONOMICS

In preceding chapters, attention has been directed to operation of the economic system, without attempting to evaluate its performance by reference to given standards of efficiency, justice, or morality. We have considered how the economy works and why it works as it does; but we have not tried to judge whether particular features of the system are "good" or "bad." We have described how the price system determines commodity outputs—and so the composition of national product—without inquiring whether or not realized results meet desired performance goals. We have considered the forces that determine the distribution of income without asking whether the resulting distribution is in any sense optimal. In this final chapter, however, it is appropriate to raise some of these questions: to survey briefly that portion of economic analysis—namely *welfare economics* —which is concerned with evaluation, and thus seeks to judge the extent to which the working of the economic system leads to results that are "desirable" by reference to accepted social goals.

SOCIAL GOALS AND THE ECONOMIC SYSTEM

All applications of scientific knowledge give rise to ethical questions of one kind or another. The moral issues raised by the development of atomic weapons afford some particularly striking examples, but similar instances might be drawn from almost every field of human knowledge. Regardless of the field of study involved, evaluation of an existing state of affairs or the consequences of a proposed action can be separated into two distinct tasks. First, it is necessary to acquire a fairly comprehensive understanding of the concrete situation that is to be evaluated. Second, it is necessary (1) to select and (2) to apply standards of evaluation. The first of these tasks, which is concerned with *what is* rather than *what ought to be,* is the main business of science as science. The first step in the second task, the selection of standards, is a part of the general field of ethics, since it involves the making of value judgments about the personal and social desirability of alternative actions. The second step, the application of ethical criteria to evaluate particular situations, involves a mixture of science and ethics. It is this mixed area of knowledge with which welfare economics deals.

For our present purposes, we shall merely assume certain ethical goals, selecting ones that appear to reflect widely accepted attitudes of contemporary society. The fact that these goals are assumed, not determined by economic analysis, must be stressed, as well as the fact that the evaluations which follow are valid only in terms of these goals. If we were to assume other goals, the evaluations would produce different results. It is also worth emphasizing that what is being evaluated are situations described by economic models. The evaluations are relevant so far as the actual economic system is concerned to the extent that these theoretical models provide an adequate description of the real world.

Three primary social goals will be assumed to be desirable:

1. Maximum freedom of choice for individuals, consistent with rights for other individuals.

2. Maximum satisfaction of wants, which requires use and allocation of resources in such a way as to permit the optimum per capita real income.

3. A pattern of distribution of income regarded as most equitable in terms of the standards of contemporary society.

In the remainder of the chapter, these goals will be explained more fully, the conditions necessary for their attainment will be indicated, and a brief evaluation will be made of the extent to which the conditions, and thus the goals, appear to be satisfied in the present-day economic system.

FREEDOM OF CHOICE

Freedom of choice in the sphere of economic activity is the right of the individual to act as he wishes in the choice of employment and the purchase and sale of goods and services. Attainment of this goal requires that a person be free to select the commodities he prefers for the satisfaction of his wants. He must be free to make decisions about the use of factor units he owns—to make them available to business firms or not, to select the type of work and the place of work he prefers among available opportunities, to divide his time between work and leisure as he pleases, to establish a business if he wishes, and to make decisions of his own choice in the operation of the business. Contemporary western society regards freedom of action to be desirable in itself, apart from the role it may play in facilitating attainment of optimum standards of living.

It must be recognized, however, that freedom of choice is a relative matter, since absolute freedom would result in serious injury to others. Freedom of choice must be exercised within the framework established to protect the interests of society as a group, and sometimes the person himself. If all persons were free to hunt deer without restriction, there would soon be no deer to hunt, and the right to hunt would become worthless. The greatest overall freedom is obtained through the establishment of certain restrictions in the interests of the group. Over the years, there has been a tendency to increase the number of restrictions of this type. Yet, in the market form of economic system, as found in the United States and Canada and much of western Europe, as well as in other areas, a very high degree of personal freedom of choice remains. In general, persons are free to buy anything they please (with the exception of a few goods, such as opium, which are likely to bring serious injury to themselves or others). Legally, they may work or not as they wish, obtain a job anywhere they can find one, and move from one area to another as they wish. People are free to start any type of business (with a few exceptions), and select products, prices, methods of production, etc., as they desire.

MAXIMUM SATISFACTION OF WANTS

The second goal is the maximization of the satisfaction of wants, or in other words, the attainment of the highest possible level of economic well-being for society as a whole, through the use and allocation of resources in such a fashion as to allow the highest per capita real income, given the resources, technology, and the preference schedules of factor owners with regard to the use of their factor units. We assume that maximization of economic well-being requires maximum per capita real income; it must be recognized that this is in itself a value judgment—one which would not be acceptable to some groups in society such as the Amish communities. There are also problems relating to measurement of increases in per capita real income, particularly as the relative output of various goods changes, and there are significant questions relating to the manner in which the increase is distributed over various individuals. But for the moment we shall disregard the question of the distribution of real income, discussing resource use and allocation in terms of the prevailing pattern of distribution. The question of the optimum pattern of distribution will be raised later in the chapter.

The requirements for optimum use and allocation of resources, given the pattern of income distribution, are often called the marginal conditions. These are noted in the following paragraphs.

Optimum Efficiency in the Use of Resources

In the first place, optimum want satisfaction requires that resources be utilized in production with the maximum degree of efficiency. This, in turn, requires:

1. The attainment of least-cost factor combinations in production, and thus the adjustment of factor combinations until the marginal rate of substitution between any two factors is equal to the ratio of their prices.

2. The use of the most efficient production techniques and the most satisfactory available methods of administrative organization and physical distribution.

3. Operation of firms at the point of lowest long-run average cost; they must not only expand plant to the size allowing lowest cost, but must also operate at the optimum capacity (lowest cost point) of this plant.

Only if these requirements are met can maximum output be obtained from given resources. If obsolete methods are used, least-cost combinations not attained, plants are too small, or firms are not operating at lowest average cost, total output obtained from given resources is less than the potential.

To what extent is the optimum organization of production attained in a market economy? This is not an easy question to answer. The profit motive provides a continuous incentive to reduce costs—one which is, of course, strongest when competition is effective, but which is present even with complete monopoly. Yet, it is probably rare that the exact least-cost combination of factors, in all respects, is attained. It is an extremely difficult task for a firm to accomplish, especially with complex industrial processes.

Theoretically when markets are purely competitive, as explained in Chapter 9, firms will operate at the point of lowest LRAC. But imperfections, and particularly lack of knowledge, undoubtedly interfere with the attainment of lowest average cost. In nonpurely competitive markets with free entry of new firms, operation at the point of lowest LRAC is impossible since the downward-sloping demand curves for the products of the firms cannot be tangent to the ⌣ -shaped average cost curves at their lowest points. Hence, there are too many firms in terms of the market (but too few to permit the markets to be purely competitive); resources are poorly utilized, and costs could be lower if the market were divided among a smaller number of firms. The waste, however, may be less than is sometimes argued. In these industries the demand curves of the firms are likely to be highly elastic, and thus the departure from purely competitive conditions may not be very substantial.

In nonpurely competitive markets in which entry is not entirely free, firms may, of course, be operating at the point of lowest cost (although price does not equal average cost); but there is no necessity for this to be so. If the industry is dominated by a few large firms, they may easily expand to the point of lowest LRAC or even beyond. If the typical LRAC curve contains an extensive horizontal segment, as is now believed to be common, the likelihood that many firms may be operating at or near the lowest average cost figure in nonpurely competitive conditions is increased.

Whenever product is differentiated, a new element in cost is introduced, namely, that of advertising and other selling activities. These elements inevitably raise cost schedules above purely competitive levels. On the other hand, advertising does convey certain benefits to consumers. Evaluation of the relative advantages of the higher costs and benefits is very difficult. In some instances in which markets would not be purely competitive even without selling activities, the development of these activities may allow the firms to operate nearer the ·point of lowest average cost by increasing their sales volumes.

Optimum Adjustment of Production in Terms of Consumer Preferences

The second requirement is attainment of a pattern of relative outputs of various commodities which conforms to consumer preferences. That is, the composition of total output—and thus the allocation of resources—must be such as best to satisfy consumer preferences. For example, if consumers desire some shoes and some luggage, all of the available leather will not be used for luggage production while people go barefooted or wear wooden shoes. The leather supply must be allocated in such a manner that consumer preferences for the two products are satisfied as completely as possible. If consumers desire both cake and bread, all flour will not be used to produce bread, but some will be utilized in cake production as well.

Optimum adjustment of production can be obtained only if, for each consumer, the *marginal rate of substitution* between each two commodities purchased is equal to the *marginal rate of transformation* between the two commodities in production, the number of units of one commodity that must be sacrificed if an additional unit of the other commodity is to be produced. If this relationship is not attained, consumer preferences will be more fully realized if some resources are shifted from the production of goods with output excessive relative to consumer preferences to the production of goods with inadequate output. In other words, the output of each commodity must be adjusted to such a level that consumers are indifferent among outputs of various goods from the marginal factor inputs used to produce them. For example, the relative output of bread and cake must be such that consumers are indifferent between bread made with the marginal units of wheat going into bread production and cake made with the marginal units of wheat going into cake production. If the preference for bread is greater at the margin, more wheat must be used for bread production and less for cake production.

This relationship at the margin between rates of substitution and rates of transformation will be attained only if several requirements are met:

1. Consumers must allocate their incomes in such a manner that marginal rates of substitution among all commodities they buy are equal to the ratios of the prices of the commodities, or, in other words, the marginal utilities of all goods purchased are proportional to their prices. Failure to accomplish this adjustment will mean that the consumer has not reached the highest indifference curve possible with his income, or, in other words, is not maximizing satisfaction.

2. Relative prices of various goods must reflect marginal rates of transformation among them, so that, provided consumers allocate incomes in such a manner that marginal rates of substitution are equal to price ratios, marginal rates of substitution will also equal marginal rates of transformation.

Relative prices will reflect marginal rates of transformation only if:

a) Factor prices equate the supply of and demand for the factors, and are uniform to all producers. If factor prices exceed the levels at which supply and demand are equal, for example, they do not reflect the real costs involved in the production of an additional unit of a commodity, in the sense of the sacrifice of other goods necessary to obtain another factor unit for the production of the particular good. The same is true if factor prices are not uniform to all users.

b) Marginal costs to firms for the production of a given product must reflect all costs to the economy arising out of its production; in other words, there must be no external diseconomies. If certain costs to society do not enter into the marginal production costs of the firms, the price of the commodity will be too low and an excessive amount of the good will be produced. The traditional example is the damage from factory smoke, which does not become a cost to the business firm operating the factory. As patrons pour out of a drive-in theater at the end of the movie, they congest traffic on the highway, cause accidents, and delay motorists and truckers. These are real costs for which the drive-in is responsible, but which are not borne by the firm operating it and are not reflected in the prices charged the patrons. Air pollution by motor vehicles is another example.

3. All benefits from the use of commodities must accrue to the persons acquiring them, that is, there must be no external economies of consumption. If some indirect benefits are gained by other persons, too little of the commodity will be purchased and thus produced, since the indirect benefits do not influence the actions of persons purchasing the units. For example, if a person kills dandelions in his lawn, his neighbors will benefit as well. But the person is not likely to consider the latter (unless in the interests of neighborhood goodwill) when he makes the decision whether or not to buy the weed killer. The more significant examples of indirect benefits, however, are social or community goods such as national defense, which convey their benefits to the community as a whole rather than to individuals separately.

Realization of These Requirements.   Complete attainment of these requirements would insure an optimum allocation of resources or, in other terms, an optimum "product mix," given the pattern of income distribution. In a purely and perfectly competitive economy, with perfect knowledge on the part of consumers and business firms, with no external economies or diseconomies, these conditions would be attained. Each consumer would allocate his income according to the MRS-price ratio rule. Factor prices would equate factor supply and demand; prices of all commodities would be equal to their marginal factor costs (which, in the absence of external diseconomies, would include all real costs); marginal rates of substitution would therefore equal marginal rates of transformation. This conclusion is essentially a statement of the invisible hand doctrine; the economy, left to its own devices, will, under the assumed conditions, best serve the interests of society as a whole. Two points must be stressed, however: the conclusions are valid only in terms of a static context, and in terms of the assumption of a given pattern of income distribution.

However, the actual economy is far removed from one of universal pure and perfect competition, perfect knowledge, and absence of external economies and diseconomies. Some of the major deviations and their significance for economic welfare are noted below:

1. Consumer allocation of incomes. Even though consumers may seek to maximize satisfaction gained from their incomes, there are many obstacles in the way of so doing. Inadequate information about the ability of particular goods to meet various needs prevents attainment of maximum satisfaction. In part, this is inevitable by the very nature of consumer wants; a person cannot tell if he likes guava pie until he tries it; and if he does not, he has not maximized satisfaction. But the economic system does not do as effective a job of informing the consumer as it might. Advertising accomplishes this in part, but is by no means adequate, and may be misleading. Some rules for the labeling and description of contents have been imposed by governments.

2. *a*) Factor prices do not always equate supply and demand. The most extreme deviation is that of mass unemployment; the real cost of additional units of output may be almost nil when unemployed workers and resources can be used to produce them; but the marginal costs, reflecting existing factor prices, will be very much higher. Such situations may be explained in part by nonperfectly competitive elements in factor markets, but primarily by the inability of factor owners to adjust their real factor prices. If workers agree to work for lower wages, the prices of products may fall, and thus real wages may not change.

Similarly, factor prices are not always uniform to all users. Wages for a given type of labor may be higher in one area than in another, perhaps because of the varying strength of unions, and thus uneconomic location of industry will result. Price discrimination practiced by monopolist or oligopolist producers of materials may also cause failure to attain this requirement, as well as monopsony influences exercised by buyers over price.

b) Marginal costs do not always reflect all costs for which production of additional units is responsible. Examples were given above in the discussion of this requirement; many others could be supplied. The social costs of alcoholism do not become factor costs to liquor producers, for example. If a factory is built in a residential area, the decline in the value of residential property is not borne by the business firm.

Governments have sought to meet this problem in several ways. They have prohibited the production of certain goods which have heavy social costs not borne by the producers, such as narcotics. They have placed taxes on the sale of other products, such as liquor, to shift some of the additional social costs to the users and thus reduce consumption. City zoning ordinances are primarily designed to prevent losses in property values by indiscriminate location of particular types of activities without reference to other property uses.

c) Equality of marginal costs and prices is attained so long as firms are selling in purely competitive markets, apart from the effects of imperfections such as lack of adequate knowledge of costs by producers. The greatest advantage of purely competitive market conditions, from the standpoint of economic welfare, is the attainment of equality of price and marginal cost.

In nonpurely competitive conditions price will exceed marginal cost. Under such conditions, characterized by downward-sloping demand curves for the products of the individual firms, at the output level at which MR = MC, price will be in excess of marginal costs, as illustrated in Figure 21–1. Therefore the prices of commodities exceed

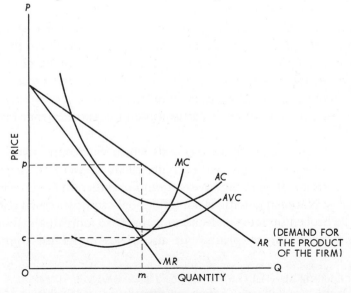

FIGURE 21–1

RELATIONSHIP OF PRICE AND MARGINAL COST, NONPURELY COMPETITIVE
CONDITIONS

the figures which reflect the real factor costs, in the sense of the sacrifice of output of other goods, and outputs of commodities are held to uneconomically low levels. This result is encountered whether excess profits are earned or not; the source of the difficulty is the downward-sloping demand curve, which causes marginal revenue to be less than price at the point of most profitable operation.

In other cases, artificial deviations between marginal factor cost and price are caused by the levying of excise taxes on the sale of particular commodities. These taxes result in prices for the commodities in excess of their factor costs—and hence in uneconomic reductions in output (if the other requirements for optimum economic welfare are attained)—unless, of course, the excises reflect costs to society which are not borne by the producers. Liquor taxes may perhaps be justified on this basis.

One basic dilemma has been noted in recent years: the case in which, when price is equal to marginal cost, average cost is not covered, and thus all costs of production cannot be recovered. An obvious example is a public utility enterprise which, although possessing a monopoly in a particular geographical area, does not have sufficient market to allow it to reach the point of lowest cost. As explained in earlier chapters, in ranges of output less than that of lowest average cost, marginal cost is less than average cost. An extreme example is provided by a toll bridge not used to capacity. Marginal cost of use of the bridge by another car may be nil, yet the average cost may be substantial. If prices are set at a level equal to marginal cost, the deficit must be made up by a subsidy financed by taxation. Since virtually all taxes presumably have some adverse effects upon the economy, the decision about pricing must be made on the basis of a weighing of the relative disadvantages of taxes versus those of departure from marginal cost pricing.[1]

3. There are many types of goods which yield important benefits to persons other than those who acquire them, or yield all or most of their benefits to the community as a whole, rather than separately to individuals. National defense is the traditional example. By its nature, it cannot be broken up into small pieces and sold to individuals. Education directly benefits the recipients, but also yields important community

[1] For surveys of the marginal cost pricing problem, see the article by R. W. Harbeson, "A Critique of Marginal Cost Pricing," *Land Economics,* Vol. 31 (February, 1955), pp. 54–74; and J. de V. Graaff, *Theoretical Welfare Economics* (Cambridge: Cambridge University Press, 1957), chap. x.

benefits as well in the form of greater social and political stability and more rapid economic development.

Because of the importance of indirect benefits from many types of activities, governments, representing the community as a whole, have found it desirable to provide such services to the community and to cover the costs of producing them from compulsory levies in the form of taxes. Private enterprise cannot produce many of these services at all, because they cannot be sold to individuals. Others, such as education, could be privately produced, but the total output would be uneconomically small if production were left in private hands because the indirect benefits would not influence purchases.

Optimum Degree of Factor Utilization

The third general condition necessary for the attainment of optimum satisfaction of wants, given the pattern of income distribution, is an optimum degree of utilization of factors. There are several aspects of this condition:

1. *Avoidance of Unemployment.* Optimum use of factor units requires that all factor units whose owners wish to have them employed at the equilibrium factor prices should find employment. Unemployment of factors obviously reduces the output of the economy and per capita real income below the optimum level. Furthermore, unemployment causes severe distress for the individuals concerned, since their source of income vanishes.

2. *Optimum Division of Time between Work and Leisure.* Optimum economic welfare does not require the absolute maximum possible output, but rather a level consistent with the allocation of time between work and leisure which persons prefer to make. Thus as real income rises as a result of increased productivity, optimum economic welfare does not require that the entire gain be taken in the form of greater output, if persons prefer to take a part or all of the benefits of greater productivity in the form of increased leisure. The argument against shorter hours that output will be reduced is not a conclusive one. If society prefers more leisure and less output, it cannot be argued that such a choice is an undesirable one in terms of the assumed goals.

In practice, the requirements of efficient production make it impossible for each individual to decide the number of hours he will work. In general, individuals must accept the working period that is standard in the particular line of employment, or work elsewhere. But as labor unions have grown in strength, workers as a whole have been in a much better position to obtain a working period that conforms to the average wishes of workers.

On the other hand, it may be argued that the growth in the importance of income (and commodity) taxes has interfered with the attainment of an optimum division of time between work and leisure. Income taxes apply to gains from work but not to those from leisure, and sales and excise taxes apply to gains from work to the extent that income is spent on taxable goods. Thus the relative gains from work and leisure are altered somewhat; some persons may seek to work more because of taxes, while others will seek to work less. It may be argued that the consequent distortion interferes with the attainment of optimum economic welfare.

3. *Optimum Rate of Capital Formation.* The optimum rate of capital formation is particularly difficult to define. It may be argued that economic welfare requires the division of total income between consumption and savings in a manner which conforms to the relative preferences for present and future consumption on the part of individuals. However, this requirement is subject to certain modifications:

a) An increased rate of capital formation allows a more rapid increase in output of consumption goods in the future. Particularly in countries with very low per capita incomes, relatively small increases in savings now may lead to very sharp rises in consumption in the future —rises that are not foreseen by the people of the society. It may be argued, in such cases, that a higher rate of capital formation than that permitted on the basis of the preferred division of income between consumption and savings would greatly increase economic welfare.

b) The preferred allocation of income between consumption and savings may prevent the maintenance of full employment and stable economic growth. If persons seek to save greater sums at high income levels than can find an outlet in investment, unemployment will develop, and optimum economic welfare will not be attained. Under such circumstances, a compromise is necessary between the requirement of allocation of income on the basis of choice of individuals and the need for maintaining full employment.

4. *Optimum Rate of Utilization of Scarce Natural Resources.* Economic welfare requires an optimum rate of utilization of scarce natural resources such as petroleum and iron ore. But this optimum rate is very difficult to define because of the conflicting interests of present and future generations. An extremely rapid rate of exploitation would exhaust supplies otherwise available for the future while an excessively

slow rate involves heavy sacrifice of present welfare for future welfare, one which may prove to have been unnecessary as new resources or alternative methods of production are developed in the future.

Attainment of an Optimum Rate of Economic Growth

Traditionally, the theory of economic welfare has been established in terms of static conditions, merely seeking to define the requirements for optimum welfare in terms of given determinants of equilibrium positions. In recent years, however, increased attention has been given to the significance of dynamic considerations for economic welfare. This attention has centered primarily on two elements:

1. *The Maintenance of an Equilibrium, Full-Employment Rate of Growth.* Generally speaking, an economy can continue to expand at a stable rate, without continuing or frequent recurring unemployment, only if balance is maintained among various determinants of the rate of development. In particular, aggregate demand for output must keep pace with growth in aggregate capacity to produce. The theory of economic growth has not reached a sufficient stage of advancement to prescribe more fully the specific requirements for stability in growth.[2]

2. *The Attainment of an Optimum Rate of Increase in the Real Level of National Income.* The economic system must provide maximum incentive for the discovery and introduction of new techniques, new methods of organization and operation, and new products, which increase the real level of national income, and aid in maintaining the volume of investment at sufficiently high levels to permit full employment.

One of the greatest advantages of the private enterprise market economy relates to innovation. A major means by which firms can gain a rate of profit higher than the average is to introduce innovations that will yield excess profits until competitors are able to duplicate the change, and may give rise to continuing monopoly profit. The pressures of competition likewise force other firms to meet innovations in order to escape losses.

Nonpurely competitive conditions may be somewhat more advantageous for economic growth than purely competitive ones, so long as some elements of competition remain. The typical firm selling in purely competitive markets is too small to undertake the research and experimentation necessary for innovations. Largely for this reason, most

[2] See F. H. Hahn and R. C. O. Matthews, "The Theory of Economic Growth: A Survey," *Economic Journal,* Vol. 74 (December, 1964), pp. 779–902.

agricultural research in the United States has been undertaken by the federal government. It is the larger firm, in situations of oligopoly and related cases, that is best able to develop and introduce improvements which allow real increases in national income.

However, pressures toward improvement and efficiency will slacken if the entry of new firms into various industries is limited, and if existing firms gain monopoly or semimonopoly positions. Many innovations are made by newcomers. If these cannot start, and if existing firms are already making a high rate of profit, development may be checked. Restrictions on entry of new firms may be more detrimental, from the standpoint of overall economic welfare, than mere differentiation of product and the presence of relatively few firms in an industry. Outright agreements among firms on methods of production, shares of output, etc., as permitted in the cartel systems of some countries, are likewise detrimental to economic progress.

INTERPERSONAL COMPARISONS AND WELFARE CRITERIA

The analysis thus far has abstracted from the problem of the relative economic position of various individuals; we have in effect assumed that all individuals have the same capacity for satisfaction, or in other words the same utility functions relating to money income. We have also assumed a given income distribution. The second assumption will be considered later in the chapter. The first assumption, if considered carefully, is seen to be essentially meaningless. It is now universally recognized that with the present state of knowledge, there is no possibility of making interpersonal utility comparisons, that is, of comparing relative satisfactions received by different persons. There is no way in which the relative satisfactions gained by two persons drinking cups of coffee can be compared, for example.

Once it is recognized that interpersonal utility comparisons are impossible, it becomes evident that the rules advanced thus far in the chapter are not adequate to allow us to state with certainty that various changes in the economy would of necessity increase economic welfare, even many which are universally regarded as doing so. Almost any type of change will benefit some persons and injure others—even, for example, readjustment of factor combinations to bring them to the optimum as defined above, or elimination of monopoly. Since the relative gains and losses of satisfaction by various individuals cannot be compared, we cannot say that the charges *necessarily* increase economic welfare, even though they bring the economy more closely in conformity with the rules of optimum efficiency and resource allocation.[3]

Thus if welfare economics is to be at all meaningful as a basis for evaluation of the economy and determination of economic policy, it is necessary to establish a suitable welfare criterion to meet this interpersonal comparison problem. There have been several approaches:

1. The Paretian optimum, based upon the work of Vilfredo Pareto, the Italian economist, who played a major role in the development of general equilibrium theory and welfare economics.[4] According to the Paretian optimum, a change may be regarded as necessarily desirable in terms of economic welfare only if the change benefits someone without injuring anyone else.[5] This is, of course, a highly restrictive assumption; even elimination of monopoly, for example, while benefitting many persons, will injure the owners of the monopoly enterprise. Changes covered by the criterion would be restricted to such instances as the lessening of unemployment, or alteration of factor inputs in such a way as to increase output with a given quantity of factor inputs, there being no change in factor prices (and incomes) as a consequence. Thus as a basis for judging efficiency or for policy recommendations, welfare economics is of very little assistance if we hold rigidly to the Paretian definition of the optimum.

2. The compensation principle: in the years immediately after World War II, the British economists Kaldor and Hicks and others developed the so-called compensation principle in an effort to broaden the applicability of welfare economics. This involved adding to the Paretian optimum case those situations in which the persons benefitting from the change would be willing to compensate those losing to a sufficient extent that the latter would no longer oppose the change. Thus, for example, owners of business firms and consumers benefitting

---

[3] For example, suppose that the building of a new highway will bring benefits to thousands of motorists, in the form of saving of time, fewer accidents, and more pleasant driving. But the building of this highway will necessitate moving the home of one family from a site for which it has strong preference and does not wish to leave, regardless of compensation offered. There is no scientific basis for stating that the total satisfaction gained by the thousands of motorists exceeds the dissatisfaction suffered by the one family —since there is no possibility of interpersonal comparisons of satisfactions. An additional criterion is necessary for determining appropriate policy on welfare grounds for building the highway.

[4] V. Pareto, *Manuel d'Economique Politique* (2d ed.; Paris: Girard, 1927).

[5] This criterion, usually referred to as "Pareto Optimality," appears to have been developed initially by F. Y. Edgeworth; see his *Mathematical Psychics* (London: C. Kegan Paul & Co., 1881).

from the introduction of improved technology might be willing to pay enough to induce the workers displaced by the technological change and having to take jobs at lower pay to end their resistance to the change. It is *willingness* to pay that is significant, not actual payment. If the latter occurs, the Paretian rule applies.

Various criticisms have been advanced against this rule. One is a technical question, as noted by Scitovsky and Little: in some instances once the change had been made, it would be advantageous for those who had been willing to allow the change to compensate the other group to return to the original situation. Scitovsky argued that the rule was valid only if after the first change it would not be advantageous to change the situation back to the original.

But more fundamentally, this rule is based upon the implicit assumption that a given number of dollars represents equal utility to all persons; otherwise the fact that those benefitting are willing to pay an amount in excess of the figure the injured would regard as adequate compensation for their injury does not demonstrate that there is a net gain in economic welfare. In effect interpersonal utility comparisons have entered in. Furthermore the rule cannot be implemented; there is typically no way in which the compensation which persons would be willing to offer and to accept could be ascertained.

3. Social welfare function: Today, the most widely accepted criterion is the social welfare function, as developed by Bergson, Samuelson, Arrow, and others. Such a function would express the optimum pattern of distribution of benefits among individuals as viewed by the consensus of thought in contemporary society.[6] The welfare function would thus establish the basis for weighing benefits and injuries of various persons—perhaps, for example, in terms of the relative numbers of persons benefitting or losing, or in terms of the nature of the gain or loss (cheaper products in preference to monopoly income, for example). The task of ascertaining an overall social welfare function embracing all aspects of the economy is obviously an impossible one, given the present state of knowledge. But it is not impossible to develop major segments of such a function; this is constantly being done as persons make judgments about the desirability or undesirability of certain policies.

Thus, we typically conclude that the benefits from the elimination of monopoly power, with consequent improvement of resource allocation, exceed the injury to those losing their monopoly profits. Restric-

[6] The function could, of course, be based upon the opinion of a dictator or some other source.

tion of the right of smelters to pour out noxious fumes is accepted on the basis that the social welfare function dictates that benefits to those living in the surrounding area are greater than the injury to the owners of the smelter and the consumers of the products made by the smelter, who must pay higher prices as a result of the costs of waste-control devices.

The principle of the social welfare function criterion has great merit in making explicit the fact that virtually any change does benefit some persons at the expense of others and that society must weigh the benefits and injuries, not in terms of any scientific principle, but upon a social welfare function resting upon value judgments. Unfortunately there are many difficulties involved in ascertaining consensus of thought, and the rule could lead to what an outsider might regard as flagrant violation of the rights of a minority segment of the population. But given the present state of knowledge there is no suitable alternative, and it is preferable to recognize that there is no scientific basis for the judgments than to make implicit assumptions which result in attachment of scientific support to purely value judgments.

THE OPTIMUM PATTERN OF INCOME DISTRIBUTION

The definition of optimum efficiency in the use and allocation of resources given in the preceding sections is based upon the assumption of a given distribution of income; this is true even with the Paretian and compensation welfare criteria. If conformity with the efficiency and allocation rules has been attained, it may be stated that the economy has attained optimum economic welfare in terms of the pattern of income distribution which prevails after all adjustments have been made—but only in terms of this pattern. What can be said about the optimum pattern of income distribution?

Aggregate Total Satisfaction? Were utility measurable, and interpersonal utility comparisons warranted, it would be meaningful to say, in conformity with the accepted goals, that the optimum pattern of income distribution would be that which would allow aggregate total satisfaction. But satisfactions are not measurable and are not comparable among individuals, and thus such a statement is meaningless. As a matter of practice, rough comparisons are frequently made; most persons would accept the argument, for example, that the transfer of one dollar from a millionaire to a starving family would increase the satisfaction of the latter more than it decreased the satisfaction of the former. But this is strictly a value judgment.

The Lerner Argument

Lerner has argued that, in the absence of knowledge of the actual pattern of distribution which will maximize satisfaction, the most satisfactory assumption which can be made is that an equal distribution would be the one most likely to maximize satisfaction from a given level of national income.[7] The argument is based upon the principle that capacities for satisfaction are distributed normally around the mode of a frequency distribution, and that an equal distribution would involve only random error, whereas any other would involve a definite bias. But this assumption likewise has no scientific foundation. Furthermore, satisfaction may depend to a large extent upon the ability to be able to outdo other persons in consumption, or to keep up with them, in a society in which such "keeping-up" is not insured by equality of distribution. Furthermore, an equal distribution is obviously not consistent with the maintenance of a high level of national income, because of effects upon incentives, nor with prevailing attitudes in contemporary Western societies.

The Attitudes of Society—the Social Welfare Function

The only feasible approach to the problem is the principle that the optimum pattern is that which is regarded as the most equitable by the consensus of opinion in the particular society, or in other words, is embraced in the social welfare function. This is a value judgment, one which cannot be derived from economic analysis, but appears to reflect most satisfactorily contemporary thinking on the question. It cannot be argued that the pattern determined in this manner necessarily maximizes satisfaction—a goal which has no meaning because it cannot be defined—but is simply one which accords with the concept of equity accepted in the particular society.

How can the consensus of thought on this question be determined? No precise method is possible; evaluation of legislation, as reflecting (perhaps rather imperfectly) the will of society, represents the only tangible approach. On this basis, certain general statements about the current consensus of opinion are possible:

1. Excessive inequality of income is regarded as undesirable. This point of view is reflected in the use of progressive taxation, in the provision of old-age pensions, relief, aid to housing, and anti-poverty programs, in minimum wage legislation, etc. Opinions differ on the question of what constitutes excessive inequality, but the general

[7] A. P. Lerner, *The Economics of Control* (New York: Macmillan, 1944), chap. iii.

principle is widely accepted that the extent of inequality which develops in the absence of governmental interference is excessive.

2. The attainment of large incomes from monopolistic "exploitation" of the public is regarded as particularly objectionable, and an attempt is made to check this by antitrust legislation, public utility regulation, etc. From the standpoint of resource utilization, the basic objection to monopoly is the restriction of output below the level at which price is equal to marginal cost. But legislation on the question has been greatly influenced by the desire to eliminate monopoly profits.

3. Complete equality of income is regarded as undesirable from the standpoint of its effects upon production, and inequitable because it denies the more efficient, hard-working persons the attainment of a higher reward for his skill and effort.

The lack of a more precise definition of the optimum pattern of income distribution reduces the significance of contemporary welfare theory, the precision and strength of its conclusions, and the force of policy recommendations based upon them. For example, on the basis of welfare principles relating to optimum use of resources, it can be argued that subway fares should be higher in rush hours than in nonrush hours because marginal cost is higher in the former (when extra cars and trains must be added to carry more passengers) than it is in the latter (when trains are half empty). But the distribution of passengers by income group is not the same in the two periods, with a heavy concentration of workers in the rush hours. Thus, opponents of such a fare system condemn it on the grounds of its effects on distribution of the costs of providing subway service by income group. Welfare theory can offer no conclusive answer to this argument.

Concluding Observations

Welfare economics is admittedly one of the least satisfactory portions of the overall subject of economics. The rules for attainment of optimum efficiency in the use and allocation of resources—given the pattern of income distribution—are clearly definable and generally acceptable. But their significance is dependent upon the nature of the social welfare function relating to gains and losses of particular individuals and groups and the optimum distribution of real income. The concept of a social welfare function is clear enough; the determination of its empirical content—which must rest upon consensus of thought in the particular society—encounters serious theoretical and practical difficulties. Thus decision as to the desirability or undesirability of certain features of the economy or policies rests in part upon the interpretations of particular persons about the nature of the social welfare function, and, of course, differences of opinion are inevitable. Judgments will be made and policies adopted, and welfare economics can make significant contributions to these actions, even if it cannot provide answers based in their entirety upon scientific analysis. But it is of utmost importance that the value judgments involved in the evaluations and recommendations be made explicit, and that these not be given a scientific validity which they do not possess.

SELECTED REFERENCES

BAUMOL, W. J. *Economic Theory and Operations Analysis,* chap. xvi. 2d ed. Englewood Cliffs, N.J.: Prentice-Hall, 1965.
> A good summary of welfare theory.

BERGSON, A. *Essays in Normative Economics.* Cambridge: Harvard University Press, 1965.

GRAFF, J. DE V. *Theoretical Welfare Economics.* Cambridge: Cambridge University Press, 1957.
> A high-level analysis of welfare economics.

LITTLE, I. M. D. *A Critique of Welfare Economics.* 2d ed. Oxford: Oxford University Press, 1957.

MISHAN, E. J. "A Survey of Welfare Economics, 1939–1959," *Economic Journal,* Vol. 70 (June, 1960), pp. 197–265.
> A very detailed review of the development of welfare theory in the last two decades, with a complete bibliography.

PIGOU, A. C. *The Economics of Welfare.* 4th ed. London: Macmillan, 1932.
> A classic presentation of welfare economics.

ROTHENBERG, J. *Measurement of Social Welfare.* Englewood Cliffs, N.J.: Prentice-Hall, 1961.

SAMUELSON, P. A. *Foundations of Economic Analysis,* chap. viii. Cambridge: Harvard University Press, 1947.
> An advanced analysis of the welfare problem.

SCITOVSKY, T. *Welfare and Competition.* Homewood, Ill.: Irwin, 1957.
> An extensive analysis of the significance of various forms of competition for the attainment of economic welfare.

> There has been extensive discussion of various aspects of welfare aspects theory in the journals in the last five years; many of these appeared in the *Economic Journal.* See for example, E. J. Mishan, "The Welfare Criteria that Aren't," *Economic Journal,* Vol. 74 (December, 1964), pp. 1014–17; and "The Recent Debate on Welfare Criteria," *Oxford Economic Papers,* Vol. 17 (July, 1965), pp. 219–36; H. F. Lydall, "Little's Criterion—an Empty Box," *Economic Journal,* Vol. 75 (June, 1965), pp. 379–87.

QUESTIONS

1. What is the nature of welfare economics?
2. How are the goals selected for evaluations of welfare economics?
3. Indicate the major goals which are generally employed as a basis for welfare economics.
4. Why can freedom of choice never be absolute?
5. Explain the term "maximum satisfaction of wants."
6. Indicate the requirements for the optimum efficiency in the use of resources.
7. Why is the operation of firms at the point of lowest LRAC essential for optimum efficiency in the use of resources?
8. Why, in purely competitive markets, will firms operate, over a long-run period, at the point of lowest LRAC? Will they necessarily do so in non-purely competitive markets? Explain.
9. Distinguish between optimum efficiency in the use of resources and optimum adjustment of production in terms of consumer preferences.
10. Why does optimum adjustment of production require equality of the marginal rate of substitution and the marginal rate of transformation? What requirements must be fulfilled for this equality to be attained?
11. Indicate some examples, other than those given in the chapter, of divergence between costs to the economy and costs to the individual producer.
12. Give examples of external economies of consumption.
13. Indicate the significance for economic welfare of the failure of price to equal marginal cost in nonpurely competitive conditions.
14. What is the objection, on grounds of welfare economics, to "luxury" excise taxes?
15. How would you justify, in terms of welfare economics, the following government policies:
    a) High excise taxes on liquor.
    b) Municipal zoning ordinances.
    c) Financing subway construction by taxes on motor vehicle use.
    d) Prevention of price discrimination.
    e) Restriction of entry of competing firms into the public utilities field.
    f) Provision of funds for agricultural research.
    g) Legislation prohibiting "featherbedding."
16. In what respects is pure competition superior to nonpure competition from the standpoint of welfare economics? In what respects is it inferior?
17. Why is it difficult to state categorically that any particular change increases economic welfare of society? What type of change is regarded as desirable in terms of the Paretian optimum? Why is this a very restrictive rule?
18. What is the compensation principle? What are the limitations of the rule?
19. What is meant by a "social welfare function?"

20. Explain the various approaches to the definition of the optimum pattern of income distribution.

21. There has been a long-standing argument over the question of whether bridge tolls be higher in rush hours when traffic is very heavy and marginal costs are high, but most of the users are workers, or higher in nonrush hours when traffic is light and marginal cost low, but the users on the average come from higher income levels. Evaluate the arguments.

Index

mplete Poems and Plays

agedy

s of Malfi

stus

: Philsater

he Major Texts

Modern Criticism

e Victorian Age

ems and Plays 1909-1950

ms

ms

ems

Poem

INDEX

A

Absolute income hypothesis, 77
Activity analysis, 423–24
Adding-up problem, 279–80
Adjustment of production, in terms of consumer preferences, 451–57
Advertising; *see* Selling activities
Agriculture
  cobweb theorem, 176–77
  purely competitive conditions in, 149
  slowness of adjustments in, 175–76
Allen, R. D. G., 59
Allocable fixed costs, 119
Allocation
  of common costs, 232–33
  of consumer income, 57–59, 383–94
Analytical principles, 13–18
Arrow, K., 462
Assumptions
  of cost analysis, 138, 140–42
  in economic analysis, 13–15
  of general equilibrium theory, 392
Average cost
  behavior of
    long-run, 133–42
    short-run, 127–29
  relation of price to, 170, 212
Average-cost pricing, 231–38
Average fixed cost, 123, 124
Average outlay, 263
Average product, 90, 264–66
Average revenue, 150–52, 182–84, 186
Average revenue product, 274–76
Average variable cost
  behavior of, 124–27
  definition of, 123
  relation of price to, 158, 164

B

Backward-sloping supply curve, 277, 287
Bain, J., 247, 248, 255
Banks, 335–36, 347
Barometric price leader, 230
Barriers to free entry, 215, 247–49
Basing point system, 244
Baumol, W. J., 33, 40, 86, 113, 240, 255, 282, 326, 402, 424, 466
Beach, E. F., 444
Bennion, E. G., 240, 424
Bergson, A., 462
Bierman, H., 327

Bilateral monopoly and oligopoly, 255
Bonds, 345–46
Boulding, K. E., 14, 366, 367
Bowen, H. R., 3, 10
Bowen, W. G., 306, 310
Brady, D., 77
Brennan, M. J., 178, 444
Budget equation, 392
Budget restraint, 65
Bushaw, D. W., 396, 402
Business losses, 249–50, 381–84
Business policy and marginal revenue product principle, 275–76

C

Calculation of return on capital goods, 316–18
Capital budgeting, 316–18
Capital deepening, 315–16
Capital equipment; *see also* Capital goods
  indivisibilities of, 107–8
  quasi rent on, 365–66
Capital formation, optimum rate of, 458–59
Capital goods
  definition of, 5, 6
  demand for, 314–27
  prices of, 323
  productivity of, 315–16
  return on, as quasi rent, 365–66
Capital requirements as bar to entry, 248
Capital widening, 315
Capitalism
  nature of, 7–9
  versus socialism, 9–10
Capitalization
  of land rents, 356–58
  of monopoly profits, 375
Carter, A. M., 311
Cassel, G., 402
Cassels, J. M., 113
Chamberlin, E. H., 178, 205, 218
Changes
  in cost, 178–75
  in demand, 48–49, 172–74
  in demand for capital goods, 323–24
  in determinants of general equilibrium, 399–400
  in factor demand, 273–75
  in interest rate level, 349–50
  in national income, 341–44
  in wages, 306–8

Charmes, A. A., 424
Chenery, H. B., 424
Chiu, J. Y. S., 34
Clark, J. M., 145, 205, 306
Clark, P. G., 424
Classifications, 20
Clower, R. W., 396, 402
Cobweb theorem, 176–77
Cobb-Douglas function, 281–82
Cohen, K. J., 23, 31, 40, 86, 113, 178, 202, 218, 255, 282, 402
Colberg, M. R., 145, 202, 255
Collective bargaining, 298–306
Collusion, 221
Commercial banks; *see* Banks
Common costs, 144, 232, 234, 249
Comparative statics, 22
Compensation principle, 461
Competition; *see also various forms,* e.g., Pure competition
   in factor markets, 278–79
   as a feature of the market economy, 8
   forms of, 36–38
Complementary goods, 61, 79
Complete oligopoly, 222–25
Complexities, in large-scale management, 110–11, 140
Conard, J. W., 351
Constant average variable cost, phase of, 126–27
Constant-cost industry
   long-run equilibrium in, 167–68
   nature of, 144
Constant returns to scale, 106, 110–11
Consumer allocation of income, 57–58, 65–66, 454
Consumer borrowing, 337
Consumer demand, 45–86
Consumer preferences
   adjustment of output in terms of, 399, 451–57
   changes in, 74–75
   significance of selling activities for, 195
Consumer satisfaction, maximization of, 28
Consumption function, 330–32
Consumption-possibilities line, 65
Convenience motive, 333
Convexity
   of indifference curves, 61–63
   of isoquants, 99–100
Cooper, W. W., 424
Correctness
   in economic analysis, 14
   of definitions, 20
Cost; *see also under specific type of per unit cost,* e.g., Average cost
   adjustability of, in response to changes in output, 119–21
   analysis of, 115–47

Cost—*Cont.*
   changes in, 174–75, 236–37
   expenditure, 117
   fixed, 119–20, 124
   nature of, 115–17
   nonexpenditure, 118–20
   of money capital, 320–21
   relation of, to price; *see* Average cost schedules; *see* Cost schedules
   types of, 117–21
   variable, 119–21
Cost Behavior and Price Policy, 115, 145
Cost conditions of industry
   nature of, 142–45
   significance of, for long-run adjustments, 167–70, 215
   types of, 142–45
Cost minimization, 266–68
Cost-plus pricing; *see* Average cost pricing
Cost schedules
   empirical studies of, 131–32, 140–42
   long-run, 133–37
   parameters of, 121–22
   short-run, 122–32
   tabular presentation, 154, 166
Costs; *see also under particular type,* e.g., Variable costs
   common, 144, 232, 234, 249
   expenditure, 117–18
   fixed, 119–20, 124
   nonexpenditure, 118
   selling, 144
   variable, 119–21
Credit expansion, 335–36, 347
Credit rationing, 317, 322
Cross-elasticity of demand, 54, 79–80
Culbertson, J. M., 351
Cutoff date, 319
Cyert, R. M., 23, 31, 40, 86, 113, 178, 202, 218, 255, 282, 402

D

Dantzig, G. B., 407
Davis, R. M., 384
Declining average variable cost, phase of, 125–26
Decreasing-cost industry, 143–44
Decreasing returns, from selling activities, 197
Decreasing returns to scale, 106, 111–12
Definitions, in economics, 20
Demand
   for capital goods, 314–27
   consumer
      changes in, 48–49, 74–80, 172–74
      concept of, 45–46
      cross-elasticity of, 54, 78–80
      definition of, 45–46
      determinants of, 57–65

Demand—*Cont.*
consumer—*Cont.*
econometric studies of, 430–32
elasticity of, 49–54
empirical studies of, 80–81
function, 48
income elasticity of, 53–54
increase in, 48–49, 172–74, 236
indifference curve approach to explanation of, 61–71
law of, 56
marginal utility approach to, 56–59
nature of schedules of, 57–65
relation of schedule of, to indifference curves, 68–70
for factor units, 262–76
for labor, 289
for money capital, 338–39
for the product of an individual seller, 150–52
Demand concepts, 45–55
Demand equations, general equilibrium, 392–95
Depreciation, 118, 371, 392
Development, economic; *see* Economic growth
Dewey, D., 214, 314, 327
Diet, optimal, 407–10
Differential theory of land rent, 358–63
Differentials, wage, 291–93, 304–6
Differentiation
in monopolistic competition, 206–7
in oligopoly, 221, 247
significance of, for demand, 47–48
Diminishing Marginal Rate of Factor Substitution, Principle of, 97–98
Diminishing Marginal Rate of Substitution, Principle of, 61–63
Diminishing Marginal Utility, Law of, 56–57
Diminishing Returns, Law of, 92–96, 127
Direct variable costs, *see* Fully variable cost
Dirham, J. B., 230
Discounted present value, 317
Discrimination, price, 190–94, 202, 244
Diseconomies of large-scale production
external, 143
internal, 110–11, 140
Distribution of income
optimum, 463–65
relation of, to factor pricing, 261–62
Division of labor; *see* Specialization
Dorfman, R., 420–424
Douglas, P. H., 281
Duesenberry, J., 77
Duffy, J., 111
Dunlop, J. T., 299, 311
Durability, significance of, for demand elasticity, 73

Dynamic analysis, 22–23
Dynamic forces, significance of, for investment, 324–27

E

Easterlin, R. A., 294
Econometrics, 427–45
Economic analysis
formulation of, 13–16
nature of, 12–13
terminology of, 20
usefulness of, 18–20
Economic goods, 5
Economic growth, 21, 459–60
Economic institutions, 3–4
Economic principles, nature of, 12–20
Economic profit; *see* Pure profits
Economic rent; *see* Rent
Economic stability, 306–8
Economic system
functions of, 6–7
goals of, assumed, 447–48
Economic theory; *see* Economic analysis
Economics, 4
Economies of large-scale production
external, 143
internal, 107–10
Edgeworth, F. Y., 461
Efficiency, optimum, 450–51
Eiteman, W. J., 132
Elastic demand, 50
Elasticity of demand
cross, 54
for factor units, 272–73
income, 53–54, 75–79
for labor, 289–90
in monopolistic competition, 207
for product of an individual seller, 182–84
price, 49–53, 71–74
significance of, for price discrimination, 190–94
Elasticity of substitution of factors, 104–5
Elasticity of supply
of commodities, 152–54
of factors, 276–77
of labor, 288–90, 293–94
Elbing, A. O., 34
Ellis, H. S., 145
Embodiment, of technological change, 316
Empirical generalizations, 16–18
Empirical studies
of demand schedules, 80–81
of long-run cost schedules, 140–41
to provide magnitudes in input-output analysis, 421
of short-run cost schedules, 126, 131–32
of wages, 302–4, 309–10

Employers
  domination of labor markets by, 294–95
  wage policies of, 298–99
Engel's Laws, 76
Entrepreneurial activity, 6
Entry of new firms
  excessive, 214
  in monopolistic competition, 212
  in oligopoly, 245–46
  in pure competition, 164–66
  restrictions on, 215, 247–49
Equilibrium
  general, 22, 389–403
  nature of, 22
  of the firm, in
    monopolistic competition, 208–10
    monopoly, 186–89
    pure competition, 158–59
  of the industry
    monopolistic competition, 210–14
    pure competition, 165–170
Errors, in economic analysis, 15
Estimation problems, 438–43
Euler's Theorem, 279–80
Excess profits, 373–81, 245–46
Excessive number of firms, monopolistic competition, 214
Executives of corporations, goals followed by, 31–32
Expansion path, 106–8
Expectations, significance of
  for demand changes, 80
  for investment decisions, 325–26
Expenditure costs, 117–18
Expense preferences, 241
Experimentation in determining demand schedules, 227
External diseconomies, 142, 453–55, 456–57
External economies, 143

F

Factor combinations, optimum, 96–106, 262–73
Factor demand, analysis of, 262–76
Factor incomes, 29–34, 326
Factor prices, determination of, 261–83
Factor substitution, 96–106
Factor supplies
  changes in, 323–24, 401
  general analysis of determinants of, 276–77
Factor utilization, optimum, 457–58
Factors of production
  definition of, 5
  demand for, 262–76
  mobility of, 39
  prices of, determination of, 261–83
  supply of, 276–77

Failures, of business firms, 381–82
Feasible diets, 407–10
Federal Reserve System, 337–38, 344
Fellner, W., 23, 145, 256, 344
Ferber, R., 75–86
Firms
  demand schedule for factors by, 269–72
  functions of, 26–28
  goals of, 30–35, 240–42
  nature of, 25–26
  new, development of, 165–66
First-degree discrimination, 191–94
Fixed costs, 119–20, 124
Forbush, D. R., 145, 202, 255
Freedom of choice, 448–49
Free entry, 164–66, 212, 245–46
Free goods, 5
Friedman, M., 86, 307
Friedman, R., 77, 78
Full-cost pricing; *see* Average-cost pricing
Full employment, and economic welfare, 457–58
Fully variable costs, 121
Functional return
  profits as, 379–80
  rent as, 364
Functions
  of the business firm, 26–27
  of the economic system, 6–7
  of the interest rate, 350–51

G

Gale, D., 424
Games, theory of, 239–40
General equilibrium theory, 22, 389–403
General price level, significance of wage changes for, 306–7
General wage level changes, 306–7
Geographical wage differences, 292–93, 305
Goals
  of business firms, 30–35, 240–42
  of consumers, 28–29
  of the economic system, 447–48
  of factor-owners, 29–30
  of labor unions, 299–300
Goldberger, A. S., 430
Goodness of fit problem, 441–42
Goods, definition of, 4, 5; *see also specific type of good,* e.g., Capital goods
Gordon, R. A., 40, 276
Governments
  borrowing by, 337
  interferences by, in markets, 177–78
  role of, in economy, 8–9
Graaf, J., 35, 456, 466
Green River ordinance, 249
Growth theory, 21
Guthrie, G. E., 132

H

Hague, D. C., 327
Hahn, F. H., 459
Haley, B. F., 344
Hansen, A. H., 351
Harberger, A. C., 288
Harbeson, R. W., 456
Haynes, W. W., 145, 203, 256
Henderson, A., 424
Henderson, J. M., 86
Hicks, J. R., 59, 63, 86, 342, 344, 351, 403, 424, 461
Hilton, G. W., 383
Hood, W. C., 427, 444
Household savings behavior, 81–85
Households, 25
Human wants, 4–5
Hurwicz, L., 240

I

Identification problem, 439–40
Identity
    of least-cost figures of firms, in pure competition, 167
    of long-run cost and supply schedules, 165
    of short-run marginal cost and short-run supply schedules, 158–60
Imitative pricing, 231
Immobility
    of factors, 39
    of farmers, 177
    of labor, 292–93, 305
Imperfect knowledge, 38–39
Imperfections
    nature of, 38–39
    in pure competition, 175–78
    in selling activities, 199–200
Implicit costs, 371–73, 382–83
Implicit interest, 371–72
Implicit rents, 373
Implicit wages, 372–73
Imputation, of monopoly profits, 374–75
Income changes, and demand, 75–76
Income distribution
    optimum pattern of, 463–65
    significance of factor pricing for, 261–62
Income effect
    of price change, 70–71
    of wage changes, 286
Income elasticity of demand, 53–54
Income inequality, 464–65
Increasing average variable cost, 127
Increasing-cost industries
    long-run equilibrium of, pure competition, 169–70
    nature of, 142–44

Increasing returns
    from selling activities, 196–97
    stage of, 93–95
Increasing returns to scale, 106–11
Indifference curve approach, 59–71
Indifference schedule, 59–61
Indirect benefits, 453, 456
Indivisibilities, 107–9, 140
Industry
    concept of, 25–26
    cost conditions of, 142–45, 167–70
    equilibrium of, monopolistic competition, 210–12, 213
Inelastic demand, 51–52
Inequalities, 415–16
Inequality of income distribution, 464–65
Inferior goods, 54, 76
Inflation, relation of unions to, 306–7
Innovations, 376–77
Input-output analysis, 419–22
Interdependency of prices, 390–91
Interest
    element in business profits, 371–72
    nature of, 328
    necessity for payment of, 329–30
    origin of, 328–30
    significance of, for investment, 320–21
    theory of, 328–52
Interest rate
    changes in, 349–51
    decisions affecting, 330–36
    equilibrium level of, 336–45
    functions of, 350–51
    relation of, to national income equilibrium, 341–44
    significance of, for liquidity, 334–35
    stability of, 339–40
    structure, 345–49
Interfirm wage differences, 304
Interindustry economics, 423–24
Internal financing, 346–47
Internal rate of return, 316
Interpersonal utility comparisons, 460–63
Introductory pricing, 238
Investment
    concept of, 316
    decisions, 316–22
    determinants of, 316–23
    induced, 324
    significance of dynamic elements for, 324–25
    significance of interest rate changes for, 321–22, 341–44
    significance of level of national income for, 321–24
Isocost line, 102–4
Isoquants, 99–107

J

Jaffe, W., 389
Johnson, H. G., 351
Johnston, J., 132, 145, 445
Joint profits, maximization of, in oligopoly, 222–25
Jureen, L., 445

K

Kaldor, N., 461
Kaplan, A. D. H., 230
Kaun, D. E., 303
Keirstead, B. S., 384
Keynes, J. M., 19–20, 79
Keynes, J. N., 23
Kinked demand curve, 227–30, 245–47
Klein, L. R., 430
Knight, F. H., 10, 377, 384
Knowledge, imperfect, 38–39, 175–77
Knowles, K. G. J. C., 303
Koopmans, T. C., 407, 427, 444

L

Labor
   demand for, 289
   immobility of, 294–95
   indivisibilities of, 108–9
   real income of, 308–10
   share of output, long run, 281–82
   supply of, 285–89
Labor unions
   goals of, 299
   policies of, 300–302
   significance of, for
      economic stability, 306–7
      real wages, 309–11
      unemployment, 307–8
      wage determination, 298–308
      wage differentials, 304–6
      wage levels, 298–308
Land
   character of, 354–55
   rent on, determination of, 354–64
   selling price of, 356–58
   supply of, 355–56
Land rent, determination of, 354–68
Lange, O., 23
Lanzillotti, R. F., 230, 233
Law of Diminishing Marginal Rate of Factor Substitution, 96–106
Law of Diminishing Marginal Rate of Substitution, 61–63
Law of Diminishing Marginal Utility, 56–57
Law of Diminishing Returns, 92–96, 105–6, 127
Leadership, price, 230

Least cost combinations of factors, 266–68
Legal barriers, to entry, 249
Leontief, W. W., 419, 425
Lerner, A. P., 464
Lester, R. A., 276
Levinson, H. M., 303, 311
Lewis, H. G., 303, 311
Liebhafsky, H. H., 282
Lindblom, C. E., 306
Linear inequalities, 415–16
Linear programming, 404–25
Linear relations, 405–6, 433
Liquid balances, 332–34, 340
Liquidation of businesses, 381, 83
Liquidity decisions, 332–34
Little, I. M. D., 462, 466
Loanable funds; *see* Money capital
Long-run average cost, 134
Long-run marginal cost, 135
Long-run period
   behavior of marginal revenue product in, 269
   cost schedules in, 133–42
   definition of, 119
   price and output adjustment in, with
      monopolistic competition, 212–15
      monopoly, 188–90
      oligopoly, 244–50
      pure competition, 164–74
   supply of labor, 293–94
Losses, 249–50, 381–84
Lowest average cost
   failure to attain, monopolistic competition, 213–14
   necessity for operation at point of, for optimum economic welfare, 450–51
   operation at, pure competition, 165–66
Lutz, F., 327
Lutz, V., 327
Lydall, H. F., 466

M

Machlup, F., 23, 276, 282
Macroeconomic theory, 21–22
Malthus, T. R., 293, 402
Management problems, in large-scale enterprises, 110–11, 140
March, J. G., 40, 255
Marginal cost
   behavior of, 129–31
   concept of, 123
   in pure competition, 164
   requirement of for optimum adjustment of production, 452–455
Marginal cost–marginal revenue rule, 159
Marginal cost pricing
   dangers of, with oligopoly, 234–35
   dilemma, with decreasing cost conditions, 201–2, 456–57

Marginal outlay, 263–64, 296
Marginal physical product, 90
Marginal product; *see* Marginal physical product, Marginal revenue product
Marginal productivity theory of distribution
  applied to land, 355–56
  nature of, 278
Marginal rate of factor substitution, 96–97
Marginal rate of substitution, 452
Marginal rate of transformation, 452–54
Marginal revenue, concept of, 152, 182–84
Marginal revenue–marginal cost rule, 159
Marginal revenue product, 264–66, 268–69, 309
Marginal utility
  approach to explanation of demand schedules, 56–59
  concept of, 56–57
Margins, retail, 233–34
Market
  concept of, 35
  imperfections, 38–39
  relationships, 35–38
Market economy, 7–9
Market period
  definition of, 150, 153
  in monopolistic competition, 207–28
  in monopoly, 185–86
  price adjustment in, pure competition, 150–57, 171–72
Market structure, 35–38
Markham, J. W., 230
Markup system, 231–38
Marshall, A., 86, 368
Mathews, R. C. O., 459
Maximization
  assumption, 28–35
  of economic welfare, 447–66
  goals, 28–35
  of joint profits, oligopoly, 223–25
  by labor unions, 299–300
  of profits, 30–34, 235–36
  of want satisfaction, 449–59
McGuire, T. W., 34
Microeconomics, nature, 22–23
Mishan, E. J., 466
Mobility
  of factors, 39
  of labor, 294–95
Model, nature of, 13, 436–37
Models, econometric, 434–43
Modigliani, F., 77, 78
Monetary theory, nature of, 21
Money, creation of, 335–36
Money capital
  cost of, 320–21
  demand for, 338–39

Money—*Cont.*
  role of, in investment decisions, 320–22
  supply of, 337–38
Money supply, 340–41
Monopolistic competition
  in labor market, 295–96
  nature of, 37, 205–7
  price and output determination in, 205–19
Monopoly
  demand for product of, 186
  nature of, 37, 184–85
  price and output determination in, 184–202
  price discrimination in, 190–94
  profits, 374–76
  regulated, 200–202
  selling activities in, 195–200
Monopsonistic competition, 252
Monopsony
  influence of, on factor demand, 264–70
  nature of, 37
  price and output determination with, 251–55
  profits, 373–74
  significance of, for wage determination, 295–98
Morgenstern, O., 239
Mortality of firms, 214
Mortgage loans, 347–48
Morton, W. A., 307
Moses, L., 424
Motives for liquidity preferences, 332–34
Multiple product situation, 144, 232, 234
Myers, C. A., 300

N

National income
  equilibrium level of, 341–44
  and the equilibrium rate of interest, 341–44
Necessary return on investment, 118, 371–72
Negative cross elasticity, 79
Negative profits, 249–50, 381–84
Negative return, stage of, 96
Neuman, J. von, 237
New products, 238
Nonexpenditure costs, 118
Nonpecuniary goals, 34, 195–200, 215–16, 242–44
Nonpurely competitive conditions; *see also specific form,* e.g., Oligopoly
  general features of, 181–84
  in factor markets, 278–79
  revenue schedules in, 182–83
  nature of, 37–39
  wage determination in, 294–310

Normal price levels; *see* Equilibrium price levels
Number of firms, changes in, 164–66, 212, 245–46

O

Occupational wage differences, 291–92, 305
Oligopoly
    complete, 222–25
    definition of, 37
    differentiated, 221
    long run adjustments in, 244–50
    nature of, 37, 220–21
    partial, 225–42
    price discrimination in, 244
    price and output determination in, 220–55
    product variation in, 242
    pure, 221
    selling activities in, 242–44
Oligopsony
    in labor markets, 297–98
    nature of, 37
    price and output determination with, 251–55
Oliver, H. M., 276
Open-market operations, Federal Reserve System, 337–38, 344
Opportunity costs, 116–17
Optimal diet, 407–10
Optimum adjustment of production, in terms of consumer wants, 451–57
Optimum allocation of income by consumers, 57–58, 65–68, 454
Optimum efficiency, in use of resources, 450–51
Optimum factor combinations, 96–106, 262–73
Optimum factor utilization, 452–58
Optimum income distribution, 463–65
Optimum organization of production, 450–51
Optimum rate of capital formation, 458
Optimum rate of economic growth, 459–60
Optimum standards of living, 449–460
Optimum utilization of factors, 450–51
Output adjustments in monopolistic competition, 205–19
    monopoly, 184–94
    pure competition, 158–62, 164–70
Overhead, 233

P

Parameters, structural, 435
Pardridge, W. C., 32, 240
Paretian optimum, 461
Pareto, V., 59, 461
Partial equilibrium theory, definition of, 22
Partial oligopoly, 225–42

Patinkin, D., 344, 351, 397, 403
Perfect competition, 38, 378
Perfectly elastic demand, 50
Perfectly inelastic demand, 52
Perfectness, in markets, 38–39
Permanent income hypothesis, 78–79
Phelps-Brown, E. H., 310, 403
Physical product, adjustment of; *see* Product adjustment
Piecewise linear relation, 406
Pierson, F., 311
Pigou, A. C., 466
Planning curve, 137
Planning problems, and linear programming, 405
Plowback, 321
Population changes, 293–94
Precautionary motive, 333
Preference maximization, 34–35
Price-consumption curve, 68
Price determination
    general equilibrium, 389–403
    in monopolistic competition, 205–19
    in monopoly, 184–94
    in oligopoly, 220–55
    in pure competition, 149–180
Price discrimination, under
    monopoly, 190–94
    oligopoly, 244
    regulated monopoly, 202
Price following, 231
Price leadership, 230–31
Price system, functions of, 8
Prices
    of capital goods, 323
    of factors, general theory of, 261–82
    of land, 350–58
Pricing policies, average-cost, 231–38
Principle of Diminishing Marginal Rate of Factor Substitution, 97–99
Principle of Diminishing Marginal Rate of Substitution, 61–63
Principles, nature of, 12–13
Principle of Returns to Scale, 106–13, 138
Probability adjustments, 319–20
Product adjustment, 194–95, 239, 242–44
Product differentiation, 47–48, 206–7
Production
    factors of; *see* Factors of production
    optimum adjustment of, in terms of consumer wants, 451–57
    optimum organization of, 457–58
    theory of, 89–114
Production functions, 89–90
Production process, 410–11
Productivity, of capital goods, 315–16
Profits
    concept of, 370–71
    as an element in cost, 371–73

Profits—*Cont.*
  excess, 373–79
  as a functional return, 379–80
  innovational, 376–77
  maximization of
    assumption of, 30–34
    significance of average-cost pricing for, 235–38
  maximum joint, 222–25
  monopoly, 374–76
  monopsony, 373–74
  necessary, 118, 371–73
  negative, 381–84
  pure, 376–78
  role of, in the economy, 380–81
  "satisfactory," 33
  theory of, 370–84
  uncertainty as source of, 377–78
Programming
  linear; *see* Linear programming
  and planning, 405
Public utilities, pricing by, 200–202
Pure competition
  concept of, 37
  conditions necessary for, 37, 149
  elasticity of demand for the product of the firm in, 150–52
  in factor markets, 262
  imperfections in, 175–78
  in labor market, 285–94
  long-run price determination in, 164–74
  in market for money capital, 339
  market price determination in, 150–57
  price and output determination in, 149–180
  revenue schedules in, 150–52
  short-period price determination in, 157–64
  significance of, for economic welfare, 453–59
Pure oligopoly, 250–51
Pure profits, 376–78

Q

Quandt, R. E., 86
Quantity demanded, 48
Quantity discounts, 194
Quasi rent, 365–66

R

Rate of interest; *see* Interest rate
Real wages, 308–10
"Reasonable" profits, goal of, 33
Reder, M., 281
Reduction in general wage level, as solution for unemployment, 307–8
Rees, A., 307
Reid, M., 76
Regulated monopoly, 200–202

Reinvested earnings, 321
Relation
  linear, 405–6, 433
  nonlinear, 405–6
  piecewise linear, 406
Relative income hypothesis, 77
Rent
  concept of, 354–55
  as generalized surplus return, 366–67
  land, determination of, 354–68
  quasi, 364–65
Replacement of capital goods, 315, 372
Reservation price, 153–55
Resource allocation, 6
Resources, optimum use of, 450–57
Restraints, on setting of full monopoly price, 200
Restrictions on entry of new firms, 215, 247–49
Retailing
  price determination in, 233–34
  rent in, 363–64
Retention of earnings, in corporations, 321
Return on owners' capital, 371–72
Returns
  diminishing, 92–96, 127
  increasing, 93–95
  negative, 96
  to scale, 106, 111–12
Revenue schedules, 150–52, 182–83
Ricardian theory of rent, 358–62
Ricardo, D., 356–358
Risk, 318–20
Robertson, D. J., 303
Robinson, E. A. G., 203
Ross, A. M., 299, 311
Rothenberg, J., 466
Ruggles, R, 23
Rule of thumb approaches to investment, 317–18
Ryan, W. J. L., 113

S

Sales maximization, goal, 33–34, 240
Sales promotion; *see* Selling activities
Sales schedules; *see* Demand for the product of an individual seller
Samuelson, P. A., 420–24, 462, 466
Satisfaction of wants, maximum, 449–59
"Satisfactory" profits, 33
Savings
  behavior of, 81–85
  ex ante vs. ex post, 331
  factors influencing, 331–32
  motives for, 330–31
Savings deposits, 334
Scale, returns to, 107–11
Second-degree discrimination, 191
Schumpeter, J., 376, 384, 402

Scitovsky, T., 466
Schultz, C. P., 300
Secular growth, 401–2
Selling activities
adjustment of
in monopolistic competition, 215–16
in monopoly, 195–200
in oligopoly, 242–44
nature of, 144
Selling costs
nature of, 144
significance of, for prices, 215–16, 243–44
Semivariable costs, 121
Separation, of ownership and management, 27–28, 31
Shackle, G. L. S., 319, 351
Shillinglaw, G., 383
Shipping schedules, 411–12
Shock models, 437–38
Short run
adjustability of factors in, 119
cost schedules in, 122–32
definition of, 119
marginal revenue product, behavior in, 268–69
price and output levels in
monopolistic competition, 208–12
monopoly, 186–88
pure competition, 157–64
supply schedules in, 160–62
Short-term interest rates, 347
Shubik, M., 240
Simon, H. A., 40, 86, 256
Simplification, in economic analysis, 14
Smidt, S., 327
Smith, Adam, 109
Smith, C. A., 141
Social cost, 453–54
Social goals, 447–48
Social welfare function, 462
Socialism, 9–10
Solomon, E., 327
Solow, R., 281, 420, 424
Specialization, 109–10
Speculative motive, 334
Spontaneous coordination, in oligopoly, 221–22
Stability, of general equilibrium, 396
Standard of living, optimum, analysis of, 449–59
Standardized product, 251
Static analysis, 22
Stigler, G. J., 11, 198
Stock, as source of money capital, 320, 346
Strategical moves, in oligopoly, 224, 229–30, 239–40
Structural parameters, 435
Structure, concept of, 437

Structure of interest rates, 345–49
Substitutability
of factors, 96–106
relation of, to cross-elasticity of demand, 79–80
significance of, for demand elasticity, 71–72
Substitution
factor
elasticity of, 98, 104
marginal rate of, 96–98
marginal rate of, 59–60
Substitution effect
of price changes, 70–71
of wage changes, 286
Sultan, P. E., 303
Supply
concept of, 152
elasticity of, 152–54
of factors, 276–77
of labor, 285–89
of land, 355
of money, 340–41
of money capital, 337–38
in pure competition
long-run period, 165–70
market period, 153–55
short-run period, 158–62
Supply equations, in general equilibrium theory, 395
Surplus, rent as, 365–67

T

Tangency
of average revenue and average cost curves, in
monopolistic competition, 213–14
oligopoly, 245–46
pure competition, 165–66
of isocost line and isoquant, 102–4
of price line and indifference curve, 66
Target return, 232
Taylor, G. W., 311
Technique of linear programming, 415–19
Technological change, 316, 324–25, 399
Terminology, 20
Theil, H., 445
Theory
of change, 401–2
of distribution, general, 261–82
economic; see Economic theory
of games, 239–40
general equilibrium, 389–402
of interest, 329–52
of production, 89–113
of profits, 370–85
of rent, 354–68
of wages, 284–310
welfare, 447–56

Third-degree discrimination, 192–94
Time lags, in adjustments of output, 175–77
Time preference, 330–32
Tobin, J., 78
Total outlay, behavior of, 50–51
Transactions motive, 332
Transitivity of indifference curves, 64
Triffin, R., 384

U

Uncertainty
  in oligopoly, 226
  significance of, for investment, 318–20
  significance of, for profit maximization, 30–31
  as a source of pure profits, 377–78
Undistributed profits, 321
Unemployment
  effect of, on economic welfare, 457–58
  and investment, 324
  unions as a cause of, 307–8
Union wage policy, 299–300
Unions; *see* Labor unions
Unitary elasticity of demand, 52–53
Usefulness
  of economic theory, 18–20
  of general equilibrium theory, 397–98
Utility
  comparison of, 460–64
  definition of, 5
  marginal; *see* Marginal utility

V

Valavanis, S., 445
Validity
  of economic principles, 14–16, 17–18
  of Principle of Returns to Scale, 112–13
Variable costs, 119, 120–21; *see also* Average variable cost

Variables, exogenous and endogenous, 434
Varying proportions, 92–101
Viner, J., 145
Von Neuman, J., 237

W

Wage bill, maximization of, 299–300
Wage differentials, 291–93, 305
Wage policies
  of employers, 298–99
  of unions, 299–302
Wages
  determination of
    with labor unions, 290–310
    with monopsony and oligopsony in the labor market, 294–98
    with pure competition in the labor market, 285–94
  real, levels of, 308–9
  relation of, to supply of labor, 285–89, 293
  union effects on, 302–6
Walras, L., 389
Wants, 4–5
Wealth-income hypothesis, 78
Welfare economics, 20–21, 447–66
Weston, J. F., 384
Whittaker, G. R., 145, 202, 255
Williamson, O. E., 40
Wold, H., 445
Wonnacott, R. J., 293
Woodham-Smith, C., 293
Worcester, D. A., 368
Wright, D. Mc., 307

Y

Yield
  on bonds, 345–46
  on stock, 346

This book has been set on the Linotype in 12 point Garamond #3, leaded 1 point, and 10 point Garamond #3, leaded 2 points. Part and chapter numbers and titles are in 18 point Spartan Medium. The size of the type page is 27 by 46½ picas.